Making Ethnicity in Southern Bessarabia

Eurasian Studies Library

History, Societies & Cultures in Eurasia

VOLUME 14

The titles published in this series are listed at *brill.com/esl*

Making Ethnicity in Southern Bessarabia

Tracing the Histories of an Ambiguous Concept in a Contested Land

By

Simon Schlegel

BRILL

LEIDEN | BOSTON

Cover illustration: Nina Kurudimova, a sixth-grade student in School Nr. 1 in Ceadir-Lunga reading from a textbook during Gagauz language class in 1959. Courtesy of the Historical and Ethnographical Museum in Ceadir-Lunga. Author photo by David Grigoryan.

The Library of Congress Cataloging-in-Publication Data is available online at http://catalog.loc.gov
LC record available at http://lccn.loc.gov/2019022537

Typeface for the Latin, Greek, and Cyrillic scripts: "Brill". See and download: brill.com/brill-typeface.

ISSN 1877-9484
ISBN 978-90-04-34990-2 (hardback)
ISBN 978-90-04-40802-9 (e-book)

This book is printed on acid-free paper and produced in a sustainable manner.

Contents

Acknowledgements

I am deeply indebted to all respondents who have provided their insights on this work. Without their patience for my endless questions, the findings herein would not have been achieved. Much more than just respondents, but invaluable and enthusiastic supporters of my research were Mikhail Sakali, Mariya Sakali, Valeriy Sakali, Mariya Khadshioglo, Zinaida Kharitova, Il'ya Kharitov, Svetlana Glushchuk, Andrey Shevshenko, Grigoriy Chilik, Larissa Chakir, and Yuri Lituchenko. I am very grateful for their support in finding information and respondents. I thank the staff of Izmail's archive and public library for their help in finding some of the key sources for this study. For their institutional and academic support I am very grateful to the late Professor Andrey Shabashov and his colleagues from the department of Archeology and Ethnography at Odessa University and to Professor Alexander Lebedenko of Izmail University. I also want to thank Lyudmila Luzanova and her colleagues from the German department of Izmail University and especially Olga Gerasimova and her theater group in the Izmail Culture House for providing the starting points of a growing network of respondents. For their friendship and unrelenting practical and moral support during fieldwork I am deeply indebted to Elizaveta Shkarupa, David Grigoryan, and Yuri Vlassishen. Earlier versions of the chapters in this book have greatly profited from the critical comments and the advice of Dittmar Schorkowitz, Deema Kaneff, Alexander Osipian, Diána Vonnák, Kateryna Budz, Philippe Blasen, and Alexander Osipov. The book has also profited very much from the thoughtful criticism of two anonymous reviewers.

Maps and Figures

Maps

Figures

Notes

A Note on Translations and Transliteration

For the romanianization of Russian and Ukrainian words, the system of the U.S. Board on Geographic Names was used.[1] Place names were transliterated from Ukrainian for areas in which, according to the census of 2001, more people speak Ukrainian, and from Russian for areas where more people speak Russian.[2] For Odessa oblast, where the field site is located, place names were accordingly transliterated from Russian. Exceptions were made for place names and names with an established spelling in English, *Moscow* instead of *Moskva*, *Perestroika* instead of *Perestroyka*, *Gogol* instead of *Gogol'*.

I refer to the Romanian language spoken in Bessarabia as "Romanian/Moldovan." Although Romanian and Moldovan can be traced back to the same roots and are easily mutually intelligible, in historical sources used for this work, it was usually referred to as the "Moldovan language." The dichotomy has become politicized since the emergence of a Romanian state beginning with the United Principalities in 1862. In the Republic of Moldova, there is today among Romanian speakers a strong preference for calling the language "Romanian," whereas Romanian speakers in the Ukrainian part of southern Bessarabia usually insist they speak "Moldovan." To underline my awareness of the dispute and of different local conceptions I refer to both Moldovan and Romanian. Unless indicated otherwise, all translations are my own.

A Note on Names and Pseudonyms

All respondents are cited using pseudonyms. An exception was made for public figures, such as politicians and functionaries, whose identity could be retraced easily, and who have made their statements during public events, in the local media, or on the internet.

1 For Russian see <https://assets.publishing.service.gov.uk/government/uploads/system/uploads/attachment_data/file/807920/ROMANIZATION_OF_RUSSIAN.pdf> (17.02.2019). For Ukrainian see <https://www.gov.uk/government/uploads/system/uploads/attachment_data/file/320286/Ukrainian_ Romanization.pdf> (17.02.2019).

2 See an according map in the results section of the Ukrainian census of 2001: <http://2001.ukrcensus.gov.ua/results/nationality_population/graphic/> (17.02.2019).

A Note on Archival Sources

The great majority of archival sources used in this research come from the state archive in Izmail. It is a branch (*filial*) of the state archive in the provincial capital Odessa, which is directly subordinated to the head of the oblast administration. Archive sources are represented with a threefold label, F, standing for *fond* (collection), whereby "Fr" codes indicate collections from the Soviet period and "F" codes indicate older collections, formed before 1944, in either tsarist Russia or Romanian times. "D" stands for *delo* (file), and "p" stands for the pages within a file. When a file is cited for the first time in a chapter, its Russian title is also indicated. A detailed list of all quoted files can be found in the references section. A number of archive files cited here stem from published source collections that concern archives in Chișinău, Moscow, St. Petersburg or Odessa. In these cases they were cited as a literature source, on the one hand to give credit to the collection's authors, on the other hand because the names of archives and the collections in them are likely to have changed.

CHAPTER 1

Introduction

During my fieldwork in southern Bessarabia in 2012 and 2013 I was often asked, exactly which of the region's many ethnic groups I had come to study. As I realized only much later, the proper answer to this question would have been that I had come to study the idea that informs this question; the idea that ethnic groups are self-contained units which are best studied separately. More specifically, this book aims to tell the story of ethnic boundaries, the story of the paradigm suggesting communion occurs primarily within groups of a very specific type: ethnic groups; whereas conflicts, occur typically between such groups. This idea was in the focus of the two-century-account of a multicultural and peripheral region, now part of southwestern Ukraine. Important questions addressed included: How have ethnic boundaries in this region emerged and how could they be preserved over time and through perpetual political sea changes? Following Fredrik Barth's example, this work is more interested in ethnic boundaries than the "cultural stuff" which they enclose (Barth, 2000: 30, 1969: 6).

Before discussing in more detail the concepts of ethnicity used in this work, a characterization of what is understood here as an ethnic boundary is appropriate at the very outset: Ethnic boundaries are the demarcation lines between social groups that are seen by their members and are recognized by outsiders as two different ethnic groups because of their diverging cultural traits (may they be real or alleged) and/or diverging geographical origins (again, real or imagined). Unlike state borders, ethnic boundaries are notoriously hard to depict on maps and even harder to demarcate on the ground. But very much like state borders, ethnic boundaries limit individual options. State borders set the territorial limit within which an individual can legally reside and enjoys civil rights. Similarly, ethnic boundaries confine a social group within which one ought to, or ought not to engage in certain activities, for instance speak a certain language, pray in church, seek political representation, or choose marriage partners. In other words, ethnic boundaries reflect a set of rules that regulates which social realms have to be kept isolated from ethnic outsiders (Barth, 1969: 16; Eriksen, 1993: 25). Boundaries therefore have, as Andreas Wimmer (2008: 975) points out, two dimensions: one that refers to classification and collective representation and one that refers to everyday networks of relationships, to individual acts of connecting and distancing. The first of these dimensions divides the social world into social groups of "us" and "them"; the second

 | DOI:10.1163/9789004408029_002

dimension informs scripts of action, how to relate to individuals classified as "us" or "them." The existence of such boundaries does not necessarily imply that groups are transparently distinguishable. Boundaries are often soft and individuals often trespass them by belonging to different categories (Wimmer, 2008: 976).

Southern Bessarabia is crisscrossed by social boundaries that, as I will show, have been increasingly classified as ethnic boundaries over the course of the 19th and 20th centuries. In some cases they run along other boundaries, such as state borders or linguistic differences, but more often these different types of boundaries cross over. The combination of an exceptionally rich "ethnic mosaic" (Lebedenko and Tychyna, 2002: 3) and a history of frequently changing statehood made this place a suitable testing ground to study how ethnic boundaries were transfigured by the tides of history. At different times, different ethnic boundaries gained in importance while others lost theirs. This study sheds some light on the nature of these ethnic boundaries and the mechanisms and rationales that drive their ongoing metamorphosis.

Most of the research was conducted in Odessa oblast, in southwestern Ukraine, in and around the town of Izmail, a river port on the Danube with roughly 72,000 inhabitants.[1] Fieldwork started in August 2012 and was completed in December 2013, covering the 16 months prior to the Maidan upheavals of late 2013. Inevitably, the events that evolved in the aftermath of the Maidan protests changed my perspective on the data gathered in this period. But the events unleashed by Maidan also changed what it means to belong to an ethnic minority in Ukraine. As so many times throughout history, new priorities were set in the political center as to how history should be remembered, what a Ukrainian identity should imply, and in which relation Ukrainian society should stand vis-à-vis other societies, above all Russia and Western Europe. History accelerated in late 2013 and throughout 2014, changing the political implications of ethnic boundaries once more. Although I was not aware of it at the time of my research, the data collected became, in retrospect, the basis for a description of a society at the edge of war. When I left Ukraine in December 2013, it was clear to anyone that life could not just go on as it did, but still every political faction believed they could turn things their way.

The protests on Maidan Square were originally caused by a general tiredness with the self-serving Yanukovich regime. The trigger of the first protests

1 Based on an estimate by the State Statistics Committee of Ukraine: <http://www.citypopulation.de/php/ukraine-odesa_d.php?adm2id=51106> (17.02.2019). The last reliable census figures are from 2001 when Izmail still had about 84,800 inhabitants: <http://2001.ukrcensus.gov.ua/rus/results/general/urban-rural/odesa/> (17.02.2019).

was a political U-turn of president Yanukovich, who in the last minute decided not to sign, after all, an Association Agreement with the European Union. In the weeks running up to this moment, he and his government had advertised the agreement loudly, despite secret meetings between the Yanukovich government and the Russian leadership were being held at the same time.[2] Already then, it became clear that the perspective of closer ties with international organizations, dominated by Western states, had the potential to deeply divide Ukrainian society. The decision not to sign a particular agreement eventually exposed much deeper rifts in culture, language policy, and perspective on the country's history. It was impossible to write about ethnic boundaries in Ukraine without asking whether these rifts ran along ethnic boundaries. Still, during fieldwork in 2012 and 2013 my focus on ethnic boundaries almost invariably produced responses stressing the harmonic interethnic relations in Ukraine. There were certainly no ethnic tensions that suggested imminent war. But many of my respondents, as well as protagonists of public discourse, unequivocally expressed their frustration with the Ukrainian government and highlighted that life could not go on like this for much longer. Very little of the grievances named to exemplify such complaints were caused by cultural or ethnic differences, by language barriers, or disputes over history. Most of the trouble mentioned was centered on corruption, clientelism, mismanagement, political hypocrisy, legal nihilism, and the resulting economic hardship. These were, I firmly believe, the deeper underlying causes of the crisis starting in 2013. The significance of ethnicity and ethnic boundaries grew when violence spread in Ukraine from early 2014 on. This is not to say that ethnic boundaries are at the root of the conflict, but they are, as I demonstrate in my research, closely tied to clientelistic local politics.

For many of my older consultants their frustration about social and economic decline was expressed through an omnipresent nostalgia for the Soviet Union. This nostalgia often came along with a moral discourse. In this discourse, corruption was seen as the cause of decline and poverty. One painfully felt consequence of the ensuing economic decline is massive out-migration of rural regions such as southern Bessarabia. The lack of working-age people creates a strain on family and village life. The result is a widespread perception of a declining communal spirit and a rise in egoistic individualism. The comparison between the more prosperous Soviet village and the present decline blends neatly into a long cultivated dichotomy between East and West, between a

2 *The Guardian* November 26, 2013, *Ukraine U-turn on Europe pact was agreed with Vladimir Putin*, available online: <http://www.theguardian.com/world/2013/nov/26/ukraine-u-turn-eu-pact-putin> (17.02.2019).

Russian-led cultural sphere and Western Europe. The latter came to stand for destructive capitalism and opportunism whereas Russia, mainly through television, maintained an image of a conservative society based on family and community values that for many seem to have disappeared from Ukraine along with the Soviet Union.

Even though, at the time of my research, I did not anticipate rapid social change, the material gathered just prior to it can provide some insight on how very tangible grievances came to be connected to concepts like ethnicity, language, and history. In Ukraine as elsewhere, these are vague and contradictory notions, receptive for political molding. Thus, in this work, for all the periods studied, it will be crucial to analyze the discourses on the overriding topics—ethnicity, language, and history—by looking at the forces that drove social change in each period.

1 Central Questions

In this study, the process of ethnic boundary maintenance (Barth, 1969: 19) will be looked at from three different angles. First, a historical perspective should clarify at what times ethnic boundaries occurred and how they changed. Second, a socio-economic perspective will focus on the implications ethnic boundaries had for people and their biographies. And third, it is vital for the understanding of ethnic boundaries to analyze the discourses used in justifying them.

These three perspectives raise the central questions which informed the research process: In a long term perspective, at what times did ethnic boundaries play a crucial role in access to resources and the political decision making process? Was the influence of ethnicity on politics a continuous one, or were there decisive ruptures? At what times and in what ways did ethnic belonging foster or impede individual life trajectories? And how was this fostering or impediment explained and justified to them and by them? Additionally, sociopolitical aspects of ethnic boundaries will be given ample attention in order to explain the motivations behind creating and maintaining ethnic boundaries: At what times and in what ways did actors who maintained ethnic boundaries gain economically or politically from this activity?

To connect the historical approach with the assumption that ethnic boundaries are culturally constructed (Anderson, 2006; Barth, 1969; Gellner, 1983; Hroch, 1998), one central question would be: Which techniques and narratives proved useful—currently and in the past—to make people perceive ethnic groups as clear-cut entities and as active subjects of history?

Ethnic boundaries, in the course of the period studied here, survived many challenges. Therefore, finally, it will be enlightening to see what makes them so resilient. How were narratives adapted if they proved to be unconvincing? When contradictions between narratives about ethnic distinctions and the observable social environment become obvious, how are they confronted by those who claim ethnic distinctions are clear-cut? The topics addressed in these questions, the varying importance of ethnic boundaries and the ways in which ethnic boundaries can be created and maintained, reappear throughout the following chapters. They can be approached with a set of three central assumptions.

First, concerning the question when, in the history of Bessarabia, ethnic boundaries reached their maximum potency, we can assume that their greatest potential to foster or impede individual life trajectories occurred simultaneously with legitimation crises of the state. This assumption makes sense if studies on the rise of ethnic nationalism in other post-socialist regions in Eastern Europe are an indication (Beissinger, 2002: 27; Brubaker, 2004: 89, 100). The assumption is therefore, that whenever the ruling political elite was unable or unwilling to provide security and economic prosperity, mistrust between the state elite and the population at the periphery soared and with it the significance of ethnic boundaries. One difficulty in testing this hypothesis is that in southern Bessarabia, since the occurrence of ethnic boundaries, times of turmoil have almost outlasted times of stability. However, stability and instability are relative, and even in bad times there were periods much more distressful than long lasting stagnant and oppressive periods. Therefore, we can conclude that there is enough ground for comparison even if it is not between two extremes, stable vs. unstable, but on a continuum in which unstable and stable were perceived according to a particular historical context. Certainly, the relations between the members of particular ethnic groups and the quickly superseding governments changed frequently enough to provide testing ground for this assumption.

Second, with regard to the techniques and narratives that created and maintain ethnic boundaries, it might turn out that there is a mechanism that represents the lowest common denominator: Ethnic boundaries are kept clear-cut by stigmatizing ambivalent identities as anomalous and by denying their partial belonging to one's own identity group (Barth, 1969: 18; Eriksen, 1993: 67). This stigmatization is likely to come in many guises, but the underlying mechanism of exclusion and inclusion may well remain unaltered. If this assumption will be found true, one goal of this study will be to identify and contextualize the different forms this mechanism has taken in southern Bessarabia's recent history.

The third assumption addresses the ways people deal with contradictions in narratives that portray ethnic groups as unambiguously bounded. Ethnic identities are based on the belief of an emotional bond between all the members of such a group (Anderson, 2006: 6; Connor, 2011: 7). Such connections can allegedly be felt, but it is hard to disclose or even prove them. Ethnic identities, even if they have become common sense, are "saturated with emotion" (Suny, 2001: 894) and emotions need no proof. Therefore, when it comes to contradictions between claims of distinctiveness of ethnic boundaries and observable social environment, the claimants will most likely seek the refuge of evidence that can be tested only by group members themselves and remains invisible to outsiders. These may be feelings or sensations perceptible only to those whom the claimants consider their own kind and unfathomable for those who challenge ethnic boundaries.

As the questions and assumptions presented above indicate, this work is at its core an exploration of reoccurring patterns of inclusion and exclusion through the modern history of southern Bessarabia. This endeavor requires collecting tangible instances of inclusion and exclusion, historical as well as modern, and subsequently analyzing these instances for their underlying patterns. Such an approach allows some degree of comparison over time.

2 History and Anthropology, Some Methodological Implications

The historic scope explored in this work begins in the year of 1812, the year Bessarabia became a part of the Russian Empire. Two hundred years is a long period to discuss by any means, but it is especially challenging to do so concerning a peripheral region, the history of which is documented scantily, controversially, and in several languages. On the other hand, the topic of this work, the creation and maintenance of ethnic boundaries, is rather narrow, merely one aspect of the much studied advent of nationalism. The rationale behind tracing ethnic boundaries—a specific but not an isolated social phenomenon—is to reveal the tirelessly working actors behind the creation and maintenance of ethnic boundaries, and the techniques they used at different times. The changing character and functions of ethnic boundaries thereby merely serve to illustrate much broader changes; the rationalization of the state, industrialization, and later the decline of the socialist economy, the advent of post-socialist nationalism, and the resulting promotion of relatively uniform national cultures. More abstractly, it also touches upon the effects of compulsory education, of social and geographical mobility, and the spread of mass media. All these phenomena have to be discussed while proceeding through history in big steps. Ignoring these indicators of change, the social mechanisms behind the occurrence of ethnic boundaries can hardly be understood. After all, ethnic boundaries have often been reinforced by references to history. Therefore, it would be impossible to study ethnic boundaries without studying the history of the society that produced them. Employing historical perspectives in anthropological thinking seemed therefore an appropriate procedure.

By starting in the early 19th century and ending with the events on Maidan, this work ran the danger of having two parts; a historical one, relying on archival sources, and an anthropological one, relying on participant observation and interviews. I aimed to dissolve the methodological boundary between history and social anthropology by adding biographical interviews to the methods, and by closely scrutinizing the way history is represented in the present. Thus I added emphasis on the idea that the present society and the ethnic boundaries in it are an outcome of the past and that the past, as we see it today, is shaped by present circumstances. Nevertheless, if we combine insights of history and anthropology, we should never take the methodology of the two disciplines for the same or believe they can readily be combined. In ethnography, the past cannot be seen. It inevitably has to be explained in terms of the present (Bloch, 1989: 2). The people of the past leave traces—if we are lucky—but beyond these, they cannot be observed nor questioned. The traces they left us are very selective, scattered to the four winds, as it were, and easily misinterpreted. In contrast to an interview, taken in the present, historical sources most often do not lend the actors the courtesy of speaking for themselves. Most of the sources were produced and stored by the state. Therefore, there is more emphasis on the views of state functionaries the further back this account reaches. With the present's flesh-and blood respondents it is hard enough to unravel the complexities of ethnic identities. One common frustration is that inquiry likely deepens complexities rather than reduce them, for instance when respondents reveal that they have ambivalent ethnic identities, that they have changed their ethnic identity at a particular point in their lifetime, or that they use different ethnic identities in different situations. These complexities are often concealed in archival documents, where information about ethnicity usually appears as boxes in tables and lists. As a rule, state documents attempt to root out ambiguities and thereby hide most of the meaning inherent in the social situation that originally produced the document. In this study, I therefore tried to focus first and foremost on the *function* of the behavior that produced a document, in order to understand its *meaning*.

One of the dangers when focusing on the functions is recognizing relicts of the past in all contemporary cultural traits. One would look for example at popular art and folklore and try to interpret what the people in the past could have meant and thought, when they created these cultural forms that have allegedly been preserved by tradition. Soviet ethnography in particular was institutionally tied to historiographical research institutions (Tishkov, 1992: 373) and it looked at "traditional" artifacts as the remains of a pure and authentic past. Present cultural forms, in this approach, represented merely a layer of dust over the authentic. It had to be wiped off in order to see the true nature of the people underneath. But rejecting the present as a mere distortion from a once undisturbed authentic society, would again divide the two disciplines, the underlying motivations for which I aim to combine here. What unites the two fields is undoubtedly the desire to grasp the ideas of people who differ from the researcher in their mindset, whether it be because they lived long ago or were socialized in a different culture. The expedition into the mind that thought long ago or far away is "the same adventure of the mind" as Fernand Braudel (2009: 184) quoted Claude Lévi-Strauss. The metaphor of the past as a foreign country was borrowed from the opening sentence of L.P Hartleys *The Go Between* (1973), a novel based on the memories of an old man, who recalls events and the social order of his childhood with the help of a rediscovered diary. The American anthropologist Clifford Geertz saw ethnographic research as an act of reading the culture of a foreign society. He employed the metaphor of a manuscript that needs to be read and understood, although it is written in a foreign language, faded and full of digression, contradictions, suspicious corrections, and tendentious comments (Geertz, 1973: 10). For historians, in contrast, such documents are not a metaphor but the real sources on which they base their insights. Still the cognitive process of interpreting the two sources of knowledge, observable behavior and historical sources is parallel in both disciplines and can be fruitfully combined.

For scholars who combine historical and ethnographic approaches, it is a time tested trick to scrutinize a foreign culture via a narrowly defined aspect but with the aim of shedding light on broader terms of social change. In the French Annales School, the historiographical movement that is now widely credited with bringing historiography and the social sciences back together, this trick has often been employed. Marc Bloch, for instance, was reportedly scoffed when he set out to dedicate an entire book (Bloch, 1973) to the supposedly marginal topic of a medieval popular belief in the healing powers of monarchs. But Bloch managed to show that this belief had far wider implications for social structure and political thought at the time (Burke, 1990: 17). Similarly, Carlo Ginzburg's (1989, 1980) portrayal of a single man's ideas could be fruitfully used to illustrate the mindset of entire layers of society in 16th century Friuli. Looking at the narrow topic of ethnic boundary maintenance, this study envisages achieving a similar effect. Traced through a long time, the belief that ethnic boundaries are natural, real, and meaningful, can reveal a lot about the time, the nature of society and the state as a whole. The narrow subject was just one ingredient in creating a historical and anthropological research design. A second ingredient was looking at a fairly long stretch of time in order to create a perspective approaching the target of a *longue-durée* (Braudel, 2009: 147). This stretch had to be limited sensibly in terms of the subject (the occurrence of ethnic boundaries). It also had to be a period of time from which sufficient sources were accessible. Southern Bessarabia as a field was chosen partly because state hegemony had changed so many times there. But one of these changes had to be chosen as a starting point in order to limit the number of states that had to be looked at to a manageable scope. The choice ultimately fell on the year 1812 as a starting point; the year, when the Russian Empire for the first time formally annexed Bessarabia. Since then, besides tsarist Russia, three more states have governed the region; Romania, the Soviet Union, and most recently Ukraine. All these states have shaped and used ethnic boundaries to their ends and thereby changed what it meant to belong to one or other ethnic group.

This process offers insight into how the state has changed over time, how its relation to the population has changed, and how ethnicity became the ubiquitous category it is today. A combination of methods and of theoretical concepts from both history and social anthropology was indispensable in this endeavor. Ethnic boundaries have been a major preoccupation of social anthropology at least since Barth's pioneering study (1969) on this subject. Slow social change, as well as shifting beliefs and practices have been the main focus of the Annales-school and its derivatives in historiography (Burke, 1990: 2).Therefore the theoretical and methodological approaches of this study are not new and can rely on a great range of established works. Neither is there much novelty in picking a narrow region and a narrow topic in order to point out trajectories of social change in a wider field. But for Ukraine—and for this nook in particular—studying ethnicity itself, and not ethnic group by ethnic group as separate phenomena, is a new approach. It runs counter to the trend of most local social science, because it treats ethnic differences not as givens but as social constructs with specific social functions. And it fills a gap in the foreign literature on Ukraine, because it anchors the study of ethnic boundaries with a focus on a rural, peripheral area, often passed over by big politics. The present rapid changes in statehood and ethnicity in Ukraine make understanding the historical roots of ethnic differences and weak statehood more relevant than ever.

This study combines a wide range of archival sources with ethnographic material. The bulk of sources come from the state archive in Izmail. They include a broad array of data on the relation between state and population from two centuries and three different states: tsarist Russia, Romania, and the Soviet Union. Since the archive had no collection on ethnicity, clues on the significance of ethnicity at various times had to be taken from census data, police reports, marriage certificates, school reports, culture house programs, minutes of village gatherings, and many other files. Some of the files that looked very promising according to the description of their content turned out to contain very little valuable information. For example, census data from the 19th century, which were described in the Soviet-era *opis'* (description) as being full of data about ethnicity, in fact contained mainly data about religious and social categories. On the other hand, files which, judging by their description, did not look as obvious candidates for information on ethnicity, turned out to be rich sources. For instance Soviet school reports from the 1940s and 1950s contained a wealth of information about the ascription of ethnic categories by educational institutions.

Sources from Izmail's local archive could shed some light on the historical particularities of southern Bessarabia. For the wider national context, however, the archive offered little and I had to rely on historical literature. Additional data used in this book stems from local newspapers. The main local periodicals since World War II are stored in Izmail's central library and are searchable by article titles thanks to a card index.

The scarcity of published literature on this specific region's history also made it necessary to use the early ethnographies, statistics and travel journals available, both as sources of information and at the same time as illustrative material how the category of ethnicity was used by them. This double function demanded a clear division between factual information about places, dates and numbers and their own interpretations of their observations. The latter became the basis of my discussion of ethnic categories and their evolution in the ethnographic literature of the late 19th and early 20th century in chapter 2. The many different contexts in which the category of ethnicity popped up in the archive alerted me to pay attention to its changing social and administrative functions. I was therefore constantly reminded of the question, what function did the phrase "I am Russian" or "you are Bulgarian" or "my neighbor is Ukrainian" fulfill at different times in Bessarabia. One conceivable answer was that this ascription was meant exclusively to transport the information which language the person in question spoke. It was also conceivable that this speech-act was meant to entitle a person with rights or obligations that others did not have. It was further conceivable that such an ascription, at times carried information about whom the specified person was permitted to marry or not, where he or she could obtain an education, where one was permitted to live or travel to. All of these conceivable functions were coupled to the category of ethnicity in the course of the two centuries since 1812. The subjects of these acts of ascriptions had to make sense of what the ethnic identity attached to their person did to them. The category had to be filled with meaning. Because these explanations happened in private, they hardly ever left a trace in the archive. To focus on function was therefore often the closest approximation one could get to the intended meaning.

The other approximation to what ethnic categories meant to people in the past came through biographical interviews. I conducted 34 interviews of this type with mainly elderly rural inhabitants of the region. Biographical interviews started with questions about language skills of the respondent and when and under which circumstances they were acquired. This proved a good entry point into biographies often shaped by a marked shift from a village-centered identity to a wider Soviet and Russian-speaking identity. Biographical interviews then usually went along the topics of how respondents acquired their professional skills, built their houses, tended their gardens, and raised their families. These recollections were occasionally interrupted by the interviewer to ask for interethnic relations, language barriers, administrative obstacles and perceived discrimination at the time concerned. This procedure turned out to be much more effective than to ask directly how ethnic boundaries had fostered or impeded a respondent's biography. It was much easier to explain to respondents what these questions meant when they were already in the course of describing a particular period of their life. Such biographical interviews were mostly conducted in villages after I had gained access to respondents there. Because accessing village respondents acquired long preparation, most of these interviews became possible only in the second half of the fieldwork period, in summer and autumn of 2013.

Data for this book also come from 16 semi-structured expert interviews with local politicians, scholars, teachers, and activists. Most of these interviews were conducted in Izmail and Odessa during the first half of the fieldwork period. Two interviews with scholars were recorded in Chișinău. Each of these interviews was tailor-made for the respective expert's background. They included questions about the changing content of education, about the history of ethnic associations in the region, about the development of commemorative culture and about local politics in general. I have also discussed all these topics outside of interview situations in countless informal conversations which subsequently informed my field journal.

I conducted all interviews in Russian, which is the most widely used language for the public sphere in the region. In one case, during an interview with an elderly Ukrainian man, I asked my questions in Russian but the interviewee responded in Ukrainian.

When selecting the four villages in which I could conduct interviews, three criteria were decisive: the ethnic composition of the population, whether I was able to find a host family, and the distance from Izmail, since traveling between villages by public transport could be very time consuming. Because interviewing and archive research were conducted as parallel activities, I had to spend about half of the work week in Izmail to work in the archive and the other half of the week in one of the selected villages in order to conduct interviews. This mode of multitasking became my schedule between June and December 2013, when the archive study, my study of the local press, and expert interviews were already at a progressed stage and when my initial contact network in Izmail also began to provide access to villages. I eventually sought out four villages for my interviews. The village of Kotlovina is inhabited predominantly with people who identify as Gagauz. It is part of Reni rayon, has roughly 2,600 inhabitants,[3] and is located about 48 km to the northwest of Izmail. Chervonoarmeyskoe in Bolgrad rayon is a village with about 6,500 inhabitants, roughly two-thirds of which identify as Bulgarians and one-third as Gagauz. Chervonoarmeyskoe is located at 65 km to the north of Izmail. In 2016 Chervonoarmeyskoe, Ukrainian for "Red Army Place," was renamed to its pre-Soviet name, Kubey, in accordance with Ukraine's de-communization laws.[4] Kotlovina and Chervonoarmeyskoe were located too far away from Izmail to travel there just for a day. Therefore in these two villages I had to rely on host families, who also allowed me to gain deeper insights into village life. I was introduced to these host families via earlier contacts in Izmail and Odessa. The other two villages were close enough to Izmail to commute. One of them was Kislitsa, a predominately Ukrainian village only 21 km from Izmail. The other one was Pershotravnevoe at 31 km from Izmail. Both of these villages today are predominately Ukrainian speaking but have substantial Moldovan minorities. Kislitsa has about 2,900 inhabitants[5] and Pershotravnevoe about 2,000.[6] The archive search was modified according to the selection of villages, so that files about the villages

---

3 Kotlovina on the website of the Verkhovna Rada: <http://w1.c1.rada.gov.ua/pls/z7503/A005?rdat1=19.03.2013&rf7571=22994> (17.02.2019).

4 Kubey on the website of Verkhovna Rada: <http://w1.c1.rada.gov.ua/pls/z7503/A005?rdat1=10.06.2016&rf7571=49952> (17.02.2019) the website also contains the parliamentary decree to rename the village on June 3, 2016.

5 Kislitsa on the website of Verkhovna Rada: <http://w1.c1.rada.gov.ua/pls/z7503/A005?rdat1=13.09.2014&rf7571=24161> (17.02.2019).

6 Pershotravnevoe on the website of Verkhovna Rada: <http://w1.c1.rada.gov.ua/pls/z7503/A005?rdat1=14.11.2015&rf7571=24181> (17.02.2019).

I regularly visited were examined first. By seeking out this combination of villages, interviews with rural respondents were feasible and could include people who identify with all the major ethnic groups in Izmail's environs.

Research also included a participant observation study of the parliamentary elections in October 2012, of folklore festivals, and memorial events. The greatest difficulty with participant observation was hearing about relevant events before they took place. Most events were not announced publicly but by word of mouth. It therefore became crucial that at the beginning of my fieldwork I spent a lot of time in Izmail's culture house, where I met well-connected people, who were regularly involved in organizing and conducting cultural events. They included the head of the drama theatre, the head of the rayon Center of Ethnic Culture, as well as folklore artists and stage technicians.

3 Locating the Field Site and Choosing a Name for It

There are many peripheral regions in Ukraine that might be studied for similar interests. In fact, most scholars today agree that the national denomination *Ukrayina* is probably derived from a word with a meaning similar to "periphery" or "borderland" (Kappeler, 2000: 17; Magocsi, 1996: 171; Plokhy, 2006: 317; Subtelny, 2000: 105). However, other regions of Ukraine have at least for one period of history been at the center of events; Kyiv as the capital of Kievan Rus', the Dnepr region as the center of the Cossack states, Galicia as the center of the medieval Kingdom of Galicia-Volhynia and since the late 19th century of Ukrainian nationalism, and the Donbas as the center of Soviet industrialization as well as the recent, Russian-backed separatism. Bessarabia has remained at the periphery throughout and still has a peripheral status in Ukraine today (Kushko and Taki, 2012: 18).

But before discussing the region's historical fate, it might be sensible to define its geographical extent. Today, the name "Bessarabia" can be found only on historical maps. Since 1918, when Russia had to cede the territory of *Bessarabskaya Guberniya* to Romania, no administrative unit has carried this name. But the denomination "Bessarabia" continued to be used in Russian as well as in Romanian (where it is commonly spelled "Basarabia") to refer to the territory of the old Russian *Guberniya*. This province and most modern references to Bessarabia, are limited by three rivers; the Prut in the west, the Dniester in the east, the Danube and the Black Sea in the south. A string of old Ottoman fortresses runs along the Danube and up the Dniester, once a line of defense against intruders and rebellious locals. The northernmost of these fortresses, Khotyn, stands at a point where the Dniester and the Prut flow parallel, with hardly 30 km of land between them. Here, the old Guberniya reached its northernmost extension and the name Bessarabia is not usually used to designate territories far beyond this imaginary line between the Dniester and the Prut.

The region enclosed by these borders has not only been a political periphery, but also an ecological border zone. Here end the vast steppes stretching from central Asia, through southern Siberia and into the Ponto-Caspian plain of southern Russia and Ukraine. Beyond Bessarabia, they pass into the more forested foothills of the Carpathians. This stretch of land represented the European end of a large steppe zone, a "Eurasian highway" for peoples and cultures (Schorkowitz, 2012: 85). For the pastoral nomads, who once roamed these lands with their herds, the three large rivers that bound Bessarabia formed an obstacle and marked a boundary for their way of life. This geographical situation might be at the origin of a second name sometimes used to designate this region; "Budjak." "Budjak" refers to the flat and dry steppes in the southern third of Bessarabia. It likely was derived from "corner" or "nook" in the Turkic languages of its earlier nomadic inhabitants (Palamarchuk, 2008: 219). Writing in 1850, the traveler and scholar Apollon Skal'kovskiy defined Budjak as the steppe regions in the south of Bessarabia (Skal'kovskiy, 1850: 255). Stepan Kornilovich who, in 1899, presented a description of the Izmail area, used "Bessarabia" and "Budjak" as synonyms.[7] The term Budjak (Budziak) appears as early as 1681 on a map by Moses Pitt. Later, on a map produced by Johann Baptist Homann in Nuremberg in 1729, "Bessarabia" and "Tataria Budziacensis" refer to the same area.[8] With the addendum of "Tataria" the cartographer reminds us that this region was then still predominantly inhabited by Turkic speaking Muslims. Today the name Budjak is still extensively used in local historiography and sometimes in folklore.[9] But it is not a widely known and well-defined term that lends itself to public reference and identity formation. "I am a Budjakian" would certainly sound rather absurd, whereas "I am a Bessarabian" is a perfectly reasonable utterance still today.[10]

Indeed, the territories known as Budjak and Bessarabia might once have been more congruent than today. The term "Basarabia," probably derived from the Walachian princely Basarab dynasty that originated in the 14th century. The region for which it was used had neither clear boundaries, nor much political relevance for a long time; but it included or overlapped with the equally

7 He wrote that Izmail belonged to "Bessarabia that is alternatively also called Budjak" (Kornilovich, 1899: 376).

8 Both maps are reproduced in Kordan (2008: 73, 83).

9 One example is the renowned folklore group of the Gagauz village of Kotlovina. They perform under the name "Stars of the Budjak."

10 An observation also made by Anastassova (2006: 60).

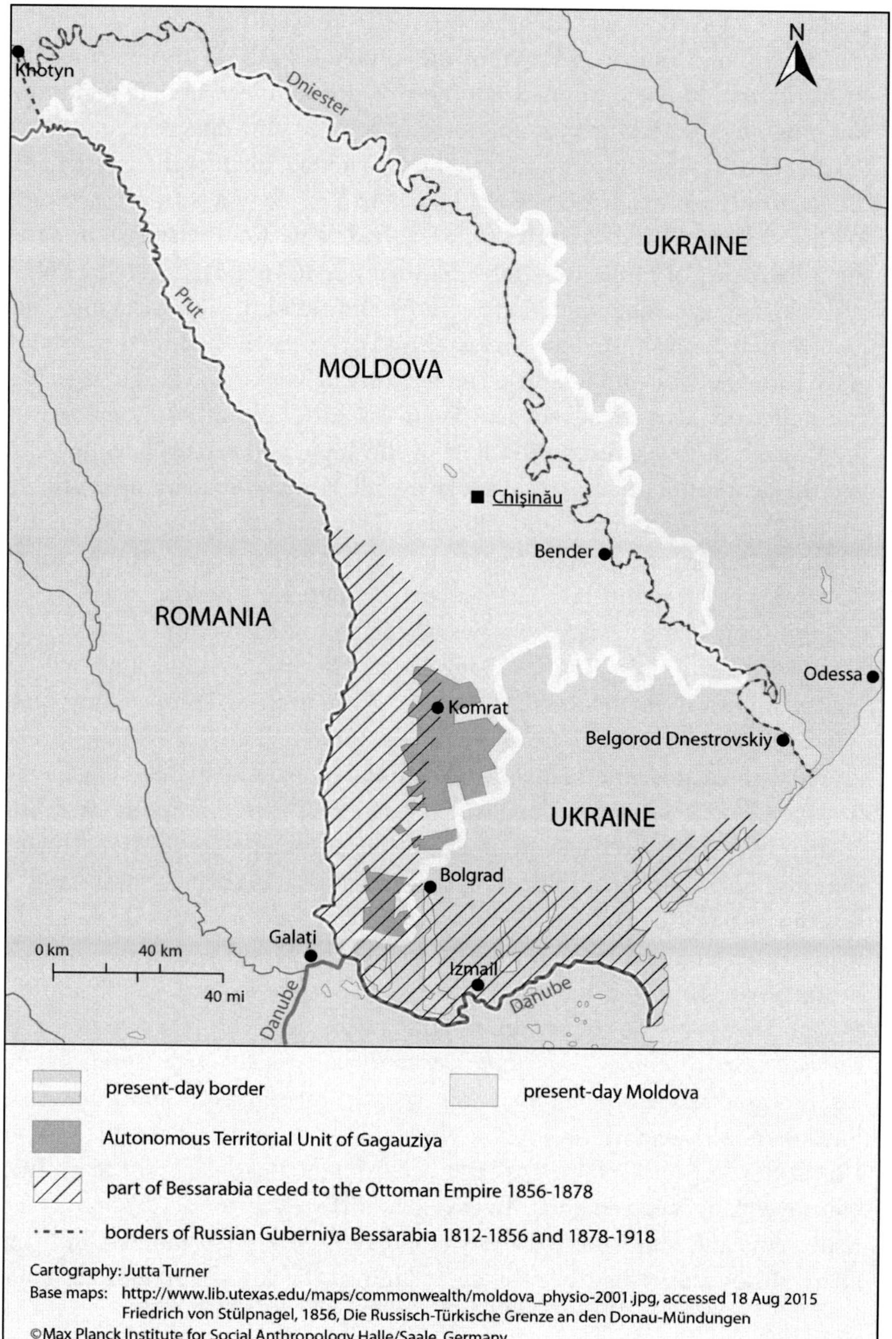

MAP 1 Bessarabia's shifting state borders since 1812

vaguely defined "Budjak" (King, 2000: 21). Before the Russian annexation, the principality of Moldova, a vassal of the Ottoman Empire, loosely controlled this land. Its influence thinned out towards the southern Budjak region that was inhabited by Muslim pastoral nomads (Kushko and Taki, 2012: 17).

After the Russian Empire annexed the area in 1812, the Russified designation "Bessarabiya" was extended beyond Budjak to a much wider area, reaching up to Khotyn fortress, across lands that so far had been simply the eastern part of the principality of Moldova (Grek and Russev, 2011: 66; King, 2000: 21; Kushko and Taki, 2012: 71; Palamarchuk, 2008: 218). Only after the Russian Empire had named their newest province "Bessarabiya," the area, limited by the three rivers, became a conceptual entity. The territory of Bessarabia had always been culturally and linguistically diverse. There was little cultural cohesion between the Russian or Jewish urban dwellers of the small and relatively young cities and the peasant population that spoke mostly Romanian or, in the south, Bulgarian, Gagauz, Ukrainian, and Albanian. Therefore, in the late 19th century, when nationalist aspirations began to test the imperial integrity of Russia, Bessarabia could hardly be considered a candidate for a new nation.

Nevertheless, the designation "Bessarabia" became a reference point in other nationalisms. In his *Historical Description of Bessarabia*, published "with the highest approval" by the Russian Ministry of the Interior, Pompey Batyushkov (1892: 78) characterized Bessarabia as an old Russian land that had finally been united with its motherland in 1812. Around the time of the first Russian Revolution 1905–07, Moldovan nationalist circles in their turn referred to Bessarabia as their core land and based their aspirations of independence from the Russian tsar on that claim. Their newspaper that was eventually prohibited by Russian authorities was named *Basarabia* (King, 2000: 29; Kushko and Taki, 2012: 285). Even much later, when Bessarabia after World War II became a part of the Soviet Union, it remained an entity of reference and justification, although there was no longer an administrative unit with that name. In the *Chronological Reference Book of the Occupation 1941–44*, a staple in local libraries, Bessarabia was characterized an "age old Russian soil" and a landscape filled with the traces of "the shining glory of Russian arms."[11] Later in the Soviet Union, this territorial claim was extended from the Russians to the Slavs. In his controversially received book, Artem Lazarev (1974), rector of Chișinău's Lenin University and the Moldovan Soviet Republic's highest ranking historian, claimed Bessarabia had been a Slavic land in the Middle Ages, long before

11 "Khronolgicheskiy spravochnik ob okkupatsii Izmail'skoy oblasti (1941–944 gg.)," 1950: 5, 83.

something like a Moldovan nation could have existed (Lazarev, 1974; van Meurs, 1994: 250).

However, with the integration into the Soviet Union, the concept of Bessarabia as an entity began to erode. In 1940, Moscow technocrats drew borders between two Soviet Republics, the Moldovan SSR and the Ukrainian SSR. The northernmost part, the lands around Khotyn, with a Ukrainian majority population, was given to the Ukrainian SSR. The large middle part, with a Romanian speaking majority, was made into the Moldovan SSR. The southernmost part, with no clear ethnic majority, was joined with the Ukrainian SSR. These administrative Soviet borders became paralyzing state borders when the Soviet Union fell apart in 1991. The southern Ukrainian part of Bessarabia is now squeezed between the Danube that has no ferries or bridges here,[12] and the Moldovan border with its unreliable and corrupt border posts. Only one road connects Izmail to the provincial capital Odessa and to the rest of Ukraine. This road has been in notoriously bad shape for many years and its renovation is a perpetual concern of local politicians.[13] After heavy snowfall, the road can be closed for days, literally cutting off the whole region from the rest of the country. This isolated appendix of modern Ukraine is the geographical framework of the present study. Even after the territory of Bessarabia has been divided between two countries, it apparently has not lost its identificatory potential. During my fieldwork the term "Bessarabia" for the region and "Bessarabian" for its inhabitants was not only used frequently but also in a wider variety of contexts than any alternative denomination. For instance, in 2011 the local weekly *Kur'er Nedeli* (the weekly courier) ran a series of photo

12 In October 2015, it was reported that construction of a ferry connection between the Ukrainian village of Orlovka and the Romanian village of Isaccea had begun: <http://bessarabiainform.com/2015/10/v-oktyabre-nachinaetsya-stroitelstvo-v-bessarabii-paromnoj-perepravy-ukraina-rumyniya/> (17.02.2019). However, similar announcements were made in the years before without materializing.

13 Mikhail Saakashvili, the former President of Georgia and the Governor of Odessa oblast between May 2015 and November 2016, in a talk show on ICTV, explained to a Ukrainian audience the extent and problems of southern Bessarabia. He said the region was "terribly poor," and that the road that connects it to rump Ukraine was "the worst in Europe." To illustrate how neglected the region was (and therefore, in Saakashvili's view, how vulnerable to separatism) he said that Putin's government had devoted much more thought to Bessarabia than the Ukrainian government. Video from on June 23, 2015, available online: <https://www.youtube.com/watch?feature=player_embedded&v=KzS3c32BRMk> (17.02.2019). In the days leading up to Saakashvili's talk show performance he had visited southern Bessarabia and listened to the complaints of citizens. Also, Anton Kisse, an MP for one of the region's electoral districts, in the days prior to Saakashvili's speech, made several petitions lamenting the bad condition of the Izmail-Odessa road. He published these on his various social media outlets.

portraits called "faces of Bessarabia."[14] The band leader of a folklore group that regularly played for German tourists on shore leave from their Danube cruise boat usually explained at the beginning of their performance "this region is called Bessarabia but the country we live in is Ukraine." A deputy to the national Parliament, Anton Kisse, who will be introduced in more detail later, addressed the crowd at a Gagauz culture festival in Odessa as "dear Bessarabians" (*dorogie Bessarabtsy*). A local artist entitled one of the paintings he contributed to an exhibition "Bessarabian scene." The painting showed a circle of friends drinking wine in the shade of a vine cover. And even the looming threat of separatism in the region after violence had broken out in Donbas brought the term up: When, in spring 2015, rumors of a local separatism movement began to circulate, the mysterious political organization behind it was called "the People's Council of Bessarabia."[15]

But of course Bessarabia is bigger than its Ukrainian part. The bulk of the former province belongs to Moldova. I therefore follow Lebedenko and Tychyna (2002: 4), two local historians from the University of Izmail, in their designation of this area as "southern Bessarabia."[16] The authors alternatively use the term "Ukrainian Danube Region" (*Ukrayins'ke Podunav'ya*). But some of the villages studied here are located far away from the river and are not Ukrainian in terms of ethnicity or language, so that "southern Bessarabia" is the more appropriate term here. Other terms that might be politically less captious, such as "southwestern Ukraine" are even less precise than "southern Bessarabia." It would certainly also include the city of Odessa and the northern part of Odessa oblast that has much closer cultural and transportation connections to rump Ukraine. Southern Bessarabia therefore remains the best term to refer to the entire region, whereas most often a particular municipality or district can be indicated. This is often in order because fieldwork activities for this study were, for the most part, confined to an even smaller area, the town of Izmail and villages in Izmail rayon, as well as neighboring rayons Bolgrad and Reni.

In the former Soviet Union, there are many ethnically mixed areas. Three main types of ethnic diversity can be distinguished: Areas where Russians are in a majority, areas where another ethnic group is in a majority, and areas

14 *Kur'er Nedeli*, 25.6.2011: <https://issuu.com/izmail.es/docs/kn26/48> (24.2.2017).

15 After the name and logo of this group appeared in April 2015, most local political and ethnic organizations quickly declared they had nothing to do with it. *Zerkalo Nedeli* April 7, 2015: <http://zn.ua/UKRAINE/sbu-nazvala-ocherednoy-lozhyu-rossii-sozdanie-narodnoy-rady-bessarabii-172266_.html> (17.02.2019).

16 Administratively, this area makes up the part of Odessa oblast south-west of the river Dniester, about half the province's territory. It consists of rayons Belgorod-Dniestrovskiy, Sarata, Tatarbunary, Tarutino, Artsis, Kiliya, Izmail, Bolgrad, and Reni.

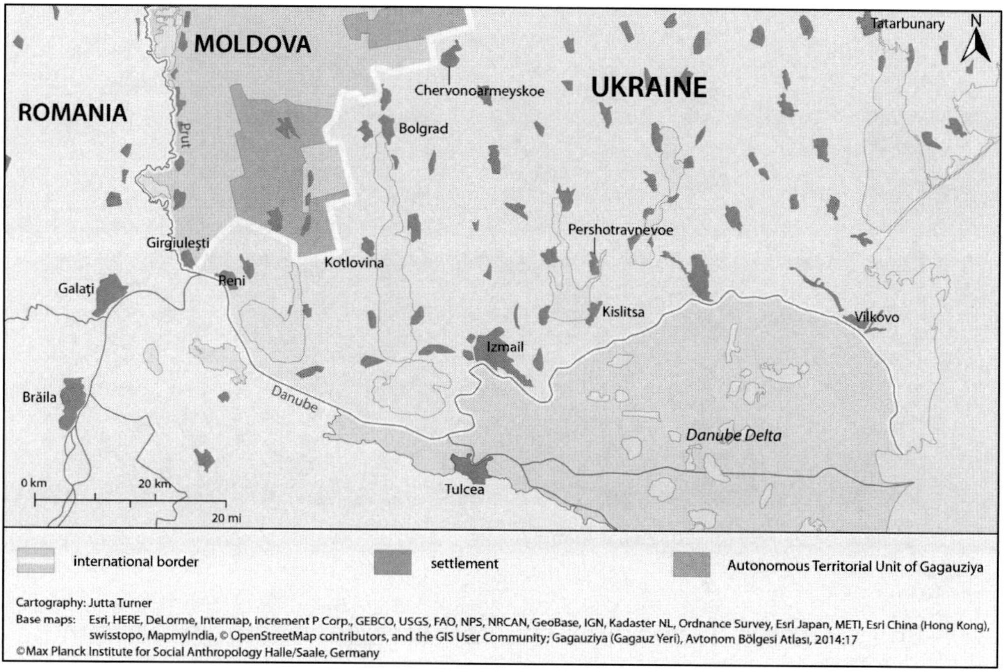

MAP 2 Southern Bessarabia

where there is no clear ethnic majority (Karklins, 1986: 8). Southern Bessarabia belongs to this last type. Its ethnic groups have lived in close interaction for two centuries. For all this time it is hard to find instances of open ethnic hatred. Harmonic interethnic relations are considered a matter of great pride in this region. The attitude many people take to ethnicity and conflict can be illustrated by an episode that occurred during a family reunion in the Gagauz village of Kotlovina in October 2013. A round of men, including the village's priest, heatedly discussed the imminent signing of the Association Agreement with the EU in Vilnius while tasting the host's new barrel of wine. When I asked them about ethnic conflicts in the region, the host raised a laugh by pointing to the barn where he stored his wine. "Ethnic conflict?" he asked, "this is where we go to sort out ethnic conflict."

The best clue of current ethnic composition in this region is given by the latest available census from 2001, in which ethnic identity was recorded based on self-identification. In towns, Russians are the biggest group, as was the case for most of the time since this region was incorporated into the Russian Empire. In the city of Izmail, Russians comprise 43% of the population. Those who identify as Ukrainians are a close second (38%). Bulgarians make up for 10% of Izmail's inhabitants. Moldovans make up around 4% and Gagauz less

FIGURE 1 A view of Kotlovina in summer 2013

than 1%. Izmail is surrounded by villages-turned-suburbs with inhabitants who largely identify as Ukrainians. The further north, the more the ethnic composition is reminiscent of the colonization of this land by settlers from the Balkans. In Izmail rayon with its 23 villages (the city is not part of the rayon) Ukrainians are the biggest group (29%), but there are nearly as many Moldovans (27%) and Bulgarians (25%). Russians are another substantial group (16%) many of whom live in the Old-Believer villages. Bolgrad rayon, to the north of Izmail has 60% Bulgarians and 19% Gagauz. Russians and Ukrainians each make up for only 8% here, with Albanians and Moldovans comprising the rest. In Reni rayon, bordering both Romania and Moldova, there are 49% Moldovans, 17% Ukrainians, and 15% Russians. Bulgarians make up 8%, but for this research the only Gagauz village in the rayon, Kotlovina (that largely accounts for the 7% Gagauz) was studied.[17]

With a history of changing statehood between the great empires of Eastern Europe and a complicated relationship between many different ethnic groups, often exploited by the ruling state, the history of southern Bessarabia also holds many clues for the whole of Bessarabia, that now belongs both to Moldova and Ukraine or for other adjacent regions, such as Bukovina, today a part of Romania as well as of Ukraine.

17 All figures from the Ukrainian 2001 census: <http://2001.ukrcensus.gov.ua/rus/results/general/nationality/odesa/> (23.02.2019).

4 A Brief Historical Outline

Bessarabia's ethnic diversity and frequently changing political powers are evidence of its long peripheral status. Since Russia expanded into the region in 1812, this territory has changed hands seven times: First after the Crimean War (1853–56), in which Russia was defeated by a coalition of France, Britain, and the Ottoman Empire, southern Bessarabia was given to the United Principalities, a forerunner of Romania, still technically under Ottoman suzerainty. Then in 1878, after the last of the Russo-Turkish Wars, it was retaken by the Russian Empire. Bessarabia was now out of reach of the Ottoman Empire, since a buffer zone consisting of two newly independent states, Romania and Bulgaria had been created as a consequence of the war. In 1918, after the Russian withdrawal from the First World War, Bessarabia was joined with expanding Romania, which managed to almost double its territory and population through the Paris Treaties that settled World War I. In 1940, a strengthened Soviet Union annexed Bessarabia according to the Molotov-Ribbentrop Treaty, just to lose it again to an alliance of Romania and Nazi Germany that attacked the Soviet Union in June 1941. After the situation on the eastern front had changed dramatically in the winter of 1942–43, the Red Army, on its way to drive out Hitler's troops, conquered and integrated Bessarabia again in summer 1944. After belonging to the Ukrainian SSR of the Soviet Union for 47 years, southern Bessarabia became part of independent Ukraine when the Soviet Union broke apart in 1991.

Before modern states systematically populated southern Bessarabia, human settlement was sparse but not absent. Like most of the Ponto-Caspian Steppe region, southern Bessarabia did not appear enticing to early peasants. The steppes offered little water sources; large trees for construction and firewood were scant. The open landscape allowed big herds of game, swarms of insects, and nomadic groups to quickly travel great distances and to endanger a peasant's crop. Prairie fires and storms were an additional hazard (Moon, 2013: 7,44; Sunderland, 2004: 90). Along the rivers, where water and timber were abundant, so were malaria-infested mosquitos.[18] Since the 16th century, Nogai nomads were the dominant group in the Bessarabian steppe, loosely controlled

18 In 1933, according to Romanian statistics, there were 3,079 cases of malaria in Izmail district, some 1,950 of which were new infections. Most cases occurred along the channels of the Danube Delta and its adjacent lakes. For almost 13% of malaria patients, the infection was fatal (Rossetti, 1934: 36). Between the end of World War II and the early 1950s Soviet administrators installed two malaria treatment centers in southern Bessarabia, one in Izmail and one in Belgorod-Dniestrovskiy, Fr 734 (for Izmail) and Fr1723 (for Belgorod) ("Putevoditel' Filial Odesskogo oblastnogo archiva v g. Izmaile," 1966: 165). In the 1940s

by the Crimean Khans (Kushko and Taki, 2012: 37). Under more direct Ottoman control were the fortresses along the large rivers; Izmail and Kiliya on the Danube, as well as Akkerman (today Belgorod-Dniestrovskiy), Bender, and Khotyn on the Dniester. When Russia incorporated Bessarabia in 1812, these were the only places in the province with rudimentary urban structures (Kushko and Taki, 2012: 198). Decades later, towards the end of the 19th century, urbanization was still very low. Of the 1.9 million inhabitants Bessarabia had at the time of the 1897 census, only about 15 percent lived in cities (Derzhavin, 1914: 15). During Fieldwork in 2012 and 2013, many villages around Izmail celebrated the bicentennial of their foundation. Izmail's own history was traced back further (during the fieldwork period the city celebrated its assumed 422 and 423 anniversaries) but this mode of counting includes more than two centuries in which Izmail was more a trading post growing into a fortress, than a fully-fledged town. The fact that most settlements which can now be found on the map of southern Bessarabia date back no longer than 200 years speaks of a history full of warfare and of a dramatic change in population structure at the beginning of the 19th century.

The Russian Empire had joined the ranks of the great European powers under Peter I when it drove Sweden out of Eastern Europe in the Great Northern War (1700–21). An episode of this conflict, the so-called Prut Campaign, saw the first Russian advance into Moldova in 1710–11. Although this time the Ottomans prevailed over Russia, the advance led by Peter I had established a Russian claim to acting as the protective force for the Christian population in the Ottoman Empire. But Russia became a serious force in South Eastern Europe only when the Empire gained access to the Black Sea. In the second half of the 18th century, under the reign of Catherine II, Russia won two decisive wars in what is now southern Ukraine. The first of these was the Russo-Turkish War 1768–74 that according to the subsequent treaty of Küçük Kaynarca, gave the empire an outlet to the Sea of Azov (Hosking, 2001: 231). But the fortress of Izmail, taken by General Repnin in 1770, had to be given back to the Ottomans. It was subsequently reinforced and gained the reputation to be impregnable (Lebedenko and Tychyna, 2002: 77). The second decisive war was the Russo-Turkish War of 1788–92, during which the Ottoman Empire unsuccessfully attempted to regain parts of the lost territory. But the Ottomans had to redraw even further, which allowed the Russian Empire to expand as far west as the Dniester River (Sunderland, 2004: 56). The 1788–92 War also proved that the Turkish fortress at Izmail was not impregnable. In December 1791, Count

lectures were given by the Izmail lecture bureau how to avoid and treat malaria: Fr415 D15, 1947, p. 4.

Suvorov sacked the fortress with his troops, a great military triumph at the time and today the single most important historical event in the historical self-consciousness of Izmailians. For all its symbolic importance, Russia once more ceded Bessarabia back to the Ottoman Empire with the Treaty of Iași in 1792 (Lebedenko and Tychyna, 2002: 80). It took another Russo-Turkish War (1806–12) to incorporate Bessarabia again into the empire. After a number of disastrous losses, the Ottoman Empire agreed in 1812, with the Treaty of Bucharest, to cease the eastern half of their vassal state, the Principality of Moldova, to the Russian Empire. This area became the oblast of Bessarabia, the last in a long line of annexed territories along the Black Sea coast. Combined, these new provinces were by that time referred to in Russia as *Novorossiya* (New Russia). This is the point in time from which a more detailed historical discussion starts in chapters two through five. Here, it suffices to mention, that the Treaty of Bucharest allowed the Russian Empire to formalize an already ongoing influx of Christian colonists, mainly from the territory of modern day Bulgaria (later they would be termed the "Transdanubian Colonists"). The colonists were given modest amounts of land, as well as fiscal privileges for the time they needed to build up peasant economies (Kushko and Taki, 2012: 168). As the region became integrated into a state with military, trade, and transportation systems, the soil of southern Bessarabia, once spurned by peasants for its exposure to the dangers of the open steppe, revealed its great fertility.

The oldest building now standing in Izmail is the former Ottoman mosque on the bank of the Danube. The fortress around it, once thought to be impregnable, can vaguely be recognized on satellite images. On the ground, there is nothing left to give a clue of it. The forces that erased the once mighty fortress of Izmail were, as so often in the history of Bessarabia, unleashed from far away. A small section of southern Bessarabia, along the border with the Ottoman vassal state of Moldova, was ceded to the Ottoman Empire again in 1856 after Russia had suffered a setback in the Crimean War. The area included 40 settlements of Transdanubian Colonists who were promised the same rights and privileges as under Russian rule (Batyushkov, 1892: 164). The Paris Peace Treaty of 1856 specified that the fortifications, before ceded to Ottoman forces, had to be torn down (Sapozhnikov, 2009: 254). In 1857 Russia had to agree to give away Izmail and a stretch of land along the Danube to the Principality of Moldova, a vassal of the Ottoman Empire, and the Danube Delta to direct control of the Porte.[19] Russia regained the southernmost region of Bessarabia after 22 years in 1878, when the last of the Russo-Turkish Wars was settled with the Berlin Treaty (Ryasanovsky, 2000: 387).

19 The agreement is reproduced in (Tsyhanenko, 2013: 160).

Izmail was transformed from a garrison fortress to a river port as the region began to be integrated into the civil communication infrastructure of the Russian Empire. Industrialization remained on a low scale, but for parts of the population it offered geographical and social mobility. Now, this relatively remote area for the first time drew the interest of Russian ethnographers, who provided us with the first systematic descriptions of the area's ethnic mosaic. At about the same time, Russia began to fear minorities' nationalism and began to russify the bureaucracy and the church (King, 2000: 25). As was true throughout its history as a part of the Russian Empire, these administrative efforts to russify society reached Bessarabia late and weakened by the sheer length of the command chain from the imperial center in St. Petersburg. But the suspicion towards ethnic minorities and their alleged tendency of separatist nationalism became a dominant theme for the relation between the local population and the two regimes that covered most of the 20th century; Romania and the Soviet Union. Bessarabia's contested status was enhanced by the fact that Bessarabia was not only contested between Russia and Romania but also between two different models of the legitimation of power. With Romania beginning to voice irredentist intentions after its independence in 1878, Bessarabia became the only Russian province that was contested between the Russian empire and a neighboring nation state. This made it also a province contested between nationalism and imperialism (Cusco, 2017: 3).

Southern Bessarabia experienced a long and devastating period of violence, insecurity, and deprivation during and between the two World Wars. The loss of Bessarabia to Romania was a thorn in the flesh of the newly founded Soviet Union, and Stalin never concealed his intention to reconquer the region. For the Romanian interwar governments the annexation of Bessarabia and other provinces was the culmination of a centuries-long struggle to unite (or as Romanian nationalists claimed, re-unite) all Romanian lands. For them, the non-Romanian minorities in Bessarabia came under the growing suspicion of acting as the Soviet Union's fifth column. The Romanian government felt confirmed after a pro-Soviet uprising of workers and peasants erupted around the town of Tatarbunary in 1924. The bloody oppression of the revolt further strained the relation of the weak Romanian state and its new Bessarabian subjects. By the time the Soviet Union acted to annex Bessarabia in 1940, far right forces had taken over in Bucharest. During the Second World War, when Bessarabia changed hands again and was for another three years occupied by Romania and her German ally, the hawks had their way with ethnic minorities. They unleashed the mass murder of the Jewish and Roma population and planned to deport large swaths of other non-Romanians, plans that were thwarted only by the return of the Red Army in the summer of 1944 (Wedekind, 2010: 65).

Bessarabia's integration process into the Soviet Union was short but not sweet (see chapter 5). Only after thousands of men had been recruited to far-away factories, and only after those who remained in their homes had lived through a severe man-made famine in 1946–47, the inhabitants of southern Bessarabia began to enjoy a period of relative prosperity and stability. During this time a Soviet education and fluency in Russian became the keys to social upward mobility. The "language of interethnic communication" (i.e. Russian) was established alongside and increasingly in the place of local languages.

In the more ethnographic stretches of this book, I treat southern Bessarabia distinctly as a post-Soviet land, by emphasizing the Soviet legacy in its institutions that deal with ethnicity and history. These cultural legacies connect southern Bessarabia more tightly to far-away regions in the former Soviet Union than to Romania, which lies just across the Danube. The lasting paradigms of thinking about ethnicity and history were shaped by Soviet institutions that were the first to have a long lasting outreach to the rural population (see chapter 4), a condition that preceding states, tsarist Russia and Romania, never quite achieved. Of course, the notion of post-socialism is an academic construct, but it was shaped by reasonable assumptions that socialism was a deeply pervasive phenomenon (Humphrey, 2002: 12). However, the Ukrainian crisis, starting in 2013, has raised doubts whether the post-socialist economic and political system, besides a few remaining cracks, can be researched as a newly emerged stable system, as Kürti and Skalník suggest (2009: 2). Rather, the crisis has drawn our attention back to perceptions of what an ethnic group is or how history should be remembered and represented. These concepts often reveal the resounding impact of the Soviet Union and its institutions on the region's culture.

This is astonishing, because in southern Bessarabia only one generation really lived all through the Soviet period. The rules changed again when Ukraine became independent in 1991. Overwhelmingly quick for many, new regulations from Kyiv had people learn Ukrainian alongside Russian if they wanted to succeed in wider society. Isolated from rump Ukraine, neglected by big politics, with the economy and infrastructure quickly falling apart, and with only a minority of Ukrainian speakers, Bessarabians showed little enthusiasm for the nation building projects of Ukraine. The region fell prey to a new class of opportunistic local patrons who followed political trends in Odessa and Kyiv. When in late 2013 the political leadership of Ukraine was about to sign an Association Agreement with the European Union, many Bessarabians viewed this with skepticism, fearing it might in time further remove them from Russia, which many see as their cultural center and historically a force of protection. With the outbreak of war in eastern Ukraine, Bessarabians began to fear a similar scenario there. The region's isolation might predestine it for separatism, but its ethnic and linguistic diversity makes a unanimous separatist claim difficult. The suspicion of separatist tendencies has nevertheless come up in the national mainly as an accusation. The impression of separatist trends was augmented by reporting about occasional clashes between the Ukrainian army recruiters and the local population when young men from the region should have been recruited for Ukraine's "Anti-Terrorist Operation" against Russian-backed separatism in Donbas.[20] However, those few people who thought aloud about adventurous attempts to break away from Ukraine were chilled in their enthusiasm by the disastrous outcomes of the war in Donbas and by the bloody end of a pro-Russian demonstration in Odessa on May 2, 2014. After this event, it became clear to everyone that Odessa would not easily fall for separatism. Local observers quickly drew the conclusion that a possible time window for separatism had already lapsed (Kosienkowski, 2015). However hard it is to reach Odessa from Bessarabia, for the local population to engage in pro-Russian separatism would also have meant to impede access to the region's pre-eminent urban center and its opportunities. What is more, most politicians depend on their Kyiv patrons and have therefore opted for Ukrainian unity.[21] As in other regions of Ukraine, the events on Maidan and the violence that followed it led to the strengthening of a civic Ukrainian identity over ethnic identities.[22] Nevertheless, in the ongoing conflict, southern Bessarabia, due to its history and ethnic diversity, has retained a geopolitical microclimate of which no one knows which way it would turn when push comes to shove.

5 Ethnicity, Natsional'nost', and Nationality: Definitions and Translations

This study deals with the history of boundaries between ethnic groups. Because this subject was pursued through two centuries and relying on sources

20 *Komsomolskaya Pravda v Ukraine*, 27.02.2015, Pod Odessoy selyane buntovali protiv mobilizatsii: <https://kp.ua/odessa/488049-pod-odessoi-seliane-buntovaly-protyv-mobylyzatsyy> (23.02.2019).

21 In a rare bout of attention similar observations were made in the *Economist*, January 3, 2015, in an article specially dedicated to the region. Available online: <http://www.economist.com/news/europe/21637415-little-known-place-interests-both-ukraine-and-russia-towards-unknown-region?fsrc=scn/fb/wl/pe/towardstheunknownregion> (23.02.2019).

22 *Local identity and inter-ethnic interaction in the south of Odessa region: problems and trends of transformation*, Ukrainian Peacebuilding School, National Institute for Strategic Studies and Organization for the Promotion of Intercultural Cooperation, Odessa, January 2015.

from a number of academic and administrative traditions, it is necessary at this point to clarify what ethnic groups and boundaries mean in the context of this book. On first sight, the obvious English translation for Russian *natsional'nost'*, Ukrainian *natsional'nist'*, and Romanian *naționalitate*, would be simply "nationality." But a closer look to the semantic content of these orthographically similar words points to substantial differences in translation. Just as the English "nationality," the Romanian "naționalitate" can have an ethnic connotation, but more commonly is used to refer to a person's country of citizenship. In Greater Romania "naționalitate," if used in official sources, was clearly used in the sense of "citizenship" and juxtaposed with people who were also *ethnically* Romanian (de origină etnică Română) (see chapter 3.). It is this second, essentialized and inheritable category that is in the focus here, not the bureaucratic category of citizenship. In Russian and Ukrainian the category of "natsional'nost'/natsional'nist'" hardly has a connotation of citizenship. In Russian "grazhdanstvo" and in Ukrainian "hromadyanstvo" would be the term of choice to refer to "nationality" as used in bureaucracy. If natsional'nost' had anything to do with the state one enjoys civil rights in, it would not have been registered in Soviet passports (since it would have been on the cover anyway). The category registered in passports clearly referred to a person's *ethnic identity* (Baiburin, 2012: 59; Kozlov, 1974: 81). In many English texts the term "natsional'nost'" is nevertheless translated as "nationality," which may be permissible if the matter is not central for the argument. For our purpose however, too much of what "natsional'nost'" means would be lost in translation. Essentially, it comes down to a problem of set theory: Every natsional'nost', in translation can be called a nationality, but not every nationality would qualify as a natsional'nost'. Therefore for example if one would take the frequently amended list of ethnic groups from which Soviet passport identities could be chosen, all of the natsional'nosti on it could sensibly be called "nationalities." Some of them are currently also nationalities as in citizenship, like Russian, Ukrainian, or Kazakh. Others are nationalities with no state to themselves and therefore would not qualify as nationality meaning citizenship, but still be commonly called a "nationality"; Tatar, Buryat, Gagauz etc. Yet this equation does not work quite as well the other way round. Some passport nationalities, typically those that have an established language with the same name, would also be natsional'nosti, like Ukrainian, German, or Hungarian. Other passport nationalities that have no language of the same name would hardly be accepted as a natsional'nost', like Belgian, Swiss, or Canadian. If in Ukraine (or probably in most other places in the former Soviet Union) a person is asked for his or her natsional'nost' and names a passport nationality of this type, then he or she will typically be asked again for his or her natsional'nost' until he or she reveals an *ethnic* affiliation within the population of the respective country.[23] If the person cannot or is unwilling to name an ethnic affiliation, the inquiring person might offer help by suggesting the name of a native language, the origin of a parent, or even a religious confession as ethnic affiliation.

In Soviet social sciences the academic term "ethnos" was introduced partly to avoid confusion with what in English is called "nationality." "Ethnos" was the academic equivalent to what in Soviet bureaucracy and in public discourse was called "natsional'nost'," an allegedly stable core that persists across time and space, despite all changes in the group's political and economic circumstances (Gorenburg, 1999: 556). The most ardent promoter of the "ethnos" term, long-time head of the department of ethnology in the Soviet Academy of Sciences, Yulian Bromley, introduced the term "politonym" (i.e. the name of a polity) for those nationalities which in his view were not ethnic groups, like the Belgian and the French (Bromley, 1983: 46). "Natsional'nost'" would not have been a suitable term to describe these, because in the Soviet perception it was tied to common traits beyond mere citizenship, typically a language, a religion, and the belief in a common ancestry qualified a group a as a natsional'nost'. This category is therefore conceptually very close to what Max Weber has called an "ethnic group":

> We shall call 'ethnic groups' those human groups that entertain a subjective belief in their common descent because similarities of physical type or of custom or both, or because of memories of colonization and migration; this belief must be important for the propagation of group formation; conversely, it does not matter whether or not an objective blood relationship exists (Weber, 1996: 35).

The main difference, of course, between Weber's concept and the Soviet one is that the belief in common descent was *subjective* for Weber, whereas in Soviet scholarship it was treated as *objective*. More importantly, however, Weber's definition points to a form of identity that in the reading of those who have it can be inherited but not acquired. For sake of precision, I therefore translate the Russian term "natsional'nost'," the Ukrainian term "natsional'nist'," as well as their Soviet academic pendant "ethnos" as "ethnicity" if it refers to a concept and as "ethnic group" if it refers to a group of people to whose identity this concept is significant. There is a Russian word with the same morphology as "ethnicity"; *etnichnost'*, but it entered the lexicon of social sciences only after

23 This was a common experience during fieldwork for the Swiss author and an observation shared by American political scientist Rasma Karklins (1986: 29).

the end of the Soviet Union and only after a "Perestroika of terminologies" (Sokolovskiy, 2003: 13).

The fact remains that most English language sources would use "nationality" rather than "ethnicity," the further back one goes the likelier. This work first and foremost traces the term "Natsional'nost'" through a local history. It is therefore crucial to stick to one translation throughout, even if the terminology of sources at the time of their creation would have been translated into English as "nationality." It is also true that terms like nation, nationality, and ethnicity have not always been used with consistent meaning (Connor, 2011: 3). Stalin is a prominent example, since he wrote an influential essay on the "Nation" (*natsiya*) in his capacity as People's Commissar of Nationality Affairs (Narodniy Kommisar po Delam *Natsional'nostey*). One of the early promoters of the "ethnos" term in Soviet academia, Pavel Kushner, used Stalin's concept of the *nation* (*natsiya*) as a synonym with his definition of *ethnos* (1951: 6). But the confusing histories of the terms "nation," "nationality," "ethnicity" and their translations cannot be taken as excuse for inconsistent use of these terms here. Sticking to "ethnicity" can lead to anachronistic uses, when referring with "ethnic group" or "ethnicity" to times when these terms were not yet common either in English or any of the languages spoken in Bessarabia. But anachronisms could hardly be avoided by using the term ethnicity interchangeably with other terms. The terms "natsional'nost'" and "nationality" have no less been used anachronistically by the people who created the sources for this study. Therefore it is most reasonable to stick to a consistent terminology, calling all those groups that claim cultural unity, common history, and common ancestry "ethnic groups." It is of course crucial to offer, wherever possible, the term used at the time and place of original utterance.

6 Chapter Structure

There are several options to structure a book meant to reveal how ethnic boundaries emerged and were preserved. One viable way would be to choose a strictly chronological structure, event by event, state by state. Another way would be strictly analytical, phenomenon after phenomenon, traced through the ages. While writing this book, I have concluded that neither of these ways is satisfying for my purpose here. Therefore, a chronological account of the policies of the subsequent states that ruled Bessarabia is interrupted twice by more theoretical chapters. The first chronological part consist of chapters 2 and 3. Chapter 2 deals with the establishment of the tsarist bureaucracy in Bessarabia during the 19th century, a time when religious categories gradually gave way to ethnic categories as the main bureaucratic label. But these then gained rapidly in importance as the region entered a phase of revolutionary upheaval that made the issue of trust between the state and its subjects on the peripheries a prime concern of imperial politics. The next chapter (3) deals with the Romanian period between the world wars, a time full of insecurity and violence, and therefore a time of great mistrust between the state and those perceived as ethnic minorities. At this point a theoretical insertion, chapter 4, becomes necessary to line out the academic roots of the ethnicity concepts that dominated Soviet academia and eventually transformed the popular conception of ethnicity so strongly that many of its echoes can still be found today. This insertion prepares us for a continuation of the chronological account through the 47 years of Soviet rule in Bessarabia, the subject of chapter 5. This period saw the arrival of a new group, the Soviet village elites, who came mainly from Russian speaking areas that already had belonged to the Soviet Union before World War II. They quickly merged with the local population as rapid economic growth set in after a brief and bitter period of famine and displacement directly following the war. The Soviet decades of relative prosperity remain the measure for many today. They were characterized by the rise of the Russian language as a means of union-wide communication and a precondition for social mobility. There is little memory of ethnic conflict in this time. Nevertheless, ethnicity as a concept gained in importance. The chaotic years since Ukrainian independence are the subject of the last of these chronological chapters (6). They include the return of ethnic rhetoric to local politics, the foundation of ethnic associations and the establishment of the clientelistic political system that has led to the crisis in Ukraine starting at the end of 2013.

To structure the past into sections determined by state rule is not to deny underlying tendencies of a more *longue-durée* character that do not change just because state hegemony changes. For example, the tendency of increasing rationalization of the state administration has started long before the period covered here. Structuring chapters state by state is merely a concession to practicability. In this way, the conditions of each new state have to be introduced only once. It is a compromise in structuring this book that should not divert attention from social trends that survived changes in state hegemony.

The first chapter and second chapter about the Romanian period are almost entirely based on an archival study and historiographical literature. The fourth and fifth chapters about the Soviet period still heavily rely on the archive, but are also based on oral history from interviews with elderly respondents as well as on newspaper archives. The last chapter of the chronological part (6) deals with the period of independent Ukraine, including fieldwork conducted in

2012–13, and is naturally the most ethnographic of all. It focuses on exploring how political clientelism can profit from sharpening ethnic boundaries and how people who exist between these categories have a hard time finding political representation.

Can this be historical anthropology? A work in which the readers start out with a tour through local history and then, as the account moves closer to the present find gradually more ethnographic insight, until they find themselves reading an ethnography? Clearly, links between the past and the present deserve more attention, more context about how contemporary practices are rooted in the past and how, on the other hand, present ethnic boundaries affect people's imaginations of the past. To underscore these links, chapter 7 again interrupts the book's chronological concept. It discusses all observed techniques and narratives used to sharpen ethnic boundaries at different times. This lays the groundwork for answering the book's guiding questions in the subsequent conclusion (chapter 8) and highlights the complex interrelations of history and memory in dominant concepts of ethnicity.

CHAPTER 2

Administering the Periphery from Horseback

In May 1812, just weeks before Napoleon's *Grande Armée* attacked Russia, Tsar Alexander I was able to settle his latest war against the Ottoman Empire with the treaty of Bucharest. This victory enabled Russia to formally extend her hegemony over Bessarabia. Russian troops had made significant land gains in Bessarabia already during the two preceding Russo-Turkish wars (1768–74 and 1787–92) but each time had to retreat again in order to reach a peace accord.[1] The conquest of Bessarabia was the farthest extension to the south-west the Russian Empire ever reached. Despite the great distance to the capital, the empire, with the help of culturally very diverse colonists, managed during the next century to radically transform Bessarabia's landscape and population. This chapter discusses how the imperial Russian state struggled with administrative ambiguities caused by the integration of its new subjects in Bessarabia. The growing social and political ambitions of the state between 1812 and 1918,[2] first led it to colonize Bessarabia and other recently acquired territories with sedentary and loyal subjects, and later demanded the creation of accurate statistical descriptions in order to administrate them efficiently. I argue that present ethnic categories in Bessarabia were a byproduct of this administrative

1 These compromises led to peace treaties of Küçük Kaynarca in (1774) and Iași (1792) (Hosking, 2001: 231; Ryasanovsky, 2000: 266).

2 For most of this time southern Bessarabia belonged to the Russian Empire. There was, however, a 22 year period when Russia's effort to push back Ottoman influence in South-Eastern Europe came to a halt. This was the time between the Crimean War (which Russia lost in 1856) and the last of the Russo-Turkish Wars (which Russia won in 1878 and which enabled Romania, Serbia and Bulgaria to become independent states). In this scantily documented period, an L-shaped strip of land along the Danube and Prut rivers belonged to the United Principalities, a forerunner-state of Romania and still formally a vassal of the Ottoman Empire (The area then was still relatively sparsely populated with only about 13,000 inhabitants (Lebedenko and Tychyna, 2002: 90)) The influence of the United Principalities in Bessarabia was even weaker than that of the Russian Empire. Neither the accessible literature nor the Izmail state archive give anything more than superficial hints on this period. We do know, however, that most rules concerning the colonists were left in place by the temporal Romanian rulers. A very telling document in this respect is a collection of evidence that the transdanubian colonists were granted the right to run their own school in Bolgrad by the Tsar (F312 D76 Documentele dreptilor Liceului din Bolgrad, 1923–40). This right and many other rights connected to it were left untouched by the United Principalities in the late 1850s. The privileges of the Transdanubian Colonists were granted but could not always be enforced (Batyushkov, 1892: 164–65).

 | DOI:10.1163/9789004408029_003

calibration effort. It was only late in the 19th century that religious and socio-economic categories gradually gave way to more markedly ethnic categories. The chapter follows this transition and discusses the reasons why and how, by World War I, ethnicity had become a category familiar to most Bessarabians.

1 The State's Hunger for Tax and Men

In the last decades of the 18th century, tsarist Russia established a strong influence over southern Bessarabia. During the reign of Empress Catherine II (1762–96) *Novorossiya*, the steppe lands that nowadays comprise parts of southern Ukraine, had become a new zone of Russian imperial expansion. The land between the rivers Prut in the west, Dniester in the east and the Danube in the south became the last province of Novorossiya. The steppe lands along the northern shore of the Black Sea used to be inhabited by nomads, run-away serfs from Russia and Poland, and by religious splinter groups escaping persecution in Russia. Most of the northern shore of the Black Sea, including Bessarabia, had been under loose Ottoman suzerainty before Russian conquest. The region began to be dragged into the Russian sphere of influence as the Ottoman Empire grew weaker, but not without considerable local resistance.

The new ports and cities that sprang up along the riverbanks and the sea coast of what is now southern Ukraine were not Ukrainian. They were not particularly Russian either. They were heavily dependent on foreigners willing to migrate to the periphery (Brandes, 1986: 171; Reid, 1997: 58). Nevertheless, Novorossiya became the most ambitious project of imperial Russia and its success eventually cemented her status as a great European power. It is not for no reason then, that the colonial denomination "Novorossiya" has recently reentered the vocabulary of the Kremlin leadership on the background of the Ukrainian crisis of 2014.[3]

Russia's expansion to the west and south-west came along with a huge military effort against Poland, against Cossack bands, but mainly against the Ottoman Empire. The Tsar's administration started to prepare a full takeover of Bessarabia already decades before the 1812 treaty of Bucharest, when the region, at least on paper, still belonged to the Ottoman Empire. Therefore

3 Russian President Vladimir Putin was shown lighting candles in a church on *Segodnya* news broadcast on the state-run "NTV" TV channel on September 10, 2014. Putin explained he had lit a candle "for those who suffered and those who gave their lives protecting the people of *Novorossiya*." Available online: <http://www.ntv.ru/novosti/1211136/> (23.02.2019).

Russian policies in the decades preceding 1812 were largely wartime arrangements.

A sizeable part of the modern population of southern Bessarabia are the descendants of so called "Transdanubian Colonists" (*zadunayskie pereselentsy*), Christians from the Ottoman Balkan provinces, who started to move to Bessarabia in the course of the Russo-Turkish wars of the late 18th and the early 19th century. By the end of the century, in 1897 when the first empire wide census was conducted, this group consisted of about 159,000 people or 8.2% of the population of the *Bessarabskaya Guberniya* (Subottina, 2011: 159).[4] Moving Orthodox people from the Balkans to Bessarabia served two of Russia's goals simultaneously: First the tsarist government could prove that the expansion to the south-west really served its propagated end; the liberation of the Balkan Christians from Ottoman Muslim domination, and secondly Russia could use Bessarabia as a military deployment zone with a welcoming population (Grek and Russev, 2011: 71; Lebedenko and Tychyna, 2002: 5). The first significant waves of new settlers from the Balkans entered southern Bessarabia during the Russo-Turkish War of 1768–74 (Derzhavin, 1914: 10; Skal'kovskiy, 1850: 228). While the war raged on, Russian armed forces became the chief agent in preparing Bessarabia for an eventual full takeover. During this campaign, in 1769, 12,000 Nogai nomads, Turkic speaking Muslims who used to roam the area with their herds, were expelled to Crimea and the Northern Caucasus (Batyushkov, 1892: 136; Berg, 1918: 64). With the Bucharest Treaty in 1812 another 1,892 nomad families were deported to the Ottoman Empire. Those who had migrated east to the northern Black Sea region were forced into a sedentary lifestyle (Amburger, 1966: 286). Continued strife between Russia and the Ottoman Empire[5] helped to eventually turn southern Bessarabia into a nearly deserted land. During the Russo-Turkish war of 1806–12 around 20,000 people had fled or were deported from Bessarabia (Berg, 1918: 64; Grek and Russev, 2011: 53). In April 1811, the commander of the Moldovan Army, M. I. Kutuzov, issued the first official document that formally permitted colonization of the southern Bessarabian steppe by "Christians, who wish to resettle from the right bank of the Danube to the left bank of that river" (reproduced in Kryzhanovskaya and Russev,

4 Since the 1897 census did not include a question about ethnicity (*natsional'nost'*), Subottina concluded from native language to ethnicity. The numbers here are the combined numbers of Bulgarians and Gagauz in all of the *Bessarabskaya Guberniya* (this includes areas that are now part of Moldova as well as areas that are now part of Ukraine). Also, these numbers do not include Albanians, who were by far the smallest group among the Transdanubian Colonists.

5 Two more Russo-Turkish Wars, 1787–92 and 1806–12, preceded the formal annexation of Bessarabia.

1957: 1). When after the war Russia formally integrated Bessarabia and intended to turn it into a tax-contributing province, there was a severe lack of manpower. At a time when peasant serfdom was still the rule in central Russia, peasants there remained tied to their master's estate. Therefore, Russian peasants could not easily be resettled to the new frontier (Derzhavin, 1914: 5; Kushko and Taki, 2012: 203). The central Russian agricultural regions likewise suffered from a lack of working hands at the time. It would have taken much too long to colonize the periphery of the empire with what little manpower Russia could spare (Klaus, 1869: 6).

Many of the new settlers from the Ottoman Balkan provinces crossed the Danube together with Russian troops, who after military campaigns there returned to Russia (Batyushkov, 1892: 142). With laws, coming into force in 1819, colonists from the other side of the Danube were granted land in Bessarabia as well as tax cuts (Derzhavin, 1914: 10; Skal'kovskiy, 1850: 242). These people, independently of the language they spoke, came to be referred to commonly as "Transdanubian Colonists."[6]

This term seemed appropriate, since the settlers came from the opposite side of the Danube and since the Russian state saw the new province as a colony. Appolon Skal'kovskiy, an early statistician, writing in 1850, elaborated on whether or not it was appropriate to call the country to which Bessarabia belonged *Novorossiya* (New Russia). He concluded that the land had been developed "with the help of Russian minds and with Russian work" and that therefore the name Novorossiya was no more unjust than Spanish colonies called Hispaniola, Dutch colonies called New Holland, or British colonies called Nova Scotia. What set Russian inland colonies apart from the overseas colonies of other European powers in Skal'kovskiy's eyes was that the "English and the Spanish have eradicated the native tribes of America," while "Russia

6 This term was in fact used as a legal denominator in official documents as early as the 1820s. In a voluminous file from the years 1821–32 dealing with the naturalization of colonists by the Izmail authorities (*gradonachal'stvo*) (F56 D112, 1821–30) the colonists are referred to as "new transdanubian settlers" (*zadunayskie novopereselentsy*) (pp. 103, 121, 123) or "Turkish subjects transdanubian colonists" (*Turetsko poddaniy zadunayskiy pereselentsy*) (pp. 84, 96, 100, 125). Klaus (1869: 294) in his description of the various colonist groups of *Novorossiya*, used the term "Transdanubian Colonists" (*Zadunayskie Pereselentsy*) to distinguish this group from other colonists. He defined the group as "not a particular people or even a separate tribe. Under this term our colonization legislation refers exclusively to colonies founded in the southern part of Bessarabia, beginning with the year of 1811…" Klaus (ibid.) also acknowledged that in Bessarabia the legal term subsumed many "elements," who had never seen the other bank of the Danube. In modern literature, the term is sometimes used unaltered (Grek and Russev, 2011) or with slight transformations, such as "*zadunayskie poselentsy*" (Transdanubian Settlers) (Kushko and Taki, 2012).

has not only saved the lives and property of Greeks, Armenians, Tatars, and Romanians but even fertilized their empty land with the work and achievements of her children: noblemen, settlers, Cossacks, or invited foreigners from abroad" (Skal'kovskiy, 1850: 206). The Russian state had a self-image as a good and protective colonizer on a par with other European powers. And indeed Russian authorities ruled in Bessarabia much like Western powers ruled their overseas colonies; by riding around their horses to implement imperial policies and inspect their results. Usually they based the decisions that they made on observations made right on the spot (Kushko and Taki, 2012: 19). On inspection rides, administrators also counted people in order to have an idea how much tax they could raise and how many young men they could recruit for the army (Steinwedel, 2001: 70). Prince Urusov, Bessarabia's governor in 1903–04, still to a large extent governed in this style. In his memoires (1904: 232) he wrote that during his inspection trips he had to "constantly permit, alter, prohibit, reprimand and confirm the most diverse of issues." He admitted that this mode of governing was vulnerable to bad decision-making.

Back in the beginning of Russia's rule in Bessarabia in the second decade of the 19th century the influence of the imperial center was still minimal. The war against Napoleon 1812–14 and the subsequent Vienna Congress 1814–15 preoccupied the empire's administration, army, and diplomatic corps. The military governor at the time, commander of the Russian Danube Army, General Chichagov, ruled "almost without any interference of the Russian state" (Batyushkov, 1892: 150). The lack of binding laws, Batyushkov goes on, led to widespread abuse of power, from which the lowest classes of society suffered most. In 1816, four years into Russian rule, Tsar Alexander I saw it fit to send a special envoy to fix the Bessarabian administration. In 1818 he himself, together with his foreign minister, paid a visit to the newly incorporated province. At this occasion the imperial ruler himself practiced the then dominant style of administration. He had a thorough inspection of the province, he then listened to the suggestions of his on-site governors, especially to Lieutenant General Ivan Inzov, since that year in charge of matters of Transdanubian Colonists in southern Bessarabia. Inzov acted as an advocate for the settlers, demanding the same rights and privileges for them as other colonists in the empire enjoyed. His report managed to convince the Tsar's envoy. On the spot, a large area of land was reserved for present and future colonists (Batyushkov, 1892: 142; Skal'kovskiy, 1850: 240). Also in 1818, a first set of administrative reforms was completed. It left far-reaching powers to the local governor and the high council, which he chaired (Batyushkov, 1892: 151).

If at first, Russian rule had the aim to secure newly acquired land and to get profit out of it, and if this basic policy was implemented chiefly by the basic method of administrators travelling the country and reacting to what they saw, what then did the state need to know about the settlers living in Bessarabia? A helpful tool to address this question is James Scott's concept of "legibility" of societies. "Legibility" means the arrangement of the governed territory and population into "units that can be identified, observed, recorded, counted, aggregated and monitored." Scott views such categories as a "condition for manipulation" (Scott, 1998: 183). Thereby the state's ambitions determine the degree to which it needs to make society "legible":

> If the state's goals are minimal, it may not need to know much about the society. Just as a woodsman who takes only an occasional load of firewood from a large forest need have no detailed knowledge of that forest, so a state whose demands are confined to grabbing a few carts of grain and the odd conscript may not require a very accurate or detailed map of society. If, however, the state is ambitious—if it wants to extract as much grain and manpower as it can, short of provoking a famine or a rebellion, if it wants to create a literate, skilled, and healthy population, if it wants everyone to speak the same language or worship the same god—then it will have to become both far more knowledgeable and far more intrusive (Scott, 1998: 184).

Russia in the 19th century saw a steady growth of the state's ambitions and therefore a steady growth in its need for "legibility" of society. For the early decades, the period of transdanubian settlement, a limited range of information was sufficient. It was certainly good to know whether the people arriving would be able and willing to perform the economic tasks they were designated to perform. Since most newcomers were given land to plow, the priority task they were meant to fulfill was growing crop that would generate taxable profit as soon as possible. Therefore it was helpful to the state to know whether or not the new settlers were peasants. Since the production entity of the peasant economy on both sides of the Danube was the household, it was interesting to invite complete families rather than single men (Klaus, 1869: 20). Another information required by the state was when exactly the person in concern had come to Bessarabia, because tax cuts that were granted to the colonists ran a limited period from 3 to 7 years after their arrival.[7] Tax breaks were only

7 Ukaz Immenoy, danniy Senatu „O poselenii v Bessarabskoy oblasti Bolgar i drugikh Zadunayskikh pereselentsev, s prisovkupleniem vedomosti Okrugam, naznachaemym dlya poseleniya ikh" *Polnoe sobranie zakonov* (PSZ) SPB, 1830 Sobranie I.-T. XXXVI (1819)—Nr 28 054, 28.12.1891: <http://nlr.ru/e-res/law_r/search.php> (23.02.2019).

interesting for the state to grant for so long as the new peasant economies were still in the build-up. Another aspect, important to know, was whether the newcomers were Christians. This in the state's eyes would ensure that in times of war against the Ottomans, the new settlers would side with the Russians (and indeed, three more wars between the two empires were to follow in the 19th century).

Many other facts about the Transdanubian Colonists could have been recorded by the state, but were not. Today's historians and ethnographers would be all too grateful if, for instance, the language of the settlers or their self-designation had been recorded in state registries. But for the state at the beginning of the 19th century such information was at best of secondary priority. Therefore ethno-cultural and linguistic features of the settlers did not enter state records. The Transdanubian Colonists were similar in their religion, in their economic status, and in their origin from the Ottoman Empire. But although they were later often subsumed as Bulgarians, they were probably much more ethnically diverse upon their arrival in Bessarabia. This is how the Russian chronicler of *Novorossya* colonies and ardent defender of the colonists' privileges, Alexander Klaus, described their origins:

> The settlements of the "Transdanubian Colonists" consisted of a motley bunch (pestroy tolpy) of Bulgarians, Moldovans, Greeks, Little- and Great Russians [i.e. Ukrainians and Russians], Arnauts [i.e. Albanians], Gypsies, Serbs, Nekrasov [Cossacks], Zaporoshian [Cossacks], Turks, and converted Jews (vykrestov iz evreev); these were the original ancestors (rodonachal'niki) of today's Bessarabian-Bulgarian colonists. This whole mob (sbrod) was united solely by their common Orthodox creed, their uniform homelessness and misery (Klaus, 1869: 310).

The imperial decree of 1819 that regulated land property and privileges for settlers in southern Bessarabia implicitly also stressed the multicultural character of what would later be seen as simply Bulgarians. It defined the group of people concerned as: "Transdanubian Colonists by which we mean Bulgarians and other foreign newcomers from across the Danube who are our fellow believers" (Derzhavin, 1914: 31). The ethnic denominator in this definition is mentioned in passing, but the colonists' common faith with the empire's majority population was their single most important unifying factor.

2 Colonists out of the State's Sight

The main feature of the system by which Russia ruled its imperial periphery was luring local elites into collaborating with the imperial government and keeping their local population under control (Löwe, 2000). This system was impossible to establish in southern Bessarabia, because after the Nogai had been expelled, there was no local elite to collaborate with. The imperial strategists had to delegate their own representatives to ensure "legibility" of the new province and its freshly arrived inhabitants. The categories employed in this effort were not ethnic. At the beginning of the 19th century, Russian law subdivided the population by social status categories (*sostoyanie* and *soslovie*). People with different occupations had different rights and duties vis-à-vis the state (Haimson, 1988; 1991, 1990). The imperial decree on the Transdanubian Colonists of 1819 therefore specified the social status of the settlers before anything else. As colonists they were a social group distinct from serfs, traders, or soldiers. They were dwellers of the countryside, not of the city. The only status category that in this time foreshadowed ethnic categorization was the status of *inorodtsy* (literally "of a foreign tribe").[8] This legal status was introduced in 1822 and reserved for non-Christian and non-sedentary peoples who had been incorporated by the expanding empire (Slocum, 1998: 174). The Transdanubian Colonists were no *inorodtsy*. Therefore the language they spoke or the customs they lived by find no mentioning in any of the state's rulings concerning the settlers. It would have been unproductive for the state to be concerned with such features by limiting the group, from which the much needed settlers could have been recruited.

Once the settlers were inside Russia and once their status, property, tax obligations, and their obligation to military service had been settled, colonists could remain out of the state's view for a very long time. There was no clear oversight of how many settlers had entered the region. The writer Pavel Svin'in, was sent to Bessarabia by the Russian Senate in 1815, and in 1816 presented perhaps the first Russian description of the new province (Kushko and Taki, 2012: 77). He lamented the fact that there was hardly any data about the region's population. For a future census he advised those who would conduct it to first gain the confidence of the population. The settlers, he asserted, were very weary to be counted since they feared recruitment or even the introduction of serfdom (*rabvstvo*) (Svin'in, 1816: 210). Living in their village and

8 Ustav ob upravlenie inorodtsev, from July 22, 1822, In *Polnoe Sobranie Zakonov* (PSZ), tom 38, no. 29.126, p. 394, available online: <http://www.nlr.ru/e-res/law_r/search.php?part=177&regim=3> (23.02.2019).

working the field, peasants hardly ever came in direct contact with a representative of the administration. Still at the turn of the 20th century, the officer and ethnographer Valentin Moshkov noted that the Russian authorities had little contact with the colonists; they would "rush in like a thunderstorm and then again disappear somewhere" (1901a: 36). Communal affairs were handled without state intervention inside the colony by a council of household heads and elected chairmen (Brandes, 1986: 174). The Governor of Bessarabia in 1903–04, Prince Urusov, wrote in his memoires (1904: 254) that the upper echelons of the administration in St. Petersburg had the "most nebulous imagination of the circumstances in Bessarabia."

When the status of people changed, when they for example inherited a house or a plot of land or when they married, the state, at least theoretically, should have taken notice. Also, people were meant to come in contact with the state when they crossed its border. In fact, however, the administrative web at the time seems to have been woven so loosely that many people might have slipped through borders without the state ever taking notice.[9] The same was very likely true for alterations in civil or property relations.

An additional source of difficulties for the Russian authorities in administering the Transdanubian Colonists came from their deep mistrust towards state institutions. Among the settlers, there was apparently wide-spread skepticism, whether or not the Russian Empire would be able to hold its newly gained territories for long. Many people were reluctant to make long time arrangements and get permanently settled. In the 1816 account of Pavel Svin'in he remarked that many of the houses built by the colonists reminded him of the ones he had seen among nomadic tribes (1816: 220). The inhabitants of many settlements refused to build churches because they feared the Ottomans might come back soon (Batyushkov, 1892: 136). A wave of rumors in 1814 and 1815 that Russia might introduce serfdom for Bessarabian peasants led to the flight of more than 3,000 families across the river Prut into Austrian Bukovina.[10] The mass exodus began to flatten only when the Metropolit of Chișinău and Khotyn, Gavril Banulescu-Bodoni, sent around a conciliatory circular in Romanian, (Batyushkov, 1892: 137; Kushko and Taki, 2012: 157; Svin'in, 1816: 211). Another wave of 3,000 transdanubian settler families returned to the Balkans

9 In 1816 Pavel Svin'in complained that the clerks in Izmail's quarantine station had no clear data how many ships had docked in the city's port that year, let alone how many passengers had travelled through it (Svin'in, 1816: 237).

10 A contemporary document written by an anonymous observer states that the fear of colonists to become the subjects of a landlord had caused many of them to leave behind their belongings and move back to the Ottoman Empire (reproduced in Kryzhanovskaya and Russev, 1957: 112–114).

after a series of poor harvests between 1830 and 1834 (Skal'kovskiy, 1850: 246). When in 1856, after the Crimean War, a part of southern Bessarabia came under the rule of the United Principalities, a state that formally was still under Ottoman suzerainty, this led to yet another flight of Transdanubian Colonists, who resettled further inside Novorossiya (Derzhavin, 1914: 11; Klaus, 1869: 294). The reasons for Russia to cede Izmail and its surroundings to the United Principalities were purely strategic. It led to a formal acknowledgement by the European powers of Russia's hegemony over the rest of Bessarabia. The loss of Bessarabia's southernmost region was often treated as temporarily in Russian public discourse (Cusco, 2017: 102–104). When this proved true after the last Russo-Turkish War in 1878 the Russian empire did not rush to russify the regained territory. The Romanian administrative and juridical structures were largely left in place (ibid: 54), not a sign that Russia had the means of quickly reforming the local administration and raise its level of "legibility."

One more indication for the state's initially sketchy oversight over its periphery was that it lost track of whole groups of settlers. In 1832 the administration of Izmail Uezd,[11] trying to optimize its tax revenues, went to look for undocumented inhabitants who had lived in Bessarabia for many years. A circular memorandum to the outposts of the administration in Izmail brought the issue to the fore. The document stated that between 1821 and 1824 up to 700 settlers had entered Bessarabia every year. All of these settlers had gone through quarantine, where they were registered and counted. In order not to lose them out of sight they were required to register with the quarantine station every six months. However, at least 350 of these settlers had not been registered anywhere, had not been paying tax, and therefore did not contribute anything to the state's benefit. This was why authorities decided, in 1830, that within a year these undocumented foreigners had to either leave Russia or agree to become Russian subjects (*poddannie*) and therefore lose the right to leave the country. They should register in the place of their permanent residence and pay taxes including the amount they had failed to pay while unregistered. Those who were willing to leave the country should not be released to do so until they would have paid their tax debt in full.[12] A year later in February

11 An Uezd was an administrative sub-entity to the province which, in imperial Russia, was called "Oblast" or "Guberniya." The Bessarabskaya oblast contained 8 Uezd. The two southernmost Uezd, Akkerman (today's Belgorod-Dniestrovskiy) and Izmail, comprised very roughly the part of Bessarabia that nowadays belongs to Ukraine. Izmail Uezd covered the southwestern corner of Bessarabia.

12 F56 D112 Delo o prinyatii v russkoe poddanstvo i poselenii v izmail'skom gradonachalstve bolgar, grekov, moldavan, bezhavshikh v Rossiyu ot Turetskogo iga v 1821–830, p. 1.

1833, a second circular was sent around as a reminder, more insistent in its tone.[13]

This episode illustrates how difficult it was for a state with a still very loose network of law enforcement structures, to keep track of who its subjects were, where they had lived and paid tax at what time. The fact that a second circular had to be sent out, emphasizing the same orders as the first, but with more and clearer explanations, also shows that outposts, in charge of enforcing orders from the center, were either not willing or not able to fulfill orders swiftly and to the center's satisfaction.

The challenges that arose for the Russian state with the integration of the Bessarabian peasantry and colonists point to one of the empire's most urgent problems in the mid-19th century; the inflexibility of its deep rooted system of serfdom. The northern two-thirds of Bessarabia belonged mainly to Romanian speaking noblemen, so called Boyars.[14] The peasants working their land were not serfs. They paid tribute to their landlord in crop or labor days, but they were in principle free. Nobles from Russia proper who obtained arable land in Bessarabia were not allowed to bring their serfs from their Russian estates to Bessarabia (Kushko and Taki, 2012: 200). In southern Bessarabia, before the expulsion of the nomads, most of the land had been used communally. It had not belonged to Moldovan Boyars and therefore became state-owned land that was given to colonists (Klaus, 1869: 308). This made Bessarabia a magnet for fugitive serfs and persecuted religious zealots from central Russia (Kushko and Taki, 2012: 200).

The great number of unregistered fugitives became a severe threat for feudal economy in central Russia. It diminished the already insufficient manpower on estates in the Russian heartland and it created a motley population on the periphery that was hardly controllable and even less taxable. Especially in times of war the number of people classified tramps (*brodyagi*) increased sharply. There were attempts to convince them of giving themselves up to authorities in turn for exemption from punishment (Kushko and Taki, 2012: 201). In this way, tramps should become registered and therefore controllable and taxable. The legal concept of the "tramp" or "vagabond" became a crucial tool to delineate those who were still not "legible" for the state administration in James Scott's sense. Being a vagabond became increasingly criminalized. In an

---

13 F56 D112, p. 30.

14 This term was consistently used by modern writers such as Kushko and Taki (2012) as well as by writers of the time such as Svin'in (1816) to designate a specific Moldovan group of land owning nobles.

agrarian economy, based on the labor of serfs, there were good economic reasons to outlaw freewheeling people.

The reasons for persecuting vagabondism changed in the course of the 19th century. In the 1920s and 1930s the state wanted to avoid the thinning out of its main workforce, the serf peasants. Towards the end of the century, and especially after formally abolishing serfdom in 1861, the state came to use the category of tramp to exert an all-encompassing control of the whereabouts and activities of its subjects. The offence was no longer to run away from the master's estate but circumventing state control and therefore compromising the state's "legibility" of its population. Although reasons for the persecution of vagabonds had changed, at the beginning of the 1890s, being a tramp was still a common legal offence.[15]

One important step in categorizing people and sharpening the state's oversight over its population was the introduction of passports. Passports had existed since the reign of reform-minded Peter I (1682–1725), aimed at giving the state better control over people who traveled away from places of permanent residence, where they were registered in church books (metricheskie knigi). But it was not until 1894 that a formal law on passports came into effect. This law named two functions for passports; to identify its bearer and to certify the right to be in a place different from the place of permanent residence (Steinwedel, 2001: 73). Passports contained the bearer's full name, estate status, date of birth or age, religious confession, and marital status. For men, passports also usually contained information on whether or not its bearer was liable for military service. Information on linguistic or ethno-cultural background had no place in passports of the Russian Empire. Passports only contained information that clerks could find out without speaking much to the passport's bearer. During the 1890s in Bessarabia and throughout the Empire, passports were pre-printed forms containing the tsar's coat of arms and an abbreviated list of his titles. Into the free spaces, a local clerk could fill information about the person concerned. These specifications were so descriptive that they were probably filled in in the presence of the applicant. Height, for example, was usually described as "tall," "medium," or "short," the chin as "shaved" or "bearded," and the face as "clean" or "freckled."[16] The only instances when information about the religious background was added were passports issued for Jews.

15 An example of how people travelling without passports or with expired travel documents were dealt with is F292 D46 Pasporta i bilety, vydannye zhitelyam goroda dlya vyezda v raznye goroda i sela Rossii, 1891.

16 F292 D46, p. 2ff. as well as F92 D47 Pasporta, vydannie zhitelyam goroda dlya vyezda v raznye goroda in sela Rossii, 1891–92.

Passports, legal documents, and administrative memorandums issued throughout the 19th century remind us that the language spoken by subjects or the ethnic group they identified with at the time was no marker for a specific category. It mattered what religion they adhered to, whether or not they had come from the Ottoman Empire, at what exact time they had arrived, and that now these people had accepted to be subjects of Russia.

3 Keep It Separate, Keep It Simple

Although the majority of settlers in Southern Bessarabia were Orthodox, there were sizable groups of different confessions including Jews, Catholic Poles, Germans, both protestant and catholic, and Old-Believers.[17] Throughout Bessarabia's time in the Russian Empire there were different rules for different religious communities. While on the lookout for early signs of ethnic boundaries, state administered segregation of religious communities is one of the promising candidates.

Since the reign of Peter I, at the beginning of the 18th century, people had been recorded in parish registers. Where different religious communities lived close to each other, their mixing confused the parish based registration system and therefore endangered the state's control. With the growing importance of precise registries, a trend to bar confessional groups from intermarrying set in towards the end of the 18th century (Cadiot, 2005: 445). In regions settled with newcomers, like southern Bessarabia, each district was initially reserved for settlers of one specific religion (Klaus, 1869: 11).

One of the reasons why it was hard to administer inter-confessional mixing was that the Orthodox Church was still the only authority that kept systematic track of individuals and changes in their civic status. Confessional minorities, such as Jews, Protestants, or Catholics did not appear in metric books of Orthodox parishes. Between 1826 and 1837 a number of tsarist decrees instructed Catholic priests, Protestant pastors, and Jewish rabbis to keep track of their communities in their own metric books. In 1874, after all other religious communities, the last unrecorded groups, the Old-Believers and Baptists were

17 The Old-Believer communities along the channels of the Danube Delta were among the oldest of the settler colonies in the region. Many of them were founded soon after the Russian church reforms under Patriarch Nikon between 1652 and 1666, with which they refused to conform (Derzhavin, 1914: 7; Kushnir, 1998: 150). In this period the region still belonged to the Principality of Moldova, a vassal of the Ottoman Empire. Most Old Believers in Bessarabia settled near the rivers Dniester and Danube and relied on fishing (Kushnir, 1998: 150).

ordered to register with civil authorities in the nearest police station (Steinwedel, 2001: 70–71).

What remained unacceptable to the state bureaucracy were individuals or entire families existing between established religious communities. In July 1835 the Russian interior ministry issued a decree prohibiting marriages between Orthodox Christians and Old-Believers. A copy of the decree was sent to the governor of Izmail Uezd for "precise and immediate implementation."[18] A second decree issued in October 1836, once more reveals how limited the state's control over affairs like marriages between subjects of different categories was. The document specified the exact procedure that should be followed in order to legalize a marital union of an Orthodox person with an Old-Believer: The Old-Believer partner first needed to convert to Orthodoxy and be re-baptized before they could get married. Unfortunately, the decree lamented, there were many cases in which the Old-Believer partner simply pledged not to lead the Orthodox spouse, or their common children, into deviation. This was no longer an acceptable practice, the decree ordered. Whoever gave his blessing to such an unseemly marriage, or allowed it to be registered in his church, chapel, or house, should be punished according to the law.[19]

Another aspect of putting religious minorities in their predefined place were rules about who could employ people of various categories. An 1839 circular, distributed by the Izmail military authority to local heads of the civil administration (gradonachalniki), can provide some insight, how such regulations were handled. The document was circulated in order to remind civil administrators of existing prohibitions for Christians to stand in the service of Jews.[20] This document shows how the state attempted to keep different religious groups separated. More importantly, it reminds us how inefficient such rules were since the state just did not have the means to enforce them. In fact, the author of the circular, military governor Feodorov, started his letter with an infuriated reminder of laws that had been in effect for many years and that were well known to the civil authorities. He then went on describing an experience from his latest inspection ride:

---

18 F56 D37 Tsirkulariya ITsD o zapreshchenii brakosochitaniy raskol'nikov s pravovernimi, 1837, p. 2.

19 F56 D37, p. 6.

20 It was in principle prohibited for Christians to permanently stand in the service of Jews. But the law also allowed for a whole series of exceptions, none of which seems to have been taken into consideration by military governor Feodorov reporting on his observations in Leovo. See Polozhenie o Evrejakh of April 13, 1835: PSZ tom 10 II, no 8054, §15, p. 310, available online: <http://nlr.ru/e-res/law_r/search.php?regim=4&page=308&part=368> (23.02.2019).

> ...in spite of that [laws prohibiting Jews to employ Christians in their service], during my last inspection, I had to notice that this law is not implemented everywhere as it should be by our weak police, and that Jews in some places, as if this law did not exist, continue to employ Christians in their service, especially women, who are ignorant that this is not appropriate for them, and who work under miserable conditions and for miserable salaries for Jews and lead the most ghastly life. The police officers, out of criminal intentions, let this evil happen, and even if they sometimes do press charges against this evil, they do so out of criminal intentions too.
>
> I discovered this evil while I was travelling in the district of Kagul, in the hamlet of Leovo, where a number of shameless women approached me to complain about the assessor Bereznitskiy, who used to allow them to work for Jews and finally prohibited it, and as a punishment for this offence (about which no one had informed them) ordered that these women should work in his own house without compensation.[21]

The military governor then went on reporting how he sacked the culprit, Bereznitskiy, right on the spot, and finally expressed his hopes that this episode should serve as an example for authorities in other districts.

The procedure of law enforcement, exemplified by this case, is very telling: A high representative of the military traveled the land and encountered the victims of an alleged abuse. He himself punished the perpetrator and then found the cause of the crime in the disregard for the separation of people belonging to different religious categories. The report of this deviation also served as a reminder to civil authorities that laws existed, that these laws were meant to prevent grievances like those reported in the circular, and that it was the civil authority's job to enforce the law. The civil authorities at the time were based in small and remote settlements and had a "weak police" to their disposal, as the circular complains. The police, however, was not only weak because it was small in number and probably poorly funded, the military governor also alleged they had "criminal intentions" that led the police to sometimes take action on a crime and sometimes look the other way. Thus the weakness of law enforcement was also the consequence of serious lack in discipline and presumably deep-reaching corruption. Not for no reasons then, accounts of the already introduced Pavel Svin'in of his 1815 journey through Bessarabia (Svin'in, 1816) were rumored to be the original inspiration for Nikolai Gogol's

21 F56 D344 Tsirkulariya Bessarabskogo voennogo gubernatora o zapreshchenii khristianam postupat' v prislugu k evreyam, 1841, p. 1.

1836 satirical play *The Government Inspector*[22] (Kushko and Taki, 2012: 132, 158). Rules of religious segregation were not only weak, they were also laxly enforced. It is therefore very doubtful whether these rules could effectively separate people along religious lines.

More rules against inter-confessional or interethnic mixing might have existed beyond the codified law, in the habitual norms of settler communities. It is not easy to establish in retrospect how isolated from one another and how endogamous among themselves confessional and ethnic groups were in fact. Several forms of endogamy are conceivable: endogamy within the village community and, if there were several ethnic groups in the community, within one of these ethnic groups. It is also conceivable that everyone in a village community, irrespective of ethnic identity, was eligible to marriage, provided of course that they were of the same religion. A third possibility is, that people, already early in the 19th century, married across village borders and across, what today would be considered ethnic boundaries. If asked today, most respondents hold strong beliefs that before the advent of socialism, ethnic boundaries were a strict barrier to marriage, and that cultural exchange between ethnic groups was minimal. Tanya Boneva (2006: 52) who has conducted ethnographic fieldwork in two Bulgarian villages of southern Bessarabia reached a similar conclusion. The economic opportunities in villages were limited, meant to serve the state and not to encourage private initiatives. Social life was largely confined to the village community and characterized by social conservatism and cultural stability. Early ethnographies of the Gagauz suggested a situation in which Bulgarians and Gagauz, even if they lived in the same village, rarely ever married each other (Shabashov, 2012: 416). In the scholarly community the paradigm that Gagauz and Bulgarians strived to remain separate is most likely based on one of the first studies of the Gagauz by a Russian General Lieutenant, member of the Geographical Society, and self-taught ethnographer Valentin Moshkov, who in 1900–02 published a series of articles about the Gagauz in

22 The subject for the *Government Inspector* was given to Gogol by Aleksandr Pushkin on Gogol's request for an "authentic Russian anecdote" ("Gogol' Nikolay Vasilevich," 1989: 595; Mulrine, 1999: xiv, xvii). For exspressing his reformist ideas, Pushkin was sent to serve General Liutenant Inzov's office in Bessarabia in 1821–24 ("Pushkin, Aleksandr Sergeevich," 2007: 191–193). Svin'in and Pushkin were friends since the early 1820s and still frequented the same Moscow circles in the early 1830s ("Svin'in, Pavel Petrovich," 2007: 519–524). Both having traveled in Bessarabia, they could have exchanged notes. However, Gogol's *Government Inspector* was set in a town with a much more Russian way of life than could have been observed in recently integrated Bessarabia. For our note here it is important that the rumor of Bessarabia being an inspiration for the *Government Inspector* was so tenacious. This fact reveals the dubious reputation such peripheral regions had among the Russian intelligentsia of the time.

the leading ethnographic journal *Etnograficheskoe Obozrenie* (Moshkov, 1902a, 1902b, 1901b, 1901a, 1900). Based on a short stopover in the mixed Bulgarian and Gagauz village Kirsova (today in Moldova), Moshkov claimed that the two groups (he used the terms "narodnost'" and "natsional'nost'" interchangeably) had always lived in hostility and mutual mistrust. In Moshkov's account even the church and the cemetery were separated into two halves in which each group stayed strictly apart. However, on the same page Moshkov described how Bulgarians and Gagauz had to collaborate to run village affairs such as the night watch. He did not claim that members of the two groups could under no circumstances marry each other, but he wondered that in spite of the close cultural similarity, marriages between Gagauz and Bulgarians remained rare in Kirsova, rarer than between Gagauz and Moldovans, two groups between whom cultural differences were considerably larger (Moshkov, 1901a: 34–35). Moshkov's account is contradictory when it comes to his claim of strict ethnic segregation between Bulgarians and Gagauz. In another section, he elaborates on the common practice for young men to seek employment with well-to-do farmers in order to earn enough money to set up a household and get married. Some young men went back to the same employers for many agricultural season and many did so in neighboring villages among Bulgarians and Germans. Moshkov reported that for many of the young labor migrants their years away from home were also years of apprenticeship during which they learned a trade, picked up new manners, and in some cases found a bride (Moshkov, 1901a: 14–15). A later student of the region, Soviet philologist Samuil Bernshteyn also traveled through Kirsova in the summer of 1947 and *en passant* repeated Moshkov's claim of totally segregated ethnic communities (without referring to Moshkov). In neighboring Komrat, however, Bernshteyn noted that the Bulgarian minority had fully assimilated to the Gagauz majority and that interethnic marriages were very common (Bernshteyn, 1949: 387). But the theme of ethnic segregation found broader interest among subsequent scholars. In another expression of the long cultivated belief in ethnic endogamy, Boneva (2006: 53) reported her respondents mentioning the bible as a source of strict endogamy rules that were observed until the Soviet period. As groups that were out of the question to marry for Bulgarians, she mentions Russians and Moldovans.

In at least two ethnically mixed villages near Izmail, the large Bulgarian and Gagauz village of Chervonoarmeyskoe[23] and the Albanian, Bulgarian and

23 In Bolgrad rayon, called Kubey in pre-Soviet times and again since 2016 when it was renamed according to Ukraine's "De-communization laws."

Gagauz village of Zhovtnevoe,[24] people speak of a past ethnic segregation within the village. In some instances the term "Mahala"[25] for quarter or neighborhood was used in Russian, Bulgarian, Gagauz, Romanian, and Albanian to delineate such formerly existing sectors. The word Mahala however is also used to refer to neighborhoods in Izmail and in villages without a narrative of past ethnic segregation. In both abovementioned villages some people even today can show where exactly the border between the ethnically segregated Mahalas used to be. There are numerous tales of mass brawls between young men from different ethnic sectors on these borders. Opinions differ, however, as to whether these brawls were interethnic conflicts or simply caused by drunkenness and jealousy. Other villages also have a history of being ethnically mixed. The two neighboring villages Kislitsa[26] and Pershotravnevoe[27] today are both considered predominantly Ukrainian villages. In both villages there are memories of a once mixed ethnic character with a large group of Romanian speakers living among the Slav majority. However, there are no memories of ethnic segregation in these two villages.

Ethnic segregation within the village seems to be a part of a widely spread narrative only in villages where ethnic groups used to have roughly equal size. In most other villages there used to be one predominant ethnic majority group with which the village came to be associated beyond its limits. Usually smaller groups of ethnic outsiders also lived in Bessarabian villages among these majorities. They were certainly too small to be endogamous both within the village and within their ethnic group.

Accessible archival materials in Izmail give only very scant insight into marriage patterns of the early and mid-19th century.[28] In rare cases certificates that proved a person's eligibility to marriage have been conserved. These documents reveal some information whom and where young men and women from Bessarabian colonies married during the tsarist period. One surviving collection of documents, certifying people's rights to marry, stems from the early

24 In Bolgrad rayon, called Karakurt in pre-Soviet times and again since 2016 when it was renamed according to Ukraine's "De-communization laws."

25 The word "Mahala," as used in Bessarabia, is derived from the Arabic word *Mahalla*, meaning "a place where one makes a halt, where one settles (for a longer or shorter time)." In Persian, Urdu and Turkish (Mahalle) took on the meaning "quarter of a town" (Bosworth et al., 1986: 1220) which comes very close to the modern usage in the diverse languages of Bessarabia that have, without doubt, taken it from Turkish.

26 In Izmail rayon, called Câşliţe-Dunăre in pre-Soviet times.

27 In Izmail rayon, called Hasan-Aspaga in pre-Soviet times.

28 Church registers, in which marriages, births, and deaths were recorded, so called metric books, have largely survived; alas access is granted only to information concerning proven relatives of the applicant.

1850s. Such certificates were issued by the colonists of a settlement and written by a scribe. They usually started with the statement "We the colonists of the colony XY testify that the below mentioned person has the right to marry." This preamble typically also contained the exact name of the local church and the name of the priest.[29] That the soon-to-be-married person was from among the colonists already suggested that he or she was an Orthodox Christian. Therefore, information concerning social estate and religious confession were often not even mentioned in such certificates. What was usually mentioned, however, was that the couple were not biological relatives (*rodstvo plotskiy*), nor in-laws (*rodstvo dukhovnyy*), and in some cases that they were in no god-parenthood relation (*kumstvo*).[30] It was also mentioned which settlement the bride and groom came from, which allows us to track their marriage patterns on the map. Other information that was usually part of the testimony, was whether or not the person concerned was about to marry for the first, or for the second time. This information allows us to establish whether when married for a second time, people did so over greater geographical and social distances than in first marriages.

The surviving files in Izmail's archive concern the transdanubian colonies administered from the small town of Bolgrad. There were 38 settlements in this district, most of which are considered Bulgarian today. Others, however, are now considered Gagauz, Moldovan, or Albanian settlements.[31] From 41 marriages, registered in these colonies between November 1851 and January 1853, roughly half (20) were arranged between different colonies, alas mostly within the district reserved for Transdanubian Colonists, i.e. most likely with a Bulgarian or Gagauz partner. Only one marriage was arranged in a village of a neighboring district.[32] In 9 cases, at least one of the partners married for the second time, when they were in their mid-30s. Seven out of nine second marriages included partners from different villages, in one case over a distance of more than 80 km. If in the 1850s only roughly half of the people married within one village, this means they most likely already had a degree of mobility and exchange between villages. One form of interaction between villages could have been the practice of young men seeking paid employment with wealthy farmers, described by Moshkov. But most marriages at the time appear to have been

29 For example F93 D332 Svidetel'stva, vydannye kolonistam na pravo vstupleniya v brak, pp. 20, 21, 22.

30 F93 D332, pp. 3, 15, 17.

31 List of settlements that belonged to the Bolgrad-administered area for transdanubian colonists in the constitution of a Bolgrad gymnasium from 1884, cited in F312 D76 Documentele dreptilor Liceului din Bolgrad, 1923, p. 63.

32 All cases recorded in F93 D332.

arranged by the parental generation (Derzhavin, 1914: 126; Kushnir, 1998: 192). Therefore at least ties of trust must have existed between villages. These ties connected villages that lay at considerable distances from one another and in which Bulgarian, Gagauz, Albanian and Romanian was spoken. Most of the southern Bessarabian villages had well under a thousand inhabitants at the time.[33] If among this small group all relatives, in-laws, and people related through god-parenthood were excluded from marriage, very likely many families had no other choice but to look for future spouses beyond village boundaries. This means that at least occasionally, people chose marriage partners beyond what today would be considered ethnic boundaries.

With even greater likelihood we can draw such a conclusion for second marriages. Here partners were apparently found quite frequently outside the village. Often these partners had themselves lost a spouse from their first marriage. This observation echoes the early ethnographic material of Derzhavin (1914: 44) who observed that exclusions from a very strict prohibition of interethnic marriage were made only for widows and widowers. Even Valentin Moshkov, who hardly contained his fascination with apparently rigid ethnic endogamy, noted that Gagauz and Moldovans sometimes did marry each other and that this was especially likely for widows and widowers (1901a: 36). Despite strong social norms against marrying culturally foreign, Derzhavin, working in the 1890s had met many couples in which one partner was Bulgarian and the other was Russian, or in which one was Bulgarian and the other Greek (1914: 45–47). This rather grudgingly admitted insight, combined with the marriage data from the 1850s, leads one to cautiously conclude that marriages across village boundaries were relatively common already in the mid-19th century. We can also conclude that there might have been local rules excluding marriage with Russians and possibly also Ukrainians, but that these norms were frequently ignored. We can be relatively certain that there were no marriages across confessional lines without one of the partner's conversion. However, popular notions of strict endogamy within the limits of the village community appear exaggerated in light of even the small amount of data accessible on this topic.

Rather different marriage patterns can be seen in a second, much later, surviving collection of marriage certificates from Bolgrad, covering the first 6 months of 1918.[34] Here, still a little less than half the couples recorded (10 out of 25) married outside the village. But now one bride came from Vilnius in

33 See Kornilovich (1899) for village population statistics from the mid to late 1820s, pp. 375 ff.

34 F292 D251 Zhurnal registratsiy brakov za 1918 god.

Lithuania, one groom from Tomsk in Siberia, one from Kursk in southern Russia, one man was a Greek from Romania, and two came from the Kingdom of Slovenes, Croats and Serbs. Certainly this new, international marriage patterns had a lot to do with World War I that had ended for Russia not long before. But it also shows that by the early 20th century endogamy, neither within the village nor the ethnic group, was a value in itself. Indeed, rigid regulations confining marriage to ethnic and confessional groups had undergone thorough criticism from within the imperial bureaucracy. Newly drafted laws accepted that new forms of interaction between ethnic groups would make interethnic mixing inevitable (Cadiot, 2005: 445). Therefore, if endogamy within one colony was a frequently disregarded rule in the mid-19th century, by the time of the October Revolution it had ceased to be even a rule. Interethnic marriage became possible and common before the Soviet Union took the region over in 1944.

Moreover, if marriage between several groups of Orthodox Christians became increasingly normal in the course of the 19th century, non-Christian groups were continually considered to be best manageable if kept separate. The Jewish communities, in particular, were treated by the state according to laws specifically issued for this group. For them, geographical segregation from Christian settlements was indeed required by the law.[35] Jews had entered the region steadily, beginning with the first Partition of Poland in 1772. In 1804 a decree on the Jews regulated their status in Russian society.[36] It was the beginning of the attempt to centralize control over all Jewish communities through unified representation of their communities vis-à-vis the state (Löwe, 2000: 60). Minority groups, such as the Jews, were integrated into imperial structures by attempting to sum them all up in a single social category that had a unified and visible body of representatives.

As with the Old-Believers, for the Jews too, the imperial administration was keen to ensure that conversion from one group to another could happen only from the minority group to the majority group. Administrative incentives such as longer military service for "unproductive elements," as which Jews were classified, made it attractive to become an Orthodox Christian. Once conversed to Christianity one was prohibited to return to any former creed (Cadiot, 2005: 445; Löwe, 2000: 64).

Regulations about Jews in Russia were also a testing ground for imperial language policy. This effort again was closely tied to the state's need for

35 Polozhenie o Evreyakh May 31, 1835, PSZ Tom 10 I, no. 8054 §65, p. 316.

36 Polozhenie dlya Evreev, 1804, PSZ Tom 28, no. 21547, p. 731, available online: <http://www.nlr.ru/e-res/law_r/search.php> (23.02.2019).

"legibility." For instance all bookkeeping in Jewish firms had to be in Russian, Polish, or German.[37] The same regulations applied to all contracts and paychecks[38] and no Jew could be elected to the magistrate after the year of 1808, if he could not read and write one of these languages.[39] Even stricter language policies were introduced in the 1830s. The background for these stiffer policies was a militant rebellion in Poland in 1830–31, suppressed by Russia only with considerable difficulties. After crushing the rebels, the tsarist government hoped to prevent future rebellions by russifying the administration and the educatory system in Poland, but even more so in the western and south-western provinces of Russia (Ryasanovsky, 2000: 332). As a consequence, after 1835, Russian became the only language permissible in official or business documents for Jews too.[40] Ultimately, making the Jewish community "legible" and therefore easier to administer went much further than only dictating what languages they had to read and write in. Jews were also categorized in four distinct social statuses (*sostoyanie*); a) agriculturalists, b) manufacturers and craftsmen, c) merchants, and d) urban bourgeoisie. Specific laws applied for each of these classes.[41] They could belong to only one of those four classes, and had to register to one of them. Nowhere in Russia would a Jew be tolerated if he was not properly registered as belonging to one of these social estates. Thus the legislations on the Jews were based on an amalgamate of religious and social status categories, ingredients that later would be processed further into an ethnic distinction.

4 Bureaucracy Evolving: the Church Gives Way to the State

A Russian state with bureaucrats mounted on horseback, traveling the land on inspection excursions, like the one to the hamlet Leovo, began to slowly transform in the mid-19th century. A new style of administration began to take shape when, in a first step, administrative territories were carved out of the landscape and, more significantly, statistical categories to characterize imperial subjects were introduced with ever more precision. More and more decisions were based on such categories, and these decisions were increasingly taken far away in imperial centers. Along with this slow transition that took the

37 Polozhenie dlya Evreev, 1804, PSZ Tom 28, no. 21547, §7, p. 731.

38 Ibid. §8.

39 Ibid. §9.

40 Polozhenie o Evreyakh, May 31. 1835, PSZ Tom 10 I, no. 8054 §18, p. 311.

41 Polozhenie dlya Evreev, 1804, PSZ Tom 28, no. 21547, §11, p. 732: the Russian terms are a) zemledeltsy b) fabrikanty i remesleniki, c) kupechestvo, d) meshchanstvo.

entire second half of the 19th century, came a general enthusiasm for rationalization (Kushko and Taki, 2012: 19).

At the beginning, the administrative and legal integration of Bessarabia into the Russian Empire was slow and intricate. Bessarabia oblast, with its capital in Chișinău, was created in 1812.[42] It was structured in 8 districts, so called Uezdi. In the few towns, city councils (Dumas) were installed, headed by the mayor (Lebedenko and Tychyna, 2002: 81). The territorial systematization only gradually led to systematization of social categories. This process began with aligning laws and later linguistic practices to the rest of the newly acquired Russian provinces. In the first years of Russian rule in Bessarabia, parts of Russian legislations were used simultaneously with parts of older legislations, stemming still from the Principality of Moldova.

Ioan Kapodistrias, a Russian foreign minister of Greek descent (in office 1815–22), was the main character behind the legal incorporation of Bessarabia into the Russian Empire. His recommendations were to use local laws and the Romanian/Moldovan language, to administer the new province. He also urged his superiors in St. Petersburg to thoroughly study their new Bessarabian subjects before issuing new laws for them (Kushko and Taki, 2012: 112). Indeed, for a long time local affairs were solved inside the colonies. The Russian state accepted that they were resolved according to local rules (Boneva, 2006: 52). Notwithstanding the trend for rationalization of legal processes, a great deal of legal pluralism remained. In this characteristic Bessarabia was no exception. All over the empire, local matters were solved by "legal processes fine-tuned to local practice and endowed with imperial authority" (Burbank, 2007: 92).

Russia and her foreign minister, Kapodistrias, had helped to stir the Greek Independence War against the Ottoman Empire (Kapodistrias was to become the first head of state of independent Greece 1827–31). But the Russian government became scared of the nationalist revolutionary spirit it had helped to create in Greece. There were fears this spirit could spread to other former Ottoman Provinces such as Moldova, to which Bessarabia had belonged until recently. Therefore, St. Petersburg initiated measures to russify the Bessarabian administration and to subjugate its church under the Moscow Patriarchate (King, 2000: 25). But for a start, between 1812 and 1828, when Bessarabia received its new legislation, the Moldovan law was used in civil cases, while the Russian penal code was used in criminal cases (Berg, 1918: 72). One important consequence of the parallel use of two legislations was that penal cases were held in Russian, while civil cases had to be debated in the Romanian/Moldovan

42 From 1873 onwards it was called "Bessarabskaya Guberniya."

language.[43] Only in 1828 legal arrangements for Bessarabia were ultimately aligned with those in the rest of Novorossiya. Therefore, the Romanian/Moldovan language disappeared from courtrooms, but it was not officially ruled out as a language of state affairs until 1834 (Berg, 1918: 74). It is important to note that different languages were used in court because legal cases were of different nature, and not because the people involved in these cases were of different ethnic backgrounds. Therefore, even when the state started to unify legal processes and the language used in them, it had no reason for knowing ethno-cultural or linguistic background the subjects of those processes had.

Compared to state institutions, churches held a much more important role as institutions of group building. In Izmail, for instance, the number and denomination of churches reflected the diverse composition of the settler population. In 1835, just 23 years after Russia's annexation of Bessarabia, Izmail had already 14 churches. There were eight Orthodox churches, one of them the former Ottoman mosque in the fortress, consecrated still during the war in 1810 (Sapozhnikov, 2009: 249). There were also 4 churches for Old-Believers along with an Armenian and a Catholic church (Lebedenko and Tychyna, 2002: 88). Most duties of local civil administration were handled by the parishes around these churches. The church registered births, baptisms, marriages, religious conversions, and deaths. Therefore the church books remained the most reliable and systematic data on the number and composition of the population. Like passports, the church registries had been introduced in the Russian Empire a century before the annexation of Bessarabia, under the reign of Peter I. His hunger for recruits to run large military campaigns, and for tax money to realize grand projects such as the foundation of St. Petersburg in 1703, made it more suitable to register the Russian population person by person, not by entire households as had been the custom thus far. In a decree from 1724 the Holy Synod ordered all priests in all parishes to register every birth, marriage, and death. But it was not until the 1830s that the metrical books came to be standardized (Tebarth, 1991: 32). From this decade onwards candidates to enter state service were required to present excerpts from church registers, proving their identity (Steinwedel, 2001: 69). Since civil status data about most people were registered in their respective churches, the data provided by parishes remained structured by confession rather than by ethnicity (Cadiot, 2005: 440). Nevertheless, the church register's systematic mode of documenting the population provided the blueprint for later registration systems along ethnic lines.

---

43 Ustav obrazovaniya Bessarabskoy oblasti. *Polnoe zobranie zakonov* (PSZ)—SPB 1830- Sobranie I –T XXXV Nr. 27357 29.04.1818: <http://nlr.ru/e-res/law_r/search.php?regim=4&page=222&part=165> (23.02.2019).

5 The Categories of the Census Taker and the Ethnographer

Beside the state and the church, in the mid-19th century a third force in the gradual rise of ethnic categories emerged; learned societies. The more the rulers in far-away St. Petersburg came to think of themselves as enlightened monarchs, the greater grew their desire to read scholarly accounts about the newly acquired territories and the people living in them (Sunderland, 2004: 64). In the depths of the Russian east, scholarly excursions had been taking place on a large scale already since the 1720s. Such excursions often included devotees of the discipline of *Völkerkunde*, evolving in Germany at the time. One of the goals of these endeavors was to study the culturally diverse subjects the empire governed (Vermeulen, 1995: 43–44). Russia's expansion to the west was accompanied by an attempt to culturally "reacquire" the newly incorporated lands. With this goal in mind the tsarist government founded a new University in Kyiv in 1834 and gave it the task to research local history, geography and culture (Magocsi, 2002: 48). With values of enlightenment increasingly influencing bourgeois urban circles, they showed increasing interest in the peasant societies, living in the hinterlands of their own cities. In 1845 educated urbanites founded the Russian Geographical Society which had an ethnographic department from the beginning. Its staff consisted partly of reputable German scholars attracted to the Geographical Society by excellent research conditions (Knight, 1998: 108–111). In the 1850s and 1860s the ethnographers of the Geographical Society saw their task not so much as a comparative analysis of human societies, but more as the meticulous collection of artifacts belonging to different ethnic groups (that were then referred to as *narod* or *narodnost'*) (Knight, 1998: 128). This added to the stock of the curiosity cabinet-turned-ethnographic museum founded as the *Kunstkamera* by Peter I already in 1714. In 1836 the *Kunstkamera* proclaimed the founding of an ethnographic department, earlier than any other ethnographic museum in the world (Vermeulen, 1995: 52). The frenzy with which early Russian ethnographers collected artifacts also led to the first Russian ethnographic exposition in Moscow in 1867 and eventually to the founding of an official ethnographic Museum, the conceptualization of which began in the 1890s (Cvetkovski, 2014a: 214–227).

Odessa was then, as it is now, the nearest and most important urban center for Bessarabians. By the mid-19th century it had become a quickly growing, cosmopolitan port city, aspiring for the status of a leading cultural center in the empire. Odessa's university was founded in 1865 as the "Imperial University of Novorossiya."

The first comprehensive description of the ecology, economy, and the population of Novorossiya was produced by the abovementioned historian and statistician Appolon Skal'kovskiy (1853, 1850). He was one of the founding members of the Odessa Society for History and Antiquity. The society, one of the first of its kind in Russia, was established in 1839 with backing from Moscow University (Kuznetsov, 2008: 22). Its members were mainly interested in excavating remains of Greek and Scythian settlements (Razgon, 1982). Skal'kovskiy, in contrast, dealt with the people of the present and their history. He described all of Bessarabia's ethnic groups one after another. The Russians and the Ukrainians he summarized in one chapter. The Bulgarians he subsumed under the chapter *Serbs and other transdanubian settlers*. The Gagauz he did not mention as a separate group at all, since at the time of his writing, the term "Gagauz" was not yet established as the denominator of a separate ethnic group (Derzhavin, 1914: 13; Grek and Russev, 2011: 73; Moshkov, 1901a: 29). On the other hand, the author discussed at length non-orthodox immigrant populations from Western Europe, that today have all but vanished from the ethnic mosaic, such as the French and the Swiss.

Skal'kovskiy's interest in the peasant was in tune with the scholarly fashions of mid-19th-century Russia. The empire, ill-prepared, stumbled into the Crimean War in 1853 and lost it in 1856. To many young intellectuals, this defeat revealed how backward Russia was and how urgently reforms were needed. The most noticeable consequence of the resulting reform drive was eventually the abolition of serfdom in 1861. In this atmosphere of transformation a new brand of young writers discovered the description of everyday culture of simple, working people as a popular new genre. They used their access to well-off, urban readers to address social grievances (Clay, 1995: 45–50). But this bout of attention for the peasant was not meant to be a one way street. The scholars who went to live with them, the *narodniki* as they were called for their interest in the *narod*, the people, also hoped to bring enlightenment to the peasants and thereby enable them to liberate themselves (Cvetkovski, 2014a: 221). But Appolon Skal'kovskiy, although interested in the local population, was not yet quite as avant-garde. Like the state servants travelling Bessarabia, he was preoccupied with counting people rather than observing them or asking them questions. His descriptions of ethnic differences remained sketchy. A later student of the region, Nikolay Derzhavin (1914: ix), referring to Skal'kovskiy's work, complained that Skal'kovskiy and other scholars have hitherto shown "hardly any interest in ethnography" and that even from the most brilliant statistical descriptions of Bessarabia, only little could be learned about the culture of the "foreigners" living there. Indeed, Skal'kovskiy's account mainly relied on state documents and parish registers. It could hardly have inspired the reader's imagination of how the *narodi*, found in Bessarabia, differed culturally from one another. To do justice to Skal'kovskiy, he might have had a hard time clearly discerning ethnic groups. When he worked in Bessarabia in the mid-19th century, several ethnic denominations still could exist parallel without raising brows. It was for instance perfectly normal that a person would identify as Russian and Little Russian, as Ukrainians were still commonly called, at the same time. Only with the spread of nationalism around the turn of the 20th century these became mutually exclusive ethnic labels (Magocsi, 2002: 46).

After the Crimean War, the imperial integration of the Central Asian steppe regions and of southern Siberia became increasingly vital for the slowly industrializing economy of the empire. It was only now that for the Russian state the information about a person's social status and religion was no longer sufficient to achieve the political goals, set for the peripheral lands. With the systematic colonization of Russia's periphery, cultural differences became an important factor, mainly where they concerned modes of subsistence. Not all groups were equally suitable to settle all territories. Some groups were chiefly peasants, other were nomads or fishermen. To make colonization at this pre-industrial stage more efficient, the state needed markers for these differences. Along with religion and social estate, modes of subsistence joined the potpourri of features that would later come to define ethnic groups. Although forms of proto-ethnic categorization began to creep into the administrative process and into public discourse, there was still no systematic definition or research what an ethnicity or a nationality was (Steinwedel, 2007: 132).

In 1897 the first and only empire-wide census took place in Russia. A second one was planned for 1915, but was cancelled due to World War I (Cadiot, 2005: 440). "The fiction of the census," as Anderson (2006: 166) observed, "is that everyone is in it and that everyone has one—and only one—extremely clear place," hence the census takers' "intolerance of multiple, politically 'transvestite,' blurred, or changing identifications." To make the census worth the huge logistical effort, the categories used in it needed to be clearly defined. Since 1857 there was an international body in which statisticians from across Europe convened to make their indicators comparable, the International Statistical Congress. Its members, since the Congress' very beginnings, struggled with questions of nationality and ethnicity. Early on, language became a widely accepted proxy for ethnicity. But disagreement remained whether to ask for *langue parleé* or *langue maternelle* to determine someone's ethnic belonging (Roth, 1991: 137–140). In both the Russian 1897 census and its unrealized 1915 successor, the Ministry of the Interior, in charge of planning and executing the census was faced with the question how to ask for cultural differences and identity in order to get valid and comparable results. The question for ethnicity was not included in either of the questionnaires. Instead, census takers asked the 129 million subjects of the Tsar for their social estate (*soslovie*), their religion, and their native language (Cadiot, 2005: 442; Roth, 1991: 144–147). In some areas of the empire, respondents named their social estate almost like an ethnic identity. Russian colonists in Siberia, for example, named their status as colonists to differentiate themselves from other Russians in their region. Religious confession served as a proxy for ethnic identity in many regions. In Central Asia many respondents answered the question for their native language with "Muslim" (Cadiot, 2005: 443–444). Ukrainian peasants, when asked about their language up to World War I, most likely would say "the language of here," rather than use the denomination "Ukrainian" (Boeck, 2005: 39). In Lithuania, census takers were instructed that Orthodox respondents counted as Russians, Jews were to be counted separately, Lutherans were counted as Germans, but that Catholics could be both Poles and Lithuanians (Cadiot, 2005: 444). For many local authorities and census takers the lack of congruence between language and ethnicity was obvious already at the time of the census. The auxiliary supplement published with the census' results advised readers to correlate native language with other categories, such as confession and territory (Roth, 1991: 144–146). But for Bessarabia even such corrective correlations would lead to more confusion than clarity. In many cases people of the same confession spoke different languages (the Ukrainians, Russians, Moldovans, Bulgarians, Albanians, and Gagauz were all Orthodox Christians) or people of the same language prayed in different churches. (In Bessarabia Russian Old-Believers and Orthodox Christians both spoke Russian but belonged to different churches). But perhaps a more important flaw of taking confession for ethnicity was that confession could be changed by conversion (and at times was actively encouraged to be changed). The imperfect congruence of confession, ethnicity, and language stood in stark contradiction to the claim for objectivity and scientifically asserted truths that statistics promised to provide (Cadiot, 2005: 441).

During the first years of the 20th century, the results of the 1897 census started to trickle in to the Russian public. In 1905 the statistical results for Bessarabia were published in a separate tome (Troynitskiy, 1905). It used, like the other publications springing from the census, native language as a proxy for ethnicity (to which it interchangeably referred as *natsional'nost'* or *narodnost'*). At a time in which nationalist tendencies were gathering momentum in several regions of the empire, concerns about the conclusiveness of the data were voiced by many contemporaries, especially concerning ethnicity. One common critique was that an imprecise distinction between native language and spoken language contorted the picture for the benefit of Russians. Many people, whose identity was not or not exclusively Russian, spoke that language best of all (Roth, 1991: 148). A Ukrainian nationalist newspaper, for instance, lamented that when Ukrainian respondents answered they spoke Russian, the census taker did not enquire further to find out what particular brand of Russian they identified with (at the time "Little Russian" was a synonym for "Ukrainian") (Cadiot, 2005: 449). For Bessarabia, an educated guess, using the method suggested in the supplements to the census, often provides the best clue to an ethnic headcount at the end of the 19th century. In her study on the demographic development of the Gagauz, Subottina (2011: 159), for instance, combined language and religion to calculate the number of Gagauz. She counted in those people who were both Orthodox Christians and native speakers of a "Turkish" language.

The flaws of defining ethnicity along religious lines became obvious already in a much smaller and much earlier statistical project. Colonel Stepan Kornilovich was in charge of a statistic survey conducted in southern Bessarabia between 1822 and 1828. The aim of the undertaking was to gather reliable data based on which the land could be distributed among colonists. The study did not seek to understand the ethnic composition of the then still very fluid population. Kornilovich's work disappeared in the archives, until in the 1890s it was rediscovered and published[44] posthumously (Kornilovich, 1899). It was a time when the definition of ethnicity and how it was to be recorded in statistics, was already heatedly debated. Therefore it is unclear whether the category of ethnicity (*natsional'nost'*) was used in the original tables by Kornilovich or whether other terms have been interpreted as ethnicity by the editor in 1899. Either way, Kornilovich's data show that in the 1820s ethnicity was conceptualized very differently from the 1890s during the empire-wide census. Kornilovich paid much attention to the social estate and confession, as was the custom in his time. In his table for the population of the city of Izmail, he used categories social estate (*soslovie*) and ethnicity (*natsional'nost'*) in one column. Therefore people were counted, for example, either as military officers or as Russians. For areas outside Izmail, he distinguished two kinds of state servants, two kinds of noblemen, and a distinction was made between peasants and colonists (Kornilovich, 1899: 369–375). Kornilovich divided up several groups that later came to be seen as one ethnic group. At the same time, he counted as one group what later came to be seen as different ethnic groups. Among those groups that later came to be subsumed as Ukrainians he distinguished Little Russians (*Malorrossiyan*), Zaporozhian Cossacks (*Kazakov zaporozhskie*), and

44 By Vladimir Purishkevich, a clerk in the Bessarabian district town of Belgorod-Dniestrovskiy (Akkerman) who understood the value of the work. For the history of the *Statisticheskoe opisanie Bessarabii...* see *Kur'er Nedeli* September 10, 2012. Available online at <http://izmail.es/article/12041/> (23.02.2019).

Danube Cossacks (*Kazakov ust-dunayskie*). The latter two categories had more to do with geographical origin and military affiliation than with language or confession. A similar distinction was made between different groups of Old-Believers who had arrived in the region in separate waves. Here Kornilovich distinguished those who followed the old rite (*Staroobryadtsi*) from the followers of Hetman Nekrasov (*Nekrasovtsi*). Both groups later came to be counted simply as Old-Believers, as Lipovan under Romanian rule, and simply as Russians under Soviet rule.

In the case of the Old-Believers it was the time of their arrival in the region rather than language or confession that led to their registration as a different *natsional'nost'*. Kornilovich did, in some cases, pay attention to language. Some groups that were Orthodox Christians were listed separately from other groups of the same confession, notably the Moldovans and the Albanians (*Arnauty*). However, other groups that spoke different languages were listed as just one group. The Bulgarians and the Gagauz were simply listed as Bulgarians in Kornilovich's work, although the languages they spoke came from entirely different linguistic families. However, both groups were Transdanubian Colonists, similar in their social status, confession, and, since they both had migrated to Bessarabia from a region called Bulgaria, they were similar in geographical origin as well. Also, their settlements were close to each other and many colonies were inhabited by both Gagauz and Bulgarians. Therefore in their case, Kornilovich's statistics ignored the linguistic difference as a potential marker for an ethnic boundary.[45]

It is important to note, that just because the Russian Empire operated with categories, some of which became later the denominators of ethnic groups, this does not mean it recorded the ethnicity of subjects in any comprehensive and systematic way, like in later years did the Romanian state (see chapter 3), or the Soviet Union (see chapters 4 and 5). That colonists, as they passed the imperial quarantine station, went through a "thorough ethnic or religious registration" as Boneva (2006: 51) observes, is only partially true. For those colonists whom the state with its loose policing structures managed to register, many kinds of ascriptions, such as "Bulgarian," "Christian," "Transdanubian Colonist," or "subject of the Ottoman Empire" (*turetskiy poddannyy*) were conceivable. Yet none of these ascriptions meant the same back then as they do today, or as they did at the time of the 1897 census. The ascription "Bulgarian" in the 1820s, as the quotation of Klaus above hints, meant a Christian person

45 In a much later description of the region, Pavel Krushevan's 1903 almanac, Gagauz were still described as a subgroup of Bulgarians and the Bulgarians were described as a group that speaks two languages (Krushevan, 1903:184–185).

from the Balkans. It did not necessarily implicate that this person spoke Bulgarian or identified as a Bulgarian.

In 1897 a consensus among statisticians about what ethnicity was might have ripened far enough to no longer use it interchangeably with social estate, confession, or language. However, ethnicity remained a highly fluid term among scholars as well as among administrators, not to mention the wider population that in many regions had not yet gotten accustomed to identify by ethnicity (Cadiot, 2010: 6).

Scholars would eventually play a key role in introducing the wider public to ethnicity as a clear-cut and essential category. For southern Bessarabia, the earliest attempt of a truly ethnographic study was a series of excursions by Russian officer and ethnographer Valentin Moshkov in the last years of the 19th century. Today's undisputed authority on the Gagauz, Mikhail Guboglo, called Moshkov's series of articles "a star of the greatest magnitude" (2012: 123). Moshkov served in Warszawa, where two of his staff came from Gagauz communities in southern Bessarabia. At least one of them accompanied Moshkov on his field trips and served as an interpreter (Moshkov, 1901a: 19). In the series of articles on the Gagauz in Bendery Uezd, Moshkov published in *Etnograficheskoe Obozrenie*, he covered a wide array of topics such as customs, family structure, beliefs, and their history. The unit of analysis in Moshkovs works was clearly already the "narod," the "narodnost'" or the "natsional'nost'," all of which he used as synonyms. He made meticulous comparisons to other groups of the same domain, above all the Bulgarians. On the bases of such comparisons, he concluded that the character of the Gagauz *narod*, despite his otherwise sympathetic portrait, was incomparably inferior to the character of the Bulgarians (1901a: 31).

Moshkov already belonged to a generation of scholars for which ethnic belonging was the main cause of how people behaved. He hardly contained his fascination with the exotic beliefs and practices of the Gagauz and he was perfectly content explaining them with ethnicity alone. Talking to Gagauz and Bulgarian respondents, Moshkov found a rich array of stereotypes the two groups held against each other. But he also found similar stereotypes the inhabitants of one Gagauz village held against the inhabitants of neighboring Gagauz villages (Moshkov, 1901a: 25). Nevertheless, he gladly embraced the ethnic stereotypes as evidence for actual norms and practices, such as ethnic endogamy. Later, Moshkov attempted a synthesis of his ethnographic excursions as well as materials from zoology, archeology, anthropology, and geology to create a new theory of the origin of man (Moshkov, 1907). This eccentric theory, like his ethnographic account, saw ethnic groups and races as the subjects of history, not individuals. It was full of racism and anthropometric discourses and might be the main reason why Moshkov fell from favor and was hardly referred to anymore until the post-Soviet era.

Two of his contemporaries published their own ethnographic accounts of Bessarabia on the eve of World War I, without referring to Moshkov. One was philologist, historian, and future rector of Leningrad University, Nikolai Derzhavin, who in 1914 published a thorough study of Bulgarian colonies that he had conducted throughout Novorossiya. Part of his field sites were the Bulgarian and Gagauz villages north of Izmail. He did fieldwork in the expedition mode, ultimately visiting every single Bulgarian colony in Russia. His research was sponsored by the Imperial Association for Archeology, by the Academy of Science, and the Ministry of Education. The publication of his book in 1914 by the state press of Bulgaria was also sponsored by the Bulgarian Academy of Science.

The other eminent pre-Soviet scholar of Bessarabia was Lev Berg, born in 1876 to a Jewish family in Bendery and therefore a native of Bessarabia. Berg's main work concerning Bessarabia (1918) was an all-encompassing description of the region starting with its flora and fauna, then touching upon history, economy, and population. At the time of research, he had been the preserver of several fishing grounds and later also worked as a private lecturer at St. Petersburg Imperial University. The two books by Derzhavin and Berg together came to shape the imagination of Bessarabia and its population for a long time. They provided rare insights into Bessarabia under the old imperial order that after the First World War was briskly altered by the advent of Romanian rule. This change in regime also meant that the works of Derzhavin and Berg remained among the very few Russian language sources on southern Bessarabia for a quarter of a century and therefore among the few works trusted in the Soviet Union. Both, Derzhavin's ethnography of the Bulgarian colonists and Berg's ethnographic chapters about the main ethnic groups in Bessarabia followed roughly the same pattern: They provided very detailed descriptions but hardly any theorizing. Both works heavily relied on earlier descriptions of Bessarabia, such as the one by Skal'kovskiy (1850) or Klaus (1869). None of them used much foreign literature except when touching upon archeological problems. Berg's work relied heavily on Nikolai Mogilyanskiy, an ethnographer native from Chernihiv in Ukraine, who studied in Berlin and Paris and later served in a short-lived Ukrainian government during the civil war. He had a tendency to biologize ethnic groups and insisted that ethnography should study whole groups as "ethnic individuals."[46] According to Kuznetsov (2008:

46 See "Mogilyanskiy Nikolay Mikhailovich," *Bol'shaya Rossiyskaya Entsiklopediya* Tom 20 (2012), p. 569.

34) he was an early proponent of the term "ethnos" and he coined the premise, eventually dominant in Soviet ethnography that neither cultures nor humanity should be the subject of the discipline but its sub-units called "ethnos."

Given that both Derzahvin's and Berg's works relied so heavily on statisticians, statistical thinking most likely informed their coining of ethnic categories. Berg started his discussions of each new group with the available demographic data, then discussed their language and went to great lengths explaining this ethnic group's alleged anthropological features and character. After that he discussed the more tangible aspects of each culture such as housing, handicraft, modes of subsistence, cuisine, and customs. Derzhavin devoted more space to the historic origin of the Bessarabian Bulgarians. Then he gave a detailed description of modes of subsistence, before discussing handicraft, and customs.

What was new about both books was their ascription of cultural aspects, beyond religion and language, to different groups that were categorized now along ethnic lines. No longer was it just group history—place of origin, social standing within the imperial order, and religious beliefs that set groups apart from each other. Since the time of the reforms in the 1860s it had become standard practice to study everyday culture (*byt*), necessary but unremarkable forms of behavior (Clay, 1995: 50; Knight, 1998: 127). Now, around the turn of the century, this mode of studying cultural differences was applied to southern Bessarabia. Tangible aspects of local *byt*, such as house construction, dresses, children's games, funeral rituals, traditional calendar etc., became markers of group boundaries. These aspects had not been of much interest to state functionaries, travelling the colonies on horseback thus far. Day-to-day culture happened out of their reach, and in languages they did not understand. Therefore, they could hardly have used such aspects to coin their categories. For Derzhavin and Berg, cultural differences were not only a matter of scholarly curiosity, they also became aspects they aligned along established statistical categories in order to structure their scholarly subject. Both authors arranged their books along what were now ethnic boundaries. Most significantly however, both works claimed unique ethnic characters for each group. This character could be found within the same boundaries as differences in anthropological feature, in language, faith, cuisine and so on. A short excerpt from Berg's description of Ukrainians may serve as an illustration:

> Their height is medium, they have dark hair, their skulls are subbrachycephal. They shave their beards. By character they are just as dull and careless as generally all Ukrainians. Those who settle in Russian Bukovina are more cleanly and spruce than the ones on the Dniester River (Berg, 1918: 108).

Berg, in this excerpt, spoke of an ethnic group as if speaking about different species of fresh water fish, with which he was more familiar. But it is not this generalizing and dismissive tone that was new to the style of both Derzhavin and Berg. (In fact, Derzhavin's book amassed a lot of praise for the Bulgarians, citing over several pages the descriptions of earlier observers who characterize the Bulgarians as devout and hard-working people (Derzhavin, 1914: 32–36)). What was new about descriptions of ethnic character is that they came as a package, tied to other cultural features, and that they were presented as systematically collected ethnographic data, along with statistical tables and physical anthropological features, like "subbrachycephal" skulls. Derzhavin and Berg combined two modes of looking at the peripheral society and thereby created a new one. One mode had so far mainly been employed by the state; the meticulous collection of data and information that helped to increase the "legibility" of society for administrators and therefore make the population more controllable and taxable. The other was the insight in every-day culture that state observers largely lacked so far. These descriptions were both detailed and distinct for each ethnic group. The "ethnic character" of each group thereby became just one more aspect of observable cultural life.

The tone of describing culture and customs in Derzhavin's and Berg's ethnographies was well-suited to the aim of creating the impression that ethnographic features were similar, or even identical, *within* a specific ethnic group, but entirely different *between* different ethnic groups. When describing a custom, although in most cases the authors named the time and place where it was documented, they then used a mode of description that leaves the reader with the impression, that the observation was representative *of all* acts of the same nature within one ethnic group. From the Bulgarian village of Chesma Varuta[47] Derzhavin described an episode of a wedding that may serve as an example here:

> The custom of shaving the groom is performed on the morning of Sunday before going to church. The groom sits on a chair, on the left arm he has a towel, the barber has a towel on the right arm. In this moment the musicians appear, a violin and a drum, decorated with a cloth; the band plays a melancholic tune, the groom starts to sob, along with him cries his mother (Derzhavin, 1914: 145).

Nothing seems to have escaped the author's attention (in the introduction he stresses his fieldwork ethos, saying he had jolted down every observed detail),

47 Today's Krinichnoe in Bolgrad rayon.

but even if one assumes that in *all* Bulgarian weddings the groom had been shaved before going to church on Sunday morning, it is probably also reasonable to assume that not in all cases the towels had been in the same place and not in each ceremony the groom and his mother started to cry simultaneously. Such descriptions stuck to the present tense and an omniscient voice. They ran over dozens of pages and included many other rituals. Inevitably, they created the impression that the author's observations of one event were generalizable *to all Bulgarian* weddings. The way Derzhavin's book was structured, suggests that ceremonies like weddings and funerals were similar not within one village or district, but that the category that made them similar to one another was ethnicity.

Adding up the two ingredients of scientific data and their ethnographic descriptions, structured by ethnic boundaries, scholars like Derzhavin and Berg helped to create the idea of an ethnic boundary that divided groups, inherently different from one another in most aspects of their culture. These groups subsequently needed to be described as separate subjects in separate books or chapters. Both these books, already before the advent of the Soviet Union, forestalled the Soviet mode of doing ethnography. It is therefore probably no coincidence that both works helped to launch brilliant scholarly careers, up to the very zenith of Soviet academia. Derzhavin became rector of the Leningrad State University and a double laureate of the Lenin Prize.[48] Berg eventually became president of the Geographical Society of the USSR, editor of the seminal *Nature in the USSR,* and a laureate of the Stalin Prize. By the end of his career he had a volcano, glaciers and mountains, as well as several dozen species of plants and animals named in his honor.[49]

So far we have looked at the natural science and at statistics as possible sources of inspiration for the categories in this new mode of ethnographic description. One more important element came from historiography, especially military historiography: Berg's overview on the history of Bessarabia claims the region for Russia. Bessarabia had fallen to Romania a few weeks before the publication of the book, a fact Berg bitterly lamented in the preface (1918: viii). At the same time he characterized the area as an ancient cradle of Russians (ibid.: vi). The intention to retrospectively claim a territory for one of several competing groups demanded a view on history in which such groups were age-old and had remained stable over time. As a consequence, in Berg's historical narrative the reader gets the impression that the ethnic groups of the present

48 "Derzhavin, Nikolay Sevast'yanovich," 2007, *Bol'shaya Rossiyskaya Entsiklopediya,* Tom 8 (2007), p. 565.

49 "Berg, Lev Semenovich," 2005, *Bol'shaya Rossiyskaya Entsiklopediya,* Tom 3 (2005), p. 339.

had acted and thought as a sovereign unit in the past. Almost as military units in the historiography of warfare, entire peoples come and go in Berg's description. They change their religion or language and engage in conflict with other groups. This paradigm, that groups have an agency of their own and even intentions and feelings, like a sovereign being, resounded well with the idea that the source of loyalty with a state was ethnic identity.

In Derzhavin's book about the Bulgarian colonists yet another new feature can be found; the ethnographer's advocacy for the people studied. Derzhavin bitterly accused local and imperial policies towards the Bulgarians, who were a people of the "same roots and faith as the Russian people." He made recommendations of far-reaching autonomy rights for the Bulgarians and for the founding of schools with Bulgarian as the language of instruction. At the time of writing, during the first decade of the 20th century, these were both innovative and courageous recommendations. Without swift reforms in agricultural and language policy, Derzhavin predicted an immediate collapse of the Bulgarian community (1914: 42–67). The advocacy in Derzhavin's work was coupled with a rigid idea of cultural purism and ethnographic authenticity. The author saw himself as the conserver of a vanishing ethnic culture. The Bulgarians, he lamented, had almost given up breeding sheep and cultivating wine, two typical modes of subsistence. The author also believed that he belonged to the last generation, able to at least partially witness the "real" Bulgarian customs such as the wedding ceremony that had fallen victim to "ethnographic assimilation" (1914: 125). As the source of evil he named the cultural contact with other groups, mainly with Russians:

> The people give up their best treasures of all kinds, their most legitimate achievements: their mother tongue and national traditions, the firmest guarantors of popular morality, and in exchange for this they get the opportunity to adopt Russian manners from the lowest of the urban philistines, and our Bulgarian people, losing their national traditions, indeed successfully assimilate to these "Russian" manners, carrying from the bazar to their native village the Russian song, learned in the town's tavern, and along with it the fitting morals with all its companions: alcoholism, excess, crime, etc., etc. (Derzhavin, 1914: 42).

With his image of a morally superior and "authentic" rural culture that becomes spoiled by the influence of ethnically different town dwellers, Derzhavin also foreshadowed one more defining feature of Soviet ethnography: a decisive distaste for ethnic mixing. This distaste was hardly ever voiced, since ethnic mixing with industrialization became all but inevitable, and regulations against it have hardly ever been suggested. However, ethnic mixing even much later, in the Soviet school of Yulian Bromley (see chapter 7), has always been portrayed as a destructive force for "real" cultures. Soviet ethnography, until the end, failed to come up with a theoretical framework that could accommodate ethnic mixing and the resulting cultural change. Even today, the paradigm of ethnography, initiated by works such Berg's and Derzhavin's, remains influential. The two studies were early examples of the idea that the ethnic boundary between groups, even if they were of the "same roots and faith," should be a dividing line for the sake of each of these groups, so they could retain their culture, a culture that was seen as natural and good in and of itself.

6 Ethnicity in Revolutionary Minds

In 1905, after an ill-fated war against Japan, Russia experienced her first revolution of the new century. The empire saw widespread strife in the two metropolises Moscow and St. Petersburg, in the Baltic provinces, in Poland, and in the Caucasus. The upheavals were brutally suppressed but eventually led to a series of reforms that would remodel the political landscape of the Russian Empire for its remaining years. The tsarist elites were familiar with upheavals caused by social and economic grievances among peasants and Cossacks. Among many old demands, the revolution of 1905 also served to voice new demands the imperial elites were not so used to dealing with; demands based on ethnic nationalism both among minorities and among Russians (Slocum, 1998: 174). The ethnic argument had entered imperial policies. As a consequence of Russification policies in the preceding decades, ethnic minorities now formulated their own demands (Cvetkovski, 2014b: 4). In Bessarabia the revolution itself was hardly felt. This was in part because Bessarabia was a very peripheral province in which both urban intellectuals and industrial workers, the two social groups teaming up for the revolution, were few in numbers. Krushevan's almanac of 1903 mentioned only some 1500 factories in the entire province of Bessarabia, employing no more than 6000 workers (Krushevan, 1903: 53). Even a much more generous estimate for the same period suggests no more than 30,000 industrial workers, a mere 1.2% of the population (Kushko and Taki, 2012: 261–278). An analytical report following the revolution authored by Bessarabia's governor, A. N. Haruzin, found that the overwhelming majority of Bessarabians were loyal to the Russian tsar and state and that what revolutionary activity there was came from a small group within the local elite (Cusco, 2017: 216).

The revolution came to bear importance for Bessarabia more in the consequences it had for imperial policy than for its local mobilization. It brought not only class issues to the fore, but also the fact, that many representatives of non-Russian and non-Christian groups in the empire felt discriminated. In many realms of local and imperial politics, but also commerce and education, non-Russians were deliberately excluded or subject to opaque quota systems. Where such groups, unlike in Bessarabia, had their own urban educated elite, these ethnic grievances helped to spark the Revolution (Cadiot, 2010: 27–28).

After suppressing the revolution, one concession the tsarist government made was to found a legislative body, the Duma. For the first convocation, a number of ethnically organized parties were elected to the Duma. These political groups campaigned for more individual rights, but also for more cultural autonomy, more freedom to use and teach their languages, and against the resettlement of ethnic Russians into their regions (Cadiot, 2005: 446). The part of Ukraine that belonged to the Russian Empire was no exception to this trend. Between 1900 and 1905 four Ukrainian parties were founded, all of which explicitly demanded more political and cultural autonomy (Magocsi, 2002: 49).

Moldovan nationalism, despite the competition of Romanian nationalism, had never been far beneath the surface among the small group of Bessarabian students who formed fraternities in far-away university towns, such as Tartu (Kushko and Taki, 2012: 262). But it was not until the Revolution of 1905 that nationalist circles could print their own newspapers. In these they demanded more space for the Moldovan/Romanian language, tried to establish contacts to neighboring Romania, and mobilize the rural masses. The latter proved hard. The years of relative liberty, directly following the Revolution of 1905, were not enough to establish a Moldovan public sphere, alongside the hitherto linguistically Russian platforms. The Moldovan peasants were almost entirely illiterate. Instead of being mobilized along ethnic lines, most of them gave their votes to right-wing tsarist parties, proponents of which had been involved in organizing the anti-Semitic pogroms in Chișinău in 1903 and 1905 (Kushko and Taki, 2012: 282).

Nevertheless, elections for the Duma and ethnic parties had helped to irrevocably put ethnicity on the political map. The fact that political parties represented ethnic groups in the Duma also further cemented the paradigm that ethnicity determines loyalty to one state or another. The administrative category of *inorodtsy* became ethnically charged and right-wing political forces began to characterize them as unreliable all together (Cusco, 2017: 26). Tsar Nicholas II himself bought into this logic. The second Duma became hamstrung in 1907 amidst accusations against a number of deputies who allegedly were involved in a conspiracy against the tsar's family. Nicholas II saw the cause in an excessive number of non-Russian deputies and their lack of patriotic spirit. His reaction was to strip non-Russian delegates to the Duma of the right to vote on "purely Russian" affairs. The new electoral law was designed to reserve a number of seats for particular ethnic groups, in order to raise the number of ethnic Russians in the Duma. In this way ethnicity became a political and legal category (Cadiot, 2005: 447). Thus, an ethnic quota was introduced and made it more necessary than ever before to reach a widely accepted definition of what ethnicity was.

Religion could no longer serve to separate people in clearly confined groups. The revolution of 1905 had also led to strengthen freedom of consciousness. Now, at least in theory, everyone could convert to any creed they liked. Among some provincial authorities there were fears that Jews would now en-masse convert to Christianity and thereby also obtain the rights of ethnic Russians (Cadiot, 2005: 450).

The question how to henceforth define ethnicity became more urgent as a new Russia-wide census, planned for 1915, approached. The results of this census were meant to determine ethnic quotas in the future. Meanwhile the results of the last census from 1897 were still being contested by different ethnic interest groups. Statisticians and authorities came to conclude that self-identification during the census would only lead to problems. Although in the last days of the empire, a consensus could not be reached, the loudest voices in this debate decided that ethnicity was not a matter of opinion or choice. A Russified Jew or Estonian would still not be a Russian in the "ethnographic" sense (Cadiot, 2010: 113). Thus between 1905 and the outbreak of World War I, ethnicity in Russia had become not only a fully-fledged political category, but also a category that, although still ill-defined, was already perceived to be scientifically (ethnographically) ascertainable and ascribable.

CHAPTER 3

Persuasion and Paranoia—Romania's Rule in Bessarabia 1918–44

On February 20, 1939 culture houses in southern Bessarabia and all over "Greater Romania" received a letter from the Bucharest based Society for the Dissemination of Culture with instructions, how to celebrate the Day of the Constitution, following a week later. February 27 1939 marked the first anniversary of a new constitution. This new constitution was intended to free Romania from the political skirmish that had allegedly slowed the country's development since the introduction of multiparty democracy in 1918. It abolished the separation of powers and gave the eccentric King Carol II dictatorial powers. Therefore, it is likely that most inhabitants of southern Bessarabia—now a region of ethnic minorities in a fiercely nationalistic state—saw little reason to celebrate that day. But the letter, circulated to culture houses, mentioned article 4 of the constitution and advised culture house staff to specially highlight it during celebrations.[1] Article 4 of the Romanian constitution of 1938 was not concerned with citizen's rights; it was concerned with their obligations. Among them, the article listed the obligation to be familiar with the constitution and to sacrifice oneself for the integrity, independence, and dignity of the fatherland. The addressees of this appeal in the constitution were "all Romanians, without regard to their ethnicity and religious beliefs."[2] Since obligations were the same for all these groups, rights ought to be equal too, or at least this was claimed in the subsequent article 5.[3] In fact, the constitution of 1938 opened the harshest years for ethnic minorities in southern Bessarabia and all of Greater Romania. Political instability created mistrust that could be used as a pretext to systematic ethnic discrimination and eventually to deportations and genocide. This chapter looks at how the years of Romanian rule in Bessarabia from 1918–40 and again from 1941–44 further sharpened boundaries between ethnic groups and how these boundaries came to be used in order to determine whom to trust and who to oppress.

During both World Wars, Bessarabia was fiercely contested between Bucharest and Moscow. The region twice came under the rule of Romania, once after

1 F1023 D4 Direktivnye ukazaniya Bukharestkogo obshchestva po rasprostraneniyu kul'tury o rabote ochaga kul'tury v sele Nerushay, p. 5.

2 Toți Românii, fără deosebire de origine etnică și credință religioasă.

3 Constituția României din 1938, published in *Monitorul Oficial*, Nr. 48/27, February 1938.

the First World War in 1918–40, and once during the Second World War 1941–44. Bessarabia was also twice taken by the Soviet Union, once without bloodshed following an ultimatum on June 26, 1940, based on the Molotov-Ribbentrop treaty between Nazi Germany and Stalin, and once during the Red Army's campaign to push Hitler's armies out of Eastern Europe in summer 1944. The incorporation of multi-ethnic Bessarabia into Romania in 1918 meant that the Region for the first time became part of a nation state. Under Romania's rule, Bessarabians experienced a ferocious political competition between democratic forces and authoritarianism. The latter eventually prevailed when King Carol II proclaimed martial law to install himself as autocratic ruler in February 1938 and in 1940 was replaced by a far-right military dictatorship under Ion Antonescu, an ally of Hitler.[4] Bessarabians also experienced a heated political debate over what status ethnic minorities—roughly a third of the population—should have in the Romanian nation state. As we will see in this chapter, policies swung between attempts of integration of minorities and their exclusion. By the time World War II reached Romania, those forces who championed exclusion and even ethnic cleansing, had taken the upper hand.

Romania emerged as a victor from World War I. Tsarist Russia, which had held Bessarabia for most of the preceding century, imploded amidst revolutionary upheaval. A bourgeois revolution succeeded in ousting the Tsar in February 1917, but was followed by the Bolshevik October Revolution in the same year. The country descended into a state of chaos and lost its grip over its western periphery. Bessarabia declared its independence from Russia in January 1918. Hundreds of thousands of impoverished and defeated soldiers roamed the country. Many of them had been stranded in Bessarabia marauding and causing havoc. Bessarabian authorities asked the Romanian army to restore order (Livezeanu 1995: 97). Russian troops, exhausted, divided, and engaged in a devastating civil war, were unable to secure the province. In March 1918 the parliament in Chișinău (*Sfatul Țării*), under a de-facto Romanian occupation, voted for union with the neighboring Kingdom of Romania (Hausleitner 2004: 363). This union was ratified in a number of Paris peace treaties in 1919–20. The victorious European powers who gave their blessings to Romanian expansion, insisted Romania would have to give equal civil rights to all her ethnic minorities, including the Jews. The Romanian government only very grudgingly accepted this condition. The country's first Prime Minister, Ion I. C. Brătianu,

4 The question whether to classify the Antonescu regime as fascist is debated, because Romania's main fascist movement, the Iron Guard (*Garda de Fier*), had been eliminated by King Carol II and Antonescu in two waves of reprisals in 1938 and 1941. I follow the description of Radu Ioanid of the regime as "totalitarian, right-wing with unmistakable fascist features" (2010: 399). Another, more concise formulation would be "fascist-type dictatorship" (Calinescu 1993: 135).

even lay down his office in protest against the European power's condition of non-discrimination of ethnic minorities (Livezeanu 1995: 22, 306). Brătianu argued that giving equal rights to ethnic minorities would compromise Romania's inner security (Hausleitner 2004: 365).

Romania, in the course of five years, had doubled in size and population. After the Second Balkan War in 1913, Romania annexed southern Dobrudja from Bulgaria. In 1918, along with Bessarabia, Romania also gained Transylvania, parts of the Banat, and Bukovina from the disintegrating Habsburg Empire. Romania's spectacular territorial gains "surpassed the fondest expectations of her most extreme nationalists" (Rouček 1932: 606). The totality of this newly stitched together country is often referred to as Greater Romania (*România Mare*). Its political and economic core was the Old Kingdom (*Vechiul Regat*) that had already functioned as an independent state since 1878. This part of Greater Romania took a primus-inter-pares role in shaping the nation. The unification was led by, and formed according to the conditions of the Old Kingdom (Livezeanu 1995: 29).

Since its unification in 1871, Germany had vowed to gain more influence in Eastern Europe, especially in resource-rich Romania. France and England on the other hand tried to drag Romania to their side. That the young state had so early come between the fronts of major European powers also shaped Romania's export-oriented economy, based mainly on agrarian production. In the mid-1930s Germany's influence over Romania eventually prevailed (Verdery 1990: 83). All political factions of some weight in interwar Romania were nationalists and save for very few exceptions all major political figures were anti-Semites (Ioanid 2010: 399). In this political constellation, the main fault line ran along factions that wanted to align the country with victors England and France and those, who wanted to align it with emerging Nazi Germany. England and France had permitted Romania's territorial expansion only on the condition that civil rights were extended to ethnic minorities. Germany in contrast would eventually encourage systematic discriminations against ethnic minorities (Haynes 2007: 118).

In 1918, the new Romanian government at first sight appeared progressive, at least when compared with tsarist Russia. Universal male suffrage and compulsory schooling was introduced, a swift land reform in Bessarabia in 1918 was meant to empower smallholders. Romania managed to build almost 12,000 schools between 1922 and 1938, but the frenetic expansion of the educational system left many schools without qualified teachers, and eventually had only a small impact on the low rate of literacy in Bessarabia (Livezeanu 1995: 35–39). In 1917, when Bessarabia's future belonging was still unclear and revolutionary tensions high, a swift land reform was meant to appease the peasant masses.

By spring 1918 two-thirds of the land formerly held by landlords had been distributed to peasants. Romanian legislations of 1920 specified that these smallholders should pay compensations to former owners, so that the land reform in the end cost many peasants more than they had gained (Hitchins 1994: 350). So for most Bessarabians the spoils of Greater Romania's short-lived reformatory zeal never materialized. Not even schooling, arguably the most urgent aspect of reforms, achieved its desired effect in Bessarabia: State-sponsored school education was offered only in Romanian, a foreign language for most people in southern Bessarabia. All told, Romanian bureaucracy was installed very quickly in the new provinces, too quickly perhaps to be effective, a shortcoming that was later attempted to compensate with ruthlessness.

The rapid growth of Romania was justified with nationalism but could not be justified by its success. Nevertheless, for many Romanian speakers, Greater Romania now appears as a Golden Age. Compared with the miserable years of late Communism in Romania, this may be not too wild an exaggeration. There were no shortages of food and consumer goods most of the time. Until February 1938, a multiparty democracy functioned and a relatively free press produced a wide range of publications. Also, unlike in communist times, people were free to travel if they had the means to do so (Livezeanu 1995: 301). In southern Bessarabia however, where collective memory is shaped by Russia-centered historiography, the time of Romanian hegemony for all its pomp and failures became remembered as a dull and oppressive age. Compared to the subsequent Soviet decades of rapid economic growth, many in contemporary southern Bessarabia see the Romanian period as two lost decades.

1 Newcomer Elites in a Hostile Land

The population of Greater Romania consisted of roughly two-thirds Romanian speakers. Most of them lived as peasants in the countryside, while the cities were mainly inhabited by ethnic minorities. In Bessarabia just half of the population spoke Romanian. Towns and cities were few and far between. Their inhabitants were mainly Jewish, Russian, or Russian speakers of other ethnic backgrounds. The Romanian language was hardly heard in Bessarabian cities (Livezeanu 1995: 90; Mihaylova 2006: 17). Because most Romanian speakers were peasants and because urban elites, although in part from Moldovan ancestry had been thoroughly Russified, there had hardly been any Romanian nationalist movement in Bessarabia before the merger with Romania (Livezeanu 1995: 95). For the Romanian state elite in Bucharest, however, it was clear that the consolidation of rump Romania (the Old Kingdom) with the newly incorporated territories (Bessarabia, Transylvania, and Bukovina) was the culmination of an age-old struggle to unite all territories inhabited by Romanians. From this historical narrative, the Romanian elite drew its legitimation to rule over Bessarabia (King 2000: 57). But the newly incorporated territories were very different in cultural make-up and heritage. The degree and nature of Romanian national consciousness differed starkly from the Old Kingdom (Mihaylova 2006: 9).

Among the state elite in the Old Kingdom, there was consensus that Romanian culture should be the only officially embraced cultural basis of the state. Romanian was introduced as the sole state language already in 1919. Public schools and theatres were now allowed to function only in that language (Mihaylova 2006: 12). The new rulers also ensured that most vital positions in state and economy were occupied by ethnic Romanians, often young staff trained in the administration of the Old Kingdom who were now sent out to the new provinces (Mihaylova 2006: 10). In 1918–20 when martial law was still in force, a compulsory Romanian language test for all state employees ensured that ethnic minorities had hardly any access to posts in the administration (Hausleitner 2004: 365). The term "*Regățeni*" became a slur for newly arrived administrators and soldiers from the Old Kingdom (Solonari 2010: 163). Bucharest was eager to replace the urban middle class and the professions in towns and cities of the new provinces (Livezeanu 1990: 167). This could be done by restricting access to higher education for ethnically Romanian students, a demand that fueled a nationalist student movement beginning in 1922 (ibid.: 177). Even without an ethnic quota system, Romanian students were privileged by affirmative means: Student dormitories enabled rural, mostly Romanian students to access higher education, while non-Romanian-speaking, urban students were increasingly discriminated against (Livezeanu 1995: 299–300). Another factor in romanianizing urban communities was a land reform that did not create rural prosperity but forced many Romanian peasants to migrate to the cities in search of employment (Livezeanu 1990: 169).

The longer Romania had to struggle with the problem of a latently disloyal urban middle class in the new provinces, the more frequently Bucharest authorities intervened directly to influence the ethnic composition of decisive institutions. The police and secret police (*Siguranța*) became accomplices in reserving the most influential positions for people from the Old Kingdom.[5]

---

5 One document that sheds some light on the systematic privileging of Romanians from the old Kingdom in Bessarabia is a memorandum circulated between secret police offices in late 1933 (F312 D49 O nablyudenii za deyatel'nost' russkoy i ukrainskoy natsional'nosti gorodov i uezda, p. 114) in which the upcoming elections to the Bessarabian chamber of lawyers was discussed: The memorandum stated that, as a rule, lawyers from the Old Kingdom were preferable to

These administrating newcomers were deeply suspicious of the population they came to rule. Many among the minorities sympathized with the Bolshevists who by then were consolidating their power in the neighboring Soviet Union. In 1920 the central government established General Secretariats in Cluj, Cernăuți, and Chișinău, the capitals of the three new provinces. Only little power was given to these secretariats and they served strictly as outposts of ministries in Bucharest. Nevertheless, they were under constant suspicion to pursue regionalist agendas and to be too mild on ethnic minorities (Livezeanu 1995: 42).

To cope with the deep suspicion between state and periphery, the new rulers established a bureaucracy that left the model of state administrators mounted on horseback far behind. They installed a hierarchy of offices and a strict chain of command that could provide swift communication from Bucharest via Chișinău to outposts like Izmail or Bolgrad and back, within just a few days. This communication took place by means of numbered and dated letters and circulars, with letterheads, signatures, and stamps of all involved offices. What instantly increased the "legibility" of new national peripheries back then also facilitates the analysis of interwar Romanian administration today. However refined Romanian bureaucracy might have been, its representatives in southern Bessarabia found themselves in remote outposts, surrounded by non-Romanians. The majority of people there spoke little or no Romanian at the time, so that the interaction of administrators with the people was difficult.

Even more difficult was the creation of a sense of belonging to the new Romanian state among the Russian, Jewish, Ukrainian, Gagauz, Albanian, and Bulgarian minorities. Since there were many Russian speakers in the area, many had easier access to texts produced in the Soviet Union, a country that looked at Bessarabia as a temporally occupied territory. In the 1920s, the Soviet Union proclaimed the policy of *korenisatsiya* (in-rooting), the political integration of each ethnic group into a socialist one-party state by their own language and culture (Slezkine 1994: 433). Also, in the neighboring Soviet Union, promises of land redistribution were beginning to materialize. Quite to the contrary, in Bessarabia previous inequalities in land property augmented social

indigenous Bessarabian lawyers. Among those there were too many doubtable characters, for example the ethnically Bulgarian attorney and political activist Petr Ganchev, or Evangelicon Antipa, who in 1922 was a member of a union that claimed sovereignty for Bessarabia, or the ethnically Russian attorney Podospiev, who was expelled in 1918 for his activism against the Romanian chief judge, or the ethnically Bulgarian attorney Rainov who had been accused of anti-Romanian propaganda.

tensions. These culminated in September 1924 in a fierce peasant uprising in and around the small town of Tatarbunary, situated halfway between Izmail and Odessa. The mutiny started with a small number of peasants occupying the town hall of Tatarbunary. It then quickly spread to nearby settlements, involving thousands of angry peasants. The Romanian government deployed large army units to the region that ended the uprising within a week. The clash between Bessarabian insurgents and Romanian troops resulted in a bloodbath that left at least 600 dead. The uprising was triggered by social grievances and by Soviet subversion. No nationalist agenda was voiced by the revolutionaries, who were from various ethnic backgrounds, including speakers of Romanian (Lebedenko and Tychyna 2002: 142). However, administrative suspicion towards the population in Romania's borderlands grew. So did the economic hardship for the rural and industrial poor, especially since after 1929 the effects of the Great Depression could be felt in Bessarabia too. Within the first three years of the crisis, average salaries dropped by 40%, while taxes doubled. Strikes became frequent in the region's factories. The most harmful one was a 10-day shutdown of Izmail's Danube river port in 1932 (ibid.: 144).

2 Spying on Minorities

It was on the background of this volatile situation that the staff of the Romanian network of bureaucratic outposts started to systematically spy on the population. Reasons for the Romanian secret police to tail on a person or an organization could be suspicion of subversion inspired by communism or nationalism. In most cases of surveillance, a very similar pattern repeated itself: Secret police regional headquarters in Chișinău or Galați sensed a problem somewhere. They then alerted all their outposts, sometimes through an intermediary branch in Izmail. They advised the staff of these outposts to investigate the problem and report back as soon as possible. Usually, the reports arrived within a couple of days, and usually they said that in the outpost's section everything was quiet and that the problem could not be located there. Most of these all-clears were followed by the assurance that local officers would keep their eyes and ears open and immediately report back, should the problem occur in the future. Mostly, these reports were very laconic and did not reveal great enthusiasm of local officers to get to the bottom of a problem. Only very rarely this attitude caused wrath from above. In June 1939, for instance, provincial police headquarters in Galați sent a report from Izmail back to the sender, stating it was not very informative and it would be really appreciated if the outposts could finally produce lists of suspicious Bulgarian nationalists.[6]

In many cases, however, detailed insight into the inner workings of minority communities might just have been impossible. Take as an example a rebuke from Galați that arrived at the secret police office in Izmail in October 1939. The classified letter said word had gotten to the provincial police headquarters that in taverns in nearby Kiliya, Russian songs were sung openly and anti-Romanian propaganda was widely dispersed there, without the local police even bothering to interfere. The letter referred to a bulletin from the year before, that had been on public display in the region and that clearly prohibited the singing of Russian songs in taverns. The police commander of Izmail was asked to personally travel to Kiliya and inspect the situation. He was also asked to report back within 10 days. The Izmail police inspector dutifully reported back that taverns in Kiliya were no hotbed of anti-Romanian propaganda and that taverns that owned a radio would play exclusively the Bucharest radio station. In some taverns, he reported, the accordion was played at times, for the entertainment of the guests, but Russian songs were never sung. He assured that local police and owners of taverns were fully aware of the content of last year's bulletin and would assure its precise implementation.[7]

This case is very typical because of the superficiality of both the suspicion and the investigation. Very often, Romanian secret police displayed frenetic activity in spotting and eliminating ostensible and easily observable expressions of disloyalty with the state, such as singing of songs in a language other than Romanian. The matter was then asked to be investigated by unsuitable methods, such as a chief inspector's visit to the taverns of a neighboring town. The nature of suspicion and the ways of investigating them could lead only to superficial insight in how the guests in Kiliya's taverns really thought about the Romanian government, and whether or not they planned to take action against it.

Other similar alerts concerned theatrical performances or Cossack horse shows which were feared to be used for Russian or Ukrainian propaganda. The trace of a band of Cossack horse acrobats can be followed through all of southern Bessarabia in the summer of 1938. They performed in Izmail, Bolgrad, and Reni with the permission of the local military commander. The shows led to different reports from police officers in these towns. In Izmail, where a crowd

6 F312 D139 Nablyudatel'noe delo za deyatel'nost' bolgarskogo natsionalisticheskogo dvizhenie v Izmail'skom uezde 1937–40 gg, p. 79.

7 F312 D138 Nablyudatel'noe delo za deyatel'nost' naseleniya russkoy i ukrainskoy natsional'nosti po Izmail'skomu uezdu, pp. 145, 161.

of 500 came to see the show, local police reported the music lacked vocals and was therefore found to be harmless. In Bolgrad the audience was described as small and consisting "of minorities." The show, according to the police report, did not spark great enthusiasm there. Only in Reni it was found to be unsuitable, because it was commented in Russian and "accompanied by Russian exclamations." The Reni police therefore prohibited a second staging of the show. To be on the safe side and as a reaction to this report from Reni, the military commander in the region prohibited all subsequent Cossack horse shows in Kiliya and Vilkovo.[8] This case shows that even if the police took action against suspected subversion, this was done on ground of piecemeal intelligence and generalized suspicions.

Two years earlier, in summer 1936, a similar fuss was caused by the theatre company of a performance artist called Vronschi, who traveled the towns of southern Bessarabia and performed Russian language plays in cinema halls. The tour had been sanctioned by the Ministry of Culture. The actors carried a letter from the ministry, proofing their right to perform.[9] But after the group had already appeared in Kiliya and Bolgrad, secret police headquarters in Chișinău sent out a classified circular to all its outposts, saying the play would "touch upon public morale" and revealed "communist tendencies."[10] All towns dutifully reported back. From Kiliya, where it was already too late to prevent the staging of the play, the local police inspector insisted, his men had found the play neither morally objectionable nor could they spot communist tendencies in it.

There were only very rare cases when more detailed intelligence from the periphery reached the center. If this happened, it usually had to do with the occasional zeal of a single local officer to report a problem. One such case occurred in 1935 in Vilkovo, then according to the secret police's data, a town of roughly 8000, three fourths of which were Russian Old-Believers, and one fourth Ukrainians.[11] There was also a tiny Romanian minority of about 300 living in Vilkovo. The local police inspector wrote, apparently without being asked to do so, in an angry and "strictly classified" report about the language situation in his town. The report stated that there were three churches in Vilkovo, in two of which mass was held according to the old rite. The third church, the former Russian Orthodox Church, now belonged to the Romanian state church and the priest there was paid by the Romanian ministry of culture. The

8 F312 D138, pp. 82–92.

9 F312 D49 O nablyudenii za deyatel'nost' russkoy i ukrainskoy natsional'nosti gorodov i uezda, p. 279.

10 F312 D49, pp. 275–280.

11 F312 D49, p. 199.

report reminded superiors that it was now 18 years since Bessarabia had been "united with the fatherland," and since 18 years the church had belonged to the Romanian state church. But in all these years, the report lamented, the liturgy had been read in Russian. The police officer then admitted that the bulk of churchgoers were Russian speakers, but he insisted that it was a Romanian church after all. The Romanians in town, the report complained, would give up the "custom of their ancestors" to go to church. To use a foreign language in a national church was a great obstacle for the "spiritual reunion" of the town's citizens and to the "nationalization" of the country's minorities.[12]

These were all catchphrases of the nation building policies that had begun almost two decades ago, and bore still very little fruit, at least in peripheries such as southern Bessarabia. The constant suspicion by incompetent state institutions, coupled with the constant pressure to romanianize the citizens of the new provinces, served to further alienate all of the minorities, or "other Romanians," as the government preferred to speak of them (Mihaylova 2006: 23).

3 Counting and Categorizing Minorities

From the early 1930s onwards the state's suspicion against certain groups within the population has to be seen in the context of a renewed threat of war in Europe. Since 1934 the police and secret police compiled lists of people who in the case of an attack by a foreign state could be armed because they did not belong to a suspicious group.[13] Since state officials feared large parts of the population for their assumed disloyalty in case of a war, it became vital to know how exactly to distribute trust and mistrust among the population. With war not immediate but looming after Hitler's bid for power, the secret police and other state institutions began to compile statistics of exactly how many people belonged to which suspicious category. There was a census of the region in 1930. Florea Rossetti, an Izmail school head master and author of a 1934 monograph on the city, thought the results of that survey were very doubtable, since many of the census takers had done a quick and easy job (Rossetti 1934: 8). For lack of better data, she too used them in her book. No longer did statisticians follow the practice of their Russian predecessors to use proxy categories

12 F312 D49, p. 267.

13 F312 Opis 'Izmail'skaya uezdnaya prefektura politsii g. Izmail s 1929 g. Izmail'skaya uezdnaya kestura politsii g. Izmail s 1939 goda, Izmail'skoe uezdnoe politseyskoe napravlenie.

for ethnicity, such as language or religion. They directly asked for and recorded the "ethnic origin" (*origină etnică*) of their respondents.

An example for a more thorough enterprise to study the minorities and their attitudes towards Romania occurred in autumn 1934. In the beginning of October, the police inspectorate in Chișinău commissioned a detailed report on all the "Slavic minorities" in Izmail district (Județul Ismail). Interestingly "Slavic minorities" did not include the Bulgarians but only Russians, Ukrainians, and Poles. The order for the report included specific instructions. It should contain a) the number of these minorities in towns and villages, b) their occupation, cultural organizations such as schools, churches, choral groups, sport clubs, religious associations, journals, newspapers, print shops, and libraries that offer books printed in Romania or abroad, c) commercial enterprises such as banks, cooperatives, and factories ran by representatives of these groups, and finally d) the attitudes of these minorities towards the Romanian state and the extent to which they presented a threat. The order also asked for an according map of the region.[14] The reports, along with statistical tables and maps, started to trickle in during October 1934. On grounds of the short time between commission and completion, one can assume that previously gathered data on the number of ethnic groups had been used, very likely no better founded than the ones criticized by school headmaster Rossetti. The statistical tables included the five towns in Izmail Județ (Bolgrad, Reni, Kiliya, Vilkovo, and Izmail) as well as 24 settlements. Only in towns, the presence of Ukrainian and Polish minorities was documented. In villages, all Slavic speakers were counted as Russians, even in villages today considered predominantly Ukrainian.[15] The according hand drawn map[16] also dates from October 1934 (see map 3). It specifies the exact number of ethnic groups (not only Slavic speakers) in addition to a blue or red colored ring that indicates friendly or hostile attitudes towards the Romanian state. The map included more villages than the report (68), of which 21 were found hostile and 47 friendly to Romanian rule. Just the fact that "Slavic minorities" inhabited a village did not make that village necessarily hostile, as might have been the suspicion among Romanian authorities. The ratio between ethnic groups seems to have mattered much more. So a Slavic majority population with a sizable Romanian speaking minority seems to be a good indicator for hostility towards the Romanian state. Sixteen out of twenty-one hostile villages displayed this constellation. It is very likely that the Romanian

14 F312 D49, pp. 195 ff.

15 On the Map on F312 D49, p. 218, Broska, Matroska, and Pershotravnevoe (then still called Hasan-Aspaga), today considered Ukrainian villages, are indicated as Russian villages.

16 F312 D49, p. 218.

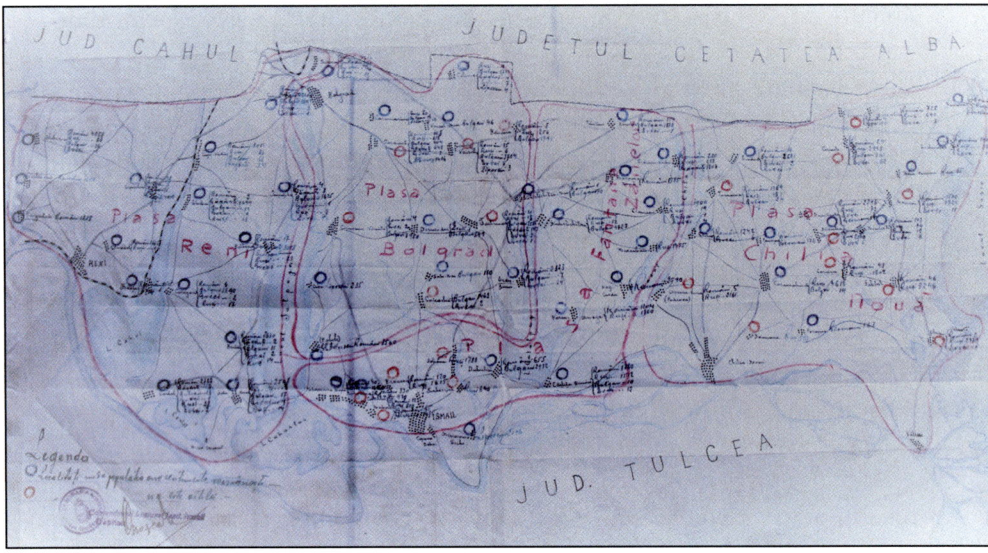

MAP 3 Ethnic map of Izmail Judeţ, created by Romanian police in autumn 1934, indicating the ethnic composition of settlements as well as the population's loyalty vis-à-vis the Romanian state with a blue circle, or their disloyalty with a red circle

police officers asked first among these Romanian speaking villagers about the general attitude towards the state. However, one village, Furmanovka, north of Kiliya (called Furmanca at the time), was hostile, although Romanian speakers were a large majority there. So all its superficiality aside, this map, the main outcome of the survey of autumn 1934, should have made it very clear to Romanian authorities, that ethnicity was an inconclusive indicator for loyalty towards the state.

The individual reports from each town confirmed that there was hardly any connection between ethnicity and loyalty towards the state. In the report from Reni, the local police inspector wrote that the town's 210 Russians were "loyal children of the Romanian state" and posed not the slightest danger to it.[17] The reports contained numbers that are not quite congruent with those on the map and those in the summarizing tables, which likely again is a hint that the Romanian state did not have the means to precisely count and control its citizens in southern Bessarabia. But the main insight the reports offer is the apparent low degree of organization the ethnic minorities could have used against

17 F312 D49, p. 204.

the Romanian state. The report from Kiliya,[18] where nearly 11,000 Russians lived at the time (many of them would be counted as Ukrainians today), denies the existence of cultural associations, separate schools, choral groups, sport clubs, newspapers, journals, or print shops. The report, however, mentioned evangelical prayer houses, one Adventist and four Baptist. The report from the Old-Believers town of Vilkovo[19] mentioned only religious institutions of significance. There was an Old-Believer's association that ran two churches in which the old rites were performed. Besides that there was only the library, named after the Moldovan 15th century King Ștefan cel Mare. But the report denies the existence of bookstores or print shops that could have distributed inflammatory material.

There may be several explanations for the lack of ethnic minority organizations in these relatively remote towns. One is probably that the Romanians prohibited such organizations. Therefore they might have gone hiding out of reach of the Romanian police. However, in bigger centers, ethnic minority organizations did exist. They circulated publications, organized events, and some of them were reported to the police. Examples are a Russian nationalist journal "The Voice of Russia" edited by a fugitive Russian colonel in Chișinău and under observation by the Romanian police since 1937.[20] Another example from March 1934 was a ring of Ukrainian diaspora activists who produced propaganda material in Berlin and distributed it in Ukraine.[21] Therefore, a more likely explanation why the Romanian secret police could find hardly any ethnic organizations in Bessarabian towns in 1934, is that, unlike religious organizations, there were still very few of them. This reminds us that only recently religion had been the main marker for different categories of people who received different treatment from the state. In southern Bessarabia this appears not to have changed much up to the mid-1930s. The meager findings of the police review on the "Slavic minorities" of October 1934 confirm this.

Nevertheless, the Romanian state continued to allocate trust and mistrust along ethnic lines. Suspicions grew more eccentric the greater the danger of a new war in Europe became, and the more influence the fascist Iron Guard gained in Romanian politics. These trends accelerated the significance of ethnicity as a denominator of state loyalty. The short-lived and fiercely anti-Semite government of Octavian Goga in 1938 introduced a quota for ethnic minorities in all institutions. Also it significantly circumvented the civil rights

18 F312 D49, p. 202.
19 F312 D49, p. 203.
20 F312 D138, pp. 41–50.
21 F312 D49, pp. 146–149.

granted to Jews in 1918 (Livezeanu 1995: 298; Hitchins 1994: 404). Shortly thereafter, in February 1938, King Carol II, reinstalled in 1930 and since then never concealing his distaste for democracy, ousted the Goga government and installed himself as the country's interim ruler, the beginning of Romania's royal dictatorship (Hitchins 1994: 421).

The shift towards autocracy and official discrimination of ethnic minorities had far-reaching repercussions in Bessarabia. The bureaucracy's fear of minorities grew ever more hysterical. In July 1938, for example, against the background of Austria's *Anschluss* and the Sudeten crisis, provincial police headquarters in Chișinău sent a sharp warning to their outposts, concerned about Ukrainians in Poland and Czechoslovakia showing increased activity. The warning came along with an "informative note" concerning the activities of Ukrainian nationalist organizations in northern Bessarabia and Bukovina. The letter said these organizations had the aim to unite all regions settled by Ukrainians into one unified Ukrainian state under a "national socialist regime." They also had the aim to prevent "assimilation to Romania" and to "block Romania's future." The note warned that such organizations often concealed themselves as commercial firms and sports clubs. It was then discussed how to avoid irredentist destabilization of Romania. Measures taken in Poland were proposed as a model practice to avoid the risk of Ukrainian irredentism. The example of the Polish province of eastern Galicia was presented as a viable way for Romania to deal with Ukrainians: In Galicia, Ukrainians made up a sizeable part of the population. But now, the document said, all ethnic Ukrainians in the state's service had been replaced. In the Polish military, Ukrainians were no longer allowed to serve as instructors and mechanized units of the army had ceased to recruit Ukrainians altogether. The note also reported that in the Polish army ethnic Ukrainian draftees were trained separately for three months. After that an entry in their military identity documents was made, so that they would be given only auxiliary tasks.[22]

Apparently, such measures were not thoroughly put to practice at the time. One of my Ukrainian informants has served in the Romanian army during the upcoming World War II, and has even received technical training from the army.[23] However, the idea to register a person's ethnic belonging in personal documents foreshadowed a watershed in ethnicity policy, even more so because this information was coupled with restricted rights and restricted career opportunities, first and foremost in the military. This was clearly a step forward

22 F312 D138, pp. 93 ff.

23 Interview in Kislitsa, November 1, 2013.

in mainstreaming the paradigm that ethnicity and loyalty were directly connected to one another.

A similar frenzy, in March 1938, afflicted local branches of the Ministry of Finance. On orders of the Ministry of the Interior, the Izmail finance administration was given the task to check whether among its employees there were people who had married a partner from an ethnic minority. This investigation was part of a much wider effort to register all interethnic marriages since 1918. A year before, in 1937, the eugenicist Petru Râmneațu published a study about mixed ethnic marriages in Transylvania. He was very alarmed at the increase of such marriages and suggested to fire all Romanian state servants in border regions, who were married to a partner of a different ethnic background (Solonari 2010: 70). The list that was commissioned in Bessarabia, was ordered to be completed within 24 hours. It should contain the ethnicity of the foreign partner (some of Romania's bigger ethnic minorities, Germans, Hungarians, Jews, Poles, Ruthenians [Ukrainians], Bulgarians, were offered as examples in the instruction). The list should also provide information about the religion of both partners and their exact professional position. In a last column of the list "observations" were to be specified ("reasons for marriage or divorce" were offered as possible entries there).[24] The lists arrived at the Ministry of the Interior swiftly, but although the instruction how to compose them had been very detailed, the resulting lists exposed considerable differences. From Izmail, a list of 32 state servants who had married ethnically non-Romanian partners arrived.[25] There were no observations made as to why these people had chosen to marry their Russian, Ukrainian, Bulgarian, Polish, and Greek partners. But the lists from small towns Reni and Bolgrad had been completed with more enthusiasm. In these two towns combined, 13 state servants had married across ethnic boundaries. In some cases these lists specified the reasons why they had chosen to do so. Two men claimed (with identical formulations) they had married women from ethnic minorities because they believed that this was the only way to create a unified nation.[26] One man laconically commented he had "married out of feelings" (*căsătorit din sentiment*).[27]

The inquiry into the ethnicity of state servant's spouses had not been taken very seriously by the administrative outposts. The lists were received with many blank spots especially in the columns for "religion" and "observations."

24 F50 D64 Spiski chinovnikov po natsional'nostyam (Izmail'skaya uezdnaya finansovaya administratsiya), p. 52.

25 F50 D64, p. 51.

26 F50 D64, pp. 60, 65, the original formulation was "A socotit, câ apropierea minorităților pentru o unitate natională se poate face numai prin căsătorii mixte."

27 F50 D64, p. 65.

Nevertheless, this inquiry of 1938 demonstrates that the effort to romanianize the state apparatus took ethnicity out of the private sphere and made it a state interest, as well as a tool of state craft. Interethnic marriage was not punished, but it now had to be declared and justified.

4 Ethnicity as a Proxy for Trustworthiness

The question of trust and mistrust between the state and its subjects soon came to bear increased significance, with the advent of a new time of turmoil and violence. The Soviet Union never acknowledged Romanian rule over the former Russian province of Bessarabia. In 1940, Romania came under pressure from both the Soviet Union and Nazi Germany. In August 1939 the two powers had secretly divided Eastern Europe among themselves in the Molotov-Ribbentrop Pact. The Soviets issued an ultimatum to Romania to cease Bessarabia on June 26, 1940. The Romanian king threatened war on the Soviet Union but was called back by Germany. There were rumors of German diplomats hinting to Romania, that the territorial loss would be only temporary (Lebedenko and Tychyna 2002: 150). Two days after the ultimatum, on June 28, 1940, the Red Army took control of Bessarabia without firing a shot. Still in the summer of 1940, the Soviet leadership drew a border between the mainly Romanian speaking bulk of Bessarabia, which was made into the Moldovan SSR, and southern Bessarabia, with no clear ethnic majority, which was joined with the already existing Ukrainian SSR. The areas settled with Bulgarians and Gagauz were divided between the two Soviet republics. The northernmost tip of Bessarabia, where Ukrainians were in the majority, was also given to the Ukrainian SSR.

The Molotov-Ribbentrop Pact also had another very significant effect on the ethnic constellation in Bessarabia. German settlers in the areas that became part of the Soviet Union were to be "evacuated." This meant that Germans, who had been an integral part of the ethnic mosaic in southern Bessarabia, were expelled within months following the Soviet takeover. Many Germans realized the lack of perspective of a life in prosperity and security in a Soviet administered Bessarabia and they mostly took the opportunity to leave. More than 90,000 people took on the way to Germany, only about 2000 opted to stay, mostly because of family ties (Hausleitner 2004: 369; U. Schmidt 2008: 317).

The resettlement was organized by a joint German-Soviet commission. The evacuees had to leave behind most of their belongings. The promise was that Germany would compensate them in their new homes. The resettlements commissions set to work only weeks after the Soviet takeover, in late summer of 1940. The ambitious plan included German peasants first bringing in their harvest, pay their taxes to the new Soviet masters and then "evacuate" before the autumn rains made the unpaved Bessarabian roads impassable (U. Schmidt 2008: 309–317). Registration for those willing to resettle began with an official call to register on September 15, 1940. It was published in Russian and German. It called those Germans willing to resettle to present themselves to one of the authorized resettlement commissioners and "if possible present a document that proves their ethnic belonging" (*natsional'nost'* in the Russian version, the German version used the term *Volkstumszugehörigkeit* that has a very clear ethnic connotation). Most families were able to present such evidence as excerpts from church registers or pedigrees (U. Schmidt 2008: 314–317). It is unlikely that these documents themselves specified the ethnicity of the people in them. It was again a group of bureaucrats—this time even from two different bureaucratic apparatuses, the Soviet and the German one—that decided on the grounds of descent and religion about the ethnicity of people.

Registering for resettlement was just the first test of their ethnic suitability that Bessarabian Germans had to pass. After their transport to the German Reich in late autumn they were interned in transit camps. There, they were screened by commissions of the central immigration office (*Einwandererzentralstelle*), a branch of Heinrich Himmler's Reich Main Security Office (*Reichssicherheitshauptamt*). The commissions split the Bessarabian Germans into two categories, "suited for the east" (*ostwürdig*) and those, who had to remain in the Reich. In examinations that were camouflaged as health checks, Bessarabian Germans were screened for traces of what was considered "non-German traits." The vast majority among them was found "suited for the east." From 1941 through 1944 these people were transported to what is now western Poland, where they were given land that had belonged to Polish farmers who were expelled to make room for them. In January 1945, when the Red Army advanced through Poland, they had to escape again (U. Schmidt 2008: 327–331).

The villages left deserted by the German evacuees of 1940 were turned into 46 new kolkhozes and settled with people from central and northern Ukraine (Lebedenko and Tychyna 2002: 156). The resettlement of the Germans gave Bessarabia a foretaste of the Soviet nationalities policy, in which an ethnicity, ascribed by government officials, could be decisive for a person's fate.

Before such a policy could fully unfold, Bessarabia once again came under Romanian rule. Now however, Romania had turned into a military dictatorship allied with Nazi-Germany and an accomplice in the German attack on the Soviet Union. Romania's military leader, General (later Marshall) Ion Antonescu, led his country towards war in a regime full of contradictions. He created a fascist-type state that was bitterly embattled with Romania's foremost fascist movement, the Iron Guard. Antonescu and his lieutenants were fiercely anti-Semitic and promoted the "final solution" in the reconquered provinces of Bessarabia and Northern Bukovina but strived to save the Jewish population of the Old Kingdom from the Holocaust.[28] Some of these contradictions may have to do with the attempt to curry favor with Germany as long as Germany was gaining ground in the east and preparing for a separate peace with the Allies once Germany lost its aura of invincibility (Glass 2014: 235–240).

The Holocaust in the territories controlled by the Antonescu regime is a tragic and often overlooked aspect of World War II. It would certainly merit its own chapter in this book. However, in order to stick to the book's main topic, the creation and maintenance of ethnic boundaries, it is important to notice that the years of World War II in Bessarabia, for all their cruelty towards Jews and Roma, for all the turmoil and uncertainty they brought to Ukrainians, Bulgarians, Bessarabian Germans and other minorities, they are sadly not an oddity. Rather they are the culmination of decades of ethnic categorization that preceded 1941. The slow introduction of ethnic categories in the tsarist administration and the fast expansion of this categorization in the years of Greater Romania now crystalized in a moment when their ultimate purpose suddenly became applicable—the exclusion of entire groups from Romanian society based on ethnic criteria. The scale of exclusion escalated quickly in the summer of 1941 from the issuing of differently colored passports for Romanians, Jews and other ethnic minorities (Glass 2014: 101) to murderous pogroms and the deportation of approximately 56,000 Bessarabian Jews across the river Dniester,[29] where they were left to fend for their survival.

Once it was clear that Romania would use military action to regain Bessarabia and Northern Bukovina, it was also openly communicated that the non-Romanians living there would be subjected to violence. In summer 1941, for instance, the Minister Secretary, the powerful number two in Romania's military regime and Ion Antonescu's distant relative, Mihai Antonescu, very openly announced that Jews would be deported. The justification of drastic measures against the Jews in Mihai Antonescu's speeches was that another chance like the attack on the Soviet Union to create an ethnically pure Romania was very unlikely to occur again anytime soon.[30] For the Romanian regime, World War II was an opportunity to quickly and violently turn Romanian society into what they thought it should have remained in the preceding centuries, an ethnically

28 Final Report of the International Commission on the Holocaust in Romania 2004, pp. 8–9.
29 Ibid., pp. 84–85.
30 Ibid., pp. 23–24.

undiluted body of people. The time to use all the bureaucratic categorization against the people the regime considered alien had come. In this the mass murder and deportations of the Second World War are not a separate chapter, but the outcome of decades of ethnic labeling.

Whereas the practices of the Romanian military regime were in many ways a logical continuation of the preceding decades, its territory had dramatically changed. The main theatre for the ethnic cleansing campaigns of 1941–44 were the two provinces regained from the Soviet Union, Bessarabia and Northern Bukovina. The northern part of Transylvania, in the interwar period one of the three new provinces of Romania, had now been ceded—with German blessing—to Hungary, another of Hitler's allies. As compensation, the Germans granted Antonescu an additional chunk of land in the east, Transnistria, which at the time referred to all the territory up to the Southern Bug River in central Ukraine. This region had belonged to the Soviet Union during the interwar years and many of its inhabitants had already developed a firm Soviet sense of belonging. The Romanian occupiers in general treated the local population not quite as ruthlessly as the Germans who occupied the rest of Ukraine (Richardson 2008: 32). Perhaps this was just due to the fact that Romania did not have the means for quick and thorough ethnic cleansing.

However, starting from October 1941, plans to expatriate members of all ethnic minorities were developed in Bucharest. The leading planner for ethnic cleansing operations was Sabin Manuilă, the director of the National Statistics Office. He planned to get rid of Romania's Ukrainians, Russians, Hungarians and Bulgarians by exchanging them for Romanian speakers from the respective countries or by offering neighboring countries small territories in exchange for receiving their ethnic brethren. For Jews and Roma, Manuilă's plan envisaged a "unilateral transfer." According to the plan, 3.6 million representatives of ethnic minorities should leave Romania and 1.6 million ethnic Romanians from neighboring countries should resettle within Romanian borders. A much smaller population exchange had already been undertaken in the summer of 1940. After Romania had to cede Southern Dobrudja to Bulgaria, more than 100,000 Romanians should move to the northern part of Dobrudja in exchange for between 61,000 and 72,000 Bulgarians,[31] who should move south (Glass 2014: 200–201).

It was no coincidence that plans for deportations of such magnitude were drawn up by a statistics authority. The clarity of statistical categories led Bucharest technocrats to believe it would be straight forward to ascribe ethnic

31 According to Wedekind (2010) the number was 61,000, according to Glass (2014), it was 72,000.

categories to actual people. In practice, systematic discrimination and large-scale deportations required introducing documents that would unambiguously prove each person's ethnic belonging. Such ethnicity certificates became a corner stone of Antonescu's ethnicity policies. But first attempts to base population exchange on such documents proved tricky. Bulgaria and Romania founded a joint commission to work out the details of who should be counted as Romanian and who as Bulgarian, but they failed to come to an agreement. Who was a Romanian in Southern Dobrudja therefore had to be determined by self-identification, which in practice meant only those people who wanted to move to Romania self-identified as Romanians (Solonari 2010: 98). 61,000 Bulgarians were deported out of Constanța and Tulcea provinces that constitute Northern Dobrudja, just across the Danube from Izmail. In exchange, 100,000 ethnic Romanians had to leave Southern Dobrudja. Some of these Romanians had been sent there as recently as the 1920s to reshape the ethnic composition in the then newly acquired province in favor of Romania (Wedekind 2010: 57). In Northern Dobrudja, the Romanian administrators hastily pushed forward with the "evacuation" of Bulgarians. People were identified as Bulgarians by episodic evidence, by hearsay and denunciation. When Romanian bureaucrats drew up the lists of Bulgarians to be deported, they identified about 75,000 people, more than double the number counted in the 1930 census. The same statistical authorities that claimed ethnic ascription was objective now proved with their own headcount that this was not the case (Solonari 2010: 102–105). So when the turn was on Bessarabia one year later, both the Romanian administrators and their new subjects realized that a lot could depend on identity documents that now specified no longer only Romanian citizenship (*de naționalitate Română*) but also ethnicity (*de origină etnică Română*).

The introduction of this new category understandingly alerted representatives of ethnic minorities, since it provided a potential administrative base for deportations and ethnic cleansing. Passive resistance became a common response. North of Izmail, in the predominately Bulgarian village of Kalcheva, for instance, a persistent rumor caused problems. It was apparently a widespread belief there in 1943 that Bulgarians from Romanian held territories would soon be exchanged for ethnic Romanians living in Bulgaria. This rumor, very likely based on the botched attempts to homogenize the ethnic composition of Dobrudja in 1940, led numerous ethnic Bulgarians to try to obtain Romanian ethnicity certificates.[32] This rumor was dismissed by the Romanian authorities as "counterpropaganda." But Sabin Manuilă's plan to resettle

32 Fr30 D193 Perepiska s Izmail'skoy uezdnoy prefekturoy primariyami i selvolosti ob ustanovlenii zhitelyam ruminskoy natsional'nosti, p. 689, p. 1077.

100,000 Russians and Ukrainians as well as thousands of Roma from southern Bessarabia to southern Ukraine were on Antonescu's desk since 1941. Only the desperate military situation, in which Romania found itself by 1943, prevented the plans from materializing (Hausleitner 2004: 371; Wedekind 2010: 65).

All in all, it had become undeniable that it was now a great asset to hold an official document, stating that one was ethnically Romanian. The right to stay in one's house and yard was but the most basic one that had now become the privilege of those in possession of such a document. Other restrictions were more than just rumors but very day-to-day matters of access to opportunities. Take for example the recruitment of trainees in the province's schools for future tractor drivers. A circular with an advertisement to enroll in such schools was sent to local administrators from the Bessarabian branch of the Agriculture Ministry in summer 1943. Conditions for boys to enroll were parent's permission, to be bodily able, and to be ethnically Romanian.[33] Other regulations had an even more straightforward effect of crowding out all non-Romanians from influential positions. Already in 1934 new labor laws required 80% of employees in each enterprise to be Romanians. For many years these legislations could be circumvented (Hausleitner 2004: 368). But now during the war, enforcement of romanianization laws became stricter. Moreover, in the summer of 1943 the Governor of Bessarabia, General Olimp Stavrat, strived to monopolize the grain trade to ethnic Romanians. He issued a decree with a list of criteria one henceforth had to fulfill in order to be issued a license to trade in grain. Requirements were to be a registered company, be in possession of the necessary stock and resale facilities; one needed to have reserves of at least five wagon loads of grain and needed to hold a letter of recommendation from the chamber of trade and commerce. On top of these preconditions one needed to be ethnically Romanian and employ exclusively ethnic Romanians.[34] That meant for everyone in the grain trade they needed to get their ethnic origin certified.

But the areas in which it became important to be ethnically Romanian were much wider than access to training or to trade. In lists of people who applied for a certificate of Romanian ethnicity in Bolgrad, the reasons for which the applicants needed their certificates were recorded. They included the need to be registered for access to state services such as marriage and pension schemes,

33 Fr30 D196 Tsirkulariya bessarabskogo gubernatora i perepiska s izmail'skoy uezdnoy prefekturoy, p. 107.

34 Fr30 D206 Perepiska s primariyami sel o kolichestve i natsional'nom sostave naseleniya, p. 240.

access to education and all sorts of licenses, such as a license to carry a gun[35] or licenses to hunt.[36] Other documents reveal that it was a precondition to be ethnically Romanian in order to be accepted by the chamber of trade and commerce.[37]

Ethnicity had become a vital administrative and legal category. So on what grounds was the decision made whether or not someone was actually entitled to hold a certificate stating he or she was ethnically Romanian?[38] It seems Romania in the 1940s had an already time-tested regulation on citizenship. However, concerning the legal basis for handing out certificates about *ethnicity*, there was considerable confusion. For all its importance, the issuing of ethnicity certificates was not based on legally enforceable legislations, but on procedures published in several issues of the official gazette (*Monitorul Oficial*) in 1939 and 1941, as well as on a number of circulars that were interpreted differently in different municipalities.

When in Autumn 1941 the practice of handing out ethnicity certificates was introduced, many different kinds of justifications were used by applicants. One Ion Dandiș wrote to the municipal authorities in Bolgrad, requesting a certificate on his ethnically Romanian origins. In his reasoning he wrote that his lineage was of "Romanian blood" and that his father had been born in 1837, near Cahul, in a village called Sarge Vechii, where even today many people bore the family name Dandiș.[39] A relative of Ion Dandiș, a medical doctor called Vasile Dandiș, applied for a certificate around the same time in spring 1942. His argumentation was not based on blood ties, but on patriotic feelings. He wrote that "even in times of oppression" he had "never lost his feelings for Romania," he had stayed in Bessarabia instead of escaping, and for a number of weeks, in 1941, he had been fighting (against the Red Army) in the war.[40] In another

35 Fr35 D178 Proshenya zhiteley o vydache im udostvoreniy o rumynskom poddanstve i natsional'nosti, p. 200.

36 The 355 applicants between March and the beginning of October of 1942 requested their certificates for a variety of reasons. In order of frequency they are "registry," "service," "commerce," "studies," "marriage," "pension," "Ministry of Finance," "police," "mail," "license to run a mill," "higher education," "license to hunt," and "others." Fr 35 D179a Prosheniya zhiteley o vydache im udostvereniy o rumynskom poddanstve i natsional'nosti tom II, pp. 394–399.

37 Fr35 D179 Prosheniya zhiteley o vydache im udostvoreniy o rumynskom poddanstve i natsional'nosti tom I, p. 267.

38 The same question also arose in the Soviet Union, where beginning in 1932, ethnicity was registered in passports. For a thorough study of petitioners who were unhappy about their ascribed nationality in the USSR, see Baiburin (2012: 59–76).

39 Fr35 D177 Proshenie zhiteley o vydache im udostvoreniy o rumynskom poddanstve i natsional'nosti, p. 7.

40 Fr35 D178, p. 270.

example Alexandru Timoșencu, a native from Bolgrad, who had become a successful entrepreneur in Bucharest, put forward not his own biography but that of his ancestors. In order to obtain a certificate about his Romanian ethnicity, he wrote to the Bolgrad municipality about his maternal grandfather who had taken part in the Romanian-Turkish War (1877–78). In Timoșencu's case the confirmation that a certificate will be issued for him has remained in the archive, so we can conclude that his argumentation was eventually successful.[41] Many applicants took their name or an ancestor's name as proof of their Romanian ethnicity. One petitioner, Nicolae Măldov, argued his mother's name was Florea and that therefore he could be nothing but a Romanian.[42] In some cases this line of argumentation worked. In the case of Liubov Seciu, municipal authorities decided that she had convincingly proven that her father was named Mihail Floresco. This name, a municipal clerk in Bolgrad wrote to the mayor, could be neither Russian nor Bulgarian, and it sounded "purely Romanian" (*pur românesc*), save for the suffix "o" instead of the Romanian "u." But this orthographic change, the clerk explained, had been a common practice among the preceding Russian administrators in order to systematically "slavicize" Romanian names.[43]

Most applicants for Romanian ethnicity certificates chose harder evidence than their feelings, names, blood ties, or their ancestor's heroism. The great majority of applications came along with excerpts from birth registers. People who had been born before 1918 (everybody who in 1941 was older than 23) had to rely on birth certificates issued by the church authorities of the Russian Empire. Such certificates were quite laconic. They contained the names of both parents, the name of the child, the place of birth, the parent's religion, and whether or not they had been married legitimately.[44] In rare cases, people who were born in the Old Kingdom handed in Romanian birth certificates from the late 1800s. These were issued by the state rather than the church. They were more bureaucratic than the Russian certificates in that they specified the exact time of birth and the parent's address. They mentioned parent's religion, but, just as the Russian certificates, said nothing about ethnicity or *naționalitate*.[45] Finally, even for people who were born under Romanian rule in the interwar period, birth certificates did not specify their ethnicity or their parent's

41 Fr35 D178, p. 280.

42 Fr35 D178, p. 142.

43 Fr35 D178, p. 178.

44 For example Fr35 D177, p. 216.

45 E.g. Fr 35 D178, p. 383.

ethnicity, because not until 1941[46] was ethnicity used as an administrative category. Now municipal authorities had to decide about applicant's ethnic belonging on the grounds of documents that specified place of birth, parent's names, their religion, and marital status, but not origin, language, or ethnicity.

There was understandably widespread confusion among municipal authorities. But it was not until late 1942, more than a year after the practice of certifying ethnicity had been introduced in Bessarabia, that the central authorities made an attempt to discipline the outposts. The police in Izmail uncovered a scandal in the village of Dunăreanca (today's Zadunaevka, in Artsis rayon). In an informative note from November 1942 the police in Izmail referred to the case of two locals, Gheorghe Andonov, and Vasile Sibov, who by way of bribing witnesses, had obtained certificates confirming that they were ethnic Romanians, although they were, in the police's opinion, clearly ethnic Bulgarians. Both of them, the report said, spoke only very little Romanian and their parents spoke "not a word of it." The authorities of the village, the report concluded, had issued these documents without even the most superficial inquiry into the two men's origins. According to the report, the ethnicity certificates enabled the two men to obtain a license to run a business. This was a clear circumvention of the laws to romanianize Bessarabia (*legea de romanizarea a Basarbiei*). But despite this crushing critique of the municipal authority's work, the report admitted that the certificates in question had been issued at least partially on the basis of legal documents. In Gheorghe Andonov's case, there was a document in the files, stating that his mother had been Moldovan (and therefore, in the reading of the time, an ethnic Romanian). Still the two men were found to be clearly not the kind of Romanians the new laws on romanianization sought to empower.[47]

The case of Sibov and Andonov illustrates that deciding who was Romanian by ethnicity and who was something else, was not an easy task, and that the whole procedure was vulnerable to arbitrariness and abuse. Two months after the case became public, in January 1943, the head of Bolgrad district wrote to all municipalities in his jurisdiction, saying there had been abuses in the practice of issuing ethnicity certificates.[48] The letter urged all municipalities to reassess all the certificates issued to date and, if necessary, recollect those that

46 In the Izmail archive, cases of ethnicity certificates first appear from early November 1941 onwards, 5 months after the attack on the Soviet Union by German and Romanian forces: Fr35 D45.

47 Fr30 D46 Perepiska s primariyami sel uezda ob annulirovanii nezakonno vydannikh udostovereniy o ruminskoy natsional'nosti, p. 43.

48 Fr30 D46, pp. 41–42.

were flawed. Swift answers from the villages denied any flaws.[49] All certificates had been issued on the basis of legal documents.

The confusion about who could be a certified Romanian and who could not was more than just a local problem. The central directorate of administration in Bessarabia became aware of widespread misperceptions already in September 1942. In a circular to all municipalities the provincial administration in Chișinău complained that there had been a series of regrettable confusions over who was eligible to Romanian ethnicity certificates and who was not. The circular blamed it on the fact, that an earlier newsletter from March 1942 had been misinterpreted by many municipal clerks. The text then openly admitted that, at the time, there were no laws to regulate ethnicity. Therefore, for the time being, all that municipalities could certify was that a person was "widely known" (*este notoriu cunoscută*) for being of Romanian ethnic origin. The circular was also quite outspoken about the aims of certifying ethnicity. This practice was meant to bridge the lack of a comprehensive legislation on ethnicity and avoid that the "Romanian elements" (*elementele românești*) were crowded out of the economic, social, and cultural life of Bessarabia, and to prevent the local minorities to occupy these "realms of national life."[50] The same communication then, "in the name of Romanian interests in Bessarabia," gave detailed instructions how to handle applications for ethnicity certificates. Generally, such certificates should be issued only in cases where Romanian ethnicity could be clearly proven with legal documents. Which documents exactly qualified as proof was not specified. As we have seen, mostly birth certificates were used, although they left it to the taste of the local clerk to decide which ethnic identity they proved. The municipalities were reminded that only people with at least one Romanian parent could be considered ethnically Romanian. If there were no such documents available because the archives had been destroyed or because of other cases of force majeure, certificates could be issued on grounds of testimony. This practice, however, should be used only in rare exceptions, strictly if the mayor knew the witness personally, and only if the witness was himself widely known to be from an ethnically Romanian family. It was specifically highlighted that witnesses who gave false testimony would be held legally responsible. In addition, the circular gave instructions in which cases never to issue ethnicity certificates. This included any case in which it was known that the person in question was of any other

49 Fr30 D46, pp. 31–40.

50 Fr35 D179a Prosheniya zhiteley o vydache im udostvereniy o rumynskom poddanstve i natsional'nosti tom II, p. 307.

ethnicity than Romanian, or if there was reason to believe, or clear evidence for an "admixture of Semitic blood."[51]

The aims of the Romanian policy of certifying ethnicity were much clearer than the legal procedures involved in it. It was meant to crowd out ethnic minorities from all the important realms of society, leaving much of the details involved to the judgment of local clerks. It is hard to imagine that these could take well-informed and fair decisions. Let us get back to the case of Andonov and Sibov who had allegedly bribed the authorities in the predominately Bulgarian village of Dunăreanca (Zadunaevka) to become certified Romanians. It is reasonable to believe that the local clerks belonged to the very few native Romanian speakers among the village population. Very likely they had arrived there only the year before (1941) as representatives of a hostile and invading government. They knew probably very little about social relations and culture in the village, and they most probably had no way of knowing which family claimed which ethnic identity. In fact it is reasonable to believe that the very notion of ethnicity was quite new for most of the village's population. So far, authorities might have counted how many people belonged to which ethnic group, but they had never issued personal documents containing such information. The combination of a lacking legal basis for, and a high value of Romanian ethnicity, could result only in arbitrary decision-making and corruption. Ethnicity had become not only an administrative category, but also an economic asset.

In the last months of 1943 and in winter 1944, when the tide of the war had turned after the Soviet victory in Stalingrad, applications for Romanian ethnicity certificates diminished sharply. This of course might be simply because everyone likely to get a certificate had already applied. Probably it was also more attractive being a certified Romanian as long as the Romanians seemed to stay for good. Now it became likely that the Red Army would be back anytime soon.

Along with their ethnicity certificates, many applicants also sought to change, or rather to romanianize, their family names. During World War II the official gazette *Monitorul Oficial* in each issue published dozens of pages of changed family names. In the small and ethnically predominantly Bulgarian town of Bolgrad, 408 people, nearly 4% of the town's population, applied to change their names between March and October 1942.[52] Name changes were usually permitted only once the person concerned had obtained a certificate of being ethnically Romanian. There were different ways to romanianize a

51 The original formulation was "când există dubiu sau indicii certe amestecului sange semit." Fr35 D179a, p. 307.

52 As can be seen from the applications collected in Fr35 D179a.

family name. The most common one was to simply alter its spelling, usually in the suffix (Gavriliuc became Gavriliu, Bratov became Bratu, and Dobrev became Dobrea). In rarer cases the meaning behind the name was translated (Melnicov became Moraru, with the core in both names meaning "miller," or Crușcov became Roată, the root of both words referring to a circle or a wheel).[53] In many cases there was no apparent connection between the hitherto Slavic and the new Romanian family name. Nonetheless, for the Romanian authorities it seemed very clear that when they were changing names, they were changing them back and thereby reinstalled justice to history. In a circular of September 1942 from the Bessarabian provincial administration to rural municipalities, authorities there were reminded that the laws on name changes were to protect the rights of those Romanians who have not yet lost their ethnic consciousness even though they had suffered Russian oppression and the forced slavicization of their family names.[54] In the registry of changed family names, the romanianized names appear in a column called "name that the applicant wishes to regain."[55] At least civil servants seemed to have deeply internalized the notion, that this territory and its people would still be Romanian, had they only be left in their natural state.

5 Bringing the Past into Line

The narrative that foreign-seeming places and people had once been Romanian was a frequently reoccurring one in Greater Romania. Already in the 1920s during a school reform that banned the use of Ukrainian from schools in Bukovina, this was justified by the claim that the Ukrainians there were actually Romanians who had forgotten how to speak Romanian (Subtelny 2000; 447). In the mid-1930s the Hungarian speaking Székelys of eastern Transylvania became the center of attention of a campaign run by the Cluj-based Institute of Hygiene and Social Hygiene. This institution specialized in eugenics and anthropometrics. Using blood tests, apparently regarded a valid scientific method at the time, the institute's scientists claimed to have proven that the Székelys were but magyarized Romanians (Wedekind 2010: 33). The scholars in charge of the study believed that the blood, unlike language or culture, remained unaltered by the vicissitudes of time (Turda 2007: 428). If once, back in the

53 All examples taken from name changing lists from the town of Bolgrad 1942, Fr35 D179a, pp. 400–403.

54 Fr35 D179a, p. 307.

55 The original formulation was "numele ce dorește a-l redobândi." Fr35 D179a, pp. 400–403.

Middle Ages, the Székelys had been Romanians, and the qualities of this nation could still be found in their blood, then there was no reason why now they should not be turned back into Romanians.

The theme of giving back to Romanians what had belonged to them already, also became the chief justification of Romanian hegemony over Bessarabia. Through a network of schools and culture houses, established in the mid-1920s, Bucharest propagandists tried to convince Bessarabian villagers that only the Romanian state could have a legitimate claim over the region. By 1927 there were 16 culture centers in the villages around Izmail, most of them in villages, where at least part of the population spoke Romanian.[56] Monthly lectures there were attended by sometimes 40, sometimes up to 250 people.[57]

Behind the idea of reinstalling "historical justice" was the concept of continuity, or put more dramatically, the survival of the Romanian people. This assumption was one of three pillars of Romanian nationalist historiography, along with the idea of an ancient symbiosis of Romans and Dacians, and the unity of the Romanian people in their age-old strife for an independent state (van Meurs 1994: 224). In a suggested lecture for a national holiday, the staff of one culture house was instructed to make their audience "remember night and day" that the Romanian people settled this area almost 2000 years ago, without ever having been weakened or broken up, no matter how its enemies tried, it remained brave and united.[58] In a lesson titled *the beauty and the riches of Greater Romania* the lecturer started with the remark that now, after many sacrifices, Romania had finally found her place within her "age-old borders." The lecture ended with the call: "May the King live, may Romania live, may the Romanian nation live and prosper, so that she forever rules the age-old soil of the Dacians, from Border to Border!"[59]

The huge territorial gains of Romania were sealed in the Versailles treaty of 1920. But this treaty came under heavy pressure after Germany started to

---

56 F1139 D1 Postanovleniya Ministerstva prosvyashcheniya o sozdanii i funktsionirovanii kul´turnikh tsentrov, p. 5. The proceedings of the culture houses in Nerushay and Galilești (today's Desantnoe), two predominantly Ukrainian speaking villages near Kiliya, have survived. These culture houses were instructed in letters from the Ministry of Education on what themes they should lecture and by which folkloristic elements lectures should be accompanied. The administration of culture houses sent their programs to a branch of the ministry of education in Izmail to have them approved. After each event the culture house staff sent a detailed report to their superiors in the ministry.

57 F1044 D1 Otchet deyatel'nost'i tsentra i doklady sdelannye uchitelyami, pp. 7, 16, 15, 38, 47, 48.

58 F1023 D4 Direktivnye ukazaniya Bukharestkogo obshchestva po rasprostraneniyu kul'tury o rabote ochaga kul'tury v sele Nerushay, p. 4.

59 F1044 D1, pp. 29–33.

openly deny its validity and breach its rulings. Under these circumstances Romanian authorities increasingly looked for narratives of a naturally shaped and ancient Romanian territory in order to justify the huge territorial gains of 1918 (Wedekind 2010: 55). The colonists of southern Bessarabia, the descendants of which must have been a significant share of the audience, were characterized as vagabonds and deserters, drifting into Bessarabia in order to evade conscription in their homelands. Because the Russian administration did not care for education, the local population had allegedly lost the ability to speak Romanian.[60] This flaw should now be corrected.

The audiences of these lectures could hardly be considered Romanians on first sight. The village of Galilești (today called Desantnoe), where the above-mentioned lecture was held in December 1927, had, according to the secret police's data, only 46 Romanian inhabitants, against 3246 Russians[61] (Today the village is considered predominantly Ukrainian). A culture house report from earlier the same year lamented that the lecture had not been a full success since the village population consisted of Ukrainians who could hardly understand Romanian.[62] Nevertheless, both the Ministry of Culture and the Ministry of Education took quite some effort to persuade ethnic minorities, like the Ukrainians in Galilești, of a new, nationalist Romanian imagination of their region's past.

6 Eugenics and Ethnic Cleansing

In the mid-1920s, on the height of Greater Romania's democratic experiment, fascist rhetoric could still mobilize only on the fringes of the political spectrum. Apart from Jews and Roma who had faced considerable hostility for many years already, orthodox ethnic minorities were still treated as past and future Romanians, or at least Romanian citizens. To discriminate too harshly against Russians, Ukrainians, Bulgarians, Germans or, in other regions of Greater Romania, against Hungarians, would only have spurred revisionist tendencies (Wedekind 2010: 28; Hitchins 1994: 423). Neighboring states Hungary, Bulgaria, and the Soviet Union had all lost large chunks of land to Greater Romania and could hardly wait for a good excuse to get them back. Therefore, alienating minorities too much could have triggered coordinated acts between

60 Dovadă că pământul Basarabiei este românesc și că străinii de aci au venit în urma noastră, in F1044 D1, pp. 5–7.

61 Information contained in the ethnic map of southern Bessarabia commissioned in 1934, F312 D49, p. 218.

62 Report on the lecture of March 20 1927, F1044 D1, p. 47.

neighboring states and their diasporas within Romania, which might have well led to the break-up of the not-yet-consolidated Romanian state.

So the orthodox ethnic minorities and the Hungarians of Transylvania were told that they were in fact just Romanians who had fallen prey to the propaganda of foreign states that by historical accident, and out of low motives, had ruled over the area. This argument presupposed a primordial conception of ethnicity. If ethnicity did not change when people changed their culture and their language, then it had to be tied to the blood and the soil, both of which had purportedly once been part of a glorious Romanian past. This past and its heroes, in the reading of Romanian nationalists, had been betrayed by letting their glory degenerate. Long before fascism became a dominant political voice in Romania, there was a widespread belief that society was in a state of constant degeneration. That many Romanians had allegedly accepted foreign ethnic identities was just the most visible sign of this degeneration. Partly, the theme of degeneration was borrowed from German mentors of fascism, particularly Oswald Spengler's *Downfall of the Occident* (Hitchins 1994: 308). Such ideas suggested that now as Romania ruled over all the territories inhabited by Romanians, this degeneration could be halted using scientific knowledge and social engineering (Turda 2011: 329). Romanian right-wing forces romanticized the peasant community and depicted it as void of urban, modern, or ethnically foreign influences. Most theoreticians who contributed to Romanian fascism had a deep suspicion for everything modern and urban. Their sources of inspiration were the Romanian peasantry and the Orthodox Church (Livezeanu 1990; Ioanid 2010: 132, 148). A notable exclusion to this rule was a tendency to exploit scientific rhetoric in order to prepare the grounds for ethnic cleansing.

After the "unification of the nation," stopping the alleged degeneration of Romanian society was the next step in reinstalling historical justice. Correcting the past was turned into a project of correcting the country's ethnic composition. The political right demanded that this endeavor was given priority in Romanian politics and that modern methods of grand-scheme planning should be applied. In this way the language of natural science, especially medicine and biology, crept into the debate about ethnic minorities and paved the way for fascism and ethnic cleansing.

By the mid-1930s Romanian politics had turned into a race of escalating demands to ethnically "purify" the nation. The fascist Iron Guard competed for power with the violently anti-Semitic National Christian Party. Both movements had made their political capital by mobilizing against ethnic minorities, first and foremost against Jews. Since 1918, the electorate of these two parties had been obsessed with the alleged degeneration of the Romanian nation and the question of how to strengthen the "national body" (Turda 2011: 347). The language of hygiene and medicine had accompanied this debate since World War I. Eventually, in the 1920s a wave of eugenic publications openly discussed measures such as sterilization, abortion, and marriage control to free Romanian society from "unwanted elements." In the mindset of those who wanted to purify the nation, the idea of an organic unit, an actual body, had become more than just a metaphor. One of the pioneers of Romanian eugenics, Iuliu Moldovan, saw the nation as a living organism and his concept of "bio-politics" as the means to regulate the relation between the state, the nation and individuals (Turda 2007: 413). In the speeches of Iron Guard leader Corneliu Codreanu the nation appeared as a being of flesh and blood, animated by the spirit of all living Romanians, as well as all Romanians who were no longer among the living, and those yet to be born (Ioanid 2010: 403). But in the 1920s, eugenics was still seen as a tool to prevent hereditarily ill or disabled individuals from procreating, whereas in the early 1940s it came to be seen as a tool to cure the "body of the nation" (Turda 2011: 349). The state came to be seen as inseparably tied to one ethnic group. All the other people living there were perceived more and more as a potential wartime hazard and therefore, in the language of national hygiene, were to be cleaned away.

Biological concepts of ethnicity had been around well before fascism. As in other European countries, in the last decades of the 19th century, Romanian nationalist thinkers sought to take on some of science's prestige by adopting racial theories. Usually these theories assumed that a group of people who lived by a certain culture would also exhibit a certain set of physical and psychological characteristics (Pârâianu 2007: 353). Following the idea that culture and biologically determined characteristics were congruent, the metaphor of the nation as an organism was not far-fetched. This organism was perceived as healthy in and of itself, but by way of social degeneration it had contracted various diseases. Eugenics was one of the cures suggested.

The figurehead of Romanian eugenics, Iuliu Moldovan, published his *Hygiene of the Nation* in 1925 in which he described the Romanian nation as a "biological reality, a human structure with its own biology and pathology" (Turda 2011: 331). The more the idea of the ethnic group was turned from an ancestral group that shared age-old blood ties, into a living organism, the less conceivable it became that those who did not feel they were part of this organism, would soon accept assimilation. It was even less conceivable that they would be talked into it by rereading history to them.

That ethnic minorities were not part of the imagined Romanian national organism became ultimately apparent in 1940, when Romania lost again much of the territorial gains of 1918, including Bessarabia. Many representatives of ethnic minorities showed little nostalgia for their 22 years under Romanian rule. In light of this new situation, Antonescu's military regime openly considered eugenic measures and ethnic cleansing in order to "rescue the nation" (Turda 2011: 343). To register people by ethnicity was a first step in putting such plans to action. The strategy of persuasion was dropped in favor of planned ethnic cleansing. Along with the strategy, the notion behind it was dropped; the idea that ethnic minorities at the fringes had once been Romanians and could choose to revive this identity.

Measures of ethnic cleansing during World War II hit the Jews and Roma hardest. There were several reasons for this: Killing Jews and Roma was a vocal goal of Romania's powerful ally Germany and required no special justification, as the deportation and mass killings of other ethnic groups might have needed. Anti-Semitism was deeply rooted in the Romanian state and especially in the Romanian military. This Anti-Semitism was reinforced in Northern Bukovina and Bessarabia, the territories that Romania reconquered from the Soviet Union in 1941, by consciously ascribing the Jews the role of traitors who had profited from the arrival of the Bolshevists, an accusation that has never been convincingly proven (Solonari 2010: 158–164). The Soviets and their alleged Jewish collaborators attracted the wrath of the Bessarabian population just days before the joint German and Romanian attack by quickly deporting between 17,000 and 22,000 people, according to completely arbitrary criteria. From the Bulgarian and Gagauz village of Kubei in southern Bessarabia, for instance, 125 men and 25 entire families were deported based on a list that was hastily completed by the chairman of the village committee just days before the attack (Solonari 2007: 771–772). Killing Jewish civilians was presented as an aspect of the war against Bolshevism. Like in neighboring Hungary and Bulgaria, the Jews in those territories over which Romania was at war with a neighboring power, were those affected harshest by the Holocaust. What in the case of Hungary applied to the Jews in the contested regions of Yugoslavia and Ukraine, what in the case of Bulgaria applied to the Jews in Thrace and Macedonia, in Romania applied for the Jews from Northern Bukovina and Bessarabia, over which Romania was at war with the Soviet Union; they were the first to be targeted (Ioanid 2000: 290).

Another important factor in the faith of Jews was whether they lived in a city or in a village. In the cities of Bessarabia and Northern Bukovina, Jews were horded into ghettos and transported to Transnistria from September 1941 onwards. In villages, Jews were often targeted by the local population rather than the military or the police. The army and the gendarmerie enabled and encouraged pogroms, plundering and mass murder of Jewish villagers. The deportation of the survivors in July and August 1941 was often unorganized and in itself caused the death of thousands (Glass 2014; Solonari 2010). These crimes are still documented only patchily and the numbers of victims varies according to sources. According to Glass (2014: 108) in July and August 1941 the joint attacking forces killed between 45,000 and 60,000 Jews in Bukovina and Bessarabia. From these two provinces combined, between 105,000 and 120,000 Jews were deported to Transnistria and killed or left to die there, along with Roma and local Ukrainian Jews. The Final Report of the International Commission on the Holocaust in Romania is cautious to state exact numbers of victims. It cites Romanian documents as the best sources. These reveal that at least 20,000 Jews were killed during the unorganized deportations in summer 1941 and by December that year at least 164,000 Romanian Jews had been deported to Transnistria, 56,000 of these came from Bessarabia. Of all the Romanian Jews deported to Transnistria 104,000–121,000 had perished by 1943.[63] Additionally, among the deportees to Transnistria, where the harsh winter of 1941–42 brought unspeakable suffering, were 25,000 Roma, of which only about 6,000 survived (Ioanid 2000: 289–299).

The southernmost stretches of Bessarabia were the last to be occupied by Romanian troops in August 1941. This gave local Jews more time to flee to the Soviet Union. In addition, the concentration of Jews was less dense here than in northern Bessarabia or in Bukovina, which led to a lower number of victims in the areas of Bessarabia that now belong to Ukraine. Nevertheless, southern Bessarabia too became the site of two large massacres that August, one in Tatarbunary with 120–140 victims and one in the town of Cetatea Albă (Belgorod Dnestrovskiy), where between 2500 and 3500 Jews were killed in a quarry outside of the town (Solonari 2010: 176–190).

The physical extermination of entire groups of people would not have been possible without the preceding ascription of ethnic categories in bureaucratic documents and in statistics that suggested clear-cut boundaries between each such category. Another important factor in the preparation of deportation and mass-murder during World War II was an amalgamate of folk theory and eugenics that proved popular in Greater Romania and that concluded that some groups could be exchanged with neighboring countries whereas other groups should become the subjects of a violent "unilateral transfer." In the camps along the river Dniester, where Jews were concentrated before they were forced across the river into Transnistria, the Romanian army and gendarmerie were eager to count each individual so as to make sure that the number of people they had identified as Jews were eventually met. They were equally careful not

63 Final Report of the International Commission on the Holocaust in Romania, 2004, pp. 86–87.

to record names of the deportees and to confiscate from them all the documents that could have revealed their identity (Glass 2014: 106). After having ascribed each person an ethnic category, entire groups of people were now completely reduced to this very category. All other aspects of their identity, their home, their citizenship, and their belongings were stripped from them to leave only their ethnicity, a category that now doomed them to death.

The years of inter-bellum Romania exposed ethnic minorities to a dangerous cocktail of nationalist frenzy, mythical historiography, and semi-scientific methods of social engineering. The re-writing of history was by far the most harmless of these. It implied that some ethnic minorities living in Romania could still be converted (or rather reconverted) into passable Romanians. In the mid- and late 1920s ethnic minorities in Bessarabia were therefore exposed to a well-meaning but lukewarm educatory campaign. But at the same time suspicion against ethnic minorities constantly grew, especially within the police. At first, folklore artists and suspected activists were targeted, but soon unfounded rumors about disloyalty became sufficient to trigger frenetic if inefficient activism within the security apparatus. When the Romanian leadership started to realize that the country might soon be caught in crossfire between the Soviet Union and Nazi-Germany, suspicion against ethnic minorities grew even further. Systematic counting and categorizing of ethnic minorities, starting from the mid-1930s, was the response. During World War II these measures were taken to the next level. The regime began—on shaky legal grounds—to hand out certificates concerning people's ethnicity. These served systematic ethnic discrimination against all minorities and prepared the grounds for deportation and ethnic cleansing. Ethnicity had become a category on the grounds of which the state decided about life or death.

CHAPTER 4

Politically Desirable Theory and Its Way into Folk Theory

There are a few very striking parallels between the Romanian military regime (1940–44) and the Soviet state that succeeded it in Bessarabia. One such parallel was that both states were dominated by an ethnic group that was in the minority in southern Bessarabia. Romanian/Moldovan speakers and Russian speakers both had been living here for many generations. The Moldovans were a rural minority. In Romanian times they were privileged over non-Romanian speakers but not quite to the extent of *Regățeni*, Romanians from the Old Kingdom. The Russian speakers, who dominated the Soviet Union, were mostly urban dwellers, save for the secluded Old-Believers in their delta villages.

Both states have tried to use minorities that were ethnically, culturally, and linguistically similar to their elites, as a justification for their presence in the region. Ethnicity statistics produced by the local Romanian administration in August 1941 reveal that in the district of Bolgrad, where Bulgarians and Gagauz made up the bulk of the population, Russians and Romanians were both a tiny minority; both representing roughly 2.4% of the population.[1] In the city of Izmail, Romanians, again by their own statistics of 1941, accounted for 14% of the population, while Russians made up 18% of the city's inhabitants.[2] So the elites of both states were locally an ethnic minority at roughly the same ratio.

There was another parallel between the two powers that replaced each other during the 1940s: Administrators in both these states believed that they could and should know how many representatives of which ethnic group lived in their jurisdiction. They were eager to acquire this kind of information because they believed some ethnic groups could be trusted, while others could not. This parallel meant that both states, nationalist Romania and the socialist USSR, in their ethnicity policy followed two basic axioms: (1) that the ethnicity of a person could be objectively determined and (2) that this ethnic identity would inevitably lead a person to identify with and be loyal towards one particular state. Following these two axioms the Soviet administration, like the preceding Antonescu regime, found it necessary to register ethnicity in personal

1 Fr30 D5 Spravki o kolichestve, natsional'nom i professional'nom sostave naseleniya po selam volosti.

2 Fr37 D26 Svedenie o kolichestve, polevom, natsional'nom sostave naseleniya goroda za 1940–41 gg, pp. 8–9.

 | DOI:10.1163/9789004408029_005

documents. In the Old Soviet Union, passports were introduced in 1932 as an instrument to control people's fluctuations, not just across state borders, but in and out of cities swelling with rural-urban migrants (Ahlberg 1991). The internal passports in combination with a system of registration lead to a maximal "legibility" of Soviet society. It enabled the state to keep people where the centrally planned labor market needed them and it also allowed to carefully engineer a city's population according to economic or ethnic criteria.

In southern Bessarabia, this meant a Soviet continuation of state ascription of ethnic categories begun by the Romanian regime. The declared goal of this ascription was the creation of an inclusive state this time, not an exclusive one as nationalist greater Romania. The effects on the category of ethnicity were similar to those under Romanian rule. Ethnicity became an ever more pervasive category.

Ethnic boundaries in southern Bessarabia appeared in the later decades of the 19th century, when both the tools and the need for social engineering were already around. Ethnic boundaries were then molded according to the needs of the different power holders at various times ever since. This chapter will argue that under the conditions of mass education and mass media that arose during the Soviet period, ethnic boundaries were no longer just molded according to the interests of the powerful, they were also propagated as one of the decisive distinctions that shape human societies. Most of the informants to this work, with or without a special interest in the topic of ethnic boundaries, would not agree that anyone ever needed to be convinced of this. The ethnic boundaries I have described as an outcome of socio-political processes, they would more likely see as a natural and essential feature of the human condition. The administrators, ethnographers and political patrons whom I have credited with producing and maintaining ethnic boundaries, they would merely credit with revealing what had been there since times immemorial. This is more than a simple misunderstanding between Western and formerly Soviet paradigms. The assumption that ethnicity is an essential part of every person's identity and that it exists whether or not the person recognizes and accepts it is crucial for the preservation of ethnic boundaries. I take the advent of Soviet power as an opportunity to pause before moving on in the next chapter with the chronological display of the development of ethnic boundaries, and to raise the question, why in multi-ethnic regions of the former Soviet Union, such as southern Bessarabia, ethnic boundaries did not just wither away. Contrary to what one would expect under circumstances of long cohabitation and increased cultural likeness, ethnic boundaries in southern Bessarabia are perceived as tenaciously persisting. Why does Bessarabia appear as a "salad bowl" rather than a "melting pot"? The answer, I believe, lies in a slow transformation process of ideas from the political needs of the respective governments in power, the academic theories they fostered and from there through the education system and the media into a broader public. Academic theories about ethnicity, especially those of the Soviet period, eventually became "folk theories," a genre described by Michael Burawoy (2009: 270) as "the theory of the people we study, (…), buried in common sense and sometimes elaborated into ideology." Folk theory contains "some truth, a practical truth." The ideology and practical truths of essentializing ethnicity were not produced within the realm of folk theory but in what Burawoy describes as folk theory's counterpart, "analytical theory." In this chapter, I therefore explore the roots of the paradigms that came to dominate analytical theory in the region.

Late Soviet theories retain a strong influence in Ukraine and other post-Soviet countries (Kuznetsov 2008: 21). The educatory and administrative systems that followed those of the Soviet Union were not nearly as pervasive as those during the Soviet period. One good way to assess whether or not the educatory system underwent a paradigm shift is to look at introductory textbooks, recommended for use in university classes by the Ministry of Education, where Soviet concepts and definitions can still be found.[3] The answer why ethnic boundaries continue to be important should therefore be sought in the conception of ethnicity in post-war Soviet academia itself. If we content ourselves with scrutinizing Bessarabia's ethnic mosaic through the lens of Western Anthropology alone, two conceptual frameworks are bound to clash, the Soviet concept of "ethnos," and the Western concept of "ethnicity." The Soviet (and to a large extent post-Soviet) strand of explanation includes very clear ideas what an ethnos (or more popularly "natsional'nost'") is, what criteria it needs to fulfill in order to be counted as one, how it emerges, and how it disappears.

The administrative needs to which Soviet ethnicity theories were tailored was to have a set of clearly bounded social categories that could be addressed with separate policies, very much akin to James Scott's (1998) notion of "legibility." As a consequence of decades of ethnographic research guided by this need, ethnic belonging is still often treated as a self-explanatory fact of life. It can be determined by observing what language people speak, what kind of clothes they wear, what god they pray to, or who they think their ancestors were (Kushner 1951: 10). Soviet scholars described the phenomenon of interethnic marriage with great demographic detail (for an overview see Gorenburg

3 A recent example is a reader on the ethnography of Ukraine (Makarchuk 2008) that introduces Soviet definitions for "ethnos," "super-ethnos," "sub-ethnos," "race," "sub-races," and describes the anthropometric features of Ukrainians.

2006a), but never questioned ethnicity as a valid census category, let alone came up with a concept of ethnicity that allowed ambiguous ethnic identities.

Dominant Western perspectives on ethnicity provide quite a contrast. In the post-war era, most Western scholars began to see ethnic identity, merely as an idea, constructed in the 19th and 20th centuries in order to structure societies and to exercise power (Fowkes 2002: 6). Rigid definitions of ethnicity and nationality, relying on a "shopping list of criteria" (Hann 1997: 27) that need to be fulfilled (as they were used in varying forms in the Soviet Union) have had a hard time being accepted in Western academia. This is for one because if we look at groups defined by certain "trait inventories" we look at cultural groups, and these are not necessarily congruent with ethnic groups (Barth 1969: 12). Criteria lists to define ethnic belonging are also problematic because for each of the definitions of ethnicity that uses a finite list of criteria, exceptions can easily be found (Hobsbawm 1990: 16). Another weakness of shopping list definitions is that they do not pay sufficient attention to the complex interrelations between the individual items on the list (Hroch 1968: 13). These items can be shared but not owned by one group. Depending on the needs of elites, such lists can be expanded or shortened and thereby inclusion or exclusion into the group can be steered (Elwert 1997: 257, 2002: 38). So if a common language is taken as a criterion to form an ethnic group or nation of the type that would qualify as *natsional'nost'*, then the Belgians, the Irish, or the Swiss do not fit into the definition. If a common territory is a precondition the Armenians, the Jews, or the Roma are at odds with it. If common religion is what counts, the Lebanese, the Albanians, or the Ukrainians fall short. If common ancestry is assumed, the Brazilians, the Americans, and many others are excluded. If it is assumed that a *natsional'nost'* can only be counted as such if inside and outside that group it is seen as different from other such groups, then the Moldovans and the Romanians, the Serbs and the Croats are out, because debates about their ethnic sovereignty are far from resolved. This list of exclusive criteria could be continued endlessly because virtually every set of common features and differences can, under the right circumstances, be used to mark ethnic boundaries, as Max Weber observed (1990: 237). Therefore, it is worth repeating his definition, which left the formulation of a list of "trait inventories" not to social scientists (as in the Soviet Union), but to the people concerned:

> We shall call 'ethnic groups' those human groups that entertain a subjective belief in their common descent because of similarities of physical type or of custom or both, or because of memories of colonization and migration; this belief must be important for the propagation of group

formation; conversely, it does not matter whether or not an objective blood relationship exists (M. Weber 1996: 35).

Hence, ethnicity in Weber's perspective is not something that a certain group of people *has*, it is something that they *do*, they "entertain a belief" in their communality. But this view on ethnicity runs into trouble in Bessarabia. If an ethnographer, trained in the West, asks an informant in Bessarabia (or probably anywhere else in the former Soviet Union) "what ethnic group do you belong to?," then only one of the participants in this conversation will likely have a concept similar to the one cited above in mind. The Bessarabian (or otherwise post-Soviet) informant will most likely understand that he or she is asked about his or her *actual* ancestry, and it will probably matter to them whether this ancestry is real or not. Therefore most post-Soviet informants have an essentialist view of ethnicity in mind, one in which ethnicity is obtained by birth and cannot credibly be obtained by choice. One could assume that such a conception is simply the product of folk-intuition, a genre in which ethnicity is likely to be essentialized (Gil-White 2001). But in this chapter, I argue that Soviet ethnicity theory (and much of what remains of it) has done a good deal to give an air of scientific credibility to what folk wisdom allegedly concludes intuitively.

Although most ethno-political movements are based on essentialist views of ethnicity and although most ordinary people have never heard of constructivist theories, social scientists have pretended essentialism was nothing to take seriously. Just for its importance and prevalence constructivists should try to understand essentialism (Gil-White 2001: 515). One way to reach such an understanding in the post-Soviet region would be to look for suitable translations of "natsional'nost'" and "etnos" as well as their connotations. In order to approach such a translation, it will be indispensable to have a closer look at the historical context in which Soviet and post-Soviet ideas about ethnicity emerged, both popular and academic ones.

1 The Imperial Roots of Diverging Ethnicity Concepts

If we want to understand the emergence of an ethnicity concept in any region, we have to reach back to the socialization of the elites that coined and disseminated these concepts. In Bessarabia these were Soviet elites who took up influential positions in politics and education after World War II. They received their own education from people who were socialized and educated in the Russian Empire. We therefore have to zoom out at least to the final decades of the Russian Empire to understand the roots of an ethnicity concept that survived the collapse of the Soviet Union.

This section discusses why after the Soviet Union's demise, concepts of ethnicity were so different on both sides of the iron curtain. It is worth therefore to first take a look at what common questions both concepts had to answer. After World War II, scholars of ethnicity in the West as well as in the Soviet Union had to make sense of cultural differences while equality in status and rights for people of all origins and cultures became an ever more urgent demand. Ethnicity concepts on both sides of the iron curtain ultimately strived to answer questions raised by the process of integrating former colonial lands into a unified nation or receiving immigrants from foreign countries.

Bessarabia was a land both of colonists and immigrants that was culturally different from the center and economically dependent on it. It was a region in which people of different origins settled land that was previously emptied out forcefully. In this *Novorossiya* was strikingly similar to the settler colonies in the New World. But there was one major difference: In the Americas, the link to the colonial power quickly became a burden to the settlers. The colonial "creole elites" formed new national identities on which they based their struggles for independence. In Central and Southern America, colonial elites even integrated the native population of the countries they had conquered into these new identities. While the colonizing states extracted more and more resources from their overseas colonies, they hardly left a share of it to their colonial administrators. They prohibited the colonies from trading among each other and systematically discriminated those born there against newcomers from the mother country (Anderson 2006: 50–57).

A very different process took place on the fringes of the Russian continental empire with its continuous territory. Whenever the Russian Empire, in its long history of expansion, conquered and settled new territories, it did so not on some far-away coast but directly beyond its established borders. One of Russia's tactics to control the newly won land and its inhabitants was to integrate the local ruling class into imperial structures and to secure their local power and freedom of action (Löwe 2000; Manz 2003: 91; Sunderland 2004: 41). If the elite in this newly conquered land was not Russian by origin, it became Russified in time, often not even by force but in order to be socially upward mobile in the structures of the Russian state (Kappeler 2000: 96). In contrast, the new elite in overseas empires was dependent on their European metropole. They payed taxes to the king, but neither were they politically represented in their respective capitals, nor did they have a chance to rise up the social ladder of the colonizing states. They were trapped in dependence in their colonial outposts. Although local elites might have been indispensable to keep up stability in the colony, they were never even considered for a career in the empire's metropolis. This made it very intriguing for local elites to call for the creation of a new, local identity that would justify the creation of new, independent states (Anderson 2006: 48–50).

With the rise of capitalism and the accompanying need for a standardized education, the careers of young elites began to be channeled inevitably through centers of learning and administration. Anderson calls these journeys of future elites "pilgrimages" (2006: 121). In these "pilgrimages" lays the crucial difference between the overseas empires of Western European powers and the continental empires of Central and Eastern Europe. The elites of Peru or Indonesia traveled from the far ends of these colonies to Lima or Batavia to hone their qualifications, but never to Amsterdam or Madrid. In the destinations of their pilgrimages they met their peers from the same colony who might have been culturally very different from them, but who received the same education through the same standardized language and eventually joined the same colonial elite. Their common interest was the formation of an all-embracing Peruvian or Indonesian identity on which they could base their struggle for independence from an exploitative colonial center.

The continental empires in the 19th century provide a glaring contrast: Here, access to the imperial elite for young socially upward mobiles from the provinces was granted by travelling to the imperial center, to Moscow and St. Petersburg, to Istanbul or to Vienna, and by receiving an education in the language dominant there. Their journey (their *pilgrimage*) is perhaps best captured by Ernest Gellner's (1983: 58–63) "lads from Ruritania" who received their education in the capital of Megalomania, the imaginary empire of which Ruritania is an obscure and linguistically foreign periphery. If they had wanted, they could have assimilated to the culture of Megalomania, as many of their compatriots did. Unlike the young lads in Batavia or Lima, the Ruritanians who became teachers and journalists in the capital of Megalomania did not recognize their *commonality* with other lads from other peripheries who had come to the capital with the same goals. Instead, they discovered how *different* their Ruritanian background made them. Aside all their heartfelt sympathy with the simple Ruritanian culture (the *Narodniki* of Russia come to mind), the few educated Ruritanians eventually understood that in an independent Ruritania they would be able to secure much better posts than most of them could hope for in Greater Megalomania, where they had to compete with scholastically more developed ethnic groups. This was when the Ruritanian intellectuals and their peers from other peripheral areas in the empire started to mobilize the masses, along cultural *differences*.

So already before ethnicity became the dominant criterion for the allocation of power, there were big differences between the territories of overseas empires and those of continental empires such as Russia: The emerging elites in overseas colonies had to stress *commonality* in order to gain momentum for an independence movement (Anderson 2006: 47–67) the emerging elites from the fringes of continental empires had to stress how *different* they were from the imperial center and from the inhabitants of other peripheral regions (Gellner 1983: 58–62). It is these diverging interests of emerging 19th century elites that we can still trace in the differing conceptions of ethnicity in Western Europe and in the former Soviet Union. When nationality became an administrative category, the emphasis on commonality began to translate into a civic concept of belonging whereas the emphasis on cultural difference began to be translated into an ethnic definition of nationality.

In overseas colonies and in the New World especially, linguistic differences disappeared, not instantly, but as a gradual concession to social mobility. New arrivals had to learn and pass on the lingua franca of the region, simply in order to have a chance to participate in the emerging labor market. The lingua franca was usually the language of the former colonists. When revolutions hit the aristocratic states in Western Europe, the concept of a civic nation that paid little attention to cultural difference, served as a model. A similar concept had already proven victorious in the American Revolution. In France, the nation came to be understood as a group of people who, independently of the cultural differences between them, expressed the will to live in a community and draw their identity from shared struggles and common achievements (Renan 2006). In this conception of the nation, cultural differences, as they existed between Paris and its peripheries, were not necessarily an obstacle to a sense of national community. However, most inhabitants of France in the late 19th century had hardly any historical education or consciousness and therefore no idea of common achievements or struggles, which, according to Renan, hold the nation together. Awareness for history and the awareness that society had evolved and will evolve in the future had first to be popularized, before it could serve identity building (Tonkin 1992: 10). National identity had to be brought to the masses in a slow but steady didactic campaign, possible only with the advent of compulsory public schooling (E. Weber 1976: 110). This process contributed to the withering away of cultural and especially linguistic differences. Around 1870, Eugen Weber (ibid.) estimated every fifth Frenchman did not understand the French standard language. Public schooling helped them to pick up some French, but as soon as they left school, they would switch back into their local *patois*. The French state of the 19th and early 20th century worked on diminishing cultural difference and to create a culturally relatively homogenous national community, as which France, and most of its neighbors, appear today.

The Russian Empire, for most of its existence, has put some effort in russifying the elites of its non-Russian territories. In order to russify the rural masses, however, the assimilatory force of the empire was not sufficient. In Bessarabia, for instance, the presence of the state in the 19th century was simply too weak to create public schools and impose its ideas on villagers (Grek and Russev 2011: 86; Cusco 2017: 56). In an 1827 law that ordered the establishment of schools in Bessarabian towns, the law's author claims there were no more than four schools in the entire oblast.[4] 70 years later, the census of 1897 showed that in the guberniya of Bessarabia only about 22% of men and 9% of women could read and write. Illiteracy was especially high among the rural orthodox population, by far the biggest group of Bessarabia's inhabitants. Among the Orthodox population only 16% of men and 4% of women were literate. Other groups that organized education around their religious institutions had far higher rates of alphabetization; among Jews 50% of men and 24% of women were literate, among Protestants it was even 66% and this among men as well as women (Troynitskiy 1905: XIX). So in education, religious institutions were still stronger than the state, which could potentially have served as a force of Russification.

Ethnic differences as something wider than confessional differences came to the attention of the imperial authorities when the idea of nationalism intruded all the big empires of Europe. Now the imperial elites, themselves multi-ethnic conglomerates, had to deal with national aspirations of their subject peoples. These were based on the cultural differences which many within the imperial elite had given up in order to join this class. In contrast to confessional groups and their champions, these new ethno-national movements demanded not just the freedom to exercise their specific way of life, they also demanded that their ethnic group should be the one to delegate the ruling class within a country regarded as the ancestral ethnic homeland. A distinction to be made here is between the ethnic groups with their own historic aristocracy, which eventually took on a decisive role in the nationalistic avant-garde, and the "peoples without history" who had no aristocracy of their own (Hroch 1968: 120). In such cases, well-educated groups like the "lads from Ruritania" were the main force behind nationalist mobilization. This latter category

4 Ob uchrezhdenii Uchilishch v Bessarabskoy oblasti. *Polnoe sobranie zakonov Rossiskoy imperii* (PSZ). SPB. 1830 Sobranie II. T.I. (1827) Nr 1520, 08.11.1827: <http://nlr.ru/e-res/law_r/search.php> (23.02.2019).

would include the Ukrainians. For an empire, their demands of political and cultural autonomy could only mean break-up into sovereign nation states. This demand, from the perspective of the imperial center, could not be just administered like religious diversity. It was a direct challenge to the legitimacy of the empire and therefore needed to be repressed. Advocates of national self-determination were directly targeted, and the existence of the ethnic groups aspiring nationhood was simply denied.

When, in this situation, the Bolshevik revolutionaries took power in Russia, there was immediate danger that the country would be fragmented into an unclear number of aspiring nations. Whoever wanted to rule the former empire as a whole needed to make concessions to those who had their priorities set on the self-determination of their ethnic group. Therefore, the Bolsheviks, from the very moment of their coming into power, advocated the principle of national self-determination. Even though most communist theoreticians saw nationalism as a bourgeoisie ideology, they appealed to a sense of national solidarity in order to mobilize a following (Connor 2011: 8). This did not mean they shied away from ruthless oppression of those national leaders who demanded more self-determination than served the purpose of the Soviet government. But in the first two decades of Soviet power, national languages and national symbols were used to firmly establish the rule of the Communist Party in most areas of the former Russian Empire (Wanner 1998: 16; Spolsky 2004: 116; Popov and Kuznetsov 2008: 226).

In Central and Eastern Europe, the Entente's victory in World War I entailed the redrawing of state borders on the territories of Germany, the Habsburg, and Ottoman Empires. Although the Entente was dominated by civic nations, their governments declared the ideology of national self-determination the guiding principle in reshaping the map of Central and Eastern Europe. But national aspirations in the disintegrating Habsburg and Ottoman Empires were based on ethnic nationalism that stressed the periphery's difference from the former imperial centers and that included or excluded people not by their will to belong to a nation, but by their cultural characteristics, above all the language they spoke. Especially in those linguistic groups, which prior to World War I had been divided between several states, the linguistic principle dominated nationalist rhetoric (Barbour 2000: 15). State boundaries, according to nationalist movements, should correspond as closely as possible to linguistic and cultural boundaries (Gellner 1983: 1). It took another two and a half decades and millions of deaths in war and genocide to come to the painful conclusion that cultural boundaries cannot be turned into clear-cut state-border-type boundaries except by the use of massive violence. It was this devastating experience that made civic nationalism the favored concept in Western Europe. Even in nations such as Germany or Italy, once claimed to be held together by their ethnic unity, a civic concept of inclusion eventually prevailed after the experience of World War II.

From the late 1960s onwards it became increasingly clear within the social sciences that ethnicity, even outside the civic nations of Western Europe, was a fluid and constantly changing concept. Anthropologists and historians became more interested how this concept was used than what it actually was. The social *function*, not the cultural *content* of ethnicity became the focus of scholarly inquiries. As a consequence of this shift of attention, the process of maintaining ethnic boundaries also became an interest. In 1969 Fredrik Barth showed that even though ethnic groups were perceived as discrete entities, their boundaries were very permeable and did not necessarily correspond closely to cultural traits. But in the post-war Soviet Union, ethnicity was used as an administrative category, a function for which it was essential that it was considered objectively ascribable. Barth's notion of the permeability of ethnic boundaries would have been highly corrosive for ethnicity's bureaucratic functions. Therefore, the political and administrative function that ethnicity fulfilled in the multi-ethnic Soviet Union, can partly explain, why it came to be seen as a firmly bounded and tangible entity by Soviet scholars.

2 Self-Identification vs. Ascription—Who Gets to Draw Ethnic Boundaries?

In Bessarabia, most people can swiftly answer the question which ethnic group they belong to. This is surprising, because according to the way ethnicity is studied by most local specialists, ethnicity is something that is inherited by every person from his or her parents. Yet many inhabitants of Bessarabia have parents of different ethnic backgrounds, and often these parents themselves were born already into mixed ethnic families. Also, some people change their ethnic identity during the course of their lives. For instance in Izmail, the share of those who identify as Ukrainians instead of Russians has increased by 7% between the two censuses of 1989 and 2001, without disproportional migration or growing birth rates of one group.[5] Much greater fluctuations have been documented elsewhere in the former Soviet Union (Gorenburg 1999).

5 Ukrainian census of 2001, results published online: <http://2001.ukrcensus.gov.ua/rus/results/nationality_population/nationality_popul1/select_51/?botton=cens_db&box=5.1W&k_t=51&p=25&rz=1_1&rz_b=2_1%20&n_page=2> (23.02.2019).

Chapter seven retraces the narratives that serve to keep ethnic bondaries clear-cut in Bessarabia in detail. But what can be forestalled here is that in order to keep up the assertion that ethnicity is a scientific category that every individual belongs to by birth, one can simply claim that those people, who actively chose their ethnic belonging, are ignorant about what they *really* are or ought to be by scientific standards. The paradigm of objective verifiability of ethnic belonging in case of doubt favors ascription from the outside over potentially wrong self-identification. Francisco Gil-White (2001: 517) uses the metaphor of the ugly duckling to analyze the assumption that ethnicity is *inside* everyone. In the tale of the ugly duckling, a swan's egg by accident ends up in a duck's nest. The young swan is raised among ducks who are, like the hackling himself, ignorant about his true nature. Everyone takes him for a duck, if an ugly one. Only when he grows up he reveals his true nature as a swan (supposedly superior to a duck) exposing everyone's mistake. Neither the fact that the swan talked and walked like a duck, nor everyone's belief in him being a duck turned him into one. When we essentialize ethnic identity we run the danger of retelling the fairy tale of the ugly duckling. If social scientists ascribe ethnic belonging in the believe of a scientifically determinable essence of ethnicity, if they claim the right to tell people what ethnic group they *actually* belong to, they lose two of their crucial arguments: One is the "native's point of view," which to grasp has been the goal of ethnographic research since Bronislav Malinovski laid out the principles of ethnographic fieldwork (1932: 25). This notion would forbid social scientists to decide by their own standards what group their informants *actually* belong to. Ironically, the other argument we lose, is the self-identification of people as a crucial ingredient in most Soviet definitions of ethnos (Kozlov 1974).[6]

Although ethnic identity in many cases seems to be chosen from a range of possible ethnic identities, many informants in Bessarabia seem to think of ethnic belonging as something quite obvious. This interpretation may stem less from individual experience than from an academic tradition that sees ethnicity as a clearly defined scientific category, the existence of which demands no further proof. It is rather objectively derivable from a list of traits every person exposes. Many of the traits on the fluctuating "shopping lists of criteria," such as common language, common religion, a belief in a common ancestry, and a sense of belonging together, have become rather ambiguous in recent decades, even in rural Bessarabia. Now, many people, independently of their ethnic

6 All Soviet definitions of 'Ethnos,' mentioned in this chapter rely on the self-identification criterion see Bromley (1980: 153), Bromley and Podol'niy (1990: 17), as well as Shirokogorov's 1922 definition, cited in Tishkov (1997: 2).

origin, speak Russian from their early childhood on. Also, many people do not practice any religion at all, and many of those, who are religious, practice a recently adopted faith, such as Baptism or Adventism. Furthermore, many people do not live in the place they or their ancestors were born in, and they might feel a stronger sense of community towards their ethnically mixed neighbors, colleagues, or politically likeminded, than they do towards the people to whom they are supposed to feel an ethnic tie. As discussed above, inventory list definitions of ethnicity fail when taken to different places. But if the traits on the inventory list wither away over time, we also have to conclude that such ethnicity definitions fail when followed back in time. Each of the above phenomena; linguistic assimilation, religious conversion, migration, and cross cutting ties, have accelerated in recent decades, but they are by no means new. It is not just since two or three generations that some people speak different languages than their ancestors did. Religious practices too have been subject to change before and migration over great distances and across all kinds of borders has laid the very fundament of Bessarabia's ethnic mosaic. In other words, ethnicity was probably never objectively derivable from a list of cultural traits. Therefore, shopping list type definitions of ethnicity neither work very well to unambiguously delimit one group from its neighbors nor can they delimit a period in the past when the "real" ethnic boundaries were still allegedly watertight.

3 State-Approved Concepts of Ethnicity in Post-War Soviet Academia

Soviet academia managed to create influential studies of ethnicity and pervasive theories of what ethnicity is, how it occurred and what it brought about. The influence of these theories, however, remained largely limited to the Soviet and post-Soviet region (with the notable exception of China (Gorenburg 1999: 556) and a limited impact on German ethno-history in the 1970s (Wernhart 1998)). Sergey Sokolovskiy (2012: 30–31) identifies two reasons for this curtailed influence: For one, the Marxist focus on 'objective realities' devaluated everything subjective and individual and sternly stuck to phenomena believed to be 'universal' and 'independent of observation,' which often impeded realistic descriptions. On the other hand, Soviet ethnography, isolated from new paradigms developed in the West, was also repeatedly diagnosed with absence of critical debate and therefore uncritical acceptance of received wisdoms (Skalnik and Krjukov 1990: 158; Tishkov 1992: 371; Sokolovskiy 2012: 31). This academic climate that preferred "objective reality" and despised its critique was liable to produce essentializing and primordial ideas of ethnicity.

The outcome should, however, not be confused with the intention. Neither the founders of the Soviet Union nor its pioneering social scientists wanted to essentialize ethnicity. The effect was an unintended consequence of a well-meant approach to address every ethnic group with a tailor-made policy. To avoid the reproach of an imperial russifying campaign among the Soviet Union's non-Russians, Soviet nationality policy, before Stalin's return to Russification in the late 1930s, ascribed ethnic identities to everyone along with the according language and culture. The rigid primordialism among social scientists of the later Soviet Union was one of the legacies of the early Soviet nationalities policy (Martin 2000: 168).

One of the reasons why Soviet ethnicity theories took roots so easily outside academia, in a broader public sphere, is that essentializing ethnicity is a rather intuitive train of thought. It is similar to our well-exercised categorization of species and substances that we also essentialize according to their hidden properties. These are usually generalizable to other items of the same category (i.e. all birds lay eggs, ceramic breaks easily, no matter whether it comes as a plate or a jar) (Gil-White 2001: 524). Therefore, essentializing theories, such as those dominant in the Soviet Union, are much easier received in a non-academic environment than counter-intuitive constructivist theories.

Since the disintegration of the Soviet Union, and the partial opening of the field to paradigm shifts, few new ideas on the nature of ethnicity have been put forward in Russian speaking academia, let alone in the public discourse. Social anthropology in post-Soviet countries has been diagnosed with a severe crisis, mainly for the tenacious preference of primordialism, for a lack of critical examination of authoritative Soviet theories, and for a persistent indifference for the present, while desperately seeking to document vanishing "traditional" societies (Tishkov 1992, 2003: 30–33; Sokolovskiy 2003: 4). Valeriy Tishkov compared post-Soviet ethnography with Moscow after it burned to the ground. Just like this calamity eventually led to the beautification of the city, ethnography eventually emerged strengthened from the collapse of Soviet institutions (Tishkov 2003: 29). This cathartic renewal, however, was very insular within the discipline and it almost completely failed to spread the word to a broader public.

The crisis of the Soviet social sciences was not caused by progressing scholarly concepts, but by the radical change of the ideological environment after the disintegration of the Soviet Union. Along with Perestroika came a rearrangement of the terminology of social sciences. Some terms were dropped altogether because they had become anachronisms (the Soviet people, proletarian internationalism), some were reinterpreted (social class, assimilation, race) and others newly entered the scholarly vocabulary (ethnicity, discourse, habitus, deconstruction, narrative) (Sokolovskiy 2003:4–13). But the renewal of the discipline is a slow process and has progressed furthest in academic centers of Moscow and St. Petersburg. In provincial centers of learning it has limited effects. There, by and large, Soviet ethnicity theories still appear to be widely in use. Therefore, this is perhaps a good place to have a closer look at them. Doing so, my attention will be directed at the connection of the Soviet state as an aggregate of planning institutions, relying on clearly defined categories, and the liability of Marxist-Leninist sociological theories to be interpreted in an essentialized way.

Soviet social sciences have gone into academic isolation during late Stalinism, and missed many paradigm shifts in Anglo-Saxon and French scholarship of the post-war decades. Before this isolation took effect, the German *Völkerkunde* was the most influential school in Russia (Vermeulen 1995: 48). Ethnography was mainly concerned with folk culture and customary life in Soviet society and secondary with the culture of non-writing peoples (Sokolovskiy 2003: 4). Ethnography in the Soviet Union never emerged as a discipline in its own right. It was a sub-discipline of history (Kuznetsov 2008: 30), the task of which was to describe the different stages of development through which human societies pass (Petrova-Averkieva 1980: 19). This disciplinary arrangement has remained largely intact after the Soviet Union's break-up (Tishkov 2003: 32).

In the post-war years, Soviet ethnography was modeled after the art genre of Soviet realism. It should provide descriptions of how the people of the Soviet Union, even in the most remote corners of the country, managed to overcome obstacles and collaborated in order to build communism. Leading Soviet ethnographers saw themselves as the builders of communist society rather than its chroniclers (Haber 2014: 194–211). Soviet ethnography studied ethnic group by ethnic group. The ethnic group (ethnos) was the very subject of the discipline's scholarly endeavors (Tokarew 1954: 7; Bromley 1980: 152). Specialists emerged for each such group. So it was not just ethnic groups that were conceptualized as clearly bounded entities, also the discipline that studied them became structured by ethnic boundaries. The relation, in which the discipline stood to the studied subject, could lead only to circular definitions: The academic discipline of *Etnografiya*, was busy defining and redefining the category of ethnos, while the discipline itself was defined as the study of ethnos (Skalnik and Krjukov 1990: 184). In the ethnographic museum, different showcases with different ethnic groups structured the exhibitions. Ethnographic encyclopedias, atlases, and library catalogues followed the same structure, in short:

> In the Soviet social sciences, ethnicity is viewed as absolutely "natural," an "independent variable" and a primary cause of phenomena. The emergence and existence of ethnic groups is a crude social fact, and such groups are classified as "ethnosocial organisms" or "biosocial communities" (Tishkov 1992: 380).

During the peak of Soviet ethnography's influence in the 1970s and 80s two figureheads of Soviet social science can be singled out as the ones shaping ideas of ethnicity that still retain a deep influence in academia as well as in wider society: One is Yulian Bromley (1921–1990), director of the institute of ethnography at the Soviet Academy of Sciences from 1966–89. Bromley not only reached the heights of Soviet academia, he also was widely read by a broad readership after he created volumes suitable for community libraries. The colorfully illustrated *Created by Mankind* (1984) and *Mankind- That's Peoples* (1990) he coauthored with the journalist Roman Podol'niy who specialized in popularizing scientific findings. The second figurehead of ethnos theory did not have this sort of institutional backing: Lev Gumilev (1912–1992), a historian and geographer who came up with the concept of *impassionedness* to explain the rise and fall of ethnic groups was widely popular among readers, but never got a firm foothold in a Soviet university (Bassin 2016: 2; Naarden 1996: 54). Gumilev preferred his own brand of social Darwinism over the dominant paradigm of Soviet historiography; historical materialism (Mühlfried and Sokolovskiy 2011: 12). Both scholars remain influential but controversial among social scientists in Russian speaking audiences. Part of the controversy around them is doubtless that their theories can be read and indeed often are read to anchor primordial or even racist concepts of ethnic groups. Therefore both theoreticians can be easily used, and indeed often are used, to justify nationalist sentiment.

The two men and their theories were connected by the central concept of "ethnos." "Ethnos" can be translated as "ethnic group" but not without partial loss of its meaning. Thus exploring the two theories and their liability to primordialism should be commenced with an attempt to give a more adequate translation of what the concept of "ethnos" contains. The term has been in use in Soviet ethnography since the beginning of the 20th century. The Ukrainian ethnographer Nikolai Mohilyanskiy, already in 1909, defined ethnos as the "object of ethnographic research" (cited in Bromley 1983: 10). Early attempts to create an all-encompassing definition for ethnos as a category were undertaken by Sorbonne-trained ethnographer Sergey Shirokogorov in the first years after the October Revolution. He worked in the Far East of the newly founded Soviet Union. Shirokogorov attempted to create a typology of different kinds of ethnos, an endeavor that after World War II might have well suited Soviet social science. But Shirokogorov was ahead of his time and fell from grace. He had to flee to China. There, he continued to publish, but lost his influence on Soviet academia. The definition for ethnos that he came up with in 1922, became influential in Russian speaking academia only after it resurfaced in Bromley's works. For Shirokogorov an ethnos was:

> A group of people speaking the same language, who recognize their shared heritage, and have a shared complex of social mores, modes of life, retained and sanctified traditions which differentiate them from other such groups (cited in Tishkov 1997: 2).

The influence of this ethnos-definition lies not so much in the first part, where the author specifies which traits group members must share to count as an ethnos, it lies in the second part, where the author names the properties these shared traits must have, so that they can define an ethnos-type group. Traditions that hold an ethnos together and notably differentiate them from other groups should be *retained and sanctified.*

Another very influential definition, strikingly similar to Shirokogorov's ethnos definition, was Joseph Stalin's definition of the nation (*natsiya*), a term that has often been used interchangeably with "natsional'nost'" and "ethnos" (see for example Tokarew 1954: 16; Kushner 1951: 16). Stalin formulated it while he held the office of People's Commissar of Nationalities Affaires, not long before Shirokogorov fell from grace.

> A nation is a historical constituted, stable community of people, formed on the basis of a common language, territory, economic life, and psychological make-up manifested in a common culture (Stalin 1994: 20).

Stalin's definition is certainly more materialistic and his is not a *sanctified set of traditions* but a *psychological make-up.* However, the similarity between Stalin's concept of a nation and Shirokogorov's idea of ethnos lies in the stressing of *stability.* Both concepts rely on the idea that a group can only be recognized as an entity if it has been such for a long time. This assumption also makes it difficult to imagine the formation of new groups of the same quality in the present. Defining ethnicity as an objectively ascertainable category with deep historical roots perfectly justified the inscription of ethnicity in a person's passport. To register an ethnos-type identity, however, also entailed the assumption that people everywhere would naturally self-identify with one (and preferably only one) stable, ethnos-type category. The prerequisite of self-identification is perhaps the major hitch to the theory. Only with a common self-identification, a group of people could become a "social organism" such as an ethnos. Historically, argued Bromley and his followers, this self-identification derived from kinship ties, however distant they might have grown over time (Kozlov 1974: 85–89). The present identification with a territory was seen as having grown out of an earlier identification with a common ancestor. Once perceived as the natural environment of one's kin, the territory assumed a more important place in ethnic identification as kinship ties grew more distant (Kozlov 1971: 93). Due to their doctrine that the origin of ethnic ties had to be sought in kinship, Soviet ethnicity theories had trouble dealing with mixing ethnic identities and their gradual transformation. Bromley admitted that a person could have more than one ethnos-type identity (Bromley and Podol'niy 1990: 18). A person could for example be Russian as well as Ukrainian if he or she exhibited traits typical for both these ethne. He however thought that this could be the case not without a special justification and that a person could have no more than two ethnic identities (Bromley 1983: 48). Bromley further argued that endogamy within the ethnos was the rule and reinforced the uniformity of people within the ethnos (1990: 21). In other writings, where Bromley experimented with the metaphor of an organism that grows and gathers strength and becomes ill and dies, endogamy within the ethnos became a "survival strategy" for the ethnic organism (Tishkov 1997: 9). The instinct to follow this survival strategy was presupposed by other Soviet ethnographers too. Even if people in the group were not aware of it, they still strived for its survival (Arutyunyan 1974: 93).

If ethnos-type belonging was seen as an ancient and inherited trait, one that was objectively determinable and stuck with a person, if interethnic marriage was seen as an exception from the rule, a rule that ensured survival of the ethnos, then consequently, inside the ethnos, some traits were shared between all members and passed on from one generation to the next. One such trait that Bromley treated with meticulous attention was the "ethnic character." An ethnic character was thought to be more than just the sum of cultural traits. It was a whole system of psychological properties that interacted with one another to create traits, unique to each ethnos (Bromley and Podol'niy 1990: 106–108). The authors considered the fact that a psyche cannot exist outside the individual and that therefore a group of people, such as an ethnos, cannot host a psyche or a complexion like a human being. They insisted, however, that the "social collective" of the ethnos acted to stress certain characteristic traits while it disguised others. The result was the observable ethnic character of an ethnos. Bromley, as did his rival Lev Gumilev, traced differences in ethnic characters to the environment in which the ethnos was formed once upon a time.

4 Gut Feeling and Folk Theories of Ethnicity

Lev Gumilev, the second theoretician who wrote extensively about ethnos, became a best-seller after the collapse of the Soviet Union (Naarden 1996: 54; Bassin 2016: 2). His theories were also widely introduced in school and university curricula, broadly discussed in the media, and constantly cited by politicians (Shnirel'man 2006: 8,16). His relevance for the ethnicity concepts that can be found in post-Soviet societies lies therefore more in the folk theories since Perestroika than in his influence over academia. His breakthrough as a widely read academic came only after his breakthrough as writer of popular science. Just as the academically more successful theories of Yulian Bromley, Gumilev saw ethnicity as one of the most durable and fundamental categories of human organization. It was neither free for choice nor could it be disposed of. No person could live outside of an ethnos (Bassin 2016: 23). Gumilev was predominantly interested in the occurrence and disappearance of ethnos-type groups throughout the course of history. This interest already suggested that entities that came to shape history, such as the "Romans," the "Greeks," or the "Tatar-Mongols" were all of the ethnos-type. An assumption that exposed Gumilev's theories to an obvious critique; that he used the modern concept of ethnos and insinuated that ancient peoples fitted that concept. Gumilev used to sweep such criticism away by stating that so far science knew next to nothing about ethnos and the nature of this phenomenon (Gumilev 2002: 31). Therefore, lack of evidence that such a type of social communion has existed for a very long time was not a hint that it was a modern phenomenon. Rather, this lack of evidence, for Gumilev, illustrated how sketchy our knowledge about ancient peoples was. He himself defined ethnos as a phenomenon on the boundary between the social sphere and the biological sphere that played a crucial role in the texture of the biosphere of the earth (Gumilev 2002: 38). Gumilev believed that an ethnos of such kind was a living being that ran on "geo-bio-chemical energy" and that obeyed "the second law of thermodynamics" (cited in Shnirel'man 2006: 8). Instances of rapid expansion of an ethnos at a particular time in history, Gumilev attributed to outpourings of cosmic energy (Naarden 1996: 76).

Thus, part of the popularity Gumilev enjoyed in the Perestroika years and especially after his death in 1992 may be due to his effort to answer in one sweep some of the most difficult questions of the humanities, using concepts of natural sciences (Shnirel'man 2006: 8). Gumilev's writings were also appealing for Russians because he described the ethnic groups of the Soviet Union and the former Russian Empire as ethnically unique but at the same time held together by a fundamental cohesion (Bassin 2016: 4). Another part of the fascination of the Russian speaking audience with Lev Gumilev is certainly his family background and his tragic biography. Lev Gumilev was born in 1912 to parents who were both renowned poets, Nikolai Gumilev and Anna Akhmatova. His father Nikolai was executed by the Soviet secret police in 1922, his mother struggled with repression and censorship for the rest of her life. Lev Gumilev spent decades in prisons and in Siberian Gulags for the sake of his family background (Naarden 1996: 54–59). In the Gulag he lived among representatives of Turkic speaking peoples of the Soviet Union. These cellmates triggered a special interest in theoretical works on why, at some times, small and obscure groups would quickly develop into the rulers of whole continents. Gumilev's quest for explanations to such phenomena also led him to turn away from the humanities and to natural science (Gumilev 2002: 29). Concepts borrowed from physics and biology throughout his theory mostly serve as metaphors, but in part as actual explanations. The most famous concept that Gumilev came up with he called "impassionedness" (*passionarnost'*), coined on the base of the Latin root for "passion." Gumilev used this concept to explain why some groups at times develop quickly, seemingly out of nothing, and why at other times they decline. He saw it as the "factor X," that social sciences ignored so far, and therefore failed to explain the occurrence and decline of ethnos-type groups (ibid.: 302). Impassionedness, Gumilev thought, was tied to the amount of energy an ethnos can absorb. He believed that there are individuals and ethnos-type groups that at times become driven by impassionedness. They then experienced a higher degree of energy and inspiration that allowed them to commit heroic deeds. Other people however, according to Gumilev exhibited a phenomenon he named "subimpassionedness" (*subpassionarnost'*). They allegedly dragged energy from others and through decadence and parasitism led whole civilizations into decline. Rise and fall of an ethnos formed a repeating life cycle for each ethnos that reoccurs mechanically, steered more by cosmic forces than by human ideas and actions. All these assumptions made Gumilev's theories vulnerable to accusations of eugenics, favoring apartheid, and even fascism (Naarden 1996: 77).

The concept of impassionedness remained inconclusive, not despite but because Gumilev wanted to tie it to science. The idea of a physical or biological force that drives people and with them the ethnos to which they belong, stood in stark contrast to the historic materialism that formed the basis of all Soviet historiography. In Soviet social science, social change could be explained only through the lens of class struggle. People reformed the societies they lived in out of the desire to free themselves from the oppression of the ruling classes. In Soviet historiography, this struggle too led to a regular succession of stages of social evolution (a characteristic shared by Gumilev's theories (Naarden

1996: 72)). Only in historic materialism of the Soviet school, these phases did not amount to a circle but to a progressive line that found its destination when a society reached the final stage of communism. Therefore, a theory that explained social change by forces of nature and social evolution as a reoccurring cycle was clearly at odds with the established social sciences in the Soviet Union (Bassin 2016: 26). Gumilev, even in times he spent out of prison, had trouble finding employment, working many years as a librarian. He completed two doctoral theses, none of which was ever accepted by Leningrad State University and he was allowed to teach only in the department of geography rather than in his preferred discipline, history (Naarden 1996: 54–55).

His relationship with Yulian Bromley was strained. Bromley's main critique of Gumilev's work was that he failed, as before him did Shirokogorov, to differentiate between ethnos and biological populations (Bromley 1983: 20). Bromley and his followers saw a flawed geographical determinism in Gumilev's theories. One of the more outspoken among them, Viktor Kozlov (1971: 96), wrote that Gumilev put all his focus on how the environment shapes people, but neglected how people shape the environment. Another major difference between the two approaches was that unlike Bromley, Gumilev saw the ethnic self-designation of people who belong to one ethnos, the ethnonym, as something secondary. For him, endogamy was a far more important marker for the ethnos-type community (Shnirel'man 2006: 12). He warned that if contact between several ethnos became too frequent and if one ethnos would intermingle into the "ethnosphere" of others, the outcome would be a "Chimera," a perverted and uprooted hybrid being, bound for decline (Naarden 1996: 61). With his views on endogamy, Gumilev exposed himself to another strand of fierce criticism. He disregarded the basic distinction between norms and practices. For Gumilev, the existence of a norm for ethnic endogamy was sufficient to assume that people would actually largely follow this norm. In this matter, according to Shnirel'man (2006: 13), he relied on "stereotypes and anecdotes" instead of data. For Bromley, in contrast, endogamy within the ethnos was not a prerequisite, but a mere "survival strategy" of the ethnos. Regardless of their differences, both figureheads contributed to an idea of ethnos, as a discrete organism, a phenomenon of nature that existed objectively and independently of the opinions and desires of people. But that Bromley's theory became accepted in Soviet academia and Gumilev's did not, was due to their contrasting ideas about the forces that drive social change. In Bromley's theory, this force was class struggle, in Gumilev's it was impassionedness.

The esoteric idea of impassionedness very likely helped to propel the immense popularity of Gumilev's books after the disintegration of the Soviet Union. To post-Soviet readers, the impassionedness motive must have been a great comfort in uncertain times. It helped to interpret the current state of decline as a phenomenon of nature, rather than of human mismanagement. According to Gumilev's cyclical theory at the time of Perestroika, Western Europe was on its last legs, whereas the Russian ethnos could expect a renaissance (Naarden 1996: 79). The idea that the ethnos is at any time going through a certain phase, whether or not the individuals within the ethnos like it, has something deeply fatalistic to it. It frees the individual of responsibility in the development of society. A resurrection of the ethnos would come in its time, independently of the actual behavior of people. Gumilev's thinking also posed the Russian ethnos in a less humiliating position vis-à-vis the West. Russia had lost the Cold War due to the West's economic prowess. But Gumilev's theory stated that money cannot buy impassionedness. While the West had a culture corrupted by the quest for profit, Russia had a new chance to recollect its cultural roots, and gather new impassionedness.

The motive of impassionedness; that strikes like a force of nature, has also been used to describe ethnic revivals like the ones taking place in Bessarabia after the disintegration of the Soviet Union. It denies that ethno-nationalist revivals are the political agendas of rational actors. In some instances, representatives of ethnic organizations referred directly to Gumilev. In an interview with a counselor of the Moldovan Academy of Sciences, herself a Gagauz and a prolific writer about the Gagauz people in southern Bessarabia, when asked about her motivation to do research on that particular ethnic group, she replied:

> …my work here let's say in the realm of science and culture… Well, naturally the future belongs to this ethnos too, and naturally the soul aches, and one wants to do one's own share, by researching something, by presenting something, and there is indeed a need for books, because on something we need to educate our youth after all, and in the university too, so people will know their customs and traditions. If we don't work that out, like we do now, then people will ask for it, there is an urge. In my point of view that is the essential stimulus, that is, the stimulus is…, well, probably ethnic… That the ethnos is now in a stage of rise (pod'em) and this ethnic rise it is, it exists in every one of us and in the whole ethnos and we want to move it in order to achieve certain results.

I: So the ethnos is like… living?
R: A living organism.
I: A living organism?

> *R:* I think so yes, absolutely. Yes. I think that the ethnos is a living organism, as said Lev Gumilev, it has predefined stages, eeeeh... birth, growth, old age, and so on, and I think that the Gagauz today are in a stage, how to say, in a stormy, active stage, and they achieve many results.[7]

The idea of the ethnos as a living organism, for this informant seems to be more than just a metaphor. The motivation to invest energy and time in making the ethnos of the Gagauz and its history better known, for her stems from the urge to do it while it is worth doing so, while the ethnos is in a certain phase that will allow it to progress.

Another idea that surfaces in this informant's explanation is that there exists a link between all the members of the ethnos, whether or not they are aware of it. They all at the same time feel an urge to raise the ethnos onto a higher level and even if the informant herself would not take the initiative to find out more about the customs and traditions, the people of the ethnos would start asking for it. A person has a primordially defined place. Belonging to an ethnos and rising or declining along with it, is not seen as a matter of individual choice.

One obvious question that needs to be dealt with, then, is how people with multi-ethnic ancestry and ambiguous ethnic identities still can hold the idea that ethnic identities are primordial and unchangeable. After all, most people who grew up in mixed ethnic families, at some point in their life, either made a (rational) choice to identify with one or other of their ancestral ethnicities, or they remain undecided and choose their ethnic identity according to the situation. If for these people ethnic belonging is primordial, then ethnic identity should manifest itself naturally, instead of being an outcome of deliberation and choice. Such an experience was revealed in an interview with an Izmail arts teacher, a woman of mixed Ukrainian and Russian ancestry who grew up in Izmail. She struggled with her ambiguous identity until a decisive moment in her childhood at 13 or 14, when she traveled to Russia with her family. There, she instantly felt at home, because she perceived people as not always friendly but always honest. "None of these dodges, none of this diplomatic veiling, none of this craftiness!" Therefore, for the first time she felt she had come to her fitting environment: "You feel it simply. I felt so relaxed. I felt as if I had breathed..., this burden..., and this is because it is in me, in the blood, in the genes." She then sharply contrasted this experience of relief with annual visits to her Ukrainian relatives, whose hypocrisy she blamed on them being Ukrainian. There she felt foreign:

---

7 Interview in Chișinău, December 6, 2012.

> *I:* This is the side of your...?
> *R:* Mum, my Mum. And we traveled there practically every year, to Mum's relatives. And I felt as if..., well maybe from the age of 5..., that I am, as if not of that sort. Well, like a white crow. And, you know, this somehow makes you feel tense.
> *I:* Did they speak a different language there than in your home?
> *R:* No. No other language. We spoke Russian. I understood Ukrainian. It's not Chinese after all. It can be understood. But the mentality itself..., this is what it is about! It makes one tense, very much. When I traveled to Russia I was just astonished![8]

In this woman's memory it was clearly a matter of feeling rather than deliberation that led her to identify as Russian and not Ukrainian. The different mentality between the honest Russian and the crafty Ukrainians may be a stereotype, but in the informant's recollection they correspond to a personal experience. Such experiences become instrumental in the choice of ethnic identity which is not a choice for the informant but a discovery of what is already there in "the genes," "the blood," "the records." The same woman at an earlier occasion already had explained to me that she and others can simply feel that she is Russian. She used the expression that Russia was "where my blood calls me." Then she said that although she had hardly been to Russia, if people from Russia saw her, she would not even have to say a word, they could say right away, "ah one of us (*nasha*)! You must be Russian."[9]

Arguing with a personal feeling also can be found in the writings of an influential patron of a Bulgarian ethnic association, Anton Kisse. In his 2006 book *The Renaissance of the Ukrainian Bulgarians* he (unlike some of my informants) admits that villages with different ethnic populations nowadays look too much alike to tell ethnic differences: "Hardly someone can precisely say in what the Bulgarian settlements in Ukraine differ from those of our neighbors...," but then he goes on arguing he could sense what one cannot see: "I simply feel this difference intuitively, I sense and emotionally react to 'our own' area" (Kisse 2006: 35). A Bulgarian Policeman and a Ukrainian history teacher also both told me that they could easily spot their ethnic brethren in a crowd. Both these informants independently from one another insisted that one had to belong to the ethnic group to be blessed with this intuition. This assumption of course excludes all ethnic outsiders from the sensation and therefore cannot be tested. The notion of a personal feeling that tells a person where he or she belongs,

8 Interview in Izmail, January 25, 2013.
9 Interview in Izmail, January 21, 2013.

rules out any objection by outsiders that ethnic groups are constructed. In line with the mechanisms of exclusion, described in the previous chapter, an insider, then, can just cite a feeling that he or she and their ethnic in-group perceive, whereas the outsider can never even hope to experience it. Systematic and scientifically verifiable ethnic differences, as purported in theories of Bromley and Gumilev would demand that these can be verified by different observers at different times. Referring to a subjective feeling that indicates to which ethnic group one belongs and where one is at odds, excludes scientific procedures such as intersubjective verification.

5 Grand Scheme Planning and the "Primordial Trap"

The link between theories with a claim to be scientifically verifiable and folk theories that can fall back on individual sentiment as evidence is that they both end up declaring primordial ethnic identities. In order to describe the theoretical dead-end all arguments that essentialize ethnicity are imperiled to get stuck in, I use the phrase "primordial trap." Soviet social sciences and most subsequent schools in post-Soviet countries repeatedly got stuck there. This is not only the fault of an academic discipline, but also of a political environment that has put heavy pressure on it (Tishkov 1992: 371). During the Soviet Union, the political environment demanded a theoretical framework that justified the use of ethnicity as an administrative category. Later, after the Soviet Union had disintegrated, the political environment in the former republics demanded a theoretical framework that justified ethnic nationalism. Theories stipulating an ethnic character that stuck to every person along with an ethnic identity, not only neatly justified the entry of ethnicity into a person's passport, they also facilitated the question how to approach ethnic diversity in the Soviet Union. Members of one ethnic group appeared to be united by a common origin and led by one motivation (Solonari 2003: 418). If one ethnic group was deemed, for instance unreliable for some reason or other, like the Gagauz and the Bulgarians during World War II, then everyone whose personal documents depicted this category could be treated in the same way. Each ethnic group was perceived as a learning organism during the long evolutionary process that ends with communist society and each is said to have developed a distinct character that makes it unique in the community of Soviet peoples (Shnirelman 2009: 114). Grand-scheme planning, the preferred mode of governance in the Soviet Union, would be infinitely more complex if state authorities would have to look whether each individual in fact exhibited a particular character or not. The proxy of ethnicity for reliability reduced decision making complexity.

This seemed especially helpful during the war, when many decisions entailed substantial risks. Categorization by ethnicity and other features may not have made Soviet administration fairer, but it certainly made it easier and cheaper.

The metaphor of a trap is fitting to discuss these theories, because they did not intentionally claim ethnicity was primordial or essential. One indication that there was no such intention is that Soviet ethnicity theories heavily rely on the concept of ethnogenesis. Soviet ethnographers closely collaborated with archaeologists and linguists to track down the history, the origins, and in some cases the disappearance and fusion of entities called "ethnos" (Bromley 1980: 160). For many ethnic groups, Soviet social sciences provided elaborate histories and precise indication at which point in time this group came into being. Soviet ethnography did therefore not claim ethnic groups had existed since times immemorial, or they were immune to change. It looked for explanations of why and when ethnic groups occurred. However, social sciences merely held an auxiliary position in the structure of institutions serving the state. One of the main tasks of Soviet ethnography was to delimit groups from one another and to ascribe a hierarchical status such as "ethnos" or "sub-ethnos" to each delimited group (Tishkov 1992: 373). This status then could be significant for the standing of the people who were registered as members of that group. In an authoritarian state, which built part of its power on such categories, to deconstruct them (as was meanwhile happening in Western social sciences), would have put the discipline at odds with party elites. Therefore, Soviet social sciences worked on constructing concepts of ethnicity that never explicitly named their essence, but implicitly assumed one.

The use of ethnicity as an administrative category not only allowed treating people of the same ethnicity in the same way, it also enabled the administration to treat people of different ethnicities in different ways. In Bessarabia, ethnic discrimination has occurred mainly during or directly following World War II. Justification for such unequal treatment only holds if these differences in alleged character are congruent with ethnic boundaries. Therefore, Soviet ethnicity theories came along with a strong, however unvoiced, reservation against the blending of ethnic groups. There was an equally strong distaste for the idea that people individually chose their ethnicity from a menu of possible ethnic identities. Bureaucratic categories are typically introduced so that people with certain givens can be treated in certain ways. Most such categories are not for choice, because state policies towards certain categories of subjects are meant to manipulate those subjects, they are not meant to *be manipulated by the subjects*. This is why, typically, people are not allowed to choose their age, gender, or tax class. By using ethnicity as a bureaucratic category, it was implicitly also imagined as something that individual people should not be allowed to choose or change.

Post-soviet countries inherited the ideas created and disseminated during a short but very intensive pedagogical campaign that took off after World War II but had passed its zenith in the Brezhnev years. The Soviet state that orchestrated this campaign had no incentive to disseminate concepts of ethnicity that would challenge its policies towards ethnic minorities or its bureaucratic practices.

What is more, besides some metaphysical polemics between the top shots of Soviet and Western social sciences there was little spirited exchange of ideas. Those Western scholars who seriously engaged with the findings of Soviet social research (good examples are the edited volumes by Dunn and Dunn 1974 and Gellner 1980) were often hampered by difficulties in gaining access to original Soviet data (Karklins 1986: 176). Without a serious impact of contrasting ideas from elsewhere, the highly centralized Soviet social sciences began ruminating their habitual concept of ethnicity. What eventually shook up this circle of self-reference was the demise of the Soviet economy and with it the Soviet state.

Besides serving the ideology of the Communist Party, the social sciences were themselves tied to grand scheme planning. Soviet ethnographers considered themselves social engineers dedicated to creating a communist society (Haber 2014: 197), and the work of ethnographers, like many other production processes, was scheduled in five year plans (as Kushner 1974: 212 indicates, lamenting ill-chosen research priorities in the projects planned for the five years to come).

Clear-cut categories were one of the most basic needs for a society engineered to fulfill centrally planned outcomes. Reading Soviet theoreticians, such as Kushner or Bromley, one sometimes gets the impression that their scholarly priority was the coining and delimitation of new categories. Each new category gave the discipline a claim to better understand society and to be able to offer finer tuned planning solutions. The concept of "legibility" of society comes to mind again. Because most states are a lot younger than the societies they administer, they need to introduce categories that enable them to "read" and eventually manipulate society (Scott 1998: 183). Programmatic thinkers in Soviet ethnography saw the discipline as a data generating machine in the pursuit of legibility and social engineering (Tokarew 1954; Kushner 1974). With the help of ethnicity statistics Kushner (1951: 18–19) wrote, administrative borders could be drawn more efficiently and school curricula developed according to local needs. Soviet scholars of ethnicity saw nothing wrong in catering to the state's need of "legibility." Most prominently they did so by creating hierarchically ordered categories of ethnic groups such as "superethnos," "ethnos," "sub-ethnos," "ethnikos," "ethnographic group," that were used along with other group categories such as "population" and "race" (split into three main subgroups, that were themselves split into 20 smaller groups that then branched into different "anthropological types"). All these categories were carefully defined by a list of characteristics attached to them. This social dimension of category building was paired by similarly bounded temporal categories such as the development stages "archaic," "slavery," "feudalism," "capitalism," and "socialism" (Bromley 1983: 14–43). Together these categories laid a grid plan of social theory over time and space. Each group at all times fitted into this grid in a specific way. Giving theoretical meaning to these categories enabled Soviet social sciences with a practical response to any problem of social engineering.

Soviet approaches, especially in the early years, strongly advocated a specific policy approach to each ethnic group in its own environment. Without the "legibility" created by social and historical categories the sheer complexity of administering a huge and diverse country towards very ambitious goals, would have simply been overwhelming. Soviet scholars such as Mikhail Sergeyev (1964: 487–492) freely admitted that categories had to be coined in order to be able to administer people. The problem in Soviet administration was not the creation and use of categories (no state can do without). The problem rather was the low degree of critical reflection upon these categories. In a state where criticism of official theories was punished, the theoretical model was increasingly taken for reality (Scott 1998: 196). If reality did not fit the theory, a new sub-category could be invented, or the contradiction could simply be denied. All ethnic groups somehow fit into the Soviet Union's grid plan, at least those inside the Soviet Union. For groups that claimed a similar status for themselves but did not fulfill the list of criteria set by the rule book, new categories substituted a discussion about the validity of established categories. The terms "ethnographic group"[10] and "sub-ethnos" were introduced to designate groups that were culturally different from an established ethnic category, but where it was inconvenient to establish a separate political approach.[11] Instead of revisiting established categories each case that did not fit created a new category. The Soviet social sciences thereby became a category coining machine and its theories became self-fulfilling prophecies. Theoreticians like Bromley

10 Still used a census category in 2001: <http://2001.ukrcensus.gov.ua/rus/regions/select_reg5/?box=5.5W&data1=1&rz=1_1&rz_b=2_1&botton=cens_db&k_t=51> (23.02.2019)

11 In Carpathian Ukraine the groups Boyko, Lemkos, and Hutsuls were sometimes described as "ethnographic groups," thereby acknowledging their cultural distinctness but denying them the status of a fully sovereign ethnos (Makarchuk 2008: 19). In Russia, the Don Cossacks or the Pomori of the White Sea coast have been described as "subethnos" of the Russian ethnos (Bromley and Podol'niy 1984: 19).

understood the pitfalls of essentializing ethnicity and he halfheartedly denied believing in an essential quality that was innate to all members of one ethnos (Bromley and Podol'niy 1990: 106). But the need for clear-cut categories in the grand scheme planning of the Soviet Union led to an academic preference of supposedly objective realities. Whenever this objectivity was challenged, Soviet scholars hurriedly invented new, allegedly clear-cut categories, and thereby renewed the claim they had found something that had already been there "independent of observation" and long before anyone realized. This reoccurring claim created a new, allegedly clear-cut category whenever the boundary between two already coined categories became too fuzzy. This claim lets the primordial trap snap shut. From the isolated Soviet academia, every theoretical attempt to deal with ethnic identities ended up here; sometimes more, sometimes less apologetic. It is certainly not an unusual process that scientists come up with ad-hoc modifications of their theories to prevent them from running into contradiction with new findings. Thomas Kuhn in his *the Structure of Scientific Revolutions* describes how a community of scientific practitioners adjusts their theories as long as somehow possible. The replacement of one paradigm with another is very costly and usually only worth the effort once the existing paradigm has run into an unresolvable crisis (Kuhn 1996: 68–78). The patching over of fuzzy social boundaries with newly coined categories in Soviet social sciences was informed exactly by this instinct. The repeated snap of the primordial trap was accepted as a cost, a cost not yet high enough to justify revising the dominant paradigm. This only became possible after a similar spirit of looking the other way in politics and economics brought down the entire Soviet system.

However, the road that led to the primordial trap was sketched out already before the Soviet ethnicity policy began to ascribe ethnic categories to individual people. Its roots are buried deep in the legacy of continental empires, where leaders of ethnic minorities insisted their groups were essentially different from all other groups in the empire and therefore needed to be governed by policies specific to this group and by leaders from within this group. This claim destabilized the Habsburg, Ottoman and Russian Empires so much, that Soviet bureaucrats decided they could guarantee stability and interethnic harmony only if they accepted ethnic differences as objective realities. In the Brezhnev era, the mere acceptance of allegedly objective realities turned into an increasingly desperate production of reality, a race to contain accelerating social change with the coining of ever new categories. Over time, the train of thought that ends in the primordial trap has become a distinctive folk theory.

CHAPTER 5

Ethnic Minorities and Soviet Newcomers

Ekaterina Chekal was 20 in 1953 when she took on the journey to Bessarabia leaving her native city in southern Ukraine to become a school teacher in the Gagauz village of Kotlovina. Some of the 46 students in her first cohort of pupils were only two years her junior and none of them spoke any Russian. The villages in southern Bessarabia had just gone through three decades of violence and deprivation caused by two world wars and the competition over Bessarabia between Romania and the Soviet Union. Nevertheless, the newcomer teacher and the village population eventually got to understand each other. In the years to come, Ekaterina instructed six-year-olds in Russian and from their chatter she quickly learned Gagauz. Until very recently, Gagauz ethnicity could have brought a man to the "labor front" into a coal shaft in the Ural, in Kazakhstan, or the Kuzbas industrial region. Ekaterina remembered people pointing out the uninhabited houses of those sent away. Now, education had become a highway to social mobility. Collaboration with Soviet newcomers, like school teachers, kolkhoz bosses, and army recruiters, was rewarded with stability and relative welfare. Under such circumstances, cultural differences were overcome quickly. Yet, ethnic boundaries were not forgotten. Quite to the contrary, they were a crucial instrument to turn the peasantry on the periphery into loyal Soviet citizens. The paradox that in the Soviet period cultural differences between ethnic groups were leveled, yet ethnic boundaries became more pronounced, is the subject of this chapter.

The Soviet period in southern Bessarabia lasted from August 1944 until the disintegration of the Soviet Union in December 1991, after which the region became part of independent Ukraine. The Soviet Union at the time of World War II had an already time-honored ethnicity policy that, compared with the Romanian ad-hoc policies, appeared downright fine-tuned. The USSR was the first state that ascribed one ethnicity to each and every of its citizens and made certain rights in certain places dependent on this category (Slezkine 1994: 415). However, the 47-year period of Soviet rule should not be portrayed as a monolith, even though it seems to be perceived as such by many in retrospect. There was a huge difference in standards of living between the beginning and the end of this period. The years of Stalinism until 1953 brought famine and deportations. Under the reign of Nikita Khrushchev (1953–64) Bessarabians began to enjoy the fruits of agricultural mechanization and education, benefits they had paid for dearly. Soviet citizens also began to perceive themselves as

 DOI:10.1163/9789004408029_006

contemporaries of- and participants in the construction of an ideal society, a society that found itself in conflict with foreign powers, trying to hamper the success of socialism. The long reign of Leonid Brezhnev (1964–82) and the short reign of his two geriatric successors, Yuri Andropov and Konstantin Chernenko (between 1982 and 1985) brought less innovation but in retrospect a kind of stability unknown to Bessarabians before and after. What is remembered now in Bessarabia as lost stability was by many perceived rather as stagnation (*zastoy*) at the time. Radical reforms by the last Soviet leader, Mikhail Gorbachev, should have revived the already moribund Soviet economy, but only accelerated the country's disintegration. The volatile times that followed from the late 1980s onwards are often remembered in sharp contrast to the years of stability in which those now in pension-age entered adulthood. The category of ethnicity accordingly changed its meanings throughout the Soviet period. Its persistent use in educatory and administrative institutions over the Soviet years formed the concept of ethnicity that remains meaningful for most people today.

1 Ethnicity and the Hierarchy of Trust in Post-War Southern Bessarabia

In southern Bessarabia, Soviet passports were introduced only in 1956 (Boneva 2006: 53). But ethnic belonging was registered well before. The Soviet use of ethnicity as an administrative category demanded that ethnic groups were clearly and exclusively bounded vis-à-vis other such groups. Belonging to an ethnic group in the Soviet Union could mean to profit from collective ethnic rights or to suffer from collective ethnic punishment. Therefore, in certain situations, very serious aspects of an individual biography could depend on one's belonging to a specific ethnic category. In Bessarabia, the most prominent historical example of the allocation of trust and mistrust along ethnic boundaries was the so-called labor front. When, with Romanian and German troops retreating, Bessarabia was again under firm Soviet control by late August 1944, lists of all men in the newly Soviet lands were produced swiftly. They served as the basis for conscription. Although the war against Germany was at that time far from over, not all able-bodied men were recruited to fight at the front. Some were sent to toil in mines and smokestack industries in the Ural, in the Donbas, in Siberia, and Kazakhstan. It seems, the decisive criteria by which a man was sent either west to fight, or east to work on the labor front, was ethnicity. Most men whose ethnicity was registered as Gagauz or as Bulgarian were sent to the labor front. Most men whose ethnicity was Russian, Ukrainian, or Moldovan were recruited into the Red Army.

In order to understand what happened to the Gagauz and Bulgarian villages in the first weeks after Soviet takeover, two contextual factors must be taken into account. The first of these is the wider Soviet practice of the *trudarmiya* (labor army), a euphemism for forced labor during World War II. It affected mainly people, who were seen as representatives of enemy nations or *neblagonadezhniy* (unreliable); Germans, Finns, Hungarians, and Bulgarians. They were forced to labor in industries and construction (Brandes, Sundhaussen, and Troebst 2010: 41–44, 281; Bulgar 2017). (However, my Bessarabian respondents never used the term "trudarmiya," referring to *trudovoy front* "labor front" instead).

The second factor that must be considered is the famine of 1946–47. A dry summer, a war devastated economy, and excessive grain exports were among the factors that caused this catastrophe. Although wide regions in southern Ukraine and Russia experienced food shortages in 1946–47, the village of Kotlovina, where all the factors causing the famine occurred simultaneously, was affected especially hard (Lebedenko and Tychyna 2002: 176–177). Some of the following examples indicate that the impact of famine in the first post-war years locally changed the meaning of forced labor. In the face of famine it was often not so much worse a fate to be far away from Bessarabia on the labor front, where food supplies were sufficient.

The case of Kotlovina,[1] a predominantly Gagauz village on the western bank of lake Yalpug sheds some light on the Soviet practice of recruiting soldiers and laborers by ethnic identity. Soviet administration of the village and the rayon of Reni, to which Kotlovina belongs, began in September 1944. The first local authorities were appointed (not elected) by army commanders. Soon thereafter a letter from the district's commander to the local authorities initiated recruitment among the male population.[2] The letter explained that every male citizen, born before 1927, was obliged to serve in the army and had to be sent to Reni, the rayon's administrative center, for basic military training. Detailed lists, produced by municipal authorities, reveal that there were 649 men in Kotlovina who fulfilled these criteria. However, two different lists were produced. The first one includes only 13 names.[3] All these men were between ages 18 and 36, and they were all ethnic Russians. According to the list, they were recruited to the 57th army to fight against Hitler on the 3rd Ukrainian Front. All the other 636 men of conscription age were registered in a separate

1 Kotlovina was until December 1944 still called by its pre-Soviet Name, Bolboka, Fr367 D3 Protokoly obshchikh sobraniy krest'yan sela za 1944–1945 god.
2 Fr367 D5 Spisok voennoobyazannykh po sel'skomu sovetu za 1944 god, p. 9.
3 Ibid., pp. 6–7.

list.[4] The list revealed their complete names, the time and place of their birth, their social status (*sotsial'noe polozhenie*),[5] their marital status and number of children, their civil profession, whether or not they had relatives abroad, and their ethnicity. All these men were registered as ethnic Gagauz. This list reveals no information about the fate of the men registered in it. Only interviews with some of the men still alive could clarify why there were two separate lists.[6]

Dmitri Petrovich Uzun, born in 1926, was sent to the labor front in 1944.[7] He was the son of a relatively well-to-do farmer, who was considered rich by the Romanians, but a *Kulak*, a class enemy, by the Soviets. His father was deported for being a *Kulak* in 1944. Dmitri Petrovich, however, was brought away with many other men, rich and poor, to eventually end up in Chelyabinsk oblast east of the Ural Mountains. Although they were brought there in box cars and without knowing where they were going, he did not see it as a deportation. In 1946 he was granted a leave and returned to Kotlovina. He found the family house occupied by strangers and the village descending into famine. He applied for a job at the village's newly founded kolkhoz, but was rejected for being a *Kulak's* son. Because of the famine looming over the village, Dmitri Petrovich easily persuaded his younger brother to follow him back to the labor front, where working hands were needed and where those who worked well ate well. He learned to speak Russian while working in the Ural and married his wife, also a native from Kotlovina, who had preferred to wait out the famine with relatives on the labor front.

4 Ibid., pp 12 ff.

5 *Sotsial'noe polozhenie* was another ascribed passport category in the Soviet Union since 1932, but it was dropped as a consequence of a passport reform in 1974 (Karklins 1986: 32).

6 The historian Stepan Bulgar conducted an archive study in 8 villages that nowadays belong to the ATU Gagauziya. He found a very similar pattern of mobilization like in Kotlovina. In each village a small minority of men was recruited into the Red Army and the large majority was sent to the labor front (Bulgar 2017: 41). In a 2016 article, Bulgar provides evidence that many Gagauz had been fighting in the war already since 1941 when they volunteered for recruitment to the Red Army before the German attack. Many of these men, he claims, were registered as ethnic Moldovans, Russians, or Ukrainians in part because recruitment officers had not heard about a group called Gagauz. The neglect to celebrate the heroism of these soldiers, S. Bulgar sees as the result of a deliberate "falsification of history" by nationalistic Moldovan historians (Bulgar 2016). Recruitment documents from 1941 that list men due to be recruited in the Moldovan SSR just weeks before the German attack, contain men of Gagauz and Bulgarian ethnicity. The lists also specify the number of "anti-Soviet elements." These, however, are listed as anti-Soviet, because they were former business owners, because they followed a "cult," or because they were classified *Kulak* (cited in Kashu 2014: 417). This would confirm Bulgar's claim that in the initial wave of recruitment in 1941, Gagauz and Bulgarians were recruited into the Red Army, but it also makes dubious his claim that they had to disguise their ethnicity in order to be recruited.

7 Interview in Kotlovina on July 12, 2013.

It is now common knowledge in villages like Kotlovina that recruitment for the labor front had something to do with ethnicity. When asked why the Gagauz were not sent to fight on the front, like most other men, Dmitri Petrovich and two of his sons who attended the interview, recollected a story that had happened before the Soviets retook the region. The story was widely told in the village and appeared in different versions. Apparently, a team of Soviet paratroopers were given the task to explore the southern bank of the nearby Danube River. They mistook longish Lake Yalpug that stands rectangular to the river for the Danube and parachuted into Kotlovina. One of the locals betrayed them when, at night, they came to the village to find out where they had landed. The Romanian army captured them. The further fate of these paratroopers is debated, but for Dmitri Petrovich and his family it was clear that this episode had made the Gagauz look like traitors and therefore unsuitable to fight at the front.

This story is a local explanation for a bigger phenomenon: Gagauz and Bulgarians across southern Bessarabia were unofficially counted as belonging to an "unreliable people" (*neblagonadezhnye narody*) and therefore sent to the labor front instead of the Red Army (Grek and Russev 2011: 98; Bulgar 2017).

In local terms the labor front was a form of conscription, not a form of punishment. Men did not go there in chains, but neither did they go voluntarily. Desertion was punished with harsh prison sentences (Bulgar 2017: 42). They were not told the reason why they had to toil, while their Russian, Ukrainian, or Moldovan neighbors had to fight, and they were never tried for treason or disloyalty. Ethnicity itself was a judgment. In exceptional cases men could be freed from their labor front obligations. So, this occurred in April 1945 when the Kisyani family in Kotlovina suffered the death of their mother, who left behind several young children. The village council acknowledged the family's severe situation and decided to write to the authorities in Chelyabinsk oblast, where the family father was serving on the labor front. In the letter, the village council pleaded to release Kisyani from the labor front so he could take care of his children.[8] In another incident, a respondent's grandfather, a Gagauz from the village of Chervonoarmeyskoe, was released for a month from his labor front duties near Lugansk, in order to bury his father. He never returned, but hid in the village until things blew over.[9]

Another labor front draftee, Valeriy Stepanovich Fuchedzhi, was born in 1928, just a few weeks too early to dodge recruitment in 1944.[10] He too was

8 Fr367 D6 Protokoly zasedaniya izpolkoma sel'skogo soveta za 1945 god, p. 13.

9 Interview in Izmail, October 14, 2013.

10 Interview in Kotlovina, July 13, 2013.

brought to Chelyabinsk oblast in a box car and without knowing where he was going. He named the number of 600 men who were brought away together with him, which fits the archived list of 636 labor front recruits quite well. Valeriy Stepanovich stayed at the labor front until 1954, working in a coal mine. In the meantime, he returned to Kotlovina twice for a leave. The first time he recruited his entire family to come to the Ural with him. In times of famine, they did not hesitate to leave behind their house and home. In the Ural industrial regions there was also a severe shortage of workers after the war. Therefore, recruiting his kin, gained Valeriy Stepanovich a bonus that allowed the family to buy a milk cow and fodder for an entire year. The milk provided a major contribution to the family's diet. On his second leave to Kotlovina, Valeriy Stepanovich chose a wife and married within a matter of days. He was 23 years old and wanted to marry a Russian girl in Chelyabinsk. But his mother, fearing that like many of his compatriots, he would never return to Kotlovina, insisted he married a girl from his native village. The marriage with then 19 years old Maria Profimovna was arranged by an aunt during the two weeks of his second stay in the village. Their first date took place under the aunt's surveillance in a mobile cinema, a vanguard institution of Soviet culture. The newly wed then returned to the labor front for another three years. Valeriy Stepanovich took pride in being a good laborer during his time in Chelyabinsk. He proudly recounted that he and his comrades, for over-fulfillment of their quotas, were called "Stakhanovtsi," after Aleksey Stakhanov, a "hero of socialist labor" with his own personality cult. On the labor front, both Valeriy Stepanovich and his wife Maria Profimovna, learned Russian. On their trip from Kotlovina back to the labor front, during a stay-over in Moscow, they were taken to see the Lenin Mausoleum, a pilgrimage site for Soviet citizens. They were also shown the Kremlin walls, behind which, they were told, Stalin sat at work.

The Kotlovina labor front returnees, like many others, became thoroughly Sovietized through their experience in centers of Soviet industry. Some of those recruited to the labor front not only learned Russian there but also received specialist training (Sakali 2013: 193). Speaking Russian and having good credentials in the process of socialist labor had quickly become a prerequisite for social mobility. Those who had stayed in Kotlovina and survived the famine had not had such a thorough crash-course of Soviet culture.

In Kotlovina most people spoke Gagauz. Only some 150 men had gone to Russian language school back in tsarist times.[11] Most of them had completed no more than two school years and those who were able-bodied were brought away to the labor front anyway. Nevertheless, meetings of the village council

11 Fr367 D5, pp. 12 ff.

and village gatherings were held in Russian from the first day of Soviet rule. The minutes were taken by men with a long-past basic education in tsarist Russia. Their orthography reveals that they were schooled before the orthography reform of 1917.[12]

By the mid-1950s the Bulgarians and Gagauz in the eyes of the Soviet administrators no longer posed a threat to the Soviet state. Bulgaria was firmly integrated into the Soviet bloc and the threat of war now came from the other side of the Atlantic, not from across the Danube. Being a Bulgarian or a Gagauz was no longer an obstacle to social mobility and those initiated to Soviet life on the labor front were in the pole position. The Gagauz and Bulgarians of southern Bessarabia hade moved up in the ethnic hierarchy of trust. But above them there was still a newly installed village elite from the old Soviet Union.

2 The Stewards of a New Model State

On September 17, 1944, less than a month after the Red Army had retaken Bessarabia, the first Soviet village gathering was held in Kotlovina.[13] It was attended by 1100 people. The only item on the agenda was to write a letter to Comrade Stalin. The letter was written "in the Name of the Ukrainian people" and spoke of the heroic deeds and the patriotic spirit of the Ukrainians that had finally been rewarded with liberation from the fascist occupiers. The letter culminated with a pledge that "we the peasants of the village Bolboka (Kotlovina's pre-Soviet name) place ourselves at the disposal of the leader of nations." The villagers then subscribed to a whole list of promises that they made to Stalin personally, such as to fertilize their fields, send all their children to school, and delegate the village's nine finest people to a village soviet.

The "promises" made by the villagers to their new leader were at the root of a catastrophe still to come. Villagers in Kotlovina and other settlements in the region "agreed" in a very similar manner to almost unbearable quotas of produce that they would deliver to the state for a fixed price. In Chervonoarmeyskoe (then still called by its pre-Soviet name, Kubey), villagers also gathered in 1944 to promise that "we the citizens of the village Kubey, (…) will honestly fulfill our obligation vis-à-vis the beloved fatherland, the Red Army, and Comrade Stalin. We are obliged to fulfill successfully before October 20 the state

12 For example in Fr367 D3 Protokoly obshchikh sobraniy krest'yan sela za 1944–1945 god, where the person taking the minutes used the old form of genitive suffix *-ago*, instead of post-reform *-ogo*.

13 Fr367 D3, pp. 3–4.

plan for grain harvest."[14] The Soviet Union exported huge quantities of grain during the following years in order to cement political alliances (to France, Poland, Romania, Bulgaria, and Czechoslovakia) even though the country was nowhere near to recovering from war (Lebedenko and Tychyna 2002: 177). This practice coincided with an unusually dry summer in 1946 (Tel'pis 2000: 12; Lebedenko and Tychyna 2002: 176). The drought affected many parts of southern and eastern Ukraine, as well as southern Russia. But only in Bessarabia it coincided with forced land collectivization, an experience, other regions in the old Soviet Union, had already painfully gone through in the early 1930s. In many villages, especially where men had been recruited for the labor front, there was a severe lack of working hands (Tel'pis 2000: 15). In 1947 the crisis turned into a devastating famine. Many people in pension-age now remember the famine vividly and most of them suffered losses in their families and communities.

The letters dictated to villagers were not so much a promise of the Bessarabia peasantry to Comrade Stalin as a promise by Stalin to his new subjects. Implicitly the letters said that the hardships of collectivization would soon be rewarded with a state that would empower laborers and peasants by calling them to meetings, sending their children to school, form kolkhozes, fertilize the fields, and elect village soviets.

These promises were represented by the Soviet newcomers who called such meetings. For a start, this new group was to dictate political decisions. The peasants then were called in to rubber-stamp them in public votes. Right after 1944, newcomers from Russia and Ukraine filled the most influential positions in Bessarabian settlements: the heads of village soviets, the directors of kolkhozes, the school headmasters, as well as the first generation of teachers, doctors, veterinaries, and agricultural managers. They were predominately people, who had proven themselves in the old Soviet Union, many of them fighting on the front.

Later in the Soviet period, villagers sent their own children to institutions of higher education in Odessa and Chișinău. And those children returned to the village as a second, a native generation of Soviet administrators. In comparison to Romanian rule, this arrangement was a progress. Under Romanian administration ethnic minorities were increasingly marginalized and discriminated against. Under Soviet rule, their opportunities of social mobility came with time and at the cost of a thorough Sovietization. The founding of Kolkhozes replaced all spaces of rural social life, the church, the fair or the tavern with state institutions. The peasants could no longer evade the state by not being "legible." It was now the state that equipped the peasants with the technology

14 Fr262 D3 Protokoly obshchikh sobraniy zhiteley sela za 1944 god, p. 10.

and data without which the Kolkhoz's way of production was impossible (Scott 1998: 214).

The two groups on the sending and the receiving end of this speedy and fundamental transformation were the Soviet newcomers and the native population of Bessarabia. But the two groups now cohabiting in Bessarabian villages were not separate castes, nor did cultural influence go only one direction from the Soviet newcomers to the native population. The already introduced teacher, Ekaterina Chekal arrived in 1953 from Ukraine's Azov Sea coast, just after having completed her education in a pedagogical institute.[15] Ekaterina had fond memories of her early years in the village. She reported to have been welcomed very warmly. In her fifth month in the village she married a Gagauz who later became an acclaimed artist. Neither her mother in Melitopol, nor her husband's parents, nor the village authorities had any objections against an interethnic marriage. Rather, there were concerns about the form of the marriage ceremony. Representatives of the modern and secular Soviet state were not supposed to take part in traditional rituals. The school's headmaster, Ekaterina's boss, boycotted the wedding because the newly-wed would sleep in a room with an Orthodox icon and an eternal light. But Ekaterina felt she had no right to change customs in her in-law's house. The phenomenon that older generations forced the younger to make compromises between their progressive Soviet attitudes and the older generation's way of life, was widely and regretfully observed by Soviet ethnographers at the time (Kushner 1974: 206). Even though Ekaterina would have enjoyed an old-style Gagauz wedding, she agreed to the school headmaster's demand of replacing the traditional white veil of Gagauz brides with the attributes of a modern, Soviet woman; a pink wedding dress embroidered with flowers.

Beginning in the first half of the 1950s, Gagauz and Bulgarian men were drafted to the army, just like men of any other ethnic group. Ekaterina's husband had served three years near Leningrad and learned to speak Russian there. The couple belonged to the class of village *intelligentsia*, the rural vanguard of a socialist society. As a young teacher, Ekaterina, notwithstanding her status as a newcomer, enjoyed great authority in the village. Many evenings she spent talking to her pupil's families. Especially for those who studied well, she made a great effort to convince parents to send their children to town for higher education.

Ethnicity, now in the absence of warfare and violence, was apparently no longer a day-to-day concern. The newcomers drew their power not from their ethnicity, but from their origin in the old Soviet Union, from their education

15 Interview in Izmail, July 9, 2013.

and their position in the Soviet state apparatus. They came not to make the ethnic minorities into Russians or into Ukrainians but to turn them into Soviet *kolkhozniki*.

Another newcomer teacher, Margarita Mikhailovna,[16] came to Bessarabia in 1969 freshly from the pedagogical institute in the central Russian city of Nizhnyy Novgorod and eventually put down roots in the large village of Chervonoarmeyskoe, where the population is mixed Bulgarian and Gagauz. Together with 41 other young teachers she was assigned to the neighboring rayon of Ceadir-Lunga, now a part of Moldova. When she left her home, she had only a very vague idea where she was going. The reason why so many young teachers were sent to this rural region was that earlier newcomers had returned home at the first opportunity. But Margarita Mikhailovna was determined to stay and to tough it out. She came with a strong sense of serving the fatherland and with the idea to "prop up the virgin soil" (*podnimat' tselinu*), a household phrase of the Soviet 1960s. When her traveling companions changed trains in the city of Bender, now in Transnistria, it dawned on her that she had arrived in a foreign land. She remembered that all the other passengers on the train were dressed entirely in black, that men wore a type of black lamb fur hats she had never seen before, and that they chatted in foreign languages. Margarita changed schools a few times. She married Nikolai, a music teacher, an ethnic Bulgarian who was part of the first native generation of Soviet educated professionals. Eventually, they moved to his native village of Chervonoarmeyskoe, where she became deputy headmaster of one of the village's schools. Although Margarita never ceased to miss her native Russia, she never planned to go back. "Women have no fatherland," her husband quipped on the issue, "they have husbands." But Margarita did not remember having been treated as an alien. When she married Nikolai, their different ethnic backgrounds were not even grounds for discussion. As a teacher, she had always been held in respect and her voice had authority in the village. She saw her mission of spreading Soviet culture on the periphery as her contribution to the common good.

3 Ethnicity Performed in Public

Even though by the 1960s ethnic differences had relatively little relevance for a single person's standing within the village community, the category of ethnicity was constantly present, be it in public discourse on the village level or in wider society. Most villagers by that time had a passport, on the fifth line

16 Interview in Chervonoarmeyskoe, October 26, 2013.

(*pyataya grafa*) of which their ethnic identity was registered. When they engaged in public functions, this feature was used in their introduction to the public sphere. Elections to municipal executive positions took place in so-called "assemblies of the working population." Each village district delegated its own candidates, who then were elected by the assembled village population, alas without opposing candidates.[17] In the documents that introduced the candidate to the public, his or her ethnicity came right behind the name and date of birth. Further information revealed the candidate's level of education, military or academic rank, place of work, and whether the candidate was a member or an aspired member of the party. In Kotlovina, in the elections of 1959 the ratio between the elect who were natives and those who belonged to the group of Soviet newcomers, were about 1:1. Of the 21 deputies delegated to the village soviet, 11 were Gagauz and 10 were either Russian or Ukrainian.[18] By 1971, the elected Gagauz had become a majority: 33 deputies were elected, 26 of them were ethnically Gagauz, three were Russians, three Ukrainians, and one was a Bulgarian. This might still not have accurately reflected the ethnic composition of the village population, but the ethnic majority now held the majority of seats. Also, by that time, the elected Gagauz deputies on average were no longer less educated than their Soviet newcomer colleagues. The only feature where ethnicity still had an effect was party membership.[19] Ethnicity was no longer a conclusive indicator for social status within the village.

Ethnicity might no longer have been a crucially category for the access to power resources, but it was a constantly present category. Even in a much wider discourse, ethnicity had a stable place in the public sphere. Take for example the official congratulations to the cosmonaut German Titov for his achievement of the first ever completed 24-hour space flight in 1961. On the front page of Soviet newspapers, including the Bessarabian local daily *Pridunayskaya Pravda*, Titov was introduced to the Soviet public by the following characteristics: "Comrade Titov German Stepanovich, born 1935, ethnicity: Russian, a candidate to join the Party since April 1961."[20] Mentioning ethnicity so high up in the list of people's characteristics has helped to produce a perception of

17 By the 1970s blanks were used as election reports. These blanks, among other details, already contained the result of the election. The bottom line of the printed form read "the candidate has been elected concordantly." For example Fr367 D210 Protokoly sobraniy o kandidatov v deputaty sel'soveta.

18 Fr367 D95 Protokoly obshchikh sobraniy rabochikh, sluzhashchikh i kolkhoznikov za 1959 god.

19 While 5 out of the 6 deputies that represented the Soviet newcomers were members of the Communist Party, only 12 out of 27 locals held party membership cards. Fr367 D210.

20 *Pridunayskaya Pravda*, Izmail, 1961, August 10, p. 1.

ethnicity as an unchangeable, tangible, and unambiguously detectable human characteristic. In the Soviet Union ethnicity became a "pervasive reality" to most people (Karklins 1986: 43). Terry Martin (2000: 168) called it a "constant routine of ethnic labeling" that "inadvertently indoctrinated the Soviet population in the belief that ethnicity was an inherent, fundamental, and crucially important characteristic of all individuals."

Despite the clear evidence to the contrary, Soviet officials emphasized very early on, that no ethnic group in Bessarabia was superior to any other. Certainly, the public insistence that all ethnic groups were equal and that they all deeply respected each other, still allowed discrimination in a less opaque manner. But publicly, ethnic diversity became a cause for celebration. The celebration of ethnic diversity became a lasting tradition in Bessarabia. Still during my fieldwork in 2012 and 2013 hardly a political speech failed to mention how ethnically diverse Bessarabians were and how well they nevertheless get along with each other. This reoccurring theme implicitly also invokes that it is an achievement to retain peaceful interethnic relations, because according to expectation ethnic differences should routinely lead to conflict. Already in 1949, when being an ethnic Bulgarian or Gagauz still meant that one was likely to toil at the labor front, the New Year's editorial in the *Pridunayskaya Pravda* ran:

> In our province, on the very periphery of the Soviet Union, on the southwestern border of the immense Soviet territories, just like anywhere else in the country, those who build up communism, Russians and Ukrainians, Bulgarians and Moldovans, Albanians and Gagauz, brick by brick assemble the majestic building of the new communist society.[21]

It was made very clear that political participation, as well as patriotic support for the Soviet state were expected to come from all ethnic groups equally. Announcing elections for people's courts, also in January 1949, the paper declared:

> In these [electoral] lists appear people of various ages and professions, Russians and Ukrainians, Bulgarians and Moldovans, members of the Party and unaffiliated [candidates]. They are all united by a boundless love for the fatherland, by their devotion to the great cause of Lenin-Stalin, the cause of communism.[22]

---

21 *Pridunayskaya Pravda*, Izmail, 1949, January 1, p. 1.

22 *Pridunayskaya Pravda*, Izmail, 1949, January 8, p. 1, similar mentions of the multiethnic Soviet electorate that all have the same aspirations have already been made during the Soviet Union's one year long rule in 1940–1941, for example in an address of the Central

With time, the fact that several ethnic groups lived peacefully together in Bessarabia became the single most important feature for the representation of the region. In the reference book *The History of Towns and Villages of the Ukrainian SSR* ("Istoriya Gorodov i Sel Ukrainskoy SSR—Odesskaya oblast'" 1978), the section about Izmail rayon began with the note that it was a multi-ethnic, but nevertheless very peaceful region.

Folklore became the main platform for the celebration of harmonic interethnic relations. It was less politicized than education, but eventually folklore began to profit from a network of institutions that had been founded with the primary goal of educating the population; schools, clubs, culture houses, and local newspapers. From early on in the Soviet Union, folklore became the single niche where ethnic particularism was not only allowed but actively encouraged. Performing ethnicity on stage demanded to form folklore collectives that specialized in the song and dance of one particular ethnic group. Folklore amateur musicians formed orchestras, choirs, and dance groups in clubs and culture houses that were founded in villages once schools and kolkhozes were established. Folklore was often performed along with acts of other genres such as political poems and Soviet battle songs commemorating World War II. Eventually folklore was performed along *estrada*, a Soviet genre of pop music. Folklore collectives sometimes had songs and dances of several origins in their repertoires, but each song and dance was labeled as belonging to one ethnic group.[23] For a long time, Soviet folklore was committed mainly to entertainment with stereotyped references to ethnicity. Eventually, in the 1980s the folkloric movement grew and began to strive for more authenticity (Cash 2011: 164).

The revival of old Bulgarian and Gagauz songs in Soviet folklore groups was also praised as a sign that these peoples had defied the oppression of the Romanian occupants and maintained their national traditions.[24] New compositions for folklore groups often had political content. They treated topics such as the Tatarbunary Uprising, gratefulness towards the Communist Party, or as expressed in a rare dissolving of ethnic boundaries, a fusion folk dance to demonstrate the "unbreakable friendship between the Russian and the Ukrainian peoples." Folklore was a genre of performing arts that allowed ethnic groups to be bounded by particular styles of songs, dances, and dresses. At the same time folklore performances were clearly political events. They provided the

---

Committee of the Communist Party in the Moldovan SSR to voters in December 1940 (cited in Kashu 2014: 216).

23 In a series of reports in *Pridunayskaya Pravda*, an early example of Soviet folklore festival is described in detail, *Pridunayskaya Pravda*, Izmail, November 18, 20, and 28, 1953.

24 Ibid.: November 28, 1953.

FIGURE 2 Danadzhi family from the village of Kazakliya performing in 1982

framework for the performance of political poems and the reading of passages from political novels.[25] Against the background of the Cold War, folklore offered an ideal tool to transport the political messages of internal unity and fierce determination towards external enemies in an entertaining and cheerful manner.

In the second half of the 1980s the region's celebrated harmonic cohabitation of different ethnic groups came under strain in the face of a severe economic crisis and an uncertain future of the USSR. In many areas, especially along the Soviet Union's periphery, ethnic nationalism rather than multi-ethnicity came to be celebrated. In southern Bessarabia however, ethnicity retained an inclusive rather than an exclusive function. None of the groups living there formed a clear majority in a continuous area. Therefore, the theme of interethnic harmony remained a strong public discourse. In 1989 the Ukrainian language was made the sole state language in the Ukrainian SSR. In an Izmail textile factory, this led to a dispute about which language should be the working language henceforth. The local daily *Sovetskiy Izmail* reported that women with over 25 different ethnic identities worked in the factory, and that

25 Ibid.: November 18, 1953.

therefore it was indispensable that Russian was kept as the working language. A local "propagandist" was sent to a worker's assembly at the factory. He reminded the staff that Perestroika was initiated to democratize the Soviet Union, not to break it up. He explained that raw materials processed in the factory, came from Russia, Kazakhstan, and the Baltic states, which he used as an illustration that only a united country could be economically strong. The factory staff subsequently discussed the matter and concluded that ethnic conflict could not be in their interest and that it was much more important to find a way out of the economic crisis.[26]

No way out of the economic crisis opened up. The Soviet state missed out on its central promise to provide economic security for everyone who did their share. The less the USSR could live up to its economic promises, the more important became the ethnic categories it had helped to establish. Soviet citizens received their passports at age 16. On the "fifth line" of the passport they inherited their parent's ethnic identity. Soviet passports recorded only one clearly specified ethnicity. Children of interethnic couples therefore had to make a choice between the two ethnic groups their parents were registered as (Tishkov 1997: 10; Ahlberg 1991: 806). Once ethnicity was registered in the passport, it was hard to change it. If it was indispensable for a party career however, a solution was usually found (Karklins 1986: 34; Gorenburg 2006b: 295). For those ethnic groups that faced a lingering hostile environment, such as the Jews or as the Armenians in Azerbaijan, it became common to change their ethnicity into one that caused them less trouble (Karklins 1986: 36; Tishkov 1997: 111). In some cases the decision about ethnic belonging was made by a clerk rather than by the citizen. A scholar from Chișinău showed me the marriage documents of his grandparents who married in 1950 near Kotovsk,[27] a small town in the north of Odessa oblast. The village where they lived belonged to the Ukrainians SSR at the time but until 1940 had been part of the Moldovan ASSR. On the couple's birth certificates that had been issued on the basis of Romanian documents, the fifth line had been manipulated on the occasion of the wedding. The word "Moldovan" was crossed out and the word "Ukrainian" was added in handwriting. A handwritten instruction on the flipside of the documents read: "change of ethnicity valid, trust!"[28] The respondent described his grandparents as "simple people who would hardly protest to a Soviet state servant." In retrospect it is hard to judge how many and which people had their

26 *Sovetskiy Izmail*, October 10, 1989.

27 Kotovsk was named in honor of Grigoriy Kotovskiy, a Bolshevist revolutionary. It therefore had to be renamed according to the Ukrainian "de-communization laws." Since 2016 the town is called Podol'sk.

28 Interview in Chișinău, December 8, 2012.

ethnicity ascribed in similar ways. Those of my respondents, who remembered the procedure of choosing an ethnicity when getting a passport, mostly went through it much later. Lidiya Mikhailovna Nikoglo was born in the late 1940s in the ethnically mixed village of Chervonoarmeyskoe. Her family identified as Bulgarian, although there were Gagauz ancestors too. When Lidiya received her first passport she registered as Gagauz, without the objection of the municipal clerk in charge. When asked why she had chosen to register as Gagauz, her ethnically Gagauz husband, who also attended the interview, interrupted laughing, "She knew that she was going to marry a Gagauz, and she made herself Gagauz." But Lidiya had a different explanation:

> My father is a Gagauz by the grandfather's lineage, but my Mum is Bulgarian…, purely Bulgarian. And we live on the Gagauz side [of the village]. And I was born on the Gagauz side. Out on the street, I spoke Gagauz with all my friends. That's why I decided that I'm more Gagauz than Bulgarian. Even though in our house we spoke Bulgarian because my mother was Bulgarian and spoke to us in her language.[29]

Especially where two groups lived in close proximity, like Gagauz and Bulgarians in Chervonoarmeyskoe, such ambivalent identities are quite frequent. Among small minorities such as Gagauz or Bulgarian neither of them offered better opportunities in the Soviet education system or state service. Whether one was Bulgarian or Gagauz mattered much less than whether one was Gagauz or Russian or Jewish. Therefore, people could guide their decision by individual preferences as in Lidiya's case.

In some regions of the Soviet Union, prestige and privilege attached to a certain ethnic identity led a majority of those who had to choose one of their parent's ethnicities to follow a particular pattern. If one parent belonged to the titular nation and the other did not, their offspring were more likely to choose the titular nation as their ethnicity. Generally, if one parent was Russian and the other was not, children tended to choose Russian as their ethnicity (Gorenburg 2006b: 295). There were exceptions with mixed ethnic marriages involving a representative of one of the "small peoples of the north." To be registered as a representative of these ethnicities offered privileges in education and taxes and was therefore gladly chosen, even over Russian (Gorenburg 2006a: 150). In southern Bessarabia, once times of the labor front were over, none of the ethnic communities offered tangible privileges. Representatives of a later Soviet generation took equality between ethnic groups for granted and saw

29 Interview in Chervonoarmeyskoe April 28, 2013.

little significance in the process of choosing a passport ethnicity. Lidiya's nephew, Evgeniy,[30] born in 1974, was registered Bulgarian in a passport he received shortly before the Soviet Union disintegrated. He said:

> In the Soviet period one could choose ethnicity… I think that, had I said I was African, they would have registered me as African in my passport. They simply asked me, how should we register you in your passport? And I said Bulgarian. That was that. They registered me Bulgarian. I think that, had I written French, they would have registered me as French or anything else. They wouldn't have asked: 'do you know that language at all…

As this example illustrates, towards the Soviet Union's end, officially ascribed ethnicity gradually lost its importance. At the same time, ethnicity became dramatically more important as a justification for political power. For the Soviet state, ethnicity had all but lost its role as an indicator whom to trust and whom to mistrust. It had, however, gained great importance for those challenging the state. The mistrust was now directed against the state by people who argued ethnically foreign elites should not be running local matters. The tables might have turned, but the essentialist logic behind the concept of ethnicity was well preserved through systematic ethnic ascription by Soviet bureaucrats.

4 Soviet Education and the Friendship of Peoples

One realm where the administrative category of ethnicity mattered throughout the Soviet period was education. In a large scale campaign that lasted from the 1960s to the late 1980s, by way of ethnic quotas, the ratio of people with university degrees was raised among the small and peripheral ethnic groups in the Union, while it stagnated among Russians and in the Russian heartland (Tishkov 1997: 39). In the older parts of the Soviet Union, from the mid-1920s to the end of the decade, Soviet nationalities policy experimented with *korenisatsiya,* the concept of "indigenization" or "nativization." This policy aimed at making ethnic differences in the non-Russian regions serve Soviet ends. It used privileges and punishment to make elites of ethnic minorities collaborate with the Bolshevists (Tishkov 1997: 35; Beissinger 2002: 50; Bilaniuk 2005: 16). Ethnic groups were counted and categorized according to the Stalinist definition of ethnicity that put primacy on a common language. Between the first Soviet census in 1926 and the second in 1939 the number of ethnic groups, from

30 Interview in Chervonoarmeyskoe April 28, 2013.

which respondents could choose to belong to, was significantly reduced. This reduction was justified by declaring that some ethnic groups were, according to new findings, merely sub groups (*subetnos*) of others (Tishkov 1997: 31).

All the 192 languages registered on the territory of the USSR in 1926 were declared official languages of a delineated area and all of them were standardized. However, during the 1930s, privileges for those local languages that did not have an administrative body with its name to it were slashed. The titular languages of Soviet republics became privileged over other languages (Fowkes 2002: 72–74). For the Ukrainian SSR, the period of *korenisatsiya* saw the Ukrainian language developed into a language of school instruction and integrated into a standardized educational system (Hrycak 2006: 73). By the time the Soviet educational system was introduced in Bessarabia in 1944, only languages that served as the titular language somewhere in the Soviet Union could be used as languages of instruction. Only languages attached to a political unit had been developed as school languages by Soviet linguists. Accordingly, there were teaching materials as well as pedagogical institutes exclusively for these titular languages. Among the languages spoken in southern Bessarabia, this was the Russian language (that served as titular language in the RSFSR), the Ukrainian language (that served as titular language in the Ukrainian SSR), and the Moldovan language (that served as titular language in the newly founded Moldovan SSR). In the immediate surroundings of Izmail several languages were used in village administrations and schools. In the two Old-Believer villages Staraya Nekrasovka and Novaya Nekrasovka, Russian was used. In the predominantly Ukrainian villages Broska, Matroska, and Safyani Ukrainian was used in schools and also occasionally in administrative proceedings. In Ozernoe and Utkonosovka the Moldovan/Romanian language was used. In contrast to the Romanian period it now had to be written in Cyrillic letters.

Languages that served as titular languages in foreign countries, such as Bulgarian or Albanian, were not supposed to serve as languages of instruction in Soviet schools, nor were languages that did not have an official status anywhere, such as Gagauz. Therefore, in the Gagauz and Bulgarian speaking villages of southern Bessarabia, as well as in Zhovtnevoe, the one predominantly Albanian speaking village, the "language of interethnic communication," i.e. Russian, was introduced as the language of instruction in schools. Since children there could not speak Russian when they entered the educational system, these village schools held "preparation classes" (*podgotovitel'nie klassy*) for six-year-olds.[31] These came to be known as "zero grade" (*nulevoy klass*).

31 Details on preparation classes were documented in rayon school reports, for example Fr445 D128 Godovye otchety gorodskikh i rayonnykh otdelov narodnogo obrazovaniya o

According to respondents who themselves have learned Russian by going to the zero grade, children there learned mainly by repeating after their teachers. One teacher, who taught zero grade classes in a Gagauz village, said children who completed it were at no disadvantage compared to children from a Russian speaking environment.

In comparison to Ukrainian or Moldovan, Russian was much better established as a language of instruction in the late 1940s. There were more teaching materials and better expertise. In fact, children who went to the zero grade and subsequently to a village school with Russian as the language of instruction performed better in their initial years than children who were instructed in their native languages.[32] The Ukrainian language that should have been taught as a second language in all schools often fell short of time and resources. Because of a lack of qualified teachers who could have taught Ukrainian in Reni rayon, during the academic year of 1951–52, neither Ukrainian nor Ukrainian literature was taught up to tenth grade.[33] In Bolgrad rayon, where the vast majority of pupils were Bulgarian or Gagauz native speakers, learning Ukrainian was abandoned all together in 1950. The ministry of education had acknowledged the exceptional linguistic situation there and allowed an exemption.[34]

Most of the teachers in the region had come here just very recently from older parts of the Soviet Union. Of the 218 teachers who worked in 1948 in Bolgrad rayon, 93 were Ukrainians, 33 were Russian, 4 were Jewish, and 88 were "others."[35] Many of the teachers of this first generation apparently were only poorly qualified. On average they had less than five years of work experience. Annual school reports were full of complaints about individual teachers and

---

rabote shkol za 1948/1949 uchebnyy god, p. 76. The ethnographer Valentin Moshkov observed similar practices already in the few schools that existed in Gagauz villages around the turn of the century. Teaching Russian to 5- or 6-year-old children started by taking them by the hand and telling them, "this is a hand" and then pointing to their nose and telling them, "this is a nose." Then they would be asked, "What is this?"—"a nose," etc. (Moshkov 1901b: 38).

32 For example Fr445 D184 Godovoy otchet Suvorovskogo rayonnogo otdela narodnogo obrazovaniya za 1950–1951 godov, p. 18, that reports on how many students in each village school had to repeat one grade over. Nowhere more than 12% of students had to repeat one grade, but the highest percentages came from villages where Ukrainian or Moldovan was used as language of instruction and children did not go to "zero grade" preparation classes.

33 Fr445 D209 Godovye otchety gorodskikh i rayonnych otdelov narodnogo obrazovaniya o rabote shkol za 1951 god, p. 70.

34 Fr445 D186 Godovye otchety rayonnykh i gorodskikh otdelov narodnogo obrazovaniya za 1950–1951 uchebnyy god, p. 126.

35 Fr445 D128, p. 78.

about entire teams. Complaints especially concerned those teachers whose native language was not Russian and who had gained their qualifications outside the Soviet Union.[36] Some teachers were criticized individually for the poor performances of their pupils. Often such complaints were explained by bad language skills of the teachers or by blaming teachers for mixing several languages and passing a mish-mash on to their pupils.[37]

But Russian language schools were still better off than schools with Moldovan as language of instruction. The Moldovan Soviet Republic had been founded only during World War II. Institutions such as publishing houses for text books or higher education facilities operating in the Moldovan/Romanian language were still very new. This resulted in a severe lack of teachers and teaching materials for village schools in Moldovan speaking villages.[38] The shortage in education resources resulted in "a lack of love of the students for their own language," as a school report lamented.[39] Moreover, the state also lacked the resources to effectively monitor these schools' work. In Artsis rayon, where there was only one Moldovan village school, an annual report complained that after having created schools according to the "principles of the Leninist-Stalinist ethnicity policies" there were now no Moldovan speaking school inspectors who could evaluate the work of teachers and students in their Moldovan language school.[40]

In the second half of the 1950s, after the gravest economic problems had been brought under control, in an attempt to tackle this unsatisfying situation in the pedagogical system, an experiment was launched. In 1957 the Odessa oblast Central Committee commissioned a report on the linguistic situation of the ethnic minorities in the Region. It revealed that 24,400 Gagauz, 79,650 Moldovans, and 132,800 Bulgarians in the oblast had not sufficient access to schooling and media in their native languages (Guboglo 2011: 115). One of the responses to this situation was the revival of a project, set aside in 1949, the creation of a standardized Gagauz language. The Academy of Sciences of the Moldovan SSR in Chișinău was tasked with the development of a suitable curriculum to teach Gagauz to schoolchildren in the Gagauz villages of the Moldovan SSR. In 1958, 38 village schools held native language courses for 14,500 Gagauz children. But problems soon became apparent. The workload on children became greater and teachers no longer had sufficient time to instruct

36 For example Fr445 D128, p. 82.

37 Fr445 D156 Godovye otchety rayonnykh otdelov narodnogo obrazovaniya za 1949–1950 god, p. 142.

38 Fr445 D128, p. 177, Fr445 D209, p. 120.

39 Fr445 D184, p. 6.

40 Fr445 D156, p. 156.

children in Russian. To have a good written command of Russian was much more decisive for educational and professional careers than the written command of a Gagauz standard language that just had been developed and that offered no career paths whatsoever. In the end, parental assemblies in Gagauz villages voted to end the experiment in 1961 (Guboglo 2011: 115–117). As was the custom in Soviet village gatherings, this outcome was reached by unanimous voting and Guboglo (ibid.: 117) suspects with some well dosed pressure from Chișinău. Nonetheless, even today Gagauz language instruction in schools is sometimes subject of parental skepticism for the same reason: It puts workload on students without providing them with additional educational or professional opportunities.[41]

Back in the 1950s education in the Soviet Union was by no means an effort confined to schoolchildren. Adult *kolkhozniki* and workers were expected to go to evening classes. The chief goal of these was giving basic literacy to the illiterate.[42] There were classes for everybody, aimed at the liquidation not only of illiteracy but also of what was seen by Soviet administrators as rural backwardness. In the second half of the 1940s, the Izmail bureau of lecturers started an evening school program in surrounding villages, with lectures in Russian and Ukrainian. Even in 1947, in the middle of a devastating famine, two dozen lecturers traveled the villages of Izmail oblast[43] attempting to fulfill a plan of 500 lessons a month. Some of these were aimed especially at peasants, workers, women, or young people. Village *intelligentsia*; teachers, doctors, and agronomists were expected to attend.[44] Villagers were gathered to hear lectures on topics as diverse as *Was there a beginning of the earth and will there be an end?*, *The natural resources of the Ukrainian SSR*, *How did life occur on earth?*, *Charles Darwin and his teachings*, or *The Stalinist constitution, the most democratic*

41 This has changed somewhat since Ukrainian citizens can travel to Turkey in search of employment and since some Gagauz language courses are available at Komrat University in the ATU Gagauziya of Moldova.

42 To get a clue of the degree of illiteracy among the population of none-Russian speaking villages, the recruitment lists of 1944 provide some insight. For example, in Kotlovina among the Gagauz men who were recruited in 1944, 40% had never been schooled. Among those who had gone to school, about half did so during Romanian reign, when Romanian was used as language of instruction. The other half had gone to school in tsarist times, more than 20 years earlier. Among the men with basic school education, 7% had gone to school for just one year, 20% for two years, 16% for three years, and 10% for 4 years. In total, among the entire male population between the age of 17 and 56 (636 men), only 36 men had completed 5 or more grades. Fr367 D5, pp. 12 ff.

43 An administrative entity that existed between 1944 and 1954, when it was merged with Odessa oblast.

44 Fr415 D10 Temy lektsii dlya sel'skikh i kolkhoznykh klubov na 1947 god, pp. 19–21.

constitution in the world.[45] Many lessons were meant to attune village audiences to ethnicity as a household category, but also to convince them of what they likely already knew; that living in a multiethnic society was nothing bad. Ethnicity was always presented in combination with the Soviet catchphrase "friendship of peoples" (*druzhba narodov*). One standard lecture was *The Leninist-Stalinist friendship of peoples.*[46] In the lesson *The Soviet state, a state of a new and higher order,* villagers were told that:

> The Soviet state is the model of a multiethnic state. The multiethnic state is based on equal rights and the friendship of peoples. The Soviet state is the organizer of friendship between peoples, of mutual assistance between peoples, the organizer of equal rights for these peoples, and their moral and political unity.[47]

From lectures like these it became clear that ethnic differences mattered and that they had to be managed. Interethnic relations, in order to be peaceful and friendly had to be organized by a patronizing state. This state, in village lectures, appeared in the guise of the Ukrainian SSR. Accordingly, many talks dealt with the Ukrainian people: *The emergence of the Ukrainian people* was an essential lesson, and so was *The Kievan Rus', the cradle of the three Slavic peoples, Russians, Belarusians, and Ukrainians*, or *The development of a socialist Ukrainian culture.*[48] But lectures also took a fierce stand against Ukrainian aspirations of independence and against ethnic nationalism: the lecture curriculum of 1947 offered *Ukrainian bourgeois nationalism, the worst enemy of the Ukrainian people*, as well as *the struggle of Lenin and Stalin against bourgeois Ukrainian nationalism*, and *the destruction of the bourgeois nationalist counter-revolution during the civil war.*[49] The fact that "Ukrainian nationalism" appeared exclusively in combination with "bourgeois" will have made it clear to even the most illiterate *kolkhoznik*, that ethnicity was only good as in "friendship of the peoples." Alexey Yurchak observed that Soviet lingo was full of such "complex modifiers," constructions that permanently tied certain nouns to certain adjectives. "Help" for instance was always "brotherly" and "participation" was always "active." By molding these pairs into fixed phrases it appeared that the reality created with such language was permanent as well (Yurchak 2006: 66).

45 Fr415 D15 Plany lektsii po istorii i literature, pp. 1–7.
46 Fr415 D15, p. 10.
47 Fr415 D22 Metodicheskie razrabotki v pomoshch' lektoram, p. 50.
48 Fr415 D15, p. 14.
49 Fr415 D15, pp. 10, 14.

There was one friendship between two particular peoples that was more important than the others, the one with the Russian people, the *outstanding nation and leading force of the Soviet Union*, as one lecture was titled.[50] The lecture program left absolutely no doubt that the Russian people had a special standing in the multiethnic fabric of Soviet society. There was *the historical role of Russia in the struggle of the Slavic peoples for their independence.*[51] But it was also made very clear that the Ukrainian and the Russian peoples had a special relation that went beyond mere "friendship of peoples": *The great historical act of unification of Ukraine and Russia in the year 1654*, or *the historical connection between the Russian and the Ukrainian culture*, or *the assistance by the great Russian people to Soviet Ukraine and her economic and cultural development*, as well as *the Leninist-Stalinist friendship between Russia and Ukraine,*[52] were all lectures meant to cement the idea of an age-old and eternal brotherly relationship between the two groups. Locally, this kind of enacted harmony, projected back into the past, must have seemed the concern of others. The centrally planned lectures said next to nothing about the Bulgarians, Gagauz, or Albanians, let alone did the lecturers speak to these groups in their respective languages. But the celebration of a multiethnic society, which became a self-congratulatory trade mark of Soviet public discourse, was certainly a well-meant attempt to give a sense of belonging even to these peripheral minorities.

Soviet education for children and adults quickly bore fruits. The generation that was born after 1950 would eventually be employed mainly in the village kolkhozes and sovkhozes. But not all of them remained rank and file *kolkhozniki*. Success in school could be rewarded with the opportunity to study on in Odessa or Chișinău. For the select few it even was Leningrad or Moscow. Provincial youth was not sent there to become urbanites or intellectuals, but to become teachers, doctors, engineers, or agronomists and then return to their native villages to contribute to the fulfillment of the quota. The generation born in the late 1940s and the 1950s was the first and the last in Bessarabia to be involved in Soviet structures from kindergarten until the pinnacle of their professional careers. Another common experience of this generation was the obligation of all able-bodied men to serve the Soviet army for two to three years. Both for civil and military education, villagers left behind an environment where their ethnicity was known and acknowledged. They entered the even more multiethnic environment of the student dormitory in the city or the

50 Fr415 D15, p. 12.
51 Fr415 D15, p. 11.
52 Fr415 D15, p. 14.

military barracks, where many of their peers and superiors had never heard that there were Bulgarians or Gagauz living in the Soviet Union.

Members of this generation were reminded of ethnicity mainly when they interacted with state institutions such as the army or the university. Ethnicity had a peculiar double nature: On the one hand it was an ascribed feature of everyone's identity. It appeared in most important identity documents and was constantly referred to in public discourse. On the other hand, most of my respondents, no matter their ethnic background, in retrospect felt that ethnicity at the time did not have an impact on one's opportunities. Compared to post-Soviet Ukraine, in the later Soviet decades it was, at least for most of my respondents, exclusively merits that could provide social mobility.

Lidiya Mikhailovna and Mikhail Stepanovich Nikoglo are a Gagauz couple from the ethnically mixed village of Chervonoarmeyskoe. They both shared the experience of studying in Odessa, Lidiya Mikhailovna to become a school teacher, Mikhail Stepanovich to become an agronomist. Both of them were born in the late 1940s. They were part of the first and only Bessarabian generation that made it from "zero grade" preparation classes to a higher education in Odessa. When Lidiya, after having completed 12 grades in the village school, departed to Odessa, some 250 kilometers to the north-east, to enroll in the pedagogical institute, it was her very first trip to the city. She felt that her rural or ethnically different background had no effect on her opportunities there:

> Maybe it's us, we who grew up and were educated in the Soviet time, and maybe it's just us who have this impression that... we had stability, we had work, our children could study, they could enter any institution without having money. No matter what disease you get, you get the treatment you need, you didn't have to pay for any operation, nor for any drug, everything was free, it was really for free. We ourselves, the children of kolkhozniki, studied for free, just for our merits, and no money whatsoever.... My father didn't know where Odessa *was*. I for example, I studied in Odessa. He didn't know where Odessa was and what this [pedagogical] institute was and through which door to enter and through which to exit. Only with your brains... you have knowledge—you enter, no knowledge—that's it, you can't enter. It was the same at work. If you work well that means they promote you, put you on the 'wall of fame,' bonuses, appreciation, holiday trips...[53]

53 Interview in Chervonoarmeyskoe April 28, 2013.

When asked whether ethnicity was an issue among students in Odessa or between them and teachers, her husband, Mikhail, answered that he had studied with representatives of very different ethnic groups and, again, all that mattered was their merits. When asked, whether later on, in the village kolkhoz, where Mikhail became a senior planner, ethnicity was ever a question, his answer was very similar:

> No, no, no! There the thing was that you need to work. There they don't ask your ethnicity, who you are. You need to work. If you appeared there, if you are a specialist, if you graduated from the institute, what do you need ethnicity for? You have to work! You show how you work. There, ethnicity meant nothing (laughs).

Interestingly, it was this perceived meritocratic Soviet society that insisted on recording and ascribing ethnicity. This insistence on ethnicity as an essential administrative category became the Soviet Union's nemesis once it slid into economic crisis and merits no longer automatically translated into prosperity.

5 Stagnation and Revived Ethnic Consciousness

Revising the concept of ethnicity and its use in administration was never less likely than in the time often referred to as "stagnation" (*zastoy*), between Brezhnev's grab for power in 1964 and the advent of Perestroika in 1985. During these years, many practices, not just ascribing ethnicity, gained a repetitive character. Life in the late Soviet Union became a collage of bits and pieces of earlier, already approved practices, cited and rearranged in a way so they would conform to a common, well-established Soviet script of doing things (Yurchak 2006). The term Yurchak uses to describe the way people talked, wrote, and represented practices in the late Soviet Union is "authoritative discourse," a term borrowed from the literary theoretician Mikhail Bakhtin. In this way of speaking and writing, the author disappeared from the text. In "authoritative discourse" everything was expressed in a tone as if it was an unquestionable, well-known truth, in no demand of any further explanation (Yurchak 2006: 70). Ethnicity and its significance in the symbolic representation of individuals and groups had become such a truth. The presence of ethnicity (*natsional'nost'* in colloquial language, *etnos* among scholars) in every deliberation about society, be it near or far, in the recent or the distant past, the explanatory power of ethnicity and its conceptual stability in time and space was neither discussed nor contradicted. This becomes evident if one looks at how ethnicity was projected into the region's past. For instance, the Soviet archivists who, in the 1960s and 70s filed documents on the Romanian and tsarist periods, gave many of the documents headings containing the term "ethnicity" (*natsional'nost'*). After examining such files, the researcher, with some disappointment, would find that most of them were in reality about confessional groups or social estates. The Soviet archivists took these earlier categories quite naturally as ethnicity. In one case, a Romanian file about an organization that defended the interests of the *Transdanubian Colonists*, the Soviet archivists in retrospect had decided that this was a *Bulgarian* organization. Therefore, in all translations into Russian, this ethnic denomination was added to the organization's name. However, neither in the proceedings of the organization nor in the secret police reports about it, does the word "Bulgarian" ever appear. In fact, nothing reminiscent of ethnicity, nationality, language, or even religion seems to have left a trace in the whole voluminous file. Some of the delegates in this organization would have been identified as Bulgarians by Soviet bureaucrats, but others might have been Gagauz, Albanian or Moldovan.[54] In a local census from 1895 for the town of Vilkovo, the archivists decided it was a about the "ethnic composition of the population." The document itself reveals religious categories and counted people by their professional affiliations, but it contains no ethnic or linguistic categories.[55] Ethnicity had come to be taken so much for granted as the chief denominator of social differences that it seemed to be a natural translation for all earlier forms of structuring society.

Soviet Society of the *zastoy* period was full of practices that had become meaningless but were continuously performed to keep up the façade of an integrated and content society. In some cases there was a degree of complicity between those in charge of the thankless task to enact façade and those who had to play along (Friedberg 1991). Take the example of participation in demonstrations or elections. Compulsory participation in parades was not a nuisance to many Soviet citizens. They enjoyed having a day off from work with their friends and colleagues, but hardly anyone paid attention to the slogans and the speeches (Yurchak 2006: 121). Like so many Soviet practices the ubiquitous reference to ethnicity had become a category of everyday life without much meaning attached to it. Not only did ethnicity no longer have any effect on the rights and duties of most ethnic groups, also the communist future anticipated a socially engineered, hard-working, non-ethnic citizen (Fitzhugh, Bilaniuk, and Lyon 1996: 1), for which cultural differences between

---

54 F312 D76 Nablyudatel'noe delo deyatel'nost'i "Soyuza obshchestv bolgarskikh kolonistov" Izmail'skogo i Kagul'skogo uezdov, 1932–1940.

55 F4 D59 Svedenie o kolichestvennom i natsional'nom sostave naseleniya, 1895, p. 8.

ethnic groups became less and less perceptible. More and more people spoke Russian in many situations and used a wide range of union-wide Soviet terms to talk about their day-to-day activities. This generation was educated in Soviet schools. Its more ambitious members could join the *Komsomol*, the Party youth organization. The large majority worked in a mode of production that could increasingly be found across the Union. The leader of the Ukrainian Communist Party, Petr Simonenko, during a campaign speech in Izmail in September 2012 spoke to a mainly grey-haired audience. He made a sweeping movement with his arm around Izmail's Soviet-era main square, where the rally was held, and reminded the audience that everything within sight had been built by this "golden generation." This claim was true, but truth might have been added by saying that Izmail's main square with its Stalinist polyclinic, its Brezhnev-era town hall, its soldier's monument and bronze Lenin[56] looked very much like any other small-town square that was built by the same golden generation anywhere else in the Soviet Union. In many ways, then, Bessarabians of this generation became culturally much more similar to other people of the same generation, living elsewhere in the Soviet Union, than to their parent's generation, that once found itself as a culturally foreign peripheral minority in the expanding Soviet state. Ethnicity stuck with them as the fifth line in their passports and as a specific "authoritative discourse."

After becoming a category almost void of meaning in the dull *zastoy* years, ethnicity had a spectacular comeback as a meaningful category, when Perestroika and Glasnost reforms allowed for political parties to be founded. Across Eastern Europe, many new parties that would become influential during the last years of the Soviet Union were founded along ethnic lines. Especially in federative states, such as the Soviet Union or Yugoslavia, ethnicity became the chief category for political mobilization, once socialist structures started to dwindle away (Beissinger 2002: 77). Indeed it was very hard for leaders of political movements, other than nationalistic ones, to establish political parties along ideological lines. For generations, Soviet citizens had been exposed to and educated in only one ideology, while all other conceivable ideologies were deemed bourgeois, imperialistic, or fascist.

In the Perestroika years with their widespread corruption, mismanagement, and food shortages, the rhetoric of a superior socialist way of life in a classless society became meaningless to most. The estrangement of the citizens from the ideology of the Communist Party became a severe threat to the power and the privileges of socialist elites who had, for the past decades, justified their

56 The Lenin statue was removed in February 2016, following Ukraine's "de-communization laws."

status with the pledge of a harmonic and just society soon to come. Ethnicity, so the dominant narrative, would become obsolete once this harmonic stage was achieved. Now the vision of an ideal society had become obsolete instead. The only refuge for elites, who thus far promised a bright future, was to turn to ethnic nationalism. Ethnicity had been cherished as an important and ever-present feature of each person. It was used to characterize each person along with achievements in socialist labor and education, military rank, or party hierarchy. Now that these officially recorded features became a burden rather than an asset, ethnicity was the only category left that could justify holding power over others (Verdery 1993b: 190, 1993a: 175; Slezkine 1994: 451; Schorkowitz 2010: 100).

Nationalist movements began to gain momentum during Perestroika years. The two Soviet republics that shared Bessarabia, Moldova and Ukraine, were no exception. In both countries nationalist movements came to pose a serious threat to the ruling party elites. Party bosses watched their peer in the Baltic republics as well as in Armenia and Azerbaijan being swept away by ethnic mobilization. Both in Moldova and in Ukraine party leaderships dealt with the threat by taking the wind out of the sails of nationalist movements and adopting their rhetoric of national revival (Kappeler 2000: 249; Fane 1993: 124). In Ukraine the mildly nationalist *Rukh* (movement) gained hardly a fourth of parliamentary seats in the first multiparty elections. Nevertheless, the parliament started to pass bills, privileging Ukrainian language and stressing nationalist perspectives on Ukrainian history. The members of parliament had remained roughly the same before and after the collapse of the Soviet Union. Only now, that nationalism was the latest craze, they had taken it up as their new legitimizing ideology (Reid 1997: 218). So even if the people in power remained the same, they "switched the we-groups" (Elwert 1997: 253) on which they based their privileges and power.

At about the same time, local ethnic minorities in southern Bessarabia started their own movements based on mobilization along ethnic lines. In the late 1980s ethnicity again came to be seen as a trait that could make a difference between several available options for the region's future. Ethnic movements that had been formed clandestinely now came out of the shadows. In many ways they were a reaction to calls for homogenization of national cultures by nationalist movements in the capitals of former Soviet republics. In the Ukrainian part of Bessarabia these movements eventually restrained from territorial claims and were turned into ethnic associations, some of which still exist. In contrast, neighboring Moldova was ripped apart by nationalist demands. A pro-Russian movement in Transnistria and the Gagauz autonomy movement in southern Bessarabia turned violent and insisted on territorial autonomy.

Both movements emerged as reactions to revived Moldovan nationalism (Demirdirek 2008b: 125). In 1989 the communist leaders of Moldova gave in to pressure from the street and promised to create an elevated status for the Moldovan/Romanian language. In the largely Russian-speaking eastern region of Transnistria, people feared they could become second rate citizens because social mobility in Moldova would soon require fluent knowledge of Moldovan/Romanian. For the Gagauz and Bulgarian regions in the south of Moldova it could mean that they soon would have to be fluent in two foreign languages, Russian and Moldovan/Romanian, in order to stand a chance of social enhancement (Crowther 1991: 194). In 1990 the Popular Front of Moldova, a spearhead movement of nationalist mobilization, was elected to the national parliament. Their radical demands in educational politics and their rhetoric of unification with neighboring Romania, caused outright panic among Russian speakers and other minorities (King 2000: 151; Demirdirek 2008a: 95). At the same time with the Popular Front of Moldova, in 1989 a Gagauz movement was founded, *Gagauz Halkı* (the Gagauz people). Initially, *Gagauz Halkı* collaborated with the Popular Front. Once pan-Romanian ideas became common among Popular Front members, the two organizations turned against each other and radicalized (Troebst 2001: 76; King 1997: 744). *Gagauz Halkı* began working on plans to separate from Moldova in 1989. The Gagauz twice declared their independence, once in November 1989 as an autonomous part of the Moldovan SSR, and once after relations had further deteriorated in August 1990 as independent from the Moldovan SSR but still a part of the Soviet Union (2012: 759). Parliamentary elections, held in February 1990, further aggravated the situation. The ballot brought many of Moldova's Popular Front candidates into powerful positions, and the new nationalist and pan-Romanian Prime Minister, Mircea Druc, repeatedly attacked the Gagauz leadership. In August 1990 another proclamation of a separate Gagauz republic followed. Gagauz parliamentary elections were scheduled for October of that year. The government in Chișinău declared *Gagauz Halkı* an illegal organization and urged Moldovan citizens to take up arms against Gagauz separatists. So called volunteer combatants were bused in from different regions of Moldova to crush the Gagauz separatist movement. In the Gagauz region, road blocks were set up and trenches dug out. Only the intervention of Soviet troops prevented major bloodshed (King 1997: 744; Hatłas 2011: 196; Fane 1993: 144). The Izmail paper *Sovetskiy Izmail* was not shy to compare the intervention to 1944. Many among the relieved Gagauz remembered the merry mood in June 1944, the paper wrote, when the Soviet liberators were greeted with salt and bread.[57] After a three-year stalemate in

57 *Sovetskiy Izmail* November 11, 1990, Opt protivostoyanie k dialogu—Miting v Bolgrade.

the conflict an autonomy status for three mainly Gagauz rayons was agreed with the Moldovan government. Inhabitants of the mainly Bulgarian rayon of Tarakliya preferred to stay in rump Moldova. This led to the discontinuous territory of the Autonomous Gagauz Territory (ATU Gagauziya) today. The government of this new territorial unit was granted far-reaching autonomy rights. Only foreign policy, defense issues, the right to naturalize new Moldovan citizens, and currency politics remained under Chișinău's direct control (King 1997: 750).

In contrast, on the Ukrainian side of the border, neither the Gagauz nor the Bulgarians came even close to such an arrangement. The perspective of shifting republic boundaries and creating an autonomous unit comprising all Gagauz and Bulgarian settlements seemed slightly ambitious and dangerous from the start. However, a leader of the Bulgarian Cyril and Methodius Society, Vladimir Petrov,[58] pushed such plans when he thought the opportunity had come. An ethnic Bulgarian from Izmail, Petrov won his degree in jurisdiction from Lomonosov University in Moscow in 1988. In the same year he helped to legalize a Bulgarian organization that had already been operating in the region clandestinely for a couple of years. The organization promoted the idea of creating an autonomous Bulgarian entity in southern Bessarabia that included all areas where Bulgarians "live compactly," be they in Moldova or in Ukraine. The idea behind this risky effort was to have resources for the development of Bulgarian culture and language that would not have to be asked for from the Ukrainian or the Moldovan authorities. But the new Ukrainian state allowed only one region, the Crimean Peninsula, to have territorial autonomy. For all other regions in which minorities lived, only modes of cultural autonomy were allowed. For Petrov and his colleagues, this was inacceptable. They believed that the Ukrainian state would not provide the resources necessary to develop Bulgarian culture and language in the region. Also, Petrov's organization took the position that Bulgarians and Gagauz, since they both came as Transdanubian Colonists and were both Orthodox Christians, were ethnically and culturally the same, just linguistically different. Therefore, for them it made sense to aspire a territorial unit for all Bulgarian and Gagauz with an area in mind that stretched across the Moldovan-Ukrainian border. An earlier project to create a Bulgarian-Gagauz autonomous Soviet Republic in 1989 had already been halted by the opposition from within Bulgarian associations in Moldova. The Organization *Vozrozhdenie* (Renaissance), based in Chișinău, dismissed the project as "absurd." The statement made clear that the Bulgarians already had a state; Bulgaria (cited in Shornikov 2012: 784). In Ukraine, a similar legal project, based

58 Interview in Izmail on April 21, 2013.

on the plans of Petrov's Cyril and Methodius Society was drafted in 1991 by Petrov and members of the Bolgrad rayon council. It was sent to Kyiv without ever being honored with an answer.

But government officials in Kyiv were not the only ones to shrug their shoulders on autonomy ambitions in southern Bessarabia. When Gagauz villages in Moldova were on the brink of civil war, there were also calls to arms across the border to their ethnic brethren in Ukraine, but to little effect. Elizaveta Derkach,[59] a history teacher in the predominantly Gagauz village of Kotlovina, remembered a truckload of guns sent to the village in 1990 from Vulcanești, the nearest Gagauz town in Moldova. No one in the village agreed to take up arms for the adventurous sake of a Gagauz independent state. Separatism from the Ukrainian SSR found no popular support. In November 1990 a rally of solidarity against the politics of Chișinău took place in Bolgrad, organized by the Cyril and Methodius Society.[60] Among the speakers were the leaders of the then still unrecognized Gagauz Autonomous Territory. One of them opted to leave Moldova and join Russia as an autonomous republic instead. Another said that the government in Chișinău was to blame for the violence. It treated the Gagauz as second-rate citizens and had permitted "pogroms" in Cahul (a nearby Romania/Moldovan speaking rayon center) where a drunken mob had vandalized the Communist Party headquarters and a Lenin monument. The representatives of the Gagauz used the formulation "Moldovan-Romanian-neo fascism," which captured the uncertainty and fear among the Gagauz in Moldova at the time. On paper, both newly independent countries, Moldova and Ukraine, granted equal citizenship rights to all their residents irrespective of ethnicity, language, or duration of residence. In both countries potential distress for ethnic minorities came not from the law but from nation building projects and reinterpretations of the region's history (Kaneff and Heintz 2006: 9). Nevertheless, the Gagauz in Moldova were without doubt under much more pressure (and therefore quicker to opt for separatism) than the Bulgarian or Gagauz in Ukraine. The Gagauz in Moldova were now the most notable ethnic minority in the country after the pro-Russian Transnistrian region had broken away to declare independence. Also, many among ethnic minorities in Moldova feared that Moldova might eventually unite with Romania. In such a scenario the Gagauz would become a tiny minority on the impoverished periphery of a foreign country, with hardly any political weight to negotiate their minority rights. In contrast to the Gagauz in Moldova, the Ukrainian Gagauz were in less danger of becoming second-rate citizens. Large parts of the population in Ukraine's

59 Interview in Kotlovina July 31, 2013.

60 Again, according to the article in *Sovetskiy Izmail* November 11, 1990.

south and east would be with them in the struggle against nationalizing projects from Kyiv, such as an elevated status for the Ukrainian language or a nationalist perspective on Ukraine's past. In short, there were intact chances to preserve the habitual way of life without grabbing guns.

Apart from the creation of a Gagauz autonomous unit (*ATU Gagauziya*) in southern Moldova, there were no attempts to redraw borders along ethnic boundaries in southern Bessarabia.[61] None of the ethnic groups that can be found here have a convincing claim for a discrete area in which they form a clear majority. Even using history as an argument, as could be observed across the Soviet Union, none of the ethnic groups that inhabit southern Bessarabia today, could credibly claim to have been here before all the others. Given the nature of the ethnic mosaic in the region with its overlapping settlement areas of ethnic groups, the fuzzy boundaries between them, and often ambiguous individual ethnic identities, the hitherto low degree of zeal to shift borders once more, can be asserted only with relief.

At the time the Soviet Union collapsed, rural Bessarabia provided neither the resources that could have served as incentives to an insurgency nor the social groups or communication networks that could have served as breeding grounds for an armed campaign. Meanwhile other attempts to redraw borders in the former Soviet Union, notably in nearby Transnistria, but also in Abkhazia, South Ossetia, Nagorno Karabakh and later in Chechnya, had turned into nightmares for the local populations there. These hapless attempts to create new republics along ethnic boundaries served those few who ever seriously thought of a Gagauz or Bulgarian state in Bessarabia as a warning. Yet, even without armed conflict, the collapse of the Soviet Union left Bessarabians in a new world order in which ethnicity had become the defining category to justify political power. This would remain so in the decades to come.

---

61 In spring 2015 rumors of separatist underground activity in southern Bessarabia resumed, but as of late 2015 did not substantiate.

CHAPTER 6

Post-Soviet Instability, Clientelism and the Persistence of Ethnic Boundaries

On a Sunday in early summer 2013, I hitchhiked from the Ukrainian border town of Reni back to my main field site Izmail. The road out of town passes Reni's large Danube river port with its dozens of cranes, storehouses, and silos. This scenery offers a sinister picture of decline. None of the cranes were moving. There were hardly any people to be seen, let alone ships on the vast river. I occasionally pointed to one of the decaying buildings to ask the driver what they once were. "The former cannery, the former winery, the former passenger port, the former Sailor's Club," he answered. "As you can see, most things here are 'former.'" Reni is a sad example even in southern Bessarabia. Situated directly on the former Soviet border with Romania, it was once an important transportation hub. Reni, now located at the end of a dead-end street, was hit especially hard by the breakaway of the state, the outpost of which it once was. However, stories of decline can be found in every single town and village, in every factory, and every family. In fact, the dominant theme of most biographical interviews with respondents, rural or urban, was the experience of decline. The present state of decline is measured against the Soviet period, perceived as having been more optimistic, even by people too young to experience it.

This chapter focuses on the decline of state institutions and their replacement with clientelistic networks. For the category of ethnicity, this process can hardly be overstated. Ethnicity along with other group denominators, such as religion and native language, enabled patrons to segment their clientele into manageable groups and they enabled clients to classify and assess potential patrons. This chapter is intended to carve out the link between decline of state institutions and the sharpening of ethnic boundaries. Therefore, the two aspects receive alternating attention throughout this chapter.

Decline is not an abstract notion in post-independence Ukraine. People in Izmail and the villages in its environs can tell uncountable stories about it. Usually they do not have to go far for examples. Most of their stories concerned respondents themselves or people close to them. Some separate realms in which decline was felt to be particularly harsh can be distinguished: Many people report a loss of ideas to live for. This loss is often connected to a perceived overall loss in morale and ethics (usually subsumed under the Russian term *dukhovnost'*). Politics is often seen as no longer governed by ideologies,

 | DOI:10.1163/9789004408029_007

but by the pursuit of personal interests. Ethnicity provides a sense of stability and continuity, which makes it a prized political currency in turbulent post-Soviet local politics. Ethnicity's air of stability is one central reason why the experience of socio-economic decline fosters the sharpening of ethnic boundaries. Furthermore, this chapter will show that in clientelistic politics clear-cut group boundaries are preferable to fuzzy ones. This is why, since Ukrainian independence, ethnicity not only retained its importance as a social category but also had its boundaries constantly mended by politicians and interest groups.

After the break-up of the Soviet Union, many institutions, on the national as well as on the local level, have ceased to fulfill their purposes or have vanished altogether. These institutions used to provide security, income, services, or as the former Sailor's Club in Reni, leisure activities. They were once funded by the state and accessible more or less equally for all citizens. Now, services such as medical care or education are accessible in satisfying quality only for the rich. The decay of infrastructure is more visible and therefore often used as a metaphor for wider social decay. Again, those parts of infrastructure that serve the common good were the first to fall apart, while other parts, that exclusively serve the private interests of a few, such as luxury housing projects, experience a boom.

In villages especially, many people reported a decline in communal spirit. Whereas in the past, people are remembered to have helped each other and were mutually obliged through reciprocal exchange in resources and support, now the dominant way to mobilize manpower is money. One common memory among villagers that illustrated bygone communal support networks was house construction. Most village homes, where the biographical interviews for this chapter were taken, were built in the 1960s and 70s. The land and some construction materials were provided by the kolkhoz, the labor by the joint efforts of several households linked to each other through kinship and friendship.[1] Not only were such communal undertakings remembered as pleasant, they also provided the capacity to build houses with very little money. The observation that nowadays one cannot achieve anything without money has become a conventional wisdom. Today, hardly any new houses are being built in villages. The main reason for this is a decline in the socio-economic standing of many families. The heavily mechanized and export-oriented agriculture in former kolkhoz villages fails to offer jobs for young people. Most of them leave their villages in search for employment in Ukraine's main cities or abroad.

1 This observation was also made by Boneva (Boneva 2006: 55) in two Bulgarian villages in southern Bessarabia.

Compared with Soviet times, there are less children growing up in villages. Many village school buildings, constructed in the Brezhnev period, appear oversized now. Houses have been built to accommodate three generations under one roof. Nowadays such households have become a rarity. Therefore, not only are there no new houses built, many of those built for children who moved away, are now falling into decay. Dmitri Petrovich Uzun,[2] a resident of Kotlovina, born in 1926, said he remembered only two periods in his life, when houses were destroyed, not built; the Second World War, and the post-socialist period. This comparison of the present with the worst years in reach of memory seems to have been fairly widespread, even before the spring of 2014, when war returned to Ukraine.

Among this all-embracing decline of ideological and social certainties, institutions, infrastructure, communities, and even families, one category, now familiar to literally everyone, seems to remain firm as a rock: Ethnicity. For illustration it is worth to recall the latest Soviet definition of "ethnos," coined by Yulian Bromley, the long-time, highest-ranking ethnographer in the USSR:

> Ethnos is a historically *stable* entity of people developed on a certain territory and possessing common, relatively *stable* features of culture (including language) and psyche as well as a consciousness of their unity and of their difference from other similar entities (self-awareness) *fixed* in a self-name (cited in Tishkov 1997: 3, emphasis added).

Whether or not in reality ethnicity was a stable category, in its academic and popular conceptualization, stability (*ustoichivost'*) over time was the feature that set ethnicity apart from other more volatile institutions such as citizenship or religion (Bromley 1983: 46). A member of an ethnos would not lose his or her sense of belonging to this ethnos, even after many generations, after political circumstances have changed, or after an individual had moved to another place. Members of political nations (Bromley named France and Belgium as examples) would lose their sense of belonging after the political entities that bear the same name would have disappeared. Also, the second generation of French or Belgian emigrants would lose their sense of belonging to what Bromley saw as the purely political community of the French or the Belgians. The same was true, he argued, for confessional groups and for language communities. After people lose their faith or no longer speak a particular language, they lose their sense of belonging to these communities. This would not happen to communities of the ethnos-type, Bromley insisted. So the

2 Interview in Kotlovina July 12, 2013.

litmus-test to differentiate an ethnos from other forms of human communion is whether the self-designation can remain even after people have changed their whereabouts, their faith, the language they speak, or after the political situation around them has changed (Bromley 1983: 47). In the Soviet interpretation of ethnos, a Russian who experienced the transformation from the empire to the Soviet Union, who moved from Russia to Estonia, started to speak Estonian there, and replaced his Orthodox Christianity with Bolshevist Atheism, still remained a Russian. The same was true for a Ukrainian, a Jew, an Armenian, or a Georgian who left their native region, became Atheists or Baptists or Buddhists, and started to speak Russian, Ukrainian, or English. Ethnicity appeared as a category immune to the chaos of the time.

In the years of Perestroika, stability became a value in and of itself. Besides ethnicity, the only other concept that provided a similar assurance of stability was religion. Both these concepts came to replace many of the functions the Marxist-Leninist ideology and its state-funded institutions had fulfilled during the decades of Soviet rule (Slezkine 1994: 451; Verdery 1993b: 191). This new set of functions that ethnicity came to fulfill, also meant that it ceased to fulfill its old, Soviet function as an administrative category. Instead, the reference to an ethnic community preserving unique and age-old values became strongly associated with continuity and stability, the one quality so many voters longed for and so many politicians claimed to provide.[3]

Many of my respondents clearly expressed their longing for stability in the near future. But they also had a way of remembering the past as much more stable than it likely could have been. For the last Soviet Generation it is rather common to associate the years of Brezhnev's rule with security, predictability, and stability (Raleigh 2012: 237). Literature on post-socialism describes many early symptoms of the decay of one-party-communism, such as an economy of shortage, nepotism, corruption, as well as pro-forma compliance in worn out rituals.[4] In stark contrast, most of my respondents described the Soviet period as monolithic and almost void of social change. Many had great difficulties to remember symptoms of imminent collapse. To Soviet citizens, the disintegration of their country was just as surprising as to most experts (Beissinger 2002: 3). Symptoms of chaos during the last decade of the USSR, or traces of stability and continuity in the post-socialist era, are hardly remembered. Many

3 One of the campaign slogans for the dominant Party of the Regions during the 2012 parliamentary election campaign in Odessa oblast was "from stability to prosperity."

4 For economy of shortage, nepotism, corruption see for example Kornai (1980), Verdery (1996), Stefes (2006), Willerton (1992), Fairbanks (1999), Eisenstadt and Roniger (1984), Kotkin (1991), for pro-forma compliance in worn out rituals see for example. Yurchak (2006), Friedberg (1991).

respondents during interviews differentiated simply between two periods: "those times" (*te vremena*) and now. Within "those times" only minimal differentiations seem to be remembered.

Thus, the mode of imagining history and the mode of imagining ethnicity are strikingly similar: Characteristics are seen as stable and alike within one epoch or one ethnic group, but they are seen as entirely different between two epochs or two ethnic groups. Differences *within* one epoch or ethnic group and similarities *between* them are easily omitted or forgotten. The opposition between "those times" and now is akin to the opposition between "us" and "them." This mechanism of thought is central in politicizing both the past and ethnic boundaries.

1 The Power of Benefaction

One big contrast to Soviet times is that now, with multi-party elections, politicians have to court people for their political support. During the Soviet Union, politicians belonged to a vanguard party. They drew their power from their party membership and their supposedly superior insight in Marxist-Leninist teachings. After the demise of the Soviet Union, the Communist Party lost its appeal and the ideological competence of its leaders lost the function of legitimizing political power. Nowadays, politicians draw their power from their role as benefactors who offer support and understanding thanks to their wealth and generosity. In the 2012 parliamentary election campaign, one of the candidates running for the Party of the Regions, then still ruling Odessa oblast and most of Ukraine, chose the campaign slogan "the power of benefaction."[5] All along the Odessa ring road, uniform billboards appeared listing the candidate's good services to the population, from repairing roads to free medical examination for the province's children. Politicians are no longer elected and esteemed because they represent and exemplify an ideology, but because they understand the people's needs and have the means to satisfy them. Ideology has all but lost its importance in Ukrainian political debates. Its place was taken by a discourse of generosity and morality.

In real democracies (as opposed to ideal democracies) voters' expectations for the politicians they elect are not so much the implementation of a party program that would serve the common good, but policies that improve the voter's own personal lot (Piattoni 2001: 193). For Ukraine, far from being an

5 The Russian original of the slogan was "Sila dobrykh del," which can also be translated as "the *force* of benefaction."

ideal democracy, this observation certainly holds true. What may set Ukraine apart from her western neighbors is the boldness with which the powerful offer personal gains instead of political visions. The benefactor who offers wholeheartedly to his voters has become the archetype of the politician. One of southern Bessarabia's most successful political patrons, member of *Verkhovna Rada*, the national parliament, Anton Kisse, described his attitude to benefaction while commenting on a power struggle between two of his subordinates:

> In this matter, my position as a politician and a citizen is very clear: For political power one should fight only with legal means. For this purpose, there are electoral processes regulated by the law. Once official elections are announced, well then one has to fight for the trust of the voter by way of tangible good deeds (*konkretnymi dobrymi delami*).[6]

Several examples of such "tangible good deeds" will be described in the course of this chapter. The purest and maybe most tangible form is to hand out money and presents to a crowd. A freshly elected deputy to the oblast parliament, Yuri Dimchoglo, has done so on several occasions during my fieldwork. At a village festival in Chervonoarmeyskoe he used a break in the football game to announce via megaphone he wanted to give a handsome sum of money to the captain of the local football team "for the development of sport."[7] The handing over of the money was followed by a short speech in which Dimchoglo said how deeply he cared about the fate of the village. He announced further gifts; air-conditioning for the village's culture house and broadband internet for the school. Even more publicly, at a village celebration in Kotlovina, Dimchoglo appeared on stage with two laptops, one for the culture house and one for the school. He also donated an icon to the local church that he had bought during a pilgrimage to Jerusalem. It is very doubtful that he could have made a similarly flattering impression among his voters, had he elaborated on his political ideas there. Nevertheless, not only the material value of the gifts but also the content of speeches, expressing affection and care for the village communities, are crucial in building the image of a patron. One way of demonstrating attention is to publish congratulatory ads on the frontage of local newspapers, and increasingly in social media. Such ads are due several dozen times a year on very diverse occasions such as professional holidays, religious festivals, and

6 Anton Kisse on his homepage July 31, 2014, commenting on a power struggle for the post of mayor in Bolgrad: <http://antonkisse.com/anton-kisse-prokommentiroval-zhurnalistam-situatsiyu-v-bolgrade/> (22.03.2019).

7 The gift was announced as 1,000 UAH, approximately 90 Euro at the time.

anniversaries of historical events. Congratulatory ads typically show members of parliament, mayors, running candidates, and the local representatives of political parties. Usually higher ranking or more influential politicians pay for bigger ads and longer texts, in which they express their affection and support for the particular group in question; the inhabitants of Izmail on the city's anniversary day, the soldiers and veterans on the day of the defender of the fatherland, the teachers on teacher's day, and the sailors on sailor's day. Influential politicians might also include in their congratulatory address the "tangible good deeds" they have recently committed for this particular group.

Mobilizing political support through generosity, politicians and their electorate have entered a relationship of patron and client. This relationship shapes a political system commonly called clientelism. Clientelism can be defined as „the proffering of material goods in return for electoral support, where the criterion of distribution that the patron uses is simply: did you (will you) support me?" (Stokes 2009: 649). The ideological parameters of such a system are hard to pin down. Clientelism is occupied with achieving and maintaining political power for those who work in it and it is judged by what it achieves, not by what it stands for (Scott 1969: 1144). Local politics in Ukraine is a very thinly disguised exchange of resources and political loyalty. In Ukraine rent-seeking structures are a symptom of the state's under-development. They bear witness to underdeveloped legal institutions, a broken welfare state, and a constrained civil society. The state's main function is that of a redistributor. At the receiving end of this redistribution, individuals, institutions, and regions are heavily dependent on the center (Gramatzki 2002: 256). Politicians, such as Kisse or Dimchoglo, are wealthy entrepreneurs who distribute their wealth and in exchange get elected to lucrative bureaucratic positions. Once they are elected, they continue to distribute their personal fortune (Dimchoglo, when asked who paid for his gifts, insisted he bought them from his private funds), but when they hold political offices, patrons can add to their private fortune the state resources over which they have leverage and the income they make from rent seeking activities. The most basic of voter's needs are usually resources and jobs that politicians attempt to provide. Next in line is the need for stability. As the Soviet Union slithered into disintegration, patron-client networks became a crucial source of security and direction for both sides of the relationship (Willerton 1992: 6). So besides piecemeal gifts on village celebrations, patrons offer the image of men (and much more rarely women) who, in the long run, will back-up their clients.

Because ethnicity is so strongly associated with stability, it has become a powerful political tool. By way of its primordial conceptualization, it refers to a long bygone time, when things were still done as they had been done always.

FIGURE 3 A Bulgarian folklore group performing in front of a World War II memorial in Izmail during city day celebrations, September 2012

The use of ethnicity in politics always comes along with narratives of history and tradition. This is usually exemplified by the use of folklore performances to refer to ethnicity in public gatherings, where political support is mobilized. As Hobsbawm and Ranger (1983: 2) observed, the wish to structure at least some parts of social life in our constantly changing, modern world as unchanging and invariant makes an "invention of tradition" so tempting. In festive occasions, in which political support is to be mobilized, the conservation of traditional aspects of culture (invented or not) is a frequently recurring element. In modern local politics in Ukraine, conserving traditional elements of culture is boasted louder and more proudly than innovation.

The regular folklore performances that frame political events illustrate this phenomenon most vividly. In a large gathering of Bulgarian folklore groups in August 2013, a veteran activist from a Bulgarian ethnic organization in Ukraine proudly announced in his celebratory address that Bulgarians in Ukraine had proven their ability to conserve their language and spirit (*dukhovnost'*). "It is not for no reason," he said, referring to the picturesque Bulgarian dialect of Bessarabian Bulgarians, "that people in Bulgaria ask me, why I speak like an old granny. It is because we are the ones who conserve our language!" This example suggests that the desire for stability in social structures can translate into a desire of stability in cultural traits. Wherever such stability can be found (real or imagined) it can become a matter of celebration. Ethnicity and an imaginary stability of ethnic features offer themselves as topics for political patrons advertising themselves as the harbingers of stability.

The interface between the process of defining ethnic culture and political clientelism is mediated by ethnic associations. In southern Bessarabia they have become the prime mover of ethnic representation in public. All established ethnic groups, even those encompassing very small shares of the population, have their own association, often even several competing ones. Depending on the group represented, such associations have ties to different centers inside and outside Ukraine. Russian associations in 2013 had ties to Moscow as well as to Crimea and the Donbas, where Russian Nationalism has been a force in politics since Ukraine's independence. Bulgarian ethnic associations usually had links to organizations in Bulgaria. Gagauz organizations were linked to the Gagauz autonomous area in Moldova but often also to Bulgaria and Turkey. Associations of smaller minority groups such as Germans, Poles, Jews, and Armenians, typically had connections to organizations in the respective countries. On top of that, many regional ethnic organizations teamed up with organizations from other regions in Ukraine, where they are also represented. Some of them form interregional umbrella organizations, based in Kyiv, such as the All Ukrainian Congress of Bulgarians, the All Ukrainian Association of Bulgarians, or the Union of Gagauz in Ukraine. Some ethnic organizations run as political parties in elections, like the Russkiy Blok in Izmail. But most such organizations just use their resources to support individual candidates. Many of them have their own constitutions in which they specify their purpose. Some organizations have narrower purposes such as language courses or folklore, but many are all-rounders, offering political representation and the fostering of folklore and language training, along with social or leisurely activities.

Maintaining what is perceived as ethnic uniqueness is certainly one function ethnic associations embrace. On the other hand, a frequently highlighted purpose of ethnic associations is also to maintain good relations with other such organizations. When one organization celebrates an anniversary, usually other associations, representing other ethnic groups, are invited to the festivities. The speeches of representatives of other ethnic associations in such occasions often enthusiastically celebrate harmonious interethnic relations.

On rare occasions, however, ethnic associations might enter into conflict with the state. Mostly, the reason for such conflicts is not the state's attitude towards ethnic minorities and their languages, but disputes over resources and property.[8] In Izmail, the Bulgarian Cyril and Methodius Society got into conflict with city authorities over a building they had rented, renovated and used

8 For a detailed study of how disputes over property can lead to reinforced ethnic distinctions in a post-socialist context see Kaneff's (1998) study of a village in northern Bulgaria.

for 20 years before the municipality wanted to sell it.[9] In a similar incident in March 2013, Ukrainian ethnic association Prosvita and Greek organization Ellada, teamed up to publicly lament the municipality of Izmail's handling of the property the two organizations shared for their office spaces. The old house lacked basic sanitation and a city official used parts of the space rented by these organizations as a private apartment. In a bitter letter to the Izmail weekly *Kur'er Nedeli*, the head of Ellada, Tatyana Mitaki, expressed the suspicion that "someone had decided to drive the Greeks out,"[10] thereby equating her organization's difficulties with oppression of the Greeks as an ethnic group. These conflicts in Izmail reflected a similar incident in the provincial capital Odessa. In 2008 the city attempted to drive the regional cultural center of Bulgarians out of a building it had been using for many years. A representative of the association hinted that the building, a historic cinema in the heart of the old town, had gained in value after it had been renovated with financial support from Bulgaria. Therefore, "business structures" (allegedly businesses connected to the city officials in charge) were interested in the property. The organization, with support from mayors of Bulgarian villages in southern Bessarabia, wrote to the Parliamentary Commission for Human Rights and Protection of Minorities, stating that the incident had harmed interethnic relations in Ukraine, and Ukraine's reputation in Europe.[11] So property related conflicts between the state and ethnic associations are very likely to be framed as ethnic conflicts, reinforcing thereby the claim of ethnic associations to be the representatives of entire ethnic communities. Yet, mostly ethnic associations and the state work together closely. In public events, representatives of the state and of ethnic associations regularly exchange pleasantries.

One reoccurring occasion for the exchange of pleasantries are award ceremonies. Such ceremonies are arguably the purest form of bringing the patron-client relationship to a public forum. Awarding ceremonies can be celebratory or serious, they can involve men, women, or children, and they can be on the scale of a classroom or a stadium. Showing off one's riches is not enough to attract clients. Because each client also propagates his patron among potential new clients it is equally important for patrons to show their prospective clients not only that they already have attracted many clients, but also that these are reputable people. The award is one way of doing so. Awarding ceremonies are a central showpiece for patrons who want to demonstrate their "power of benefaction." In this chapter they will serve as the foundation for

9 Personal communication from the organization's chair, Vladimir Petrov, April 21, 2013.
10 *Kur'er Nedeli*, March 8, 2013.
11 *Pridunayskie Vesti*, February 7, 2008.

the subsequent discussion of strategies in local politics. This discussion also involves the question why the public display of ethnicity matters in a political structure in which symbolic exchange, such as the exchange of awards, needs publicity, whereas resources exchanged for political support is preferably done in the dark. Looking at awarding ceremonies is therefore a bit like looking at the tip of a clientelistic iceberg.

It can hardly be overlooked by an outsider who visits a number of offices and waiting rooms in post-Soviet countries; the walls are often covered with awards and diplomas for all kinds of achievements. If one discusses awards with the person they were granted to, they may well reveal that their walls can impossibly host all of them and that they have stacks more in their drawers. Often just the most recent and valued awards are displayed on walls. Awards and diplomas have been described from the point of view of official display of gratitude and social recognition (Habeck 2011: 55, 62). How do functionaries and ordinary people in post-Soviet countries earn so much social recognition? Where do all these awards come from?

Awards mostly come in the form of an elaborately decorated diploma (*gramota*). Sometimes they take the form of medals, which has the benefit that they can not only be sported on one's wall but also on one's chest in public events. A tradition of awarding loyal clients and granting titles to compliant functionaries, scientists, and state-sanctioned artists, dates back far into the Soviet period. According to Yurchak (2006: 94) diplomas and awards in Soviet times were cherished as signs of recognition for an achievement. Diplomas were handed out more restrictively then and they were contrasted by harsh public criticism for those who did not live up to expectations. Therefore, the Soviet version of the awarding ceremony also involved shaming those who have fulfilled their tasks inefficiently or showed little commitment.[12] In the Soviet ceremony, the award was an instrument to stimulate production by honoring outstanding achievements and measure it against mediocre performance. Today, public shaming in an awarding ceremony would be unthinkable. Even folklore collectives that earn themselves the silent scorn of the

12 One example is a series of reports about a big folklore group gathering in an Izmail theatre in the newspaper *Pridunayskaya Pravda* November 18–20, 1953. In the event, 150 folklore collectives from the region were honored with an award. But one group from Belgorod-Dniestrovskiy was publicly reprimanded because its singers knew their lyrics so poorly. The management of the according culture house was publicly told to improve their work. Another collective from Sarata was also publicly frowned upon. There, the management of the culture house was just not committed enough, the newspaper commented. Public awarding and shaming was also observed by Caroline Humphrey (1998: 376) in kolkhoz gatherings in Siberia.

audience are politely applauded. They are just as likely to be given a *gramota*, as anyone else. Although I argue that awarding during ceremonies is a deeply political act, political dispute has no place in them. In private, people are often very explicit about the shortcomings of local politics. But such criticism is hardly ever voiced during a ceremony. That the award in post-Soviet society is assigned without the counterweight of public criticism indicates that it has adopted a new function in the post-Soviet clientelistic state. Today, it seems, awards are no longer a stimulus to excel, but a symbol of mutual trust between patron and client, the public performance of a reciprocal relationship.

Awards today, as in Soviet times, are issued by a person or an institution that claims the authority to judge the value of someone's achievements. The award links the awarding and the awarded. Not unlike a contract, it contains the names of both parties. This procedure's impact is greatest if conducted publicly. Awarding institutions can be state related and base their authority on their official status. Very often however, awards are handed out by institutions not directly linked to the state, such as ethnic associations. In those cases, their authority to judge whose achievements to distinguish stems from their role as representatives of a group they themselves help to shape and limit.

Awards can be directed both from patrons to clients and from clients to patrons. The patron awards his clients for their work, support, and loyalty. Clients sometimes in their turn award the patron for sponsorship, political patronage, or simply his or her presence in the ceremony. In some cases patrons are awarded in absentia, by their clients. In such a case it is often patrons of a lower level who attend the ceremony and are asked by their clients to pass on the award to their own patron. So if given from a patron to a client, an award means a sign of attention and gratefulness for loyalty and support. If it is given from a client to a patron, an award is a sign of gratefulness for sponsorship and patronage and therefore also a sign of loyalty.

Since awards function as a currency in clientelistic exchange, they are handed out in especially rich quantities at occasions where two levels of the exchange get together in one room. For instance when representatives of municipal, rayon and oblast level appear in one event, as is the case of annual rayon gatherings of national cultures, where the municipal delegates for culture houses and schools are awarded for their achievements by their superiors in the rayon's department of culture and in return sometimes award their superiors for their sponsorship.

Such ceremonies usually include a formal opening and closing, marked by everybody getting up to sing the national anthem. Another reoccurring feature is reference to higher levels in the state apparatus. At the rayon gathering of national cultures for Izmail rayon in August 2013, for instance, a representative of the rayon authorities gave a speech pointing out the local administration's successes during the last year. He praised the initiatives taken by his own superiors in the Odessa oblast government. He said that initiatives by the Odessa governor were backed by the president in Kyiv. These initiatives had led to better education, improved infrastructure and medical care. He also explained that the rich harvest anticipated in the weeks to come would not have been possible without the support of the government. The speech ended with words of gratefulness to the veterans of war and labor and with praising people in southern Bessarabia for their harmonious inter-ethnic relations and tolerance.

This was an example for a ceremony when patrons served their clients with recognition for their work and thereby ensured that they will continue their support for the kinds of activities that were honored with an award. This happened both very publicly and very formally, surrounded by flags, national dress, fanfare, and framed by ceremonial opening and closing. Hierarchy was a carefully stressed aspect of the ceremony, referring specifically to the governor and through the governor to the president.

Similar events, on the scale of an entire stadium, took place twice in autumn 2013 on two consecutive Saturdays the ethnic associations of the Bulgarian and the Gagauz respectively celebrated their day of Bulgarian Culture and Day of Gagauz Culture in Odessa's Spartak stadium. These events involved more layers of hierarchy, since diplomas came in some instances directly from the Ministry of Education in Kyiv. They also involved more transnational ties: Diplomas were exchanged with ministries and cultural institutions in Bulgaria and the ATU Gagauziya. These hierarchies were, like in the much smaller events, carefully stressed for example by switching from Russian into Ukrainian to announce a diploma awarded by a Kyiv ministry. In events of this kind, the awarding ceremony can sometimes last for several hours and often involves awards for nearly everyone, who has some part in the event.

Why is it that this exchange of a commodity that itself bears very little material value is so central to public ceremonies? This question is more significant even if one thinks of the huge material value of other commodities that are also exchanged between patrons and clients, albeit less publicly. The reason why the material side of the exchange happens clandestinely (and therefore out of the ethnographer's sight) is of course that it is much harder to legitimize the exchange of valuable resources for political support. It is sufficient to just imagine how outrageous it would be if a patron on a festival stage would hand out jobs and licenses instead of awards. Handing out licenses or positions in the state bureaucracy to only those clients who politically support the patron is often an inefficient allocation of resources and therefore ethically doubtful. This side of the exchange can therefore not be paraded. The legitimacy of

FIGURE 4 Gagauz from southern Bessarabia celebrating the Day of Gagauz Culture in Odessa, September 2013

exchanging awards, however, is hardly questionable. Instead of an exchange of material goods it is an exchange of symbols that indicate mutual trust. It is essential to patrons to demonstrate trust towards others, a demonstration that strengthens their own trustworthiness. Patrons and clients are, after all, not necessarily similar to each other in terms of ideology or ethnicity. All the more they need to stress their *personal* loyalty to each other. The award is a powerful symbol of mutual appreciation.

2 The Roots of Clientelism in Ethnic and Non-Ethnic Networks

Clientelism was not new to this part of the world when the Soviet Union collapsed. The phenomenon has been described for pre-modern societies by historians (see for example Kettering 1988). In feudal Russia, clientelism was a driving force in political alliance building (see for example Hosking 2000; Shlapentokh 1996 for a comparison between feudal and post-Soviet Russia). During the Soviet Union as well, many a party career depended on the goodwill of a political mentor (for a thorough study see Fairbanks 1978). In a political system as secretive and opaque as the one-party Soviet state, obscure reciprocal alliances between politicians and bureaucrats thrived (Willerton 1992: 9). But during the Soviet Union, political power had to be justified, at least seemingly, with achievements in institutions like the Party, the military, or a state enterprise. Clientelism could exist only clandestinely. Although most party careers depended on the secret patronage of higher officials, in public the powerful needed to advertise their competence (by achieving planned outcomes) not their *personal* generosity. Now, boasting gifts and favors as publicly as possible is not only desirable, but necessary to become, and to remain a patron. The change from a clandestine form of clientelism towards a more attention-seeking form has started during the years of the Perestroika. Clientelism has been described both as cause for and effect of the collapse of the Soviet system. I agree with Stefes (2006: 1) that clientelism was not a mere side effect of the USSR's break-up, but rather its main cause. Also the unwritten rules, by which clientelism works, have hindered the growth of institutions, vital for the emergence of democracy and market economy. Rule of law, allocation of resources, entitlement of rights and duties, all came to be affected by clientelistic exchange. The roots of clientelism in the later years of the Soviet Union lay in what Kornai (1980) described as an "economy of shortage." Unlike in the market economy where production of resources and services is restrained by demand, the Soviet command economy was usually restrained by scarce supply of resources. Whereas in the capitalist economy, miscalculating demand would force an enterprise out of business, in the planned economy not producing sufficient output would still leave an enterprise in the market, especially if its managers had the necessary connections to the political leadership. So in command economy, miscalculations in the production process did not lead to bankruptcy but rather to an allocation of more resources, provided managers and political planners had a good personal relationship (Kornai 1980: 27). The way of getting access to scarce goods and services through personal relations, came to be known as "blat" in Russian. To do things *po blatu* (using one's connections) often was the only way to get things done at all. And since everybody did it, those who missed out just punished themselves (Raleigh 2012: 228). Alena Ledeneva (1998: 3) described *blat* as "the 'reverse side' of an over-controlling center, a reaction of ordinary people to the structural constraints of the socialist system of distribution—a series of practices which enabled the Soviet system to function and made it tolerable, but also subverted it."

In the "economy of shortage," the scarcest resource was always the limiting factor to the volume of output, and therefore it depended on this resource whether or not the planned output goal could be reached. To obtain such resources at the time needed, personal *blat* relations between managers and bureaucrats were crucial. If one crucial resource could not be obtained in time it was substituted with another, inferior resource to still fulfill the plan. So for example if qualified workers were not at hand, they were substituted with less qualified workers, or if a durable material was not available, it was substitute with one of lower quality. Kornai (1980: 37) called this mode of production "do-it-your-self at an industrial scale." This system produced not what was in the plan, but what could feasibly be produced with the available resources. It eventually led to an even less reliable supply of processed goods. A vicious circle of deficit was the outcome. Thus, barter economy, commodity for commodity, emerged as the most reliable way to obtain the resources needed at the time needed.

This puzzling, semi-legal market chimes with Clifford Geertz's (1978: 29) observation about the bazaar economy, where information is the name of the game. In the bazaar, spatial localization and ethnic specialization help reduce the effort of information gathering. Not unlike in a bazaar, finding adequate information was the key to survival in the unforgiving post-Soviet barter economy. Some people at the source of information or in positions to control the flow of resources began to use the situation for their private gain and to deliver scarce resources and information first to those who could pay more (Eisenstadt and Roniger 1984: 158). These private profits could then be reinvested in building patron-client relations. In Ukraine, the Kuchma government (1994–2005) firmly established such relations between the President and oligarchs. Their political loyalty was rewarded by privileged access to the booty of privatization. Political disloyalty was punished by a closer look from the prosecutor, who was an instrument of the government rather than the judiciary (Schneider-Deters 2008). Political loyalty for people, who did business "*po blatu*," served as protection from the law, as a "roof" (*krysha*) that protected one's operations from state interference. State officials could provide such a protection for a share in the business. The more important the operation was, the higher the *krysha* had to be (Varese 2001: 59). When, as a consequence of such schemes, the Soviet Union collapsed, barter trade became the dominant form of economy amidst heavy inflation and an insecure financial sector. In this new situation, where only possession of valued goods, information, and contacts (not membership in a party or visionary political leadership) could attract clients, it became useful to show off one's own riches and the riches of one's clients as publicly as possible.

Mutual trust was a crucial precondition to do things "*po blatu*." If one obtained information on which to base a risky deal, one needed to be sure the informant was trustworthy. Also, one could pass on valuable information only to trusted allies. Such secure connections were often built on family ties, among old friends, neighbors, party colleagues, or military comrades. In many areas of the former socialist bloc, such ties most likely occurred within one ethnic group. Catherine Verdery has demonstrated this mechanism in Transylvania (1993a), Webb showed a similar tendency for the North Caucasus (1994). In Ukraine however, where interethnic ties had been tight and most people were thoroughly integrated to Soviet society, ethnicity mattered much less than in these areas (Wanner 1998: 51).

If in other regions of the socialist bloc common ethnicity was often a ground for preferred choice in trusted relationships, there should be a good explanation why in Ukraine this phenomenon was less marked. One possible explanation comes from the idea that ethnicity in many settings can be used as an information-shortcut, a proxy with which people think they can conclude to other characteristics of a person, such as trustworthiness or aggressiveness. An information-shortcut also allows clients to better predict how a potential patron might act in the future. Whereas costless information about an individual's ethnic identity is readily available in most settings (speech, name, etc.), information about other, non-ethnic characteristics (class, profession, income, etc.) are harder to come by (Chandra 2004: 33). But in post-Soviet Ukraine, including southern Bessarabia, ethnicity provides a poor information-shortcut. Here appearance and dress hardly purvey information about ethnic backgrounds. Speech may provide a clue, but most people can conceal their native language at will by speaking standard Russian, thereby increasing the cost of inquiry. Family names are commonly believed to carry information about a person's ethnicity, but are in fact hopelessly inconclusive indicators.[13] To learn about a person's ethnic identity in southern Bessarabia is by no means costless, except if people parade their ethnicity in public events. Therefore, in

13 Family names considered very typical for one ethnic group are often just as likely to be found among members of other ethnic groups. Take the example of a Gagauz respondent whose maiden name is the allegedly typical Bulgarian Kurteva and who obtained her equally typical Gagauz family name, Khadshioglo, by marrying a Bulgarian. The same is true for suffixes considered typical among one group, such as *-oglo* indicating a Gagauz name, *-ov*, *-ev*, *-in* indicating a Russian name, or *-ko* indicating a Ukrainian name. Many Russians have family names ending on *-ko*, as many Bulgarian names end on *-ev* or *-ov* etc. Not even family names that contain an ethnonym are reliable indicators of ethnicity. (In Bessarabia perfectly common family names are Bulgar, Gagauz, Moldovan, Moldavskiy, Arnaut, Russu, Grek, Unguryan, Moskalenko, Tsiganenko, Kozak, and others). One ethnically Ukrainian respondent was called Moldavskiy, the Kyiv-based head of one Ukraine-wide Gagauz ethnic association is called Dora Arnaut (i.e. Albanian), the association of Gagauz writers is headed by the historian Stepan Bulgar, etc. Even the heavily essentializing Valentin Moshkov, in his ethnography on the Gagauz in Benderi Uezd of 1901 had to admit that family names are an inconclusive key to a person's ethnicity (1901b: 5).

southern Bessarabia, and other areas of the former Soviet Union where people's ethnicity is not easily recognizable, another type of information-shortcut has evolved: Not a person's appearance or speech are decisive factors, but a person's behavior. It was important that through one's behavior a person was recognizable as "one's own kind" (*svoy*) or "one of us" (*nash*) (Wanner 1998: 56). Being *svoy* means that one would very likely not cause problems and act in a predictable, comprehensible way (Yurchak 2006: 109). Bribery is strictly illegal and can occur without a lasting trusted relationship, since both involved parties are interested in keeping the bribe a secret. Doing things *po blatu* on the other hand, occurs in a semi-legal shadow economy, where the law could be used to the benefit of one side. Such deals usually happen between people, who see each other as *svoy* and therefore count on each other in the long run (Ledeneva 1998: 39–40). Being *svoy* and behaving like *svoy* helped both patrons and clients to shape realistic expectations how their counterpart would act. Referring constantly to ethnicity and different ethnic characters became one way of performing *svoy* in Bessarabia. Another way is to proudly refer to ethnic diversity and interethnic tolerance in the region. On the other hand, stirring up ethnic conflict would not be seen as the behavior one expects from "one's own kind." This would cause trouble for one group of potential clients and is therefore less likely to mobilize a big and well-connected group of clients. A patron, who is *svoy*, cherishes ethnic particularities and never excludes potential clients for exhibiting them. He showers his benefactions as broadly as possible. Yet, although ethnic boundaries do not restrict the groups from which clients can choose their patrons and patrons recruit their clients, they still serve to structure the exchange of favors and political support between clients and patrons.

3 Ethnicity in Local Politics: Three Strategies

After voters have given away their vote to a particular patron, they need to maximize the value of their electoral investment by pressuring the patron to deliver on his pre-electoral promises and by making sure that a share of the patron's favors reaches them *personally*. The patron, on the other hand, faces the problem that he can serve his clients with political favors, but then does not know whether or not they will support him at the ballot box. Also, the patron is interested in recruiting as many clients as possible, while disseminating as little of his limited resources as possible (Chandra 2004: 54–56). Both these problems can be solved by forming groups with internal hierarchies and by sharpening the boundaries of such groups. In the following section, I will argue that ethnic groups are a category that can help solve these structural problems of clientelism.

Whether or not, and how ethnic boundaries can be beneficially used in clientelistic politics, depends on ethnic group consciousness, interethnic relations, and the ethnic composition of the region. This point I want to illustrate by referring to the example of the Ukrainian parliamentary election campaign in autumn 2012, in which two different patrons employed two different strategies to win a parliamentary mandate: in electoral district 143, represented by Yuri Kruk since 1994,[14] there are no clear ethnic majorities. The district includes the city of Izmail, where Russians are the biggest group (43%) closely followed by Ukrainians (38%). In the rural areas of this electoral district Moldovans, Bulgarians, and Ukrainians each make up roughly a fourth of the population, while Russians and other groups comprise the last fourth.[15] In such a setting it is hard to play on the ethnic identity of voters. Yuri Kruk, the incumbent candidate, neither during his election campaign nor on his official website[16] revealed his own ethnic identity. He was very visible in the region in the weeks running up to the election. He served numerous patron-client networks with real or promised resources during September and October 2012. Most visibly he inaugurated a freshly repaved road in Izmail during city-day celebrations, he promised better perspectives to the workers of Izmail's Danube river port, he had playground facilities repainted all over Izmail and put a sign with his name on each, he sponsored the renovation of several churches in the area, for which he was granted a high religious award just days before the election.[17] None of this prevented Kruk from using ethnic networks additionally. He, for instance, also sponsored a trip of a group of local Bulgarians to a village in eastern Ukraine, to which they trace historic kin ties.[18]

A strategy that was much more visibly ethnic in character than Yuri Kruk's, worked out in neighboring electoral district 142, where Anton Kisse won the parliamentary seat in 2012. Because in this electoral district Bulgarians are the

---

14 Kruk represented a different electoral district for a five-year period. In 2014, after the Maidan upheaval has swept the Party of the Regions out of power, Kruk lost his seat in parliament.

15 Electoral district 143 comprises the city of Izmail, rayons Izmail and Reni, and parts of Bolgrad rayon. All of these rayons are part of Odessa oblast'. For ethnic census Data of these areas see the Ukrainian census of 2001: <http://2001.ukrcensus.gov.ua/rus/results/general/nationality/odesa/> (16.11.2015).

16 http://kruk.org.ua/obo-mne/ (16.11.2015).

17 *Kur'er Nedeli*, October 20, 2012, p. 1.

18 On Yuri Kruk's Vkontakte feed, September 21, 2012: <https://vk.com/wall173409888?offset=1340> (23.02.2019).

majority,[19] Kisse could wholeheartedly use his Bulgarian ethnicity during the election campaign. Not only does Kisse often mention his ethnic belonging, he is also the prominent head of the Association of Bulgarians in Ukraine. He had already proven his firm Bulgarian identity by authoring the widely distributed book *The Renaissance of the Ukrainian Bulgarians* (2006). One week before the election, hundreds of people came to Bolgrad, the main Bulgarian town in the region, to see Mr. Kisse inaugurate a monument, the construction of which he had organized and sponsored. The monument stands in memory of volunteer Bulgarian militias (*opolchentsy*) who supported the Russian army in the Russo-Turkish war 1877–78, the war that led to Bulgarian independence from the Ottoman Empire. The spectators who had gathered around the monument on the square in front of Bolgrad's church could listen for several hours to countless speakers from local politics, from the Orthodox Church, from the military, from the provincial capital, from neighboring Moldova, and not least from Bulgaria. They all praised the Bulgarian freedom fighters, in whose memory the monument was erected, and the patriotic spirit of the candidate, Anton Kisse. The week after, he was elected with a comfortable margin, even against an incumbent candidate from the then still powerful Party of the Regions.

The municipal council of the city of Izmail has yet another strategy to address ethnic diversity. Careful not to side with one ethnic group, city officials have for many years put "interethnic harmonization" in the focus of their activities. In a special program dedicated to the city's "more than 80 ethnic groups" the municipal administration offered financial and administrative resources for a number of ethnic groups. These include the Poles, Greeks, Ukrainians, Jews, Russians, Germans, and Bulgarians, who each have ethnic associations based in Izmail. Each of these associations organizes their "day of national culture" over the course of the year. It is an explicit goal of the program to "preserve the ethnic uniqueness" of these groups and to "ensure their harmonic relations by way of supporting their officially registered ethno-cultural societies."[20]

The diversity of political strategies in dealing with ethnicity illustrates that ethnicity is an important group denominator, even in a region where there are many ethnic groups to satisfy. Supporting one group does not automatically

19 Electoral district 142 comprises rayons Artsis, Tarutino, Sarata, parts of Bolgrad rayon, and parts of Kiliya rayon. For ethnic census Data of these areas see the Ukrainian census of 2001: <http://2001.ukrcensus.gov.ua/rus/results/general/nationality/odesa/> (23.02.2019).

20 The 2015 budget for the "Program of harmonization of interethnic relations on the territory of Izmail and support of the ethno-cultural societies" was granted by the city council with decision Nr. 229-VII on December 24, 2015, as published on the municipal council's homepage: <http://www.izmail-rada.gov.ua/2010-05-05-12-39-15> (23.02.2019).

FIGURE 5 Inauguration of a monument commemorating Bulgarian fighters in the Russo-Turkish War 1877–78, Bolgrad, October 2012

mean to be renounced by other groups. Quite the opposite may be true. The more visibly a patron supports one ethnic group, the more attractive he becomes for other groups as a potential patron. Anton Kisse also supports a Gagauz association, who form the second largest ethnic group in his electoral district. One of his more visible protégés is Yuri Dimchoglo, the organizer of the "Day of Gagauz Culture" and head of a Gagauz ethnic association. So serving several ethnic groups can be a useful strategy for patrons, in such an ethnically diverse setting as southern Bessarabia. But none of these political strategies would work if ethnic boundaries dissolved.

In contrast to Soviet times, no political figure in independent Ukraine claimed that ethnicity was not important, or that it will one day go away, or that ethnic boundaries are not congruent with significant cultural boundaries. Even after ethnicity as an official, passport-registered category was dropped (in

Ukraine in 1995) a new, more fluid conception of being Ukrainian based on civil criteria emerged only very slowly (Kappeler 2000: 274). And although a civil Ukrainian identity has been clearly strengthened by the events on Maidan and the subsequent violence (Portnov 2015: 729; Sasse and Lackner 2018), Soviet scholarly paradigms on ethnicity cast a long shadow in academia and beyond (Sokolovskiy 2012: 36). Some politicians of post-soviet Ukraine have even expressed their nostalgia for the "fifth line" in the Soviet passport, the line that specified ethnicity. In 2009, Volodymyr Litvin, then the speaker of the Ukrainian Parliament, was cited saying "I want the fifth line to be reintroduced. We need it, so we know who our forefathers were. Why would anyone be ashamed of that?"[21] The far-right Svoboda Party demands the reintroduction of a person's ethnicity in identity documents high up in their party program.[22]

One reason for such nostalgic recollection of unambiguous prescription may be the relationship between ethnic groups and the clientelistic state with its need to cater to clearly identifiable groups. Popular imagination of ethnic groups and their boundaries relies on a metaphor in which the state, as something tangible and perceptible, stands for the more abstract concept of ethnicity. States, particularly in the former USSR, carry the name of the ethnic majority group, often called the "titular" group. They comprise the territory of- and provide the political guidance for the titular ethnic group. Also, they can easily be portrayed as acting subjects. They arrange treaties with other states, they engage in trade and warfare. Similarly, ethnic groups are often portrayed as clearly bounded and steerable entities. They come into contact with other ethnic groups, subjugate them or assimilate to them, move from one place to another, take on new lifestyles, faiths, and languages, fight for their independence and, ultimately, establish states of their own. Using the state as a metaphor for the ethnic group helps imagining the ethnic group as clear-cut. The state after all is bounded by a clearly demarcated state border. State borders are guarded and present a perceptible obstacle. This feature is often taken as self-evident for ethnic boundaries too. They somehow must present an obstacle. They cannot just be trespassed without justification.

---

21 *Ukrainskaya Pravda* April 24, 2009: <http://www.pravda.com.ua/rus/news/2009/04/24/4482170/> (23.02.2019). Yuriy Hnatkevich an MP of Blok Yuliy Timoshenko publicly supported Litivn's idea: Zhytomyr info, April 24, 2009: <http://www.zhitomir.info/news_39333.html> (23.02.2019).

22 See item 1.11 in Svoboda's party program at <https://svoboda.org.ua/wp-content/uploads/2018/08/PZU_actual_text_1-44.pdf> (23.02.2019).

4 Political Representation and the Pressure to Choose a Clear-Cut Ethnic Identity

Contradictions between the conceptualization of ethnic boundaries as perfectly unambiguous facts of life and the frequent experience of their fuzziness and permeability are unavoidable. The urge to keep one's ethnic identity clearly defined, and ultimately the ethnic group sharply bounded, does not stem from some kind of enthusiasm for exclusive ethnic identities. It is rather caused by a lack of imaginable alternatives. During all the years of independence, Ukraine has never developed a concept of a multiethnic state that goes beyond the mere tolerance of ethnic minorities. The idea that these ethnic minorities might mix with the majority of Ukrainians, and thereby change what it means to be Ukrainian, is often presented as undesirable to both the minorities and the majority group. Although the peaceful coexistence of different ethnic groups is often hailed, their intermixing and thereby the gradual leveling of ethnic differences, is seen as a loss, a threat even, to Ukraine's future. This fear resonates well with Yulian Bromley's ideas about organism-like ethnos, with an agency of its own. A state disappears when its borders dissolve. Likewise an ethnic group without a clear boundary ceases to exist (Bromley 1983: 36–49). The idea, that features of one particular ethnic group together with the features of other ethnic groups would form something new, so far seems to be unacceptable. Many ethnic groups hold on to a narrative of such a merger between two or several groups in their theory of origin (the Dacians and Romans into Romanians, the Thracians, Slavs, and Bulgars into the Bulgarians). That is, such mixing, in the dominant post-Soviet perspective, occurs before an ethnic group takes on its present identity, and it means irretrievable loss of the identities prior to the mixing. So ethnic intermixing is frequently portrayed as something that belongs into a mythical past but that becomes a threat once ethnic groups have formed their present identities. The identities offered by the Ukrainian state are either a Ukrainian ethnic identity or a civil Ukrainian identity, combined with an ethnic identity of one of the many ethnic minorities. The basic contradiction in which Ukrainian ethnicity policy is stuck is that on the one hand it still uses Soviet imaginations of ethnicity (that even back then stood in stark contrast to the social reality) on the other hand it lacks a prospect that promises to resolve current contradictions in the future. There is no vision for a future society without current ethnic distinctions, nothing comparable to the once anticipated "Soviet People" that would one day emerge from currently existing ethnic groups, when the country will have reached its aspired final level of development.

There are, I believe, two political mechanisms that help explain the persistence of established ethnic categories. The first of these mechanisms is caused by political elites who base their power on ethnic categories (as many do increasingly since the break-up of the Soviet Union). If the "people" is sovereign and entitled to delegate political power, it needs to be limited in some way. Since the French Revolution this once diverse society, within which *fraternité* was the basis for political consent, was increasingly defined as an ethno-national group (Rothschild 1981: 11–12). The elites who draw their power from representing such groups cannot have a meltdown of its boundaries. Would this category disappear, or worse even, merge with the category of their political rivals, they would have to find yet another way to justify their power (as if the sudden break-away of the Marxist-Leninist ideology had not been trouble enough). Therefore, there needs to be a mechanism to discipline those who dissolve the border between ethnic groups. Fredrik Barth observed that one such way was reprimanding people of unclear ethnic identity:

> … Just as both sexes ridicule the male who is feminine, and all classes punish the proletarian who puts on airs, so also can members of all ethnic groups in a poly-ethnic society act to maintain dichotomies and differences (1969: 18).

In post-Soviet Ukraine, such disciplinary measures are reported regularly. A notorious example is the story about a member of an oblast parliament, Iryna Farion, visiting a kindergarten in L'viv in 2010. The parliamentarian of the far-right Svoboda Party was filmed instructing toddlers how to properly call each other in order to avoid unpatriotic (i.e. Russian) nicknames. In one scene, Farion tells the children never to use the name Masha (the Russian nickname for Mariya). If anyone wanted to be called Masha (instead of Marychka, the Ukrainian equivalent) they should "go where those Mashas live."[23] A video of the incident was aired on a popular program of Russia's state owned first channel and therefore reached millions of viewers throughout the former Soviet Union and went viral on the internet. It was widely scandalized and one of my respondents presented it as an example, why she despised Ukrainian nationalists. The episode was seen as an epitomization of what one woman expressed as her feeling that people in western Ukraine (where Iryna Farion is based) seemed to believe everybody not quite as Ukrainian owed them something.

23 Broadcasted most notably by state-run *Perviy Kanal* of Russia on February 24, 2010: <http://www.1tv.ru/news/world/149194> (23.02.2019)

In multiethnic southern Ukraine politics demands different strategies. Local politicians, representing a multiethnic electorate, have no business telling people with which ethnic group or language to identify. It would clearly hurt their political standing. Nevertheless, local politicians do actively help to reinforce ethnic boundaries. This, however, happens not because they base their power on a particular ethnic group they serve, but because they, for efficiency's sake, need to structure the large group of their clients into well-arranged subgroups.

This brings us to a second, more significant political mechanism for ethnic boundary maintenance in southern Bessarabia. This mechanism affects patrons and clients equally. For clients it starts with the notion that those unattached to existing categories often lack political representation. For patrons this mechanism is significant, because those who do not firmly belong to one group are harder to serve efficiently. Besides ethnic groups, many other types of groups also qualify for clientelistic exchange, as long as they have an internal hierarchy and it is clear who belongs to them and who does not. Most notably, these are churches, trade unions, or the workers of state institutions. With ethnic groups it is a bit trickier. They do not necessarily have internal hierarchies and since the fifth line in the passport was dropped, there is no longer such a thing as an ethnic "membership card." Ethnic associations can help to solve this structural problem. They provide a hierarchy and by performing ethnicity in public they demarcate the line of those who belong and those who do not. Those who do not belong, because they do not expose the defined membership criteria, have no organizations and no figureheads to speak for them. There are no institutionalized links between ethnically or religiously unattached people that could create a sense of community.

A good illustration for the situation of those with ambiguous ethnic identities can perhaps be found in a linguistic parallel, the speakers of mixed languages. In Ukraine, such language varieties that dissolve the boundary between the Ukrainian and the Russian standard languages are pejoratively deemed *Surzhyk*[24] (Bernsand 2001: 38). Standard languages are often portrayed as per

24 *Surzhyk* literally means a mixture of rye and wheat used in times of poor harvest to bake low-quality bread. The term is used to pejoratively refer to mixed languages and occasionally to children of mixed ethnic ancestry (Flier 1998: 115). *Surzhyk* comes in many guises (for an exhaustive analysis see Bilaniuk (2005)). *Surzhyk* should not be confused with a pidgin or a creole. A pidgin is an auxiliary language with strongly reduced grammar, used to bridge a linguistic boundary between two mutually unintelligible languages. A creole is a pidgin that develops into a mother tongue with its own grammatical rules (Grosjean 1982: 41). *Surzhyk* can be learned as a mother tongue or it can occur spontaneously. It can be used by people who have no problem understanding Ukrainian or Russian or both and

se pure and good. The speakers of standard Ukrainian or standard Russian in Ukraine both have several zealous organizations for the advancement of these languages. Unlike that, the speakers of *Surzhyk* varieties, lack not only such organizations, but even the concept of a speaker community that would be the basis to form a representative organization. This is also true for other sub-standard varieties of Russian, such as *Prostorechie*.[25]. This can be illustrated by the impossibility to correct other speakers of sub-standard language varieties, and therefore to limit and reproduce the speaker-community (Marszk 1999: 632). It is absurd to say „in good, grammatical *Surzhyk* we would say...," or "in *Prostorechie* this would correctly be called..." Although millions of people make all kinds of utterances in these language varieties, neither one refers to a set of poems or songs, the common knowledge of which could create a sense of community. Just as absurd as correcting speakers of *Surzhyk* or *Prostorechie* it would be to say, "We, the speakers of *Surzhyk* have a beautiful song that goes like this..." or, "In *Surzhyk* there is an old saying that reminds us of..." Established languages, in contrast, have such a common stock of cultural references. The learning by heart of poems, the reading of novels, the citing of proverbs and catchphrases, the singing of songs all contribute to an "imagined community" (Anderson 2006: 145). Thanks to a common stock of such cultural tarits, an individual can hold the imagination of a community with the other members of this group, although they are far too many to be possibly acquainted with (ibid.: 6).

As the speakers of language varieties on the blurred boundaries of standard languages do not have representation (and do not see the need for it), so people who find themselves between established ethnic communities are out of the focus of ethno-politicians who are looking for followers. For nationalist politicians, like Iryna Farion, it would be impossible to tell them how to behave, because they do not claim to belong to a community with a shared cultural code. But more significantly, for the case of southern Bessarabia; ethnically unattached people lack representation. Just imagine the absurdity of an association for the ethnically mixed or a club that represents the interests of the unaffiliated or a museum for the folklore of the sovietized masses. No such organizations exist and no one claims *common characteristics* or a *common culture* for the people who have no clear ethnic affiliation.

---

it is not necessarily simpler in its grammar than these standard languages (Bilaniuk 2005: 121).

25 *Prostorechie*, freely translated, means "simple speak." It refers to a widely spoken sub-standard variety of Russian, used by people, who never learned to fully master the Russian standard language. One of its main features is that it tends to ignore irregular grammatical forms (Marszk 1999: 630).

It is a useful exercise to recollect at this point the structural problems clients and patrons face when they trade their resources for political support. Clients need to form groups in order to ensure that their patrons will deliver. If a client becomes a member of a recognizable group, there is still no guarantee that he or she *personally* will receive favors from the patron. But it significantly increases his or her chances because *some members* of the group will be served, otherwise the group as a whole can punish the uncooperative patron by shunning him the next time he needs support. Therefore, to be part of a group is in any case more beneficiary than being a free-floating client (Chandra 2004: 54).

For the patron, on the other hand, it is not easy to ensure the political support of free-floating clients. In secret ballots the political decision of an individual voter can only be established at great cost. If the patron relies on a group and its hierarchical structures, the actual voting behavior of single group members can be controlled much more efficiently through intermediaries, for example big employers or the representatives of ethnic associations. If hard-to-control, free floating individuals still manage to profit from the patron's favors, they also become free riders on the patron's expense. The patron is probably unable to serve all individuals evenly. But even if he would serve individual clients, then every neglected client would likely vote against him. If he chooses whole groups, those group members who end up empty handed, at least see that other group members had been served as promised, and they will count on their personal gain the next time their group is served. Therefore, many voters will probably still support the patron even if they personally do not gain at each round of favors (Chandra 2004: 56).

Ethnic associations in Bessarabia, along with many other organizations like churches, or worker's unions, serve as facilitators for the clientelistic exchange between local patrons and their clients. They are receivers of favors and resources, which they pass on to subgroups and individual clients. Relying on their internal hierarchies they also help the patron ensure compliance of the voters among the ethnic group they claim to represent. Yet their most crucial task in the clientelistic system is to define who is a member of a particular ethnic group and who is not. Thereby they shape the concept of what it means to be Bulgarian, Gagauz, Russian, Ukrainian, or Moldovan, but they also ensure for the patron that he does not have to deal with free-floating individuals somewhere at the frayed margins of a poorly defined group.

5 When Clear-Cut Boundaries Encounter Fuzzy Identities

For those who build their political following on the assumption that ethnicity is objective and unambiguous, it is unavoidable to run into contradiction. This can come from dealing with people of mixed ethnic ancestry, people who have changed their identity at some point in their biographies, or people who do not expose the allegedly typical features of a particular ethnic group, but nevertheless claim to belong to it. More confusion can come from comparison with other countries, where ethnicity is defined and used differently, or where it plays hardly any role at all. In the following paragraphs each of these sources of contradiction will be discussed and I describe five observed ways of dealing with them.

Mixed ethnic ancestry is the most common challenge to essentializing concepts of ethnicity in southern Bessarabia. Interethnic marriage was never barred or even actively discouraged in the Soviet Union. None of the interviewed, who have married a partner from a different ethnic group, reported hostile reactions by the state and only very few reported antagonism from their families. Interestingly, many people, who have not married a partner from another ethnic group, told me they could never have done so, or their parents would never have let them. The diverging judgment of those who have lived in an interethnic marriage and those who have not, suggests that if one starts to build an intimate relationship to a person from another ethnic group, prejudice towards this group might be revised. Some respondents also named a number of ethnic groups from which they could marry a partner and another number from which they would not. Two respondents, one Moldovan and one Bulgarian, said that people from their ethnic group could never marry a Gagauz. Both respondents reasoned this was because their ethnic group had been oppressed by the Turks for so long. But of course the Gagauz also emphasize their suffering from Turkish (Ottoman) oppression. And in spite of the reservation against "Turks," in Bolgrad rayon, where Gagauz and Bulgarians live in close proximity, marriages between them are very common. Official functionaries and official policies carefully avoid judging or ranking ethnic groups by their eligibility to marry. In the late Soviet period, interethnic couples were even portrayed as harbingers of progressive Soviet values (Gorenburg 2006a: 149).

Nevertheless, children of mixed ethnic families pose a challenge to the assumption that ethnicity is essential and unambiguous. One response to this challenge is the idea of an established mechanism, how ethnicity is passed on from one generation to another. A local history teacher, for instance, insisted only women could pass on their ethnicity. Another way is assuming that children with mixed ethnic ancestry do not mix their identities, but keep them inside themselves as separate entities. One woman with an ethnically mixed identity, who married a man with several ethnic backgrounds, explained that in her children there were five ethnicities. She could also name her children's personal traits which came from one or the other ethnic disposition. The assumption of clearly defined ethnic characteristics lives on in this conceptualization, albeit within an individual instead of a society.

Another way to dodge contradiction stemming from interethnic marriage and resulting mixed ethnic identities is to assume that they are a very recent phenomenon. To many respondents it seemed perfectly obvious that before World War II, people had married exclusively within their ethnic group. As I have demonstrated in chapter two, interethnic marriages were not uncommon even in the mid-19th century. The persistent assumption that interethnic marriage became possible only recently, at least acknowledges the trend towards greater rates of ethnic mixing caused by increasing social and geographical mobility. Although this assumption does not solve the contradiction, it restricts it to a more recent past. Therefore, an essentialized concept of ethnicity remains applicable for earlier decades.

People who change their ethnic identity at some point in their lives also pose a contradiction to established concepts of ethnicity. It is a well-studied fact that ethnic statistics in the former Soviet Union fluctuate not only because many who resettled during Soviet times returned to their historic homeland, but also because many people changed their ethnic affiliation when political circumstances changed. In Ukraine, the share of Russians between the censuses of 1989 and 2001 fell by 5%, without an according exodus of Russians. This probably means that people of mixed ethnic origin, who preferred the prestigious Russian ethnicity in the fifth line of their Soviet passport, have reconsidered their identity since Ukraine's independence (Rjabtschuk 2005: 25; Simon 2008: 7). Studies of people who changed their ethnic identity have been presented among others by Bilaniuk for Ukraine (Bilaniuk 2005: 37–44), Karklins for Soviet Germans (1986: 34), and Gorenburg (1999) for Bashkortostan.

To people who consider ethnicity an essential and unchangeable trait, adapting ethnic identity to political circumstance reeks of opportunism. One young man told me that every honest person ought to know which ethnic group he or she belongs to. Presented with examples of people from his village, who changed their ethnic identity, he replied they had changed merely their *passport-ethnicity* and that the passport was but a piece of paper. A young woman, who for herself chose her father's Ukrainian ethnicity over her mother's Bulgarian, discussed the ethnic identities of (German-born) Empress Catherine II. She said that maybe Catherine had become a *citizen* of Russia, but one could not *become* a real Russian, just because one chose to. Asked about her own choice of ethnicity, she said that now, after she had firmly chosen Ukrainian as her ethnicity, she could no longer reconsider. So separating ascribed or chosen ethnicity from the concept of an essentialized, inner and inherited ethnicity is another strategy to avoid contradiction.

Occasionally, conflicts and contradictions in the conceptualization of ethnicity occur because someone does not, in the opinion of others, exhibit the characteristics of the ethnic group he or she claims to be part of. The most common case of this conflict is that someone has forgotten or never learned the language associated with the ethnicity he or she feels to belong to. Those who sharpen ethnic boundaries in southern Bessarabia are fond of repeating that if the language disappears, the ethnic group will disappear too.[26] The head of the Bulgarian Cyril and Methodius Society told me that if someone does not speak Bulgarian, there was no reason to identify as Bulgarian.[27] Bulgarian ethnicity has recently experienced increased popularity, since the opportunity to get a Bulgarian passport offers access to the European labor market (Demirdirek 2008a: 100). Therefore, suspicion of opportunism is never far for those who have only recently discovered their Bulgarianness. It is then easy to simply exclude those considered unworthy of an ethnic label by reducing the items on the list of membership criteria. One ethnically Bulgarian school teacher reported a dispute he had on an organized tourist trip to Bulgaria. He had overheard a local man talking on the phone about the busload of "Russian pigs" along with which the respondent had arrived. This apparent exclusion from those worthy of being Bulgarians, provoked the Bessarabian Bulgarian school teacher to explain to the offender that *he* had long ceased to be Bulgarian by joining the EU and by drudgingly enduring 500 years under the Turkish yoke. His own forefathers, the teacher informed his opponent, had at least taken their fate in their hands, leaving for Bessarabia in search for a better life. In this dispute, the two men clearly had different ideas of what it takes to be a Bulgarian. In such a case it is not the situative choice of ethnic identity that liberates one from contradiction, but the situative choice of characteristics one needs to expose in order to belong.

One more source of confusion is the comparison of an essentialized ethnicity concept with groups and countries which either place less significance in

26 This theme is repeated for the Ukrainians in Serbens'ka's and Terlak's (1999) Ukrainian reader for russophone beginners. Yuri Dimchoglo, the Gagauz local politician who organized and sponsored the "Day of Gagauz Culture" on this occasion reminded the audience (in Russian) that the disappearance of the Gagauz language would mean the disappearance of the Gagauz people.

27 Interview in Izmail, April 21, 2013.

ethnicity or conceptualize ethnicity differently. These include the countries with a civil (not an ethnic) conceptualization of nationhood, such as France, Belgium, or Switzerland, as well as the nations that grew out of settler colonies in the New World. These countries claim nationhood without providing a consolidated ethnic genealogy. This is hard to square with the essentializing Soviet concept of ethnicity. In his ethnos theory (see chapter 4), Yulian Bromley called identities such as French or Belgian "politonyms" (i.e. the name of a polity), stressing their political rather than ethnic character. Unlike ethnic identities, these forms of identification would disappear, as soon as the person ceases to live in the respective polity (Bromley 1983: 46). For this concept it is similarly difficult to accommodate national identities, the ethnic basis of which is akin to neighboring nations. Soviet concepts of ethnicity are at odds with an Austrian national identity or with south-Tiroleans who self-identify as Italians. One respondent, a trained geographer who has lived and worked in Austria, was convinced no Austrian could sincerely feel different from a German. He explained the prevalence of what he believed was an artificial identity with historical ignorance and the suppression of a pan-German identity out of political correctness. Many among Moldova's nationalists, especially those who would like to see their country merge with neighboring Romania, are fond of the Austrian analogy. One history student from Chișinău, who wants the "artificial" border between the two countries removed, told me that in Austria there was a similar situation like in Moldova; those people who had learned their history knew that they were in fact Germans. Interestingly, those who oppose a Moldovan merger with Romania do not rely on the idea of a political or civil Moldovan national identity, but more likely cling to the Soviet doctrine that Romanians and Moldovans are two different ethnic groups that speak two different languages. With this insistence they seemingly prove the point of Moldovan nationalists, that two different countries must contain two different ethnic groups in order not to be "artificial."

If ethnicity is objectively ascertainable, as Bromley insists (1980: 151, 1983: 48), then those who fail to recognize it are simply wrong. Therefore, Soviet ethnography resented the "bourgeois" reduction of ethnicity to self-identification, because this notion denies hereditary membership of the group one "objectively" belongs to (Bromley 1983: 49). This brings us to the last technique to eliminate contradiction between the conceptualization of ethnicity and the frequently confusing practices of self-identification: one can simply exclude those who hold confusing identities from the circle of people who have authority to speak about it. Following this strategy of exclusion, those who do not subscribe to an essentialized conceptualization of ethnicity are simply accused of overlooking (intentionally or not) the objective existence of ethnic characteristics. By excluding the opposition of people who dissolve ethnic boundaries because they simply have no say in the matter, clear-cut ethnic boundaries take on the air of an indisputable reality (Suny 2001: 865).

This leaves us with five main strategies to avoid contradiction between concepts of ethnicity: Firstly, people who have mixed ethnic ancestry can be portrayed as not exposing a mixture of ethnic identities but as containers of several clearly bounded ethnic identities that play out in their character through clearly identifiable traits of character, each associated with one of their ancestor's ethnicities. Secondly, ethnic mixing can be portrayed as a very recent phenomenon and therefore blamed on industrialization or globalization. This preserves the claim that ethnic groups were clearly bounded and endogamous two or three generations back. Thirdly, one can strictly separate between bureaucratic identity and essential identity. If a person changes his or her identity in the course of their lives, this new identity can simply be dismissed as a "paper identity," chosen for opportunistic reasons. People who dilute someone's definition of an ethnic group can be excluded from the "real" members of this group by situatively shortening or lengthening the list of membership criteria. Fifthly, if someone holds an ethnic identity that contradicts essential and primordial concepts of ethnicity, he or she may be excluded from those able to see the objective reality.

So if essentialized concepts of ethnicity run into contradiction, the reaction by those who defend it is usually an act of exclusion: This can involve to rule out the actual mixing of ethnic identities, it can be the exclusion of those with a mixed ethnic identity from the group of people who live according to their ancestors' endogamous ways, it can be the exclusion of those who adopted a new ethnic identity from the group of sincere people on the grounds of their alleged opportunism, it can be the exclusion from the "real" members of an ethnic group because a person in the eyes of the observer has ceased to fulfil the criteria of belonging, or it can be the exclusion from those with the authority to assess membership of an ethnic community. By excluding all of these people who dilute the idea of clear-cut ethnic groups, most contradictions can be neutralized.

CHAPTER 7

The Narratives and Techniques that Maintain Ethnic Boundaries

If ethnic belonging is essential and an undeniable characteristic of each person (as most of my respondents would unhesitatingly agree), this means that every person's ethnic identity is somehow predefined and located someplace; the blood, the bones, the psyche, or the mentality are frequently suspected loci. There must be techniques to reveal such inner dispositions, and there must be narratives that explain how they affect the way people behave. This chapter is meant to list and discuss such narratives and techniques, as they are employed in southern Bessarabia.

The idea that there is something within a person that encodes information about ethnic identity lends an air of science to essentialist concepts of ethnicity. If such features are encoded within each person, making predictions how these act out, would indeed require some degree of specialized knowledge. Even to understand relatively trivial but non-obvious facts of life, such as that glass chips are not diamonds or that dolphins are not fish, we need a degree of learned expertise about qualities inside the object we look at, simply because these qualities are invisible to the naked eye: "An essence is the unique, typically hidden property of an object that makes it what it is, without which it would have a different identity (e.g., the chemical composition of water, the DNA structure of an elephant)" (Gelman and Wellman 1991: 215–214). So the very concept of essence, requires a narrative to demonstrate or explain it, and if we want to make it visible (which is not always possible), a technique is needed in order to disclose what is hidden inside. In contrast to the natural sciences, narratives about ethnic belonging are not easily tested and techniques not easily replicated. They rely on cultural practices determined by a locality and its history. The following analysis of fieldwork materials is an attempt to lump together the suggestions made to me during fieldwork, as to what the essence of ethnicity might consist of, where and how it might be found.

In the field, I have come across five systems in which ethnic essence is assumed: language, religion, common historical experience, folklore, and DNA. Each of these provides the basis for a strand of narratives what ethnic essence consists of, and the basis for a technique of inclusion and exclusion used to maintain ethnic boundaries. The chapter is structured by these five systems

 | DOI:10.1163/9789004408029_008

and discusses the techniques and narratives of ethnic boundary maintenance they imply. In a second step, every section discusses how, in the region's history, the relevant techniques and narratives have evolved and how they were shaped by changing political priorities.

Narratives, as I use the term here, means a story that is "... attached to cultural and institutional formations larger than the single individual, to intersubjective networks or institutions, however local or grand, micro- or macro- stories. (...) Public narratives range from the narratives of one's family, to those of the workplace (organizational myths), church, government, and nation" (Somers 1994: 619). Narratives, as they manifest themselves in ethnographic fieldwork are retold in similar or identical versions by different people and at different times with the aim of bringing across similar arguments. These narratives can be based wholly or partly on true stories, they can be ad-hoc collages of earlier narratives, or they can be deliberate lies, in other words any illustrative tale that reoccurs similarly in form and intention.

Techniques to make ethnic markers seen and thereby to maintain ethnic boundaries are subtler. They can be any reoccurring patterns of behavior that marks ethnic boundaries, intentionally or unintentionally, explicitly or implicitly. Such techniques are tied to social norms that people imply on themselves or demand compliance with from others. Because such norms usually exist outside the codified law, they can be employed as it best fits the respective situation. Many people have no manifest desire to maintain ethnic boundaries but do so unintentionally. Others loudly champion ideas of ethnic boundary maintenance but may still sometimes act otherwise. Since ideas about the essence of ethnicity and about ethnic authenticity are so varied, it is only natural that ideas about how and why ethnic boundaries should be maintained differ substantially. That the intention to maintain ethnic boundaries is not always there, and not every time it is indeed there, it is openly declared, makes exploring maintenance techniques a tricky endeavor. A good starting point is to look at the possible locus where the essence of ethnicity is believed to reside. Once these are identified, it becomes easier to analyze the measures employed to keep this essence in place and protected from dilution.

1 Pure and Impure Language

The most significant marker of ethnic boundaries in southern Bessarabia, and throughout the former Soviet Union, seems to be language. Linguistic differences in many cases were directly translated into ethnic boundaries by Soviet nationalities policy. A common language was a decisive criterion in the definitions of what a nation or an ethnos is, including Sergey Shirokogorov's definition in the 1920s, Joseph Stalin's in the 1930s, Pavel Kushner's in the 1950s, and Yulian Bromley's in the 1980s (for more on these definitions see chapter 4). On the other hand, language is an evident candidate to be the bearer of the ethnic essence, because anything we do can be thought and discussed only using language. Because thoughts are encoded in a language and behavior is based on thoughts, behavior can be influenced by the language a person thinks in, as well as the metaphors and wisdoms engraved in it. If two groups of people use different languages and are perceived to behave differently, one conceivable explanation is that the different languages they use are at the roots of their differing behavioral patterns. A Bulgarian language teacher from Izmail, for instance, explained alleged behavioral differences between Bulgarians and Gagauz with this train of thought.[1] She is of mixed Bulgarian and Gagauz descent but inclined to call Gagauz her native language. The only difference between Bulgarians and Gagauz, in her opinion, lies in their different languages and psychology. The latter, she explained, derived from language directly. The Gagauz were slightly more aggressive than the Bulgarians, given the large amount of words for fighting and warfare in their lexicon. The Bulgarians had more words for love and tenderness in their vocabulary and therefore behaved accordingly. Because we do what we think, she argued, the language, in which our thoughts are thought, has a direct effect on the way we act. In the respondent's perception, the language a person learns first, determines how people act, and therefore people who speak different languages will act differently. This explanation for ethnic differences however, still does not explain how one ethnic belonging becomes dominant over another in the case of mixed ethnic origin and bilingual upbringing (as in the case of the respondent herself).

In several instances, one technique to detect in which language the real identity of a person is engraved into his or her mind was suggested: One can look at moments of unconscious speech. One man of Bulgarian and Gagauz descent, who runs a Sunday school for Bulgarian children in Chervonoarmeyskoe, said he knew for sure that he was a real Bulgarian after a stay in hospital, during which his roommate overheard him speak Bulgarian in his delirious sleep.[2] At another episode of the interview this man named drunkenness or great pain as conditions in which the "true" ethnic nature of a person reveals itself. In these situations a person would no longer be able to deliberately choose a linguistic code but would use the one that was engraved in his or her mind deepest. The respondent here specifically referred to a scene in the

1 Interview in Izmail, November 14, 2012.

2 Interview in Chervonoarmeyskoe, September 19, 2013.

popular Soviet spy-vs.-spy TV series *Seventeen Moments of Spring* (1973), in which a female Soviet spy in Nazi Germany is uncovered while giving birth. It was her agonized screams during labor that betrayed her as a native Russian speaker. Consequently, no matter how many languages a person learns to speak and how fluent they become in them, the language learnt first, remains the one formative for their "true" identity, the one people fall back on when they lose the ability to obstruct it.

Following from the assumption that ethnic identity is engraved in a language, the arguably most basic and most obvious of all forms to keep ethnic boundaries clear-cut is to demand, from all those willing to be identified with a particular ethnic denominator, to use a pure form of one particular linguistic code in all social spheres and situations. The Ukrainian and Russian languages have long traditions, both of linguistic mixing and of linguistic purism. The language varieties that dissolve the boundary between Russian and Ukrainian are most commonly called *Surzhyk*. To demarcate the linguistic boundary between the Russian and the Ukrainian standard languages there is a time-honored practice to shame language mixing (Bernsand 2006; Bilaniuk 2005). The starting point for this technique is the assumption that there are clearly bounded ethnic communities that speak pure and authentic languages. These languages are seen to be better suited for the ethnic group in question than any other language. So language purists build their activism on the assumption of a hierarchy, in which pure language varieties are at the top and all other varieties can be measured against them. If there is a hierarchy of differently valued language varieties, pure language varieties index high social values (Bilaniuk 2005: 2). With language mixing, the notion of dirt or impurity is never far. Most respondents name "clean language" (*chistiy yazyk*) as the opposite of *Surzhyk*, meaning the standardized varieties of either Ukrainian or Russian. One Odessa language teacher said speaking *Surzhyk* was like walking around in untidy clothes. Other Odessa respondents said that hearing *Surzhyk* "hurts in my ears" or "bangs my psyche." The abhorrence for language mixing is a very real sensation to many people in Ukraine. Many of my respondents maintained that speaking *Surzhyk* was a sign of low social status and of rural origin.[3]

Yet, the degree of impurity is often in the eye of the beholder. People are sometimes quick to classify the language of others as impure and mark it with the *Surzhyk* label. At the same time, many people admit that their own language is not perfectly pure, but overwhelmingly reject the notion that it might be *Surzhyk*. In the two predominately Ukrainian villages near Izmail, where interviews for this study were taken, most people are aware that the language

3 Bernsand (2001: 41) also locates Surzhyk where rural life and city life meet.

they speak is not standard Ukrainian. Still many reject the label of *Surzhyk*, while others accept it laughingly or grudgingly.

But it is not peasants in villages who most often are targeted by language purists. People from whom it is expected that they should embody the attributes of Ukrainian ethnicity are much more likely to be targeted by purists; public national figures and representatives of the state. Former presidents Yushchenko and Yanukovich were often criticized for speaking Surzhyk in public (Bilaniuk 2005: 197). Many figures in Yanukovich's cabinet had linguistic habits particularly disturbing to purists. Yanukovich recruited most of his entourage from his home region, the largely Russian-speaking Donbas. Language policy had been a dominating topic of his presidency, culminating in the reform of Ukrainian language policy in 2012, giving Russian an enhanced status on the regional level. Yanukovich himself learned to speak proper Ukrainian only when already in office. His language was a frequent subject of ridicule. The popular comedy show *Vecherniy Kvartal*[4] featured one actor, Alexander Pikalov, specializing almost exclusively in lampooning Yanukovich's brand of speaking *Surzhyk*.

One criticism often accompanying ridicule of high-ranking *Surzhyk*-speakers is that their hapless attempt to speak Ukrainian is also an attempt to conceal their true nature as Russian-speakers: With this attempt they make their way into the ruling class of Ukraine that in the opinion of many should be reserved for people who speak "pure" Ukrainian.

Public ridicule, naming and shaming of prominent *Surzhyk* speakers, the association of language mixing with dirtiness, with rural-urban migration, and poor education are all mechanisms that force people to either deny that they speak *Surzhyk*, or to purify their language. If people do so, they also have to decide for one out of two possible "pure" languages. This choice forces people to take sides in the never-ending debate about the appropriate language in Ukraine. So shaming impure language in effect forces people to choose the quintessential ethnic marker, and not stand in-between established linguistic and ethnic categories.

Although mixing of Russian and Ukrainian is often portrayed as a serious danger to the existence of the Ukrainian language, other regional languages are much more endangered. The Gagauz language has been standardized only after the Second World War and is systematically taught in schools only since 2006. Linguistic purism here is largely a top-down concern. As with Ukrainian,

4 The show's hard to translate name derives from the name of the founding comedy troupe "95-y Kvartal" (the 95th district) an area in their hometown Kriviy Rih. See the show's website: <http://kvartal95.com/history/> (23.02.2019).

the Russian language is the main competitor to the Gagauz language. Although there is no demeaning term, like *Surzhyk*, to designate Gagauz with admixtures of other languages, Margarita Tanasoglo one of the interviewed Gagauz language teachers from the village of Kotlovina also used the metaphor of dirt and impurity to refer to mixed language. She insisted people should refrain from using Russian loanwords in their Gagauz, especially if there is a Gagauz equivalent for the term. She told her pupils in school to be attentive, but also asked them to tell their parents at home that a Gagauz expression existed and that there was no need to use a Russian word in its place. If she overheard a linguistically mixed conversation she had a hard time to contain the urge to meddle in the conversation and correct the speakers.[5]

Because language seems to be perceived as one of the most essential markers of ethnic identity, linguistic purity has become a major concern for those who use language as an ethnic marker. Linguistic purism was initially an instrument to discipline the huge masses of yet-to-be-schooled children and adults, who became subjects of educatory campaigns, first on a very modest scale by Romania, later to a much greater extent in the Soviet Union. Certainly, a decisive threshold in the transformation of ideas on linguistic purity was the advent of compulsory schooling after 1944. Prior to schools, improper language may have been the subject of ridicule, but there were no formal institutions to enforce linguistic purity. Institutionalized enforcement of linguistic purity typically occurs at times of rapid social change and at times of national consolidation (Jernudd 1989: 3). But efficient purification of linguistic behavior presupposes powerful and intrusive institutions. In rural Bessarabia of the tsarist period, such institutions did not exist. For more urban areas, we can at least assume that speaking decent Russian, the sort that could be obtained only in state institutions of higher education, was a precondition to enter state service. The mixed language variety *Surzhyk* is probably as old as the linguistic contact between Ukrainian village dwellers with the Russian-speakers in the cities of southern and eastern Ukraine that were founded mostly in the late 18th century (Bernsand 2001: 41).

During the Romanian phase of Bessarabian history, rudimentary educatory institutions began to take shape. Romania had vastly expanded her system of public schooling between 1920 and 1938, without reaching deep into the population (see chapter 3). So rather than purifying the language of the newly acquired Romanian citizens, the Romanian government needed to teach many of them to speak Romanian in the first place.

5 Interview in Kotlovina, July 30, 2013.

In the same period, in 1936, in what today is western Ukraine, but at that time belonged to Poland, Ivan Ohienko, a cleric, linguist, translator of the Bible into Ukrainian, and a member of the Ukrainian exile government, published his *ten commandments of the native language*. In the 1990s they were included in the Ukrainian school curriculum (Bernsand 2001: 42). The "commandments" read like a nationalist's guide to linguistic purism. The fourth of Ohienko's rules was, "the use in literature only of dialects strongly damages the cultural unity of the nation." The sixth commandment was, "Every nation can have but one standard language, one pronunciation, and one orthography." According to Ohienko's ideas, the state of the national language revealed the state of the nation itself and an individual's degree of sophistication could be judged best from how he or she spoke the national language. Therefore, his commandment was, "every conscious citizen has to know in practice his united standard language, its pronunciation, and united orthography, as well as recognize and fulfill the native language obligations to his nation" (cited in Bernsand 2001: 42). The emergence of linguistic purism among the intellectual elite, paved the way to exclude those who spoke deviating language varieties from the nation or ethnic group altogether.

In southern Bessarabia, linguistic purism was introduced less as a means of exclusion and more of a means of disciplining people to stick to administrative categories used by the Soviet school system. When Soviet schools were established in Bessarabia starting in 1944, one problem for the authorities was to find teachers that were fluent in Ukrainian and Russian standard varieties. Many of the newcomer teachers had graduated from institutions in the Ukrainian SSR where Ukrainian was the main language of instruction. According to an annual school report from 1949, many in the first cohort of Soviet teachers spoke very poor Russian.[6] The Russian language of a teacher in the village of Voznesenka-Pervaya was allegedly so "interspersed with Ukrainian words" that 31 of her fifth graders did not make it to the next grade.[7]

Some linguistic confusion was caused by the policy of using Russian as a language of communication with ethnic minorities in the post-war Ukrainian SSR, where theoretically Ukrainian was used as a language of administration. Some official reports in the early 1950s were still typed in Ukrainian, a practice largely abandoned in later years. Village gatherings were usually held in Russian, although in the early years of Soviet rule, the bulk of the population

6 Fr445 D128 Godovye otchety gorodskikh i rayonnykh otdelov narodnogo obrazovanie o rabote shkol za 1948/1949 uchebnyy god, pp. 78, 82.

7 Fr445 D156, Godovye otchety rayonnykh otdelov narodnogo obrazovaniya za 1949–1950 god, p. 142. This village is situated in Artsiz rayon. The practice of naming and shaming bad teachers or culture house workers was rather common in annual school reports of the 1940s and 50s.

would have had a hard time understanding Russian. In Ukrainian speaking villages, administrative documents remained inconsistent in their language.[8] So the legal and practical ambiguity around the use of languages combined with a lack of resources made purified linguistic codes a distant goal.

In Soviet days, there was a clear hierarchy of languages: the Russian language as the "medium of interethnic communication" on the top, Ukrainian as the language of the republic a distant second, and the local language, reserved almost exclusively for informal communication. A new form of linguistic impurity, and an according panicky response by purists, came when this hierarchy of languages collapsed with the new status of Ukrainian as the only state language in Ukraine in 1989. Now Ukrainian, the language of the nation, claimed a status on a level playing field or even above Russian. This claim shaped Ukrainian politics through all the years since independence and it has turned upside down linguistic strategies of upward social mobility. By rights, if one wanted to join the ruling class, one no longer needed to speak just spotless Russian but preferably also a refined variety of Ukrainian. Many of those who were already in the upper echelons of power had no intention of leaving, just out of a newly felt linguistic incompetence. They started to speak their own version of *Surzhyk* in order to still be eligible as members of the elite. This variety, produced by people well educated in Russian, who picked up Ukrainian late in their lives in order to enhance their credibility as good Ukrainians, can be used most purposefully to demarcate ethnic boundaries. Bilaniuk (2005: 134) christened this variety "post-independence Surzhyk." *Surzhyk* that once was the city dweller's stigma for the peasant migrant had now been turned against the post-Soviet elites, still rooted in a Russian-speaking state, and it pointed to what many saw as not only linguistic impurity, but an attempt to veil an origin in a Russian-speaking past.

2 Religion's Ambiguous Role in Marking Ethnicity

Not quite so simple to grasp are the techniques of ethnic boundary demarcation that evolve around religion. Religion never was a reliable marker of ethnic difference here. In the second half of the 20th century it became even less so. Before World War II two local groups, the Jews and the Bessarabian Germans

8 For example, the files in Fr1807 Ispolnitel'niy komitet Gasan-Aspagskogo sel'skogo soveta 1947–1985, or in F 445 D156, pp. 21 ff. Where the Soviet administration only owned a typewriter with a Russian keyboard layout, and where Ukrainian "i's" therefore had to be replaced with the number "1."

had a different religion than the rest of the population. The overwhelming majority of all the other groups settling southern Bessarabia were Orthodox Christians, with the Old-Believers as a fiercely independent subgroup. Among the Orthodox groups, a sizable number of believers, urban as well as rural, have in recent years turned to evangelical congregations or to Adventists and Jehovah's Witnesses. In many villages, the old Orthodox churches have been destroyed under Soviet administration and were never rebuilt. After the iron curtain fell, prayer houses, financed by foreign churches, were built in most villages. Often there is more than just one prayer house per village, and as a rule they are the most lavish buildings there.[9]

Nevertheless, like language, religious beliefs and practices are perceived to leave an imprint on a person's nature. Some respondents also suggested that a psychological make-up remains within a person descended from a specific religious group, even after conversion to a different creed. In a discussion of two young market traders in Izmail, one of whom said he was Orthodox while the other had converted to a New-Age practice, the Orthodox man said that even if one converted, one would remain Orthodox by ethno-psychology. This was something that every person had and that could not be denied no matter how hard one pretended. Therefore, descent from one religious group can be essentialized and sometimes people do so, but the boundaries marked in this way are wider than the ethnic boundaries between local ethnic groups in southern Bessarabia.

In the late Soviet Union, with its atheist state ideology, publicly practicing religion was a similar statement of opposition as insisting on speaking Ukrainian in public (Knudson Gee 1995: 386). But nowadays almost all forms of ethnic nationalism, in Ukraine as well as in Russia and Romania, come along with calls for religious revival. Therefore, displaying one's religiosity in public can no longer serve as a statement of opposition against a state, nor can it serve to take sides for or against a particular ethnic group.

If Orthodoxy alone cannot mark local ethnic boundaries, it is certainly suited to mark a series of other boundaries. These are, for example, religious institutions, associated with different political camps in Ukrainian politics. In 1992 a Kyiv Patriarchate branched off from the Moscow Patriarchate, in order to give the newly independent polity of Ukraine an independent religious

9 Some Baptist prayer houses were established before Soviet rule and have survived. For instance, the Baptist congregation in the village of Pershotravnevoe, according to the head of the village council, had continuously existed since 1918. Another example are the four Baptist and one Adventist prayer houses in the town of Kiliya, mentioned in a Romanian police report from autumn 1934: F312 D49, O nablyudenii za deyatel'nost' russkoy i ukrainskoy natsional'nosti gorodov i uezda, p. 202.

hierarchy. Tensions stemming from church politics reached a new high point in late 2018, when President Poroshenko managed to get the Patriarch of Constantinople to grant a merger of the Ukrainian Autocephalous church and the Kyiv Patriarchate the status of autocephaly. The *tomos* from the Patriarch of Constantinople might stimulate individual parishes to switch to the newly legitimized Ukrainian Church. However, most parishes in southern and eastern Ukraine belong to the Moscow Patriarchate, which in some instances will continue to trigger fierce conflicts over church property and doctrine. One long standing quarrel between the Kyiv and the Moscow Patriarchate was over the language used in liturgy. The Moscow Patriarchate saw Church Slavonic as the appropriate language, while the Kyiv patriarchate insisted on using the language of the people (i.e. Ukrainian), pointing to the examples of the Georgian, Cypriot, or Greek Orthodox Churches (Wilson 2002: 243). In Southern Bessarabia, practically all parishes belong to the Moscow Patriarchate. Most priests, independently of the predominant ethnicity of their parish, use Church Slavonic for the liturgy, while the language used in the (usually short) sermons can differ. In the village church of Kotlovina, a predominantly Gagauz village, the liturgy is performed in Church Slavonic and Russian by the Gagauz priest. The only Gagauz language element in mass is the "Our Father" which is recited in Gagauz. The exact linguistic arrangements of ceremonies in village parishes seem to depend on the preferences of the local priest and parish. The Moscow Patriarchate does not prohibit the use of local languages in liturgy. Differences between village parishes of the Moscow Patriarchate may be just as big as differences between parishes belonging to different Patriarchates. So belonging to different branches of the Orthodox Church may be a viable technique to mark ethnic boundaries on the national Ukrainian level, but not on the local Bessarabian level.

Politicians use the church and its representatives to enhance their own credibility and reputation. In election campaigns, church authorities sometimes make direct recommendations whom to vote for.[10] Rich patrons often recommend themselves to the support of the church and believers by building

10 See chapter 6 for an example how the church in Izmail awarded Yuri Kruk, the local Party of the Regions incumbent candidate for parliamentary elections, with a religious award just days before the elections in October 2012. Another example from the same election involved Kruk's political rival Vladimir Bodelan. The Izmail weekly *New City* printed a direct recommendation to vote for Bodelan by Metropolitan of Odessa and Izmail (at the time himself a member of the oblast Parliament and of the Party of the Regions). September 14, 2012, available online: <http://www.izmacity.com/novosti/politika/3834-mitropolit-agafangel-lvo-vlasti-nuzhny-molodye-energichnye-i-gramotnye-lyudir> (23.02.2019).

churches on their expense or by organizing the restoration of dilapidated church buildings. If such projects are sufficiently tied to the name of one patron, they can help delimit a certain district as this patron's realm of influence. One example of marking a political realm with the help of the church is Sergey Kivalov, one of Odessa's most powerful patrons, a former member of parliament, once chairman of the national electoral committee, and the rector of Odessa law school. He built St. Tatyana Church right on the law school's campus. There, each year on Tatyana's Day, Kivalov after church offers free lunch to students and church goers.[11]

Another example is Vladimir Bodelan, the oblast chief of emergency services, son of a former Mayor of Odessa, and unsuccessful candidate for parliament in 2012. He built a small chapel on a highway junction outside Odessa. In his blog, Bodelan wrote about the sanctification of the church in June 2012, "From all entry roads into Odessa, this one was the only one without a sign that Odessa is an Orthodox Christian city."[12]

Rather than referring to ethnicity, the stressing of one's religious belonging identifies one with a set of values that are informed by religious beliefs and practices. But ultimately being an Orthodox Christian in southern Bessarabia is rather a denominator of a wider Orthodox and conservative community. That the Moscow Patriarchate stands for a supra-ethnic community of believers is manifested for example in the Patriarch's title, Patriarch of Moscow and all of Rus (*Patriarch moskovskiy i vseya rusi*) or more profanely in the title of the Patriarchate's women's magazine *Slavyanka*. Such denominations clearly refer to a group bigger than the Russians or the inhabitants of the Russian Federation. This reference is more suitable to differentiate oneself from evangelical Christians and, more importantly, to delimit the border to nonbelievers who reject religion as a source of moral guidance and who are often associated with Western materialism.

Through the course of history, religious institutions changed their role in demarcating ethnic boundaries, usually rather abruptly. They were accessible for the peasant population long before institutions of education. On the other hand, during the Soviet period, churches of all religious denominations were quickly and violently replaced by schools and other institutions that promoted rationalism and scientific atheism. Therefore, religious ties underwent a very rapid transformation from one of the most important markers of identity

---

11 See *Komsomolskaya Pravda v Ukraine* on January 26. 2012, available online: <https://kp.ua/odessa/321841-v-tatianyn-den-v-yurakademyy-uhoschaly-ryboi-y-barankamy> (23.02.2019).

12 For Bodelan's blog see <http://bodelanvladimir.blogspot.de/2012_06_01_archive.html> (23.02.2019).

during the tsarist and the Romanian time, to a marker that could, at best, be displayed in private. The spectacular rise of language as the most important marker of ethnic identity was to a large part caused by the spectacular fall that religious institutions experienced in the middle of the 20th century. Like with language, the Soviet newcomers insisted on a pure form of atheism.

In 1951, 7 years after the Soviets had taken power in Bessarabia, a school report from Kiliya rayon lamented that on church holidays, up to 70% of school pupils remained absent from school and attended church instead. This situation was blamed on a lack of anti-religious education.[13] Another school report from the early 1950s demanded agitation should be intensified among parents in the town of Vilkovo, with its substantial Old-Believer population, since the town's population was overtly religious and uncultivated.[14] This form of atheistic purity could not demarcate ethnic boundaries, but it did divide those who were on a promising path to Soviet integration from those who needed harsher enforcement of Soviet manners.

The intensity with which religion resurfaced after the fall of Soviet power is all the more surprising. In many families religious practices had survived. Most people who started to regularly attend church after 1991 were no raw recruits to religion. However, with newly won freedoms and an abundant choice in congregations, not all of them joined an Orthodox parish. This fact is sometimes polemically debated by those who see Orthodox Christianity as a key ingredient of ethnic authenticity. To underline such a position, adherents of evangelical prayer houses can be lumped together under the label "sectarians" (*sektanty*). This is as much a pariah-etiquette as that of *Surzhyk*. In some cases, people who are not Orthodox are implicitly excluded from the "real members" of an ethnic group. To delineate the Gagauz identity, for instance, Orthodox Christianity is frequently cited as one of its pillars, even by Gagauz who themselves are not religious (Anikin 2009: 23). An example of this idea was the lecture of a scholar from the Gagauz University at Komrat during the World Congress of the Gagauz in November 2012. In a talk entitled *the cultural code of the Gagauz,* the speaker said that this code was made up of the Gagauz language, the strong influence of the Russian language, the Gagauz traditions, and Orthodox Christianity. The latter had now come under pressure due to the "dictate from European bureaucrats" and "liberal European ideas." Implicitly this also means that a weakening of religion would ultimately dissolve ethnic

13 Fr445 D186 Godovye otchety rayonnykh i gorodskikh otdelov narodnogo obrazovaniya za 1950–1951 uchebnyy god, p. 212.

14 Fr445 D209 Godovye otchety gorodskikh i rayonnykh otdelov narodnogo obrazovaniya o rabote shkol za 1951 god, p. 59.

boundaries. This fear has also been voiced by a clergyman speaking on the same congress. The fear that if a group loses its traditional faith it would also lose its identity mirrors similar fears about the loss of linguistic boundaries.

Most explicit about being Orthodox as a precondition to take on an ethnicity-like identity are the various Cossack associations. In order to join the Izmail branch of the Ukrainian Registered Cossacks one needs to pledge allegiance in Izmail's Cathedral, swearing that one "will serve God and the people of Ukraine to the final breath."[15] In order to join the ranks of the Bessarabian Cossack Regiment, one needs to be of age and baptized in an Orthodox Church.[16]

Religion, one can conclude, has come to serve not to distinguish the members of one ethnic group from another. Instead, the degree of a person's religiosity is used by some to distinguish what they deem the "real" members of an ethnic group from all the rest.

3 Common Historical Experience and Collective Memory

It is a familiar observation that people who have been through a lot together adopt similar characteristics and a spirit of communality. In a classic definition of the nation by Ernest Renan, national unity was produced, among other things, by the shared memory of struggles lived through together (Renan 1994: 17). In the former Soviet Union too, common historical roots were seen as one of the preconditions to call a group a nation.[17] As with other criteria in Soviet definitions of ethnic groups, common historical experience is widely perceived as an origin of ethnic ties. Since history has become a focus of national politics and a matter of passionate debate in post-Soviet Ukraine, knowledge of an official historical narrative has also become a condition of belonging to the nation (Richardson 2004: 116).

When asked for the locus of the ethnic essence, some people stress common historical experience first of all. Such experiences are thought to be conserved in people over many generations and to shape people's characters, even within

15 *Uezdniy Telegraf* October 16, 2013, Za veru, Ukrainu i kazachestvo.

16 *Kur'er Nedeli* November 10, 2012, O kazakakh vchera i segodnya.

17 See the already mentioned definitions for nation by Joseph Stalin: "A nation is a historical constituted, stable community of people, formed on the basis of a common language, territory, economic life, and psychological make-up manifested in a common culture" (Stalin 1994: 20) and later for an "ethnos" by Yulian Bromley: "Ethnos in the general sense of the word may be defined as a historically formed aggregate of people who share relatively stable specific features of culture (including language) and psychology, an awareness of their unity and their difference from other similar groups, and an ethnonym which they have given themselves" (Bromley 1980: 154).

large groups in which group members do not directly interact. One narrative derived from this belief is that the historic experience of living in a particular environment predestines people of one ethnic group for a particular economic niche. Bulgarians in Bessarabia, for instance, have long been associated with growing vegetables and wine (Kushnir 1998: 169). During fieldwork, several of my respondents associated tomato growing with Moldovans. In a series on local history that ran in the *Kur'er Nedeli* newspaper in 2012 the idea that different ethnic groups traditionally occupied different economic niches was a reoccurring theme.[18] Soviet ethnography has ascribed ethnic arsenals of skills to an ethnic character that in turn was shaped by the environment in which the ethnic group is believed to have originated (Bromley and Podol'niy 1990: 46, 106–110). An application of this theory is the idea that frugality, a characteristic sometimes ascribed to Bulgarians, stems from their century-long oppression by the Ottoman Empire (Kushnir 1998: 177). The idea that the experience of living under Ottoman rule was deeply engraved in the behavior of contemporary Bessarabians is fairly widespread. For instance, one frequently mentioned particularity of Bulgarians is their allegedly specific attitude towards women. The leader of the League of Bulgarian Families, a Bulgarian ethnic association in Izmail, called what in her view is the typical Bulgarian attitude towards women, a "cult of the mother and the mother-in-law." She explained the emergence of this specific trait with the century long struggle against the Ottomans: "Because the men…, well five centuries, 500 years, the men are fighting and the women are in the house, and therefore, naturally, the mother held the whole family together."[19] Two more respondents, both with mixed Gagauz and Bulgarian ancestry, pointed out that the often alleged ethnic endogamy of Bessarabian Bulgarians was a direct consequence of their experience of oppression in the Ottoman Empire. A Bulgarian schoolteacher saw this experience as the reason why Bulgarians had been reluctant to marry the Turkic speaking Gagauz. The narrative of still perceptible consequences of Ottoman oppression also comes as a Gagauz variety. The director of the Kotlovina culture house, when explaining the differences between Gagauz and Bulgarian folk songs, said the Gagauz songs were even more melancholic than the Bulgarian ones, because the Gagauz had been even lower in the pecking order of the Ottoman Empire. The Ottoman oppression appeared in the context of other ethnic groups too: A Ukrainian history teacher explained what he perceived as hatred between Moldovans and Gagauz with the fact that the

18 *Kur'er Nedeli* April 16, 2012, Novaya istoriya Bessarabii 1812–2012: <http://www.izmail.es/article/10594/> (23.02.2019).

19 Interview in Izmail April 4, 2013.

Moldovans too had been subjects of the Ottoman Empire and Gagauz were speakers of a Turkic language.

In all these explanations, a long-gone social order has become an allegedly stable characteristic of Bulgarians, Gagauz, Moldovans, and of the relations between them. The relations between ethnic groups appear like relations between individual people, formed by personal experiences. In this perception, it seems there is a mechanism that engraves certain cultural traits in the minds of everyone within an ethnic community, even if the formative experience was made by distant ancestors. If common historical experience is really formative for contemporary ethnic cultures, then it must have been passed down the generations by constant and profound practices of memory, which enabled later generations to relive the experiences of their ancestors. Any technique to maintain an ethnic boundary created by common historical experience would therefore include some form or remembrance rituals, part of what has been described as commemorative culture (*Erinnerungskultur*) a lose set of practices that are resistant against the findings of academic historiography (Troebst 2006: 69).

In southern Bessarabia, we can trace such rituals of commemorative culture at least since the Romanian period. In order to get locals to identify with Romania, the most obvious common struggle was the War of Independence against the Ottoman Empire 1877–78. To honor the heroes of this war, a pillar with the figure of an eagle sitting on top, was erected on Izmail's river front in 1929 (Rossetti 1934: 56). Such a monument had very little to do with the collective memory of Izmail's inhabitants. The city's population had experienced this war as a hinterland position for the Russian troops and finally as a price for Russia (not Romania). The city's Russian-speaking population was therefore hardly very passionate about Romanian independence and hardly saw the struggle for it as a common endeavor uniting them with the rest of Romania. The Romanians also renamed most streets in central Izmail to give them the names of medieval rulers in Moldova and Walachia, names of the princely family of Romania's recently established monarchy, or leaders of the national awakening campaign (Rossetti 1934: 27). In this case, the alleged common struggle was merely an ascription of commonality to people who first needed to be taught that these were the struggles they had gone through together.

In the Soviet Union, practices of commemorative culture were steered by a centrally planning state. There were two hierarchically structured realms in which solidarity needed to be created by way of remembering common historical experience; the ethnically unspecified Soviet people and the ethnically essentialized constitutive ethnic nations that formed the Soviet people. Therefore, memorization of commonly experienced struggles was used to mark civil as well as ethnic ties. This became possible by giving different ethnic groups in the Soviet Union their own historiography and thus their own particular history. The struggles stressed most in these histories could be remembered publicly in events or around monuments, provided of course, that the struggle had not been against the Russians or the Soviet Union. If there was an established narrative how the struggle of one group connected it to the rest of the Soviet people, these places of memory could refer to a particular ethnic community. In Soviet Ukraine, for example, monuments and place names remembering Cossack Hetman Bogdan Khmel'nitskiy (1595–1657) were frequent. Khmel'nitskiy led the Zaporozhian Cossacks against Poland-Lithuania and into Union with Muscovy. Therefore, his legacy did not contradict the Soviet tale of an age-old aspiration for unity of the Eastern Slavs. However, another influential Cossack Hetman, Ivan Mazepa (1639–1709) who changed sides in the Northern War, turning away from Russia to align his troops with Sweden instead, was remembered nowhere in Soviet Ukraine. This changed after the break-up of the Soviet Union when Khmel'nitskiy and Mazepa both were displayed on the banknotes of the newly introduced Ukrainian Hryvnia.

Most prominently remembered in the public sphere of the Soviet Union were historic events experienced by Soviet citizens of all ethnic identities. The one outstanding event, the memory of which remains omnipresent even in small villages, is World War II (or the "Great Patriotic War" as the period of the Soviet Union's involvement in the conflict, from June 1941 to May 1945 is commonly called in most successor states). But other defining moments, such as the October Revolution, the Civil War, the first manned space flight, or the War in Afghanistan, were also very common points of reference. They helped to prepare the grounds for an anticipated, post-ethnic Soviet identity.

After the disintegration of the USSR, independent Ukraine followed a more markedly ethnic paradigm to rename places, shift state holidays, and alter the school curriculum. (Locally, however, many Soviet street names and monuments remained in place until the de-communization laws that were implemented in 2016). Among all Ukrainian campaigns to rearrange practices of commemorative culture, the one event that took most attention and debate was the devastating man-made famine of 1932–33. In order to make this event and its memory into an ethnic marker for Ukrainians, one had to deal with it not so much as a crime against humanity, but as a crime committed by ethnic Russians against ethnic Ukrainians. When Ukraine became independent, the hitherto omitted famine was reintroduced to public memory by adding a couple of pages to Soviet history books. There, the blame was put entirely on the commanders in Moscow while local actors, often ethnic Ukrainians, were portrayed as will-less cogs in the wheel (Wanner 1998: 95). Another step in making the famine into an exclusively Ukrainian trauma was to recognize it officially as genocide. A parliamentary commission reached such a conclusion in 1993. Subsequent governments introduced a nationwide commemoration day (in 1998) and a bill that prohibited the denial of the fact that the famine had been genocide (2007). The bill itself was never finally adopted, but its reading in parliament was accompanied by an explanation that it would help to unite the Ukrainian people and to tackle intolerance. In many largely Russian-speaking regions, the presidential order to publicly remember the famine each November was widely ignored (Kasianov 2010). The debate whether or not the Holodomor was a centrally planned extermination campaign against Ukrainians spilled beyond the narrow circles of historians after the publication of Anne Appelbaum's *Red Famine* (2017) and a debate between her and Sheila Fitzpatrick that was virally commented on in Ukraine and beyond.[20]

In 2015, the nationalist Radical Party of Oleh Lyashko introduced sweeping laws on the commemoration of history. These were approved by parliament in their substance. The new laws reinstituted the famine of 1932–33 to the status of genocide of the Ukrainian people, committed by the totalitarian regime of the USSR, "which led to the deaths of Millions, destroyed the social basis of the Ukrainian people, ruined its age-old traditions and spiritual culture, and destroyed its ethnic uniqueness."[21] Although the fact of the trauma of Holodomor is now largely beyond controversy, these new laws declare it the trauma of one specific ethnic group.

Bessarabia suffered its own trauma of a man-made famine. At the time of the Holodomor the region belonged to Romania and therefore was spared from the 1932–33 famine. After Bessarabia had become a part of the Soviet Union, the region became exposed to the same forces that had provoked the famine of 1932–33. All arable land was collectivized, and in 1946 an unusually dry summer, combined with impossible production quotas imposed on peasants, caused a famine that ultimately cost some villages a third of their population (Tel'pis 2000). This famine, that in attenuated form also affected other agricultural areas of the USSR, has no commemoration day. There are commemorative monuments on some village graveyards and the nation-wide commemoration day on the fourth Saturday in November officially also includes

20 Following Fitzpatrick's review of *Red Famine* in the *Guardian*, August 25, 2017: <https://www.theguardian.com/books/2017/aug/25/red-famine-stalins-war-on-ukraine-anne-applebaum-review> (23.02.2019).

21 See preamble of the *law on the condemnation of the communist and national socialist (Nazi) totalitarian regimes in Ukraine and the prohibition of the propagation of their symbols*, published on the homepage of Verkhovna Rada, April 3, 2015: <http://w1.c1.rada.gov.ua/pls/zweb2/webproc4_1?pf3511=54670> (23.02.2019).

the victims of the famine of 1946–47. But the symbols, speeches, TV-specials, and newspaper columns that reoccur each year in late November, clearly focus on the large famine of 1932–33, the one that hit vast areas of Ukraine and is politically much more loaded. Institutions in Bessarabia, such as libraries, schools, municipalities, local newspapers, commemorate the victims of all famines each year. But because many of the speeches and pamphlets are blueprints from Kyiv, they often end up commemorating a famine that past the region by and neglect the famine that devastated southern Bessarabia. In this way, by centralizing commemorative culture, the periphery's history gets overshadowed by the narratives of the center. Whoever lives in the periphery has to subscribe to the center's historical priorities in order to belong. Practices of commemorating the famines caused by land collectivization illustrate how selecting certain events for collective memory and omitting others, can turn historiography into a tool of group boundary maintenance. In the case of the Holodomor, these group boundaries have increasingly been marked in ethnic terms. Ethnic boundaries, in this way are drawn according to who sincerely commemorates a certain historical portrayal of a particular event and who does not.

The notion of common historical experience as the essence of ethnic belonging is closely connected with an all-encompassing education system. All scholars associated with the deconstruction of national and ethnic identities, in some way or another point to the significance of mass education. In the revised edition of *Imagined Communities* Benedict Anderson (2006: 163–185) singled out the census, the map, and the museum as the three most powerful institutions creating a sense of communion.

The Museum is of particular interest here, because it is an institution one can find in many villages. Often such museums are attached to schools and culture houses and function as a continuation of the classroom. As history lessons in school, the museum usually also employs the division of the past into the history of one's own group and the history of others. The history of village museums as didactic institutions dates back to the Romanian period, when at least Izmail's leading middle school, the St. Dmitry Gymnasium for boys, offered such a history museum (Rossetti 1934: 110). In Soviet Schools, while the exhibits were replaced, the function of such museums remained similar; to remind its visitors of past events that should be commemorated in such a way that they entail a sense of communion and continuation.

4 Processed Folklore

One reoccurring narrative is that people of different ethnic identities show different emotional responses to folkloric performances. A history lecturer from the University of Izmail told me a story about an experiment he said he has conducted.[22] The story was about an infant boy born to a Russian father and a Gagauz mother. In order to determine the boy's "true" ethnic nature, he played different brands of folklore music to him. The boy, according to the teacher, did not show any reactions neither to Russian nor Ukrainian songs, but when a Gagauz song was played, "his mother had difficulties holding him." This story might well be a cliché, especially because it is a version of a scene from Tolstoy's *War and Peace*, in which protagonist Nataliya Rostova cannot resist to dance to a Russian folk tune, although she was brought up to French manners (Figes 2002: 17). Even if this was just an old story, retold in what might have been an ad-hoc tale, this does not change the fact that the respondent believed that the essence of ethnic belonging could be determined by looking at folkloric taste. During a Bulgarian folklore festival in Odessa, a Ukrainian acquaintance who accompanied me, said the music and the dances made him feel foreign. When asked how the songs and dresses differed from the ones that make him feel at home, he pointed to his heart and said that the main difference was there, inside.

One more example comes from a middle-aged Bulgarian teacher and entrepreneur from the Bulgarian and Gagauz village of Chervonoarmeyskoe. He told me, his father was Gagauz and his mother Bulgarian. He had, however, decided that his "true nature" was Bulgarian. When asked how he had reached this conclusion, he explained: "…I am drawn more towards the Bulgarian culture, because it agitates my blood more when there is Bulgarian folklore, music, dances! …More than the Gagauz ones. That means, in me, there is more of the Bulgarian. I can feel it. It acts out in the blood."[23]

So taste in folklore is sometimes believed to expose the "true ethnic nature" of people, are they of mixed ethnic origin or not. Walker Connor (2011: 114) points out that what constitutes an ethnic group can hardly be explained rationally, and that therefore the emotional realm of music is often believed to reflect a specific past and the genius of an ethnic group. Taste itself can act only as a litmus-test to expose what is believed to be a hidden quality "inside," where

22 Interview in Izmail, January 24, 2013.

23 Interview in Chervonoarmeyskoe, September 19, 2013. In the last cited sentence, the respondent used the Bulgarian word for "blood," (krav).

it seems, the essence of ethnicity can be found according to wide-spread assumptions. In this perception, ethnic essence is carried by the values and morals put across in the folklore of different ethnic groups, and allegedly these values and morals are different for each ethnic group.

One technique to mark the border between different forms of folklore is labeling folkloric performance with an ethnic marker. Today, folklore is a vital part of representing ethnicity in public. The folkloric movement is well organized around clubs and culture houses. Folkloric groups in the Izmail area perform a genre sometimes called "processed folklore" (*obrabotanniy fol'klor*). Processed folklore brings pre-modern cultural traits to the stage in a modern and appealing form. It consists mostly of dances and songs, performed in replicas of historic dresses, shinier and more becoming than they likely were in the time referred to, and to the background of synthesized, prerecorded music. The performance on stage therefore can be called "artificial" because it is so detached from the "real" life, but also because it is artistic, designed to show the talent and creativity of the performers rather than claiming ethnic "authenticity" (Habeck 2011: 67). Gregoriy Chilik, the head of the Izmail Center of Ethnic Cultures, who organizes many of the region's folklore festivals, explained where the raw material for processed folklore comes from:

> Among other things we also do folkloric expeditions. We travel..., well let's say, in this year we have planned to do this in two villages, in one Moldovan, and in one Bulgarian, [...]. We go to old people. There are 90-year-olds there, Grandmas and Grandpas, and we ask them folkloristic questions. 'How were those customs back then, marriage, baptisms, all kinds of..., how did this go, how did that go,' and they don't only tell, but some of them also have..., they know a lot of songs. And we collect this material and that's it, one after another. After that, we do a bit of..., we process the material and we keep it here. One of the folklore collectives needs it—'Aha! Please here we have songs and what you want from the people.' One can look and listen to that Grandma. They can make a modern adaptation of it, or it can be purely ethnographic like she herself had sung it. Feel free, do as you like.[24]

24 Interview in Izmail, April 10, 2013, a very similar procedure was described by a Gagauz folklore performer from the village of Kotlovina and graduate from the Kyiv academy of music in an interview on October 7, 2013 in Izmail.

This method for collecting the ethnographic raw material of processed folklore seems to be fairly wide-spread. A detailed account of a folkloric expedition to a number of villages in a nearby region of Moldova was provided by Jennifer Cash (2011: 110–121). It is notable that already in the process of collecting the material, described by the head of the Center of Ethnic Cultures, it becomes clearly ethnically labeled. Expeditions take place to a Moldovan and a Bulgarian village, where then folkloric material representative of these groups is collected. Solo artists and groups who perform processed folklore usually specialize in the repertoires of one ethnic group. If a collective or a solo artist is announced on stage, usually it will also be announced from which town or village they are and which ethnic group they represent. Therefore, the genre is structured and organized along ethnic boundaries. This does not mean that the people belonging to one or other folklore group necessarily need to identify privately with the ethnic group in question. It is more important to stay faithful to the rigid format of the genre (Habeck 2011: 66–67).

Cash also describes some of the ways in which songs and dances can be adapted between an excursion and their performance on stage. In some instances the instrumentation of a piece of music was adapted,[25] in some cases the choreography of a dance, sometimes the gender and age of the performer were altered according to an ensemble's options. But perhaps a more significant aspect of processing folklore was labeling songs and dances with the name of a village and an ethnic group. Even in cases where the village, with which a song was associated, was unclear, folklore ensembles chose one of the available options. The same was true if the ethnic group, from which a dance originated, remained unclear. The processed and performed version of a song or dance may often erase many of the subtleties in its ethnic origins. Still, usually, one ethnic label is chosen for it (Cash 2011: 115–121).

Hence, processed folklore is also a way to process ethnic boundaries from their subtle and complex expressions found in villager's songs, dances, dresses, and jokes, to the clear and shiny form in which they appear on a stage. This processing does not keep folklore groups with different ethnic labels from sharing one stage or one festival, or from collaborating with each other. Even after the disintegration of the Soviet Union and the rise to prominence of ethnic nationalism, folklore performances could still be used to promote ethnic pluralism (Cash 2011: 12). But each group has its ethnic label attached to their performance.

25 In my own fieldwork, I witnessed almost exclusively synthesized music as accompaniment of folklore song and dance, which, needless to say, alters the nature of a piece of music.

In rare cases a folklore ensemble can perform songs attributed to different ethnic groups. In such a case, however, each new song would be announced with the information with which ethnic group it is associated. This mode of performance could be witnessed during the summer months in Izmail's Art Gallery. Every second day, groups of German tourists arrived on Danube cruise boats. Their short, guided land trip inevitably ended with a visit to the gallery, including a concert by the folklore group *Kob'zarska Duma* (the bard's song). This group specialized in the celebration of ethnic pluralism. They performed explicitly as a "Bessarabian" ensemble, singing Russian Cossack songs, Ukrainian folk tunes, a Jewish wedding song, and finally the German *Lorelei-song*.[26] Importantly, however, this group too introduced each of their songs with an ethnic label.

There are, as one would expect in a multiethnic region, instances of one song being performed in several languages,[27] but I have never witnessed in public performances, someone introducing a song or dance as belonging to several ethnic groups. In a folkloric culture that is so strictly structured by ethnicity, the conclusion that each ethnic culture is essentially different from the others is not a far leap, and from there it is only logical that these essentially different cultures would cause different reactions from people who themselves are inherently different by their ethnic disposition.

Like the local history museum, state-organized folklore performances that served as public reminders for ethnic unity or ethnic diversity can be traced back to the time of Romanian rule. The culture centers in the villages around Izmail held frequent lectures to convince the ethnically non-Romanian population that they should identify with Romania as their motherland (see chapter 3). Such lectures often could not be fully understood by the local population, since many of them spoke little or no Romanian. In order to attract bigger audiences, lectures were usually accompanied by amusements, such as comical plays, acrobatic performances, and folklore performances. At the same time state institutions were terrified of public performances of other ethnic group's folklore. A main concern was Cossack horseshows, a popular entertainment in the 1930s. The Romanian secret police saw the travelling Cossack artists as a threat because they might have a subversive effect on the audience. Therefore,

26 With this last song the folklore group included the Germans as one of the constituent groups of the Bessarabian ethnic mosaic. This usually caused a grateful and emotional response from the German tourists, many of which came to Bessarabia on a root-finding-mission as the descendants of deported Bessarabian Germans.

27 A song best known in its Ukrainian version *ti zh mene pidmanula* was sung in Albanian by a group of elderly women in the predominantly Albanian-speaking village of Zhovtnevoe (renamed to its pre-Soviet name of Karakurt in 2016), Bolgrad rayon.

they were prohibited at will.[28] In any case, police kept a close eye on them, sometimes by sending undercover police to folklore shows.[29] So we can assume that in southern Bessarabia, folklore performances already in the 1930s were a tool to mark ethnic boundaries. Therefore, they were a potential medium to express the grievances of ethnic minorities and to promote minority concerns and more self-determination.

The celebration of ethnic pluralism using folklore goes back to the early years of Soviet rule in Bessarabia. Singing and dancing in folklore groups became a leisure time activity since the foundation of clubs and culture houses from the mid-1950s onwards. A 1953 article in *Pridunayskaya Pravda*, the Izmail local edition of the party newspaper, reported that there were already over 300 clubs in the oblast in which 13,000 people engaged in singing and dancing.[30] The article cited one *kolkhoznik* from the village of Ogorodnoe, saying that he was so well-off that he wanted to sing and dance all the time. Therefore, he joined the local folklore collective. The article said that in the area around Ogorodnoe, Bulgarian Songs and dances had survived the oppression of the "Romanian-Boyar Occupation." Now the Bulgarian folklore groups there had the opportunity to bring the great songs they had collected onto the stage. The Soviet Union also institutionalized musical education. Folklore traditions were studied and taught in music academies. Many songs were arranged for professionally trained orchestras and recorded for a broader audience. This process of academization also went strictly along ethnic boundaries. Folklore shows and exhibitions were organized all over the country in order to strengthen ties between the different peoples in the Soviet Union (Slezkine 1994: 447). But friendship between peoples did not mean dissolving the boundaries between them. Quite to the contrary, the Soviet principle of "national in form, socialist in content" increasingly became a "cult of form" (Slezkine 1994: 451; Szporluk 1998). The show of interethnic harmony silenced a critical discussion of ethnic stereotypes and in fact might even have helped reinforce them (Habeck 2011: 66).

The roots of the folkloric movement lie in this time, when culture houses were built and later equipped with stage prop and electronic sound systems. So the birth of this particular genre fell into a period when ethnic identities

28 For example in March 1937, F312 D138 Nablyudatel'noe delo za deyatel'nost' naseleniya russkoy i ukrainskoy natsional'nosti po Izmail'skomu uezdu, pp. 8–11, or in May and June 1938, ibid., pp. 88–92.

29 In October 1934, the Romanian police station in the Danube port of Reni sent undercover police to a guest performance of the Cossack choir "Gusari" F312 D49, p. 220.

30 *Pridunayskaya Pravda* November 28, 1953 Rastsvetayut narodnye talanty Izmail'shchiny.

were already officially ascribed and used for administrative purposes. Therefore, it made sense for state funded culture houses to organize folklore collectives along ethnic boundaries. The genre remained structured along these lines long after the Soviet state disappeared.

5 Genetic Narratives of Ethnic Belonging

A more powerful and potentially more harmful argument is that the essence of ethnicity is biological and enclosed in the genome. Until the late Soviet years, it remained mysterious which substance connected the members of one ethnos to each other. Soviet ethnographers already operated with the term "gene" and used it as an explanation for ethnic differences (see for example Arutyunyan 1974), but to wider audiences the insights of genetics and the nature of DNA were yet unknown. Since then the field of human genetics has made huge progress and the concept of DNA is widely used. The dissemination of genetic insights naturally also exposed them to distortion by interested groups. For those delimiting ethnic boundaries, the concept of DNA seemed to provide the missing link between hard science and their gut feeling that some people naturally belonged together and were essentially different from others. With the technology to detect a person's DNA, a new scientific tool emerged that allowed to decode a person's inherited traits. This was certainly a conceivable candidate for the substance that encoded features believed to be characteristic for a specific ethnic group.

Also, certain ways of behavior that are believed to be found particularly within one ethnic group can be attributed to genes. Such ideas often come along with a very common misunderstanding about DNA; that the cultural behavior of the ancestors was comprehensively recorded in their DNA and therefore the ancestor's acquired qualities would be reflected in their offspring's DNA. One commonly held belief springing from this misinterpretation is the idea that a language can be learned more easily if it was the native language of an ancestor. One respondent, a researcher at the Izmail local Museum, told me that Bulgarians and Moldovans find it easier to learn Russian than Ukrainian. She explained that this was because their ancestors had been used to the Russian language as a state language for centuries, but to the Ukrainian language only since a decade or two. Therefore, she explained, the ability to learn Russian was already "engraved in their genes."

Modern technology and genetic knowhow can indeed provide some information about a person's ancestry.[31] Recently, big-number studies such as the National Geographic Society's Genographic Project profit from the curiosity of individuals who send in samples of their DNA in order to learn about their own ancestry.[32] Other projects that sample large quantities of human DNA put their focus more on research of inheritable disease, such as the Harvard-based Personal Genome Project.[33] The company DeCode Genetics concentrates on the research of genetic disorder, but has produced a small number of publications about the genetic particularities of the population of Iceland, where the company is based.[34] Knowledge about early settlement patterns of humans clearly profited from genetics and large scale research projects. The Genographic project can, with some justification, promise to reveal "which branch of the human family tree" an individual belongs to. However, no serious study claims to reveal a person's "true" ethnic or national identity. One manifest reason for this restriction is that the genetic mutations that structure the ancestral patterns revealed through genetic tests, are much older than even the most pretentious nationalists would claim their nations to be. Even if an individual combines the two known ways of ethnic ancestry tracing (through mitochondrial and Y-chromosomal DNA), this still reveals next to nothing about the ethnic identity of the vast majority of his or her ancestors: Combined mitochondrial DNA and Y-chromosomal DNA contain information only about two direct lines of ancestors, since the mitochondrial DNA was passed on exclusively from mothers to their children, and the Y-chromosomal DNA was passed on only from fathers to

---

31 There are two widely accepted procedures to trace ancestry through many generations and to reveal common ancestors of large groups of people that have lived many generations ago. For individuals of both sexes the maternal line can be traced using mitochondrial DNA (mtDNA), which is inherited from the mother and is much shorter and therefore easier to analyze than nuclear DNA (Willermet 2006: 876–878). For men, there is also the possibility to trace the paternal line along the DNA in the Y-chromosome, which is passed on from fathers to sons (Lavender 2006: 2355–2356). The DNA in all other chromosomes is inherited in a random mix of equal proportions from mother and father; therefore, it is virtually impossible to trace one lineage. But mtDNA and Y-chromosomal DNA can be traced back along patterns of mutations for many millennia. As a result, statistics and maps can be produced that illustrate the pattern of human settlement on the planet. Coupled with archeological findings and linguistic research, these insights can reveal hitherto unknown pages of the human story.

32 See the Genographic Project homepage: <https://genographic.nationalgeographic.com/about/> (23.02.2019).

33 See the Personal Genome Project homepage: <https://www.personalgenomes.org/#about> (23.02.2019).

34 See the homepage of deCODE genetics: <http://www.decode.com/publications/> (23.02.2019).

sons. If one goes back only to the fifth generation, there are 32 ancestors in it, 16 female and 16 male. However, mitochondrial DNA was inherited only from one of these female ancestors and Y-chromosomal DNA only from one of the male ancestors, while all the other 30 individuals have equally contributed to the overall genome (Brodwin 2002: 328). Therefore, the belief that ethnicity can be determined by looking at a person's genome presupposes that the person's ancestors were strictly endogamous within an ethnic group.

Despite all these complexities, identity builders have been seduced by genetics because they offer the "cachet of science as the ultimate guarantor of truth" and they appear to be "more stable over time than more putatively accidental aspects of identity" (Brodwin 2002: 328). Therefore, DNA as a concept has been used wrongly or confusingly not only on the local level to explain everything inexplicable so far, but also in the nation-wide discourse about the origin of Ukrainians and the origin of differences between Ukrainians and Russians. A very telling example for the uninformed use of DNA as a determinant of ethnicity was a documentary aired in November 2012 on Ukrayina, a TV channel controlled by Ukraine's richest Oligarch, Rinat Akhmetov. It was called "DNA Portrait of a Nation" and announced days ahead as the "scientific sensation of the century."[35] The filmmakers collected hundreds of DNA samples from Ukrainian celebrities and people with allegedly ancient Ukrainian family names (which, in the Slavic convention, are inherited from the father and thereby, just like the Y-chromosome, carry information about only one line of male ancestors). The documentary claimed, without explanation, that "like most other ethnicities, Ukrainian ethnicity is passed on by the father to his children." Therefore, when choosing candidates with ancient Ukrainian family ties, the male lineage was decisive. The choice of the DNA specimens was justified by saying these were especially authentic Ukrainians, since their great grandfathers had already identified as Ukrainians. The collected specimens were analyzed by "the best geneticists in the world." Based on this analysis, the documentary did away with the "Soviet propaganda" that all three Eastern Slavic nations, Russia, Belarus, and Ukraine, had their roots in mediaeval Kievan Rus. Instead, the documentary claimed that Ukrainians were not Slavs at all. Rather, the film asserted, they were the most ancient branch of Arians, a people that, according to the film, originated from Ukraine and spread from there to other parts of Eurasia. The documentary also included reenacted scenes from a bronze-age Ukraine. These showed the dramatic encounters of the different peoples that would come to form the modern Ukrainian people. The

35 The documentary is available in *Ukrayina's* web archive: <http://kanalukraina.tv/ru/programs/p/396#episode/> (23.02.2019).

film neither stated that there was no country called Ukraine in the bronze-age, nor that the people living in its territory would not call themselves Ukrainians for another 5000 years. The four peoples that allegedly teamed up to form the Ukrainians were represented by actors, each dressed up in the array of one particular bronze-age people and each representing one virtue that can allegedly be found in modern Ukrainians.

A talk-show that followed the airing of the film[36] was attended not by scientists, but by politicians and by some of the arch-Ukrainian TV-personalities who had their DNA analyzed. The talk-show was accompanied by screened charts, statistics, and maps meant to reinforce the claim of scientific validity that pervaded the entire broadcast. One politician, who took part in the talk-show and eventually stormed out angrily, doubted the connection between DNA and ethnic identity. He criticized that the geneticists in the movie had been translated and cited misleadingly. The host shouted him down calling "so you deny the validity of genetics, so you don't believe in science?" One of the maps screened during the talk-show explained the distribution of the genetic traces of one common ancestor (again, one out of many) within parts of the population (by no means all of the population). These traces were spread more or less evenly across Eastern Europe but thinned out (but by no means disappeared) in Russia. One of the guests, Dmitro Korchnsky, a representative of the far-right party UNA-UNSO,[37] jubilantly concluded that now, finally there was scientific proof that Ukrainians were "a people of great ancestry" and that Russians were of different origin.

The broadcast's content and conclusions may not have been assumed to be factual by the better part of the audience. For instance, the staff of Izmail's local museum watched the film together and according to one of the employees had "a good laugh on it." Certainly, it was also understood that the guests invited for the subsequent talk-show were there not for their expertise but for their polemics. However, the spirit, in which genetics and ethnicity were discussed, clearly reinforced the idea that ethnicity was a category of natural science that can be determined using genetic analysis.

Along with this idea comes the belief that each ethnic group possesses a pool of genetic material that, like cultural traditions, is unique to this group and that comprises a value in and of itself. One example for this paradigm stems from a heated discussion about same sex marriage, in which a young

36 The talk-show is available at *Ukrayina's* web archive: <http://kanalukraina.tv/ru/programs/p/396#episode/> (23.02.2019).

37 An abbreviation standing for "Ukrayins'ka Natsyonal'na Asambleya—Ukrayins'ka Narodna Samooborona" (Ukrainian National Assembly—Ukrainian People's Self-Defense).

history teacher in one of Izmail's vocational schools asked how one could stop the decline of the "gene pool of the nation" (*genafond natsii*) if same sex marriage came to be legalized. A similar idea was expressed in a column in Izmail's weekly *Uezdniy Telegraf*: The columnist made his point against what he thought was exaggerated spending on social benefits. He argued that the social spending program to increase the birth rate did nothing to the quality of new Ukrainians: "Is it not a tragedy that in order to get these payments, the most miserable people started to give birth to more children, drunkards and socially degenerated families who hardly can improve the *gene pool [genafond] of the Ukrainian nation…*" (emphasis added).[38]

The ease with which lay people, politicians, and journalists talk about genetics in Ukraine points to an observation made by Brodwin (2002: 326) that references to genetics can be used freely to prove or disprove old wisdoms about one's own ethnic identity and the identities of others. The very complexity of genetics is an invitation for ethnic entrepreneurs to pick the proof they need to support their own narrative and to undermine the narratives of others.

Genetics is a young scientific field. Before it took its place among the established disciplines, ethnic boundaries were marked with more basic biological rhetoric. Anthropometric studies of large groups with the intention to distinguish ethnic groups and races on the bases of scientific data were common already in tsarist times. The study of Dmitry Anuchin (1889) attempted to find physiognomic differences between Great Russians, Belarusians, and Little Russians (Ukrainians) by measuring their skulls. In 1908 Fedir Vovk presented an anthropometric study about the features of different ethnic groups in western Ukraine which concentrated on the pigmentation of skin and hair (for a discussion of the two studies see Makarchuk 2008: 334–335).

In the 1930s, under Romanian rule, scientists in a fiercely nationalistic academia believed they could determine a person's ethnicity by analyzing their blood. In 1935, a study that analyzed the blood of the Hungarian speaking Szekler minority argued that only the blood could reveal true ethnic origin since it was the one "source untouched by the vicissitudes of time" (cited in Turda 2007: 428).

Still in Soviet times, there was a plethora of aspiring sciences that sought to explain the link between heredity and the characteristics of a person. The last generation of Soviet anthropologists, still very much read today, operated with the ideas of race as well as ethnic characters. Lev Gumilev, who was shunned by Soviet academia but emerged as the era's most influential thinker about

38 Andrei Potylko in *Uezdniy Telegraf* April 10, 2013.

ethnicity, described *ethnos* as a "phenomenon on the fringes of the social and the biological sphere" (Gumilev 2002: 38).

Genetics would have been both a relief and a disappointment to all these pseudo-scientific predecessors. It demonstrated that DNA was indeed the stuff on which human characteristics were encoded. It also made it possible to trace back common origins of large groups of people. However, the disappointment would have been in the fact that the boundaries of these ancestry groups hardly correspond to ethnic boundaries (Brodwin 2002: 328), let alone to modern state borders.

6 Generalizing the Inside, Omitting the Outside

The five markers of ethnic boundaries as they appear in the narratives of respondents in southern Bessarabia; language, religion, shared historical experience, folklore, and genes, were all endowed with elaborate folk theories, how they can be detected, how they act out, how they can be acquired and reproduced, and finally how ethnic boundaries can be maintained with a separate technique for each ethnic marker (see Table 1, below). Why is it these five markers that came to serve as the stuff of which narratives of ethnic distinctions are made? They all have in common that they are perceived to be essential qualities of every person. They retain their influence on a person's character regardless of individual choices. They are engraved in an essential and unchangeable core of a person's identity. If a person adopts a new language, a new religion, or a new way of life, this according to the narratives analyzed here, would not change their inner dispositions. This is demonstrated by Table 1 that shows the folk theories about how each of the five aspects discussed here shapes a person's essential qualities, how such qualities are ostensibly acquired, transmitted and maintained.

The one technique of ethnic boundary maintenance that reappears in all the narratives mentioned above is a mechanism of exclusion. If competing narratives contradict each other, one of them needs to be disavowed. The most common way of doing this is to exclude those, who disseminate a conflicting narrative. They can be excluded from the circle of people, who are competent to speak about a certain group. People who are portrayed as having forfeited their membership in a certain group, because of the way they live or the values they hold, can easily be denied the competence of seeing, detecting, or sensing true members of a group and the boundary to those who are not.

This form of exclusion entails a claim to possess better techniques of detecting ethnic essence than people with competing narratives. If new techniques appear, such as when genetics entered the field, it is crucial to realign these with existing narratives. Complex academic paradigms like genetics, linguistics, or history offer sufficient dubiety to make them essentially self-service stores of narratives for those with the power to exclude competing narratives.

Another important technique of boundary maintenance that reappears in all the above-mentioned narratives has more to do with inclusion. It starts with the claim that a certain characteristic is very typical for inside an ethnic group, while omitting that it is similarly typical outside an ethnic boundary. Fredrik Barth found this mechanism typical of ethnic boundaries:

> The boundary schema (…) constructs an assumption of shared homogeneity within the group and cultural difference between groups, with great potential consequences for the social life of larger communities and regions (Barth 2000a: 30).

This may be done with a characteristic seen as a positive feature of one particular ethnic group, such as passion, industriousness, or generosity. But perfectly banal practices can just as well serve as ethnic markers with this technique. An example could be the use of hand towels. Hand towels are used in many cultures around the world in similar ways. Without even denying this trivial observation, it is possible to elevate the use of the hand towel as a marker of ethnic identity if one wishes to do so. All one needs to do is to claim that inside an ethnic group everyone uses hand towels in a specific way (or at least traditionally did so, in an unspecified past, when people still used to behave according to principles unique to their ethnic group). At the same time one can just remain silent about identical or similar practices outside the ethnic group. This technique, applied on the hand-towel-example, was used by Oleksandra Serbens'ka, a prominent Ukrainian educator[39] in a Ukrainian language reader designed for Russian-speakers. Most grammar exercises in this volume contain patriotic motives or are based on poetry from the era of romantic nationalism.[40] One particularly interesting exercise on the use of participles employs a

---

39 Serbens'ka made a name for herself as an ardent language purist. She wrote *Antisurzhyk*, a book opposing the common practice of mixing Russian and Ukrainian into *Surzhyk*. This book was published by the Ukrainian Ministry of Education in 1994. Here, Serbens'ka described Russian loanwords in the Ukrainian language as a virus that worked after a Soviet plan to commit "linguicide" on the Ukrainian language (cited in Flier 1998: 114).

40 The technique of sneaking ideological content into grammatical exercises was not new to independent Ukraine. In the early 1950s many of the Russian grammar exercises, used to teach Bessarabian elementary school pupils, contained unveiled Cold War Soviet propaganda slogans. Fr445, D184 Godovoy otchet suvorovskogo rayonnogo otdela narodnogo obrazovaniya za 1950–1951 godov, p. 35.

TABLE 1 Predominant narratives about the location and qualities of ethnic essence

	Function	Manifestation	Mechanism of enclosing ethnic essence
language	communication, identification	speech, especially when uncontrolled	The matter of thought is language; thought is the basis of behavior.
religion	spiritual, social	observance	Religion informs values, value inform behavior.
shared historical experience	inter-generational connection	practices of commemoration	Values derived from a commo experience inform behavio
folklore	recreation, identification	performance	Values engraved in song, danc and tale inform behavior.
genes	biological	phenotype	Genes shape character.

text entitled *the Ukrainian hand towel.* While on the lookout for participles the Russian-speaking student reads:

> A sign of cleanliness and industriousness of every housewife is a tidy house and a clean hand towel. It is a custom all over Ukraine to cover bread on the table with a hand towel (Serbens'ka and Terlak 1999: 152).

None of the practices in this excerpt are particularly Ukrainian. In fact, wherever people use hand towels, their cleanliness can be interpreted as an index for a tidy house. Moreover, the familiar fact that a loaf of bread remains fresh longer under a piece of cloth makes hand towels likely to cover bread wherever the two items occur together. But in this use as an ethnic marker, the hand towel, its cleanliness, and use to keep bread fresh, become charged with a meaning beyond the material function of the item. This meaning, the author then claims, exists "all over Ukraine." Whether it also exists beyond Ukraine we do not know from the cited text, but the neglect of everything outside the realm of Ukraine, creates the impression that caring about the tidiness of hand towels or using them to cover bread, stops at the Ukrainian border.

If a laudable characteristic, like cleanliness, is chosen for this technique, it has the additional effect of marking the ethnic boundary with an advantage

Mode of acquisition	Mode of reproduction	Mode of maintenance
from linguistic environment during childhood	teaching, insisting on one language	linguistic purism
conversion, initiation	mission	church politics
learned from specialists, media, and lay	commemorative culture	regulating commemorative culture
learned from cultural insiders	popularization	ethnic labelling of folkloric performances
inherited from parents	sexual	endogamy within the ethnic group

the ethnic in-group allegedly has over the ethnic out-group. If a more doubtful quality, like impulsiveness, is chosen, it can be reinterpreted by the other group as a positive quality, say passion. Similarly, tenacity can be reinterpreted as stubbornness, industriousness as pushiness etc. Often the auto-stereotype of the group informs the stereotype that outsiders ascribe to the group, with the only difference that from the inside the stereotypical qualities of the group are painted in a more positive light. Psychologists have found that not only do we perceive the outgroup as endowed with less desirable characteristics, we also perceive them as more homogenous (Hilton and von Hippel 1996: 247).

Since the early ethnographic descriptions of Berg and Derzhavin (see chapter 2), Bessarabian Bulgarians are renowned for, and pride themselves on their industriousness. Abstract qualities like industriousness or hot-bloodedness (a quality often ascribed to the Gagauz, who in some cases proudly accept the ascription) are hard to substantiate or measure and therefore do not usually have to be proven. It is sufficient to prove that everyone *knows* about these characteristics among different ethnic groups. Qualities with a double nature, that can be used in stereotype and auto-stereotype equally, are especially suitable for the technique of internal generalization and external omission in order to mark an ethnic boundary. One more example comes from the leader of the Association of Bulgarians of Ukraine, MP Anton Kisse. He uses this technique in his widely disseminated book *The Renaissance of the Bulgarians in Ukraine*. In the chapter *the Father's House and the Homeland* he refers to the industriousness of the Bulgarians:

> As long as I can think, the [father's] house was constantly upgraded and renovated. Later, I learned from reading one of the explorers that house construction is a distinguishing feature of the Bulgarians. Ask any Bulgarian how many rooms there are in his house. As a rule, he will answer with a delay, trying to think of all the rooms he ought to know about. But then he names the number … it is often more than 10. And all that because renovations and extensions are going on almost constantly (Kisse 2006: 31).

It is true that houses in Bessarabian villages are big. There are often more rooms than people can afford to heat. But it is certainly false that the many rooms are a distinguishing feature of the Bulgarians and therefore mark an ethnic boundary. By omitting that most village houses in Bessarabia—built from mud bricks and rush mats—require constant mending, no matter the ethnicity of their tenants, the author reinforces a stereotype and helps to maintain an ethnic boundary between Bulgarians and the unnamed other. No one will likely systematically conduct the experiment suggested in the excerpt, to ask a large sample of Bulgarians the number of rooms in their houses. But if someone would, the resulting statistic would certainly prove that the size of houses or the hours spent renovating, hardly correspond to ethnic boundaries. But stereotypes are not meant to be examined. Not because the result would be considered uninteresting, but because what everybody knows, needs no proof.

The five realms that proved to be at the basis of the narratives why ethnic groups are different from one another are all susceptible to stereotype. Historically, however, all five realms could be effectively used for the construction and maintenance of ethnic boundaries only after they were institutionalized. Without standardized education there could have been no linguistic purism. Without the establishment of national patriarchates there could be no church politics. Without an academy of sciences, that sets the agenda for historical education, there could be no selective teaching of history. Without the organizations that create "processed folklore" there could be no ethnic labeling of song and dance. Without large number DNA samples and mass media there could be no public discourse about the purported genetic uniformity of ethnic groups.

During the Romanian and Soviet periods the relevant institutions were under tight state control. The Soviet Union's institutions were eventually more intrusive in southern Bessarabian society. This is the main reason why the Soviet state proved more effective in marking ethnic boundaries by ascribing standardized languages, historical experiences, and folkloric repertoires to ethnic groups. Each of the latter was associated with a set of unique traits, passed down through the generations by a then yet to be determined substance, for which later DNA was happily and mistakenly embraced. Soviet institutions proved so intrusive that a lot of the theories and concepts disseminated through them can be found today in barely modified forms.

CHAPTER 8

Conclusion—Delimiting Ethnic Groups as a Tool of Statecraft

This study has been complicated by the long timeline it aspired to cover. Many findings could only be put in context by focusing on very particular circumstances during a specific period somewhere along this timeline. In this last chapter I will zoom out again and focus on the broader patterns that emerge when answering the questions raised at the outset of this study, for the entirety of the two centuries I was concerned with. Which patterns are persistent over all these times and how can this persistence be explained? This reflection then leads us to the lessons we can draw for the situation in Ukraine after Maidan.

As one takes more distance from the specific periods discussed in this book, some patterns transcend the changes in statehood and start to appear as a continuum. The factors that drove this long-term change and that caused it to slow down or accelerate are in the focus of this last chapter. A good starting point is to remind ourselves of James Scott's observation that states have to make societies "legible" as their ambitions grow. For Bessarabia the growth of the state's ambitions and the accordingly growing efforts to achieve "legibility" are not a smooth or linear process. But the causality between state's ambitions and its pervasiveness, "the greater the manipulation envisaged, the greater the legibility required to effect it" (Scott 1998: 184) is a suitable framework to analyze the relation between the ambitions of statecraft and the nature of the state's categories.

1 The Significance of Ethnicity: Continuities and Ruptures

Structuring a historical work, by the periods of alternating state rule, as I have done here, tempts one to draw the conclusion that accelerated social change occurred simultaneously with the changes in state hegemony. Yet, after looking at how ethnicity was used in statecraft of the successive governments ruling over Bessarabia, one has to assert that oscillation in ethnicity's importance were by no means congruent with changes in statehood. Administrators in late imperial Russia used ethnicity as a crude tool of administration, very much unlike bureaucrats of the same state five decades earlier, but very similarly to bureaucrats of a new, Romanian state after the Empire's collapse. Romanians

 | DOI:10.1163/9789004408029_009

refined the use of ethnicity in their administration, and when, in 1938, the Romanian constitutional monarchy was replaced by a royal dictatorship, ethnicity gradually was turned into an officially ascribed category that determined a person's rights and obligations. This practice was not abandoned when an ideologically opposed state, the USSR, came to rule the area during and after World War II. The practices attached to ethnicity and ethnic boundaries remained strikingly similar in both these states. The practice to register ethnicity in everyone's personal documents in Bessarabia was initiated by Romania but sustained and refined under Soviet rule. The practice became increasingly unnecessary as cultural differences were gradually leveled in Soviet society, but it survived until the collapse of the Soviet Union. Although the social consequences of belonging to one or the other ethnic group became less articulated in the four and a half decades of Soviet rule, it continuously served to uphold Soviet administrative routines organized along ascribed social categories. Ethnicity held a prominent place among all ascribed categories. The collapse of the Soviet system was accelerated by wide-spread clientelism and corruption in Soviet political and economic institutions. While the state broke to pieces, politicians started to patronize ethnic groups, gaining political capital out of ethnic differences, which they zealously began to reproduce. This form of clientelistic mobilization has its roots in the Soviet state but has survived its collapse by a quarter of a century now.

One of the central tasks this work addresses is to clarify at what times ethnic boundaries played a crucial role in access to resources and political power, and whether the importance of ethnicity was continuous, or whether there were decisive ruptures. What we can see clearly from comparing the ethnicity policies in imperial Russia, interwar Romania, the Soviet Union, and independent Ukraine, is that it was not the changes in statehood that led to changes in the use of ethnicity as a tool of statecraft. Rather states improved and adjusted their use of ethnicity to changes in the economic and social structures they administered. These varying circumstances demanded different forms of legitimizing political power. In an agrarian empire, such as Russia in the 19th century, ensuring productivity and taxability of peasants was more important than knowing what language they spoke or with which group they privately identified. It was assumed that they would side with the tsar rather than with a neighboring ruler because they prayed to the same god. Another more materialistic train of thought was that the tsarist government had invited these people as tax contributing peasants and therefore was interested in their prosperity. Only in the last decades of the Russian Empire and especially after the revolution of 1905, the imperial government grew suspicious of people who identified as anything else than Russian. Although initially vague and full of inconsistencies, state institutions gradually began to develop a concept of ethnicity that could first be used as an analytical category, later as an administrative category. Increasingly, ethnicity came to be seen as a source of loyalty or disloyalty vis-à-vis the state.

Romanian authorities followed suit after World War I. As leaders of a nation state, they drew the legitimation for their power from the idea of unifying all Romanians and all Romanian lands in one state. They needed to convince part of the non-Romanians to "rediscover" their Romanian ethnic core and exclude other parts, primarily Jews, from political power and eventually from basic civil rights. In the first years of Romanian rule in Bessarabia, attempts to convince ethnic minorities prevailed. The Entente governments had, after the First World War, grudgingly allowed Romania to double its territory. In the first years the leaders of the newly stitched together country were therefore still eager to convince the Entente powers that they could live up to the terms of the enlargement, that included equal rights for all inhabitants irrespective of their ethnicity or religion. With the military dictatorship of Ion Antonescu, Romania's policies tended to follow those in Hitler's Germany. In the tumult of the war years, ethnicity came to be seen as a direct indicator of trustworthiness and loyalty vis-à-vis the state. Both Romania and the Soviet Union, which ruled over Bessarabia for one year in 1940–41, mistrusted members of some ethnic groups. In Romania this was because creating an ethnically homogenous population and, more importantly, an ethnically homogenous elite, was an explicit goal. In the Soviet Union, in contrast, the political elite was not ethnically homogenous. But some ethnic groups were in practice excluded from joining the Soviet Union's upper echelons, because they had no titular administrative body inside the Union. This was true for the Bulgarians and the Gagauz. In southern Bessarabia these were the ethnic groups most vulnerable to the suspicion of functioning as a fifth column.

After the World War II, the need to control people, to integrate them in a new socialist mode of agricultural production, and to educate them made it advantageous to ascribe an ethnic attribute to every individual. This was accompanied and fostered by the advent of ethnicity as a scientific category based on large-scale research projects and theorized as an objectively ascertainable characteristic of each individual. Ascribing exclusive ethnic categories to everyone prepared the ground for the next stage of using ethnicity; late Soviet and post-Soviet clientelism. The idea that every person had to have an ethnicity and could have only one, helped to shape ethnic groups as clearly bounded entities. Such groups could easily be represented, efficiently be served and held accountable for their political partisanship.

2 When Ethnic Boundaries Become Obstacles

Closely linked to the question whether the importance of ethnicity and ethnic boundaries grew continuously or in a staggered manner was another central question asked in the introduction: At what times, and in what ways, did ethnic belonging foster or impede the life trajectories of people? And, how was this fostering or impediment explained to them and by them?

This question became most relevant at times when ethnicity was connected to trust and mistrust between governments and the population. These were the periods when ethnic boundaries were made into obstacles for some and hindered whole groups of people in their social mobility, while privileging others. Even though it is hard to establish when exactly ethnic boundaries first became an obstacle in southern Bessarabia, we can safely say that this happened after 1812, the year Russia took control of the region. One could of course argue that the settlers, who came to establish the ethnic mosaic of the region, left their homes because an ethnic boundary impeded their development there. This however would dilute the term "ethnic boundary" as I have used it in this study. I have tried to clearly distinguish ethnic groups from confessional groups, linguistic communities, people inhabiting a common territory, social class, and geographical origin. All these groups exceed what has come to be conceived as ethnic boundaries. In this region, people who adhere to the same religion, inhabit the same region, belong to one social class, and have similar geographical origins, might still identify with different ethnic groups. They might in fact, as some researchers claim for the Bulgarian and the Gagauz, one day have been referred to simply as Bulgarians (Grek and Russev 2011: 73; Hatłas 2011: 194). In the eyes of modern states, however, they were seen as two ethnically different groups. In the still influential Soviet tradition, language is the most significant marker of ethnicity. But now that many people in Bessarabia have lost the ability to speak their ancestral languages, they have not necessarily lost their ethnic identity. Moreover, some groups that speak traditionally the same language, like the Old-Believers and the Russians or the Moldovans and the Romanians, are considered different ethnic groups by most. Therefore, using the term "ethnic boundary" makes sense only starting with the period when the concept of ethnicity could be used to demarcate them. I have argued that in southern Bessarabia this happened in the last decades of the 19th century with the arrival of field ethnographers who interpreted cultural differences as a direct consequence of ethnicity. Different ethnic groups, in their portrayal, did not only have different names and usually spoke different languages, they also had essentially different ways of doing things, different cultures, an observable indicator of different inner dispositions. Essentialized in such a way, ethnicity entered into the use of bureaucracy of the Russian Empire, and it was then that ethnic boundaries could become an obstacle, even if they were not congruent with linguistic, religious, or class boundaries.

The first period when this became evident was the aftermath of the Revolution of 1905. The state Duma, founded as a concession to revolutionary demands, entailed the legalization of ethno-political parties. When the Duma fell out with tsar Nikolai II, he blamed it on the excessive number of non-Russians represented in it, an early expression of equating ethnicity with loyalty towards the state. The subsequently introduced ethnic quota was certainly a case of ethnic boundaries as an obstacle. It did not affect Bessarabian peasants, but it foreshadowed ethnic exclusionism as it became common in the region throughout the first half of the 20th century.

The tsarist state, until its very demise, never managed to coin a unified definition of ethnicity, let alone a consistent practice for its use in administrating ethnic minorities. The same task was failed by the Romanian state that annexed Bessarabia in 1918. Although this administration accelerated the use of ethnicity as a bureaucratic category and although towards the end of Romanian rule, ethnicity could be very fateful, its definition kept changing, and a coherent legal basis was never established. Although ethnic boundaries kept non-Romanians from many jobs in the administration and in commerce, the new rulers initially had the aim to convince some of their ethnically non-Romanian subjects of their underlying Romania ethnicity. The Jews were exempted from this integrative effort. All Romanian interwar governments coupled their respective brand of nationalism with Anti-Semitism. No other group was so severely affected by the Romanian-German occupation of Bessarabia as Jews. While the Jewish communities were all but wiped out, many Bulgarians, Gagauz, Ukrainians, and Russians feared a similar fate. Their fear was not unfounded: When World War II loomed over the not-yet-consolidated Romanian state, mistrust against ethnic minorities became momentous again. Romanian ethnicity became a precondition not just to hold state offices, but for basic civil rights. Plans to deport non-Romanians out of Bessarabia were thwarted only by the return of the Red Army in summer 1944. The German colonies of southern Bessarabia also ceased to exist in 1940 when the Germans were "evacuated," a measure Germany had agreed on in an addenda to the Molotov-Ribbentrop treaty. This policy fitted the *zeitgeist* of the 1940s both in Germany and the USSR: ethnically homogenous nations were preferable to mixed ones: Their inhabitants were hoped to reliably be on the side of the country in which their own ethnic group dominated.

Interestingly, the ideologically so opposed Soviet Union also mistrusted its citizens and its mistrust was ultimately founded on the same train of thought.

It was during the last year of the war and in the immediate post-war years when ethnic boundaries kept Gagauz and Bulgarian men in coal mines rather than in Red Army trenches, to where their Moldovan, Ukrainian, and Russian neighbors were sent. From the late 1950s onwards ethnic boundaries were still cultivated in Soviet public discourse, in folklore and in the social sciences, but they ceased to be a substantial hindrance for social mobility.

Only when the cherished stability of the Soviet years gave way to post-Perestroika chaos, ethnicity became a potential obstacle again. Now elites were not necessarily replaced, but they again started to carefully stress their ethnic identity and target political adversaries for their unfitting ethnicity and language. This was a defining theme of politics in independent Ukraine. It affected the upper echelons of Ukrainian politics more than local politics in southern Bessarabia, although there too, patrons sometimes employed markedly ethnic strategies when they catered to an ethnically homogenous group of clients. As Ukraine slithered into war in 2014, many people, and public figures especially, found themselves forced to take sides. This again led to a tightening of ethnic boundaries. Anyone who stressed his or her Russianness now had a hard time to appear as an integer public figure.

One can therefore conclude that the degree to which ethnic boundaries became obstacles depended not so much on the ideology of the state as on the stability of its reign. Whenever it was felt in political centers, that the government lost its grip over peripheral regions, local and regional elites desperately clung to ethnic boundaries which helped them separating the allegedly trustworthy from the potentially dangerous. The peaks of this phenomenon can be seen between the Revolutions of 1905 and 1917, before and during World War II, when the Soviet Union consolidated its reign over newly acquired regions in the second half of the 1940s, when economic crisis eroded state power such as in the late 1980s and again since the devastating financial crisis of 2008.

The widespread idea, that ethnicity and loyalty determine one another, addresses the second part of the question; how ethnic discrimination was justified and explained. Interestingly, the reasoning that loyalty and ethnicity were linked became internalized by large parts of the population. This is especially evident in explanations of why men of some ethnicities were not permitted to fight in World War II. To many people who were affected by this policy, it appeared as a sensible precaution to keep those who had ethnic ties to a country allied with the enemy, away from arms. The reasoning may not have been as clear at the time, when Bulgarian and Gagauz men got their first taste of Soviet authoritarianism and were transported out of their villages to toil in mines and factories. But in time they also became subjects to Soviet education. This included to be exposed to a specific concept of ethnicity still influential today.

This concept became second nature to most Soviet and post-Soviet scholars and deeply rooted within "folk theory." It is a clearly essentialized concept in which ethnic origin determines character and ultimately behavior.

This finding brings us back to an assumption stated in the introduction: Ethnic boundaries reach their greatest potential to foster or impede individual life trajectories simultaneously with legitimation crises of the state. That is, whenever the ruling political elite was unable or unwilling to provide security and prosperity, mistrust between the state elite and the population at the periphery soared and with it the momentousness of ethnic boundaries. In the light of the evidence from some of the periods discussed here, this hypothesis seems to hold true. Ethnic boundaries became especially troublesome when the legitimacy of governments was severely challenged. Usually not all ethnic groups were hindered by their group boundaries to the same extent. In late imperial Russia, ethnic Russians seemed more trustworthy than all ethnic minorities. But more importantly for the case of Bessarabia, those ethnic minorities which had been privileged because of their status as colonists, seemed more trustworthy than Ukrainians and Moldovans. The latter two groups both formed ethnic majorities in adjacent regions. Both were candidates to become fully-fledged nations at the beginning of the 20th century. This could have resulted in claims over the territory of southern Bessarabia. During the interwar reign of Romania, speakers of Romanian were privileged compared to speakers of ethnic minority languages. But local Romanian speakers were considered less reliable than Romanians from the Old Kingdom. During the Soviet Union, Russians had a primus inter pares status, but in Bessarabia being a Ukrainian or a Moldovan, two groups with their own republic, was nearly just as good. After the time of the labor front, Bulgarians and Gagauz were no longer discriminated against and most became loyal Soviet citizens. Some members of these minorities even retrospectively justified the hardship of the labor front with the logic of trust and mistrust. During the nationalist frenzy of the late Perestroika years, many discovered or rediscovered their Ukrainianness and Moldovanness because these ethnic groups promised to become the foundations of new, independent, and legitimate states. The Russians, the dominant group of the crumbling USSR, found themselves struggling for their status and some would escape this struggle by crossing an ethnic boundary and becoming Ukrainian or Moldovan.

3 Ethnic Boundaries, Whom Do They Serve?

The political use of ethnic boundaries for state elites, whose legitimacy is in question, brings us to one more central question: At what times and in what ways did actors who created and maintained ethnic boundaries gain economically or politically from this activity?

The formulation of the question contains two presuppositions; that ethnic boundaries were in fact created and maintained (instead of evolving and conserving naturally), and that maintenance of ethnic boundaries did serve someone's ends. After having analyzed the history of ethnic boundaries in southern Bessarabia, it became clear that ethnic boundaries evolved through political processes and changed their function with changing social environments. It has been convincingly shown in the literature that ethnic boundaries are an outcome of activities by people who have an interest in them (Barth 2000b: 12; Brubaker 2004: 10). Studying ethnic boundaries in southern Bessarabia confirmed this assumption. Ethnic boundaries were maintained for a reason and there were people who profited from it. Therefore, to ask the question how and why these actors profited seemed sensible.

However, the nature of both the profit and the profiteers varied considerably over time. Ethnicity evolved from being an auxiliary category for describing and studying people, to a category used to predict people's loyalty. Later the use of ethnicity as an administrative category was refined and largely stripped of its function to allocate trust and mistrust. It became a category to allocate rights and duties instead. Eventually, ethnicity became a category to claim political power. Therefore, the first to profit from allegedly clear ethnic boundaries were those who attempted giving comprehensive descriptions of the region, above all census takers. Then gradually, weary administrators, in charge of distributing state resources, used ethnic boundaries to facilitate their task, and finally political entrepreneurs delineated their clientele along ethnic boundaries. Put more subtly, the emergence of ethnic boundaries was assisted by the need to make sense of cultural (above all linguistic) differences. Until the last decades of the 19th century, most administrative tasks that involved talking directly to the rural population had been delegated to village councils, and religious authorities. These institutions counted households and later individuals in their parishes. Therefore, if representatives of the state needed data about their subjects, they turned to church registries. The data they used was structured by religious differences. Only as the state penetrated deeper into rural settlements, other cultural differences became significant. The first to structure people along ethnic boundaries were ethnographers who had a more direct record of linguistic differences, and variances in day-to-day culture. For them, ethnic boundaries were helpful to make sense of cultural diversity. One handy explanation was to treat ethnicity as a cause of cultural diversity. This explanation also allowed generalizing cultural features within ethnic boundaries.

From there it was a small step to also generalize behavior vis-à-vis the state for entire ethnic groups. This facilitated the work of administrators in the last years of imperial Russia, in interwar Romania, and in the Soviet Union, during and directly after World War II. The idea of ethnic quotas for the state Duma, the discrimination of ethnic minorities in Romania and the selective spying on their activities by the Romanian police, as well as the Soviet decision not to recruit Gagauz and Bulgarian men to the front, all were shortcuts for administrators. It facilitated their work, but it complicated or even threatened the lives of people seen as potential traitors. This suspicion is part of the price paid for "legibility," James Scott's term to describe the state's fine-tuning of categories as its institutions grow more ambitious and more pervasive. But the state's pursuit of "legibility" entails more dangers: It also leads elites to take the categories they created for reality. They thereby enter a cycle of self-fulfilling prophecies to which they tend to respond with ill-informed planning solutions (Scott 1998: 196). The perception of absolute "legibility" leads to overtly high expectations and ambitions combined with flawed planning, the cocktail that set in motion the Soviet Union's collapse.

Although, after Stalin's death, the fateful implications of ethnicity gradually disappeared, the state insisted on cultivating ethnic boundaries in administration, in social science, and in folklore. One of the reasons was that the Soviet Union had painstakingly created its own logic of territorial subdivision along ethnic lines. Some of these ethnic lines, such as the one between Moldovans and Romanians had been created specially to fit the Soviet administrative map. To challenge carefully crafted ethnic boundaries would have put at stake not only the territorial subdivision of the country but also the theories of Soviet leaders and scholars. In the time of *zastoy*, many basic assumptions of Soviet society, including conventions about ethnicity, were no longer open for debate or questioning, but repeated to the point when they lost any contestable meaning.

The Perestroika reforms in the second half of the 1980s, initially meant to democratize Soviet society, eventually just sped up its collapse. From the ruins rose a society in which institutions were formed to serve patronal networks. The now firmly established category of ethnicity and the thoroughly demarcated ethnic boundaries served both patrons and clients. Whereas in many regions of the former Soviet Union, political entrepreneurs profited from exclusive nationalism, in southern Bessarabia, where the population is ethnically very diverse, the benefits of ethnic boundaries for clientelism were subtler. For most political patrons in southern Bessarabia, catering to just one ethnic group would alienate members of all remaining groups and therefore not recruit enough political followers. More successful patrons redistribute resources to different ethnic groups, which are often represented through their respective associations. Maintaining group boundaries helps patrons to allocate their limited resources more efficiently, and to ensure these groups' political support. The clients for their part have an interest in joining a clearly bounded receiver-group to enhance their chance of profiting from the patron's handouts. Therefore, having no clear ethnic (but also religious, linguistic, professional, etc.) affiliation leaves a person politically unrepresented and empty-handed in the clientelistic exchange. We can therefore conclude that in post-Soviet Bessarabian society, patrons as well as their clients can and do profit from sharpening ethnic boundaries.

4 Narratives and Techniques

If the maintenance of ethnic boundaries is so profitable, then how can it be effectively accomplished? To focus a bit closer on the process of crafting ethnic boundaries, we must return to another initial research question: What techniques and narratives are used—now and in the past—to make people perceive ethnic groups as clear-cut entities and as active subjects of history?

Again, the question includes the presupposition that ethnic boundaries *are in fact* produced and maintained by people and do not evolve naturally or automatically. Only if this presupposition is accepted, can we take a closer look at *how* people produce ethnic boundaries. While most of the authors cited in the more theoretical stretches of this book would certainly agree to this constructivist presupposition, most of my respondents probably would not. For many who use ethnic boundaries themselves, the narratives and techniques I have described are not unknown. Yet they think of them as practices that *reveal* something that is already there, rather than *producing* something new. I have extensively discussed therefore the differences between the view on ethnicity as an essential feature of every human being and the view of ethnicity as a relatively recent phenomenon, the outcome of social construction, closely tied to industrialization, the centralization of bureaucracies and the advent of mass education. This discussion has led to the conclusion that the dominant local view on ethnic boundaries is rooted deeply in the Soviet paradigm on the nature of ethnicity. Both history and ethnography have put ethnic groups, not society, not cultures, and least of all individuals at the focus of their inquiries.

Groups of the "ethnos"-type were the object matter of ethnographic research (Bromley 1980: 152). Would ethnography become obsolete if its objects turned out to be just social constructions (as I was challenged once in a heated discussion with a local colleague)? I have attempted to show, that it is just as interesting to look at *how* exactly people produced what they believe had evolved all by itself.

The techniques and narratives I have listed in chapter 7 are an integral part of this production process. They too suffer from a paradox: I believe to have observed them because they were in fact there, whereas others, presumably the people who apply them, would claim they are but my subjective interpretation. In their view, the creators of ethnic boundaries do what they have to do; they delimit and preserve something natural and good. This view also rejects the suspicion that the creators of ethnic boundaries follow their own personal interests. In helping to preserve what had been there anyway, they altruistically serve the common good. But what is it that makes people create and maintain ethnic boundaries? Some of the narratives address this question and provide an answer, as to what forces create ethnic boundaries (once people and their interests are excluded). The narratives I have listed, all in their own way, hold that people have an inner disposition that forces them to act in an ethnically specific manner. Language, religion, common historical experience, and DNA are mentioned as the forces that create these inner dispositions. Taste in folkloric performances was one of the indicators mentioned, that can reveal which inner ethnic disposition is prevalent in a particular person. All these narratives tell us that ethnicity is *within* a person and can therefore not be disposed of or changed.

What these cognate narratives have in common is that they all stress homogeneity within the ethnic boundary and difference across ethnic boundaries. If a certain cultural trait expands beyond the ethnic boundary, it must be ignored or denied. Also, if cultural differences are observable within the ethnic boundaries, they need to be overlooked or downplayed. In such a way, cultural unity within the ethnic group becomes exaggerated and essentialized, and cultural difference between the in-group and the out-group appears as the natural consequence of ethnic difference. This technique comes in different guises and it has been applied ever since ethnicity was used as a determinant of loyalty towards the state. The technique of unifying the inside of an ethnic group while denying commonalities with the outside was especially likely to be used when relations between the state and its subjects on the periphery became disturbed by mutual mistrust.

By identifying and listing the narratives and techniques that maintain ethnic boundaries I have addressed the second assumption introduced at the outset: There must be a mechanism that can be recognized as the lowest common denominator: Ethnic boundaries are kept clear-cut by stigmatizing ambivalent identities as anomalous and by denying their partial belonging to one's own identity group. In Ukraine, this mechanism is manifested most clearly in the stigmatization of impure language. The titular language in Ukraine is relatively close to Russian. Therefore, small differences matter a lot and small amounts of admixture are often portrayed as a threat to the Ukrainian and less acutely to the Russian language. Therefore, the country has a long history of linguistic purism highlighting the superior value of standard languages over mixed linguistic varieties. With religious behavior as a second powerful marker of social group ties (but not necessarily ethnic identity) it is harder to stigmatize those who do not fully belong but at the same time do not fully exclude themselves. Church authorities might mark those patrons who have dedicated attention and resources to their church so as to make them recognizable for religious voters. They also may condemn those who behave ungodly in their view. But unlike in linguistic purity, the line between practices approved and disapproved by religious institutions is neither sharp nor congruent with ethnic boundaries.

The commemoration of historic events and figures is charged with similar difficulties: patrons recommend themselves to one particular group (again, not necessarily an ethnic group) by sponsoring and organizing rituals that commemorate particular events. But commemorative practices can unite elements that at the time commemorated would have mutually excluded each other. One example could be the role clerical figures take in remembering the watersheds of Soviet history. In memorial ceremonies for World War II and the war in Afghanistan it is not uncommon that priests play a central part. Another example of such a blend would be Ukrainian symbolism in the celebration of Russian imperial figures. On city day celebrations in Izmail for example, municipal authorities, clerics, and military officers lay down wraths and flowers on the monuments of General Suvorov, the conqueror of Izmail fortress and of General Lieutenant Tuchkov, the city's first governor. Such ceremonies are usually flanked with Ukrainian flags and ribbons and with the singing of the Ukrainian anthem. Practices that use the symbolisms of two once antagonistic entities are not necessarily perceived as "mixing" and are therefore not necessarily punished by the stigma of impurity. Only if a particular historic event was conceptualized radically different among two ethnic groups and only if for one of these ethnic groups a particular way of memorizing is an important ingredient in group identity, such a stigmatization might be applied. In Ukrainian nationalism, for example, the famine of 1932–33 is strongly conceptualized as a Russian attempt to ethnically cleanse parts of Ukraine. If a nationalist Ukrainian politician would shun events, where this version of history is commemorated or if a Russian nationalist would take part in an event where the famine is publicly remembered, this would probably incur the wrath of his voters. Only if historical events are exclusively claimed by one specific ethnic group, does this mode of stigmatization work. In many other events, especially those around World War II, members of many ethnic groups are concerned. Remembering the shared Soviet victory and the hardships that led to it is therefore better suited to stress interethnic harmony and challenge ethnically particular versions of history.

Similarly in folklore, it is more important to praise and attend folkloric performances in order to appear as a true representative of a group, than to show preference for one particular ethnic style. Most events include folkloric performances associated with more than one ethnic group, and many of them are, in fact, celebrations of harmonic interethnic relations. Because folkloric particularities are hardly common knowledge, stigmatization in this realm cannot readily be supported with allegedly dreadful examples of distortion, as is common in linguistic purism. Nevertheless, all folkloric performances are clearly ethnically labeled. The differences between performances attributed to different ethnic groups might be rather subtle, and it might well be that elements deemed typical for one group appear in the performances of another. In folklore it is therefore not the mixing of the "cultural stuff" that is stigmatized, but the omission of a clear ethnic label. This confirms Barth's observation (2000b: 30) that in ethnic discourse, cultural differences are vastly overstated. Ethnic boundaries serve to sustain a social organization of differences, not as descriptions of the actual distribution of "cultural stuff."

The last realm where the assumed stigmatization could occur is genetics. Narratives of ethnic essence encoded in the genes are strongly linked to the belief that interethnic marriage was a very rare exception at least until recently. Interethnic marriage is sometimes privately loathed, but also often praised. A closer look at interethnic marriage reveals that it probably has been quite common, at least since the time ethnicity became a meaningful category in Bessarabia. Between members of different religious groups it was forbidden in tsarist times, but hardly ever actively opposed between members of linguistically different groups. Thus, most of today's ethnic boundaries hardly posed an enforceable barrier for marriage. The demeaning term "Surzhyk" has been reported to designate children from mixed ethnic parents (Flier 1998: 115), but in my own fieldwork I have never come across this usage. Some people very consciously choose a partner from their own ethnic group, and sometimes claim they could not live with someone from another ethnic group. It remains hard to assess how, in the face of alternative choices, such principles are modified.

It has become fashionable in recent years to use DNA as a substitute for other loci where ethnic essence might be located, such as the blood or the heart. Genetics is not a good guide to stigma, because phenotypes in the Bessarabian setting hardly give direct clues about ethnicity. But the belief that every ethnic group commands a unique collection of genomes implies the idea that this collection can be diluted by ethnically mixed families or, if guarded carefully, be passed down the generations. The widespread use of terminology such as "gene pool of the nation," "genetic population," or "impassionedness" alone do not yet prove a distaste for mixing, but they indicate a certain obsession with the idea that members of different ethnic groups should be genetically similar to other members of their own group and genetically different from members of other such groups.

To sum up the findings on the validity of the second hypothesis, it can be stated that the mechanism of stigmatizing the in-between or the mixed most readily applies to languages, where it certainly holds true. In other realms that regularly help to sharpen ethnic boundaries the respective "cultural stuff" that is supposed to remain unmixed is less clearly defined and therefore offers more scope. It is more difficult to stigmatize mixing of religious practices, practices of commemorative culture, folkloristic practices, or genetic pools, because the characteristics and symbols involved in these realms are not as clearly ethnically marked as language. In these realms it is more important to clearly attach ethnic labels to practices than to avoid the mixing of their content.

5 The Trouble with Fuzzy Boundaries

Since ethnic boundaries are frequently fuzzy in southern Bessarabia (as they certainly are in many other regions) their conceptualization as clear-cut and objectively ascertainable phenomena frequently runs into contradiction. Dedicated to the handling of these contradictions was the last research question: When contradictions between narratives about clear-cut ethnic distinctions and the observable social life become obvious, how are they confronted by those who claim ethnic distinctions are clear-cut?

There are several possible constellations that can produce such contradictions. One common source of contradiction is when there are only unclear ethnic markers, such as in people with ambiguous ethnic identities, in villages with mixed ethnic population, in folklore performances with elements claimed to be typical for several ethnic groups, or in linguistic behavior that dissolves the boundaries between standard languages. One of the assumptions offered in the introduction stated that when it comes to contradictions between claims of distinctiveness of ethnic boundaries and observable social environment, then those claimants will most likely seek the refuge of evidence that can be tested only by group insiders and that are hidden to outsiders. I have named observations of people referring to feelings *within* as a way out of this contradiction. The environment wherein the contradiction occurs then is to blame for it. While hidden from sight, deep inside the soul, the heart, the genes etc., the clearly structured "true" relations remain free of contradiction. Private feelings are hard to observe and document and therefore it is hard to prove or disprove them. Therefore, claiming that what one cannot see can be felt, and that this feeling can distinguish the pure from the diluted, makes any argument obsolete. These sensations can be claimed to be perceptible only to those whom the claimant considers his own kind and inaccessible for those who challenge or dissolve ethnic boundaries. It can then be claimed that if ethnic boundaries seem fuzzy, this was only due to the blindness of the ethnic "other," or to the confusion brought about by careless ignoramuses who have lost the right to consider themselves members of the ethnic group in concern. It seems all handling of contradiction in ethnic boundary maintenance functions through some manifestation of this exclusion mechanism. In this way, those who are admitted the right to include and exclude other people can be limited at will. If a dispute occurs who is within and who is outside a certain ethnic boundary, a change of the list of membership criteria can shift the ethnic boundary, excluding the allegedly unjustified claimant. The inventory list of symbols can be shared but not owned. By selecting certain criteria, group boundaries can be widened or narrowed. This technique that can be observed quite frequently confirms the third assumption, at least on an individual level. In a dispute between individuals, ethnic boundaries can therefore be drawn quite arbitrarily. On a more collective level, disputes take place more publicly and therefore face more constraints. There, accepted knowledge and established experts have set more narrow frameworks from which markers of ethnic identity can be chosen.

It is another common strategy to discredit the group or individual who doubts the validity of ethnic boundaries. If someone claims, for instance, that the ethnic boundary between Ukrainians or Russians or between Romanians and Moldovans was artificial and modern, those who believe these ethnic boundaries are ancient and natural can blame dishonest motives behind their opponent's claims. Hence, the underlying mechanism of ethnic boundary maintenance can be identified as exclusion, either on the ground of the doubter's inability to perceive clearly bounded ethnic groups, or because the doubters are portrayed untrustworthy due to their questionable motives.

Soviet academia likewise developed elaborate strategies to deal with contradictions arising from fuzzy boundaries. It became a routine to coin new, allegedly primordial and clearly bounded categories to patch over any older boundaries that became blurred by social realities. With this technique, Soviet academia kept its own paradigms functioning and kept nurturing folk theories built around essentialized ethnic categories.

6 Ethnicity as a Beacon of Stability

Most Bessarabians, when asked to sketch the recent history of their region, draw a sinister picture of steady decline. This decline is felt in economy, because it is hard to find a reasonably paid job. A decline is felt in state institutions; because of endemic corruption in schools, courts, and hospitals. The quality of these institution's services erodes while costs rise. Culture too, is often described as declining, because locally produced culture has an ever harder standing against more powerful cultural forms, produced far away and transported via TV and internet. With the virulent destabilization of Ukraine, beginning in late 2013, even the last cautious optimists were ready to believe it could get only worse. The war in the country's east between Ukrainian forces and Russian-backed separatists even called into question the prided friendship of peoples in the region. Most people very decidedly rejected the notion that there had been ethnic conflict in this region before. The very notion, that Bessarabians should get into a fight over their different ethnic origins appeared absurd to most of my respondents. Interethnic harmony after all had long been the region's signboard.

Nevertheless, anyone could see in 2013 that Ukraine—and southern Bessarabia with it—were in a precarious economic situation. The revival of the local economy, promised time and time again by officials in Odessa and Kyiv, never materialized. Potholes in the road, the embodiment of decline for many, were busily paved over before parliamentary elections, but they also quickly reappeared. There was no writing on the wall that a war was imminent, but in late 2013, when the Yanukovich government was about to sign the Vilnius Association Agreement with the EU, people began to realize that the politically loaded question whether to build closer ties with the EU or with Russia, was to be addressed more urgently than ever before. That this question even came up was seen as a sign of decline by those who thought that the cultural and historical ties to Russia should stand above any deliberation of economic prosperity. Others may have seen a great progress in the mere fact that they had a choice between different politicians, with different answers to these questions. That these politicians then cared so little about the rights and needs of their electorate was all the more disheartening. The disappointment was so deep that many people used "democracy" as a swearword. "Rights we have really plenty now," said one woman, "but they are merely a piece of paper." If she would raise her voice against those who stole and sold the former kolkhoz's property, she thinks retaliations would start from a stone thrown in her window, but they might quickly escalate from there.

In light of this disappointment, the Soviet past, which offered little rights and freedoms, seemed not so bad after all. The build-up years of the Soviet Union with their famine and deportations came to be seen as a time of unprecedented progress, guided by an idealistic vision for the future. The dull years of Brezhnevian stagnation now appear to many as a time of social security and affluence. Add the idealized representation of Soviet history, still felt today, and it is little wonder that the Soviet Union appears as the Golden Age from which decline started. This view seems to be shared by many people, both from generations who lived to see the Soviet period as well as those who know about it only from hearsay. Given the present state of Ukraine and its Bessarabian periphery, this interpretation is certainly not altogether implausible. The Golden Age against which a rather bleak present is measured, is not so much a particular period in the past, but an amalgamate of yearnings the present fails to satisfy; political stability, economic prosperity, and a set of broadly accepted cultural values.

Ethnicity is often characterized as a source of exactly these qualities. It is seen as an entity stable over many centuries within which a collection of unique cultural values is passed down the generations. The assessment of the history of interethnic relations in Bessarabia must be seen against this background. The projection of unambiguous ethnic boundaries into this past is best comprehensible with the current insecurity in mind. The supposedly pure and consistent moral guidelines engraved in the traditions of sovereign ethnic groups, are a product of the current absence of credible ethic principles. The yearning for greatness that members of all ethnic groups project into their own group's past, has a lot to do with the bitter experience of decline, a decline that started from nothing less than what was propagated to be the greatest country in the world.

The memory of this former greatness lived on in street names and monuments until the summer of 2016, when a law to de-communize Ukraine came into force and mayors were asked to rename streets, squares and towns with names reminiscent of the Soviet past. The memory of a Brezhnevian Golden Age still lives on in real memory of people and their tales. These are often told in comparative terms; the number of children that attended village school then and now, the number of workers that came to the cannery at every shift changeover before it was closed, the headcount of cattle the kolkhoz possessed before it shut down, the passenger airplane that served as a lift to town, where now there is not even a reliable bus service. The comparison of prices then and now is often employed to illustrate economic decline. People remember the cost of a kilo of good sausage or the bedroom suite bought at marriage, and they are stunned at how little this money can buy today. It is not surprising that people who could afford good sausage for special occasions and who could build and furnish a house at the time of their marriage, must sense something has gone terribly wrong if their children are hardly able to find a paying job. One cannot blame people who have been disappointed by history for wanting former greatness back. And greatness meant not only the stability and security it provided, but the promise to live and work for the sake of an ideal future society.

The bitterness, with which many people describe decline, brings us to its perceived causes. These causes are often held to parallel the causes for ethnic conflict. Most people, if asked whether they could remember when they first thought that things were going wrong, named the disintegration of the Soviet Union. When asked whether they had observed any signs of decay before that, most respondents denied that. One elderly couple in Kotlovina repeatedly mentioned Khrushchev's policy to export food supplies at the people's expense, as an anomaly of the Soviet state. However, the subsequent ousting of Khrushchev was seen as proof that the Soviet system indeed worked. The deep structural problems of the Soviet Union described by economists (Kornai 1980), the epidemic nepotism and corruption plaguing the USSR in its last years (Eisenstadt and Roniger 1984; Willerton 1992; Fairbanks 1999; Stefes 2006) or the widespread practices of stealing state property and evading state control (Friedberg 1991; Kotkin 1991; Raleigh 2012) were not remembered as forbearers of an imminent crash, or they were so thoroughly relativized by the subsequent post-Soviet chaos that in retrospect they seemed hardly worth mentioning. This seems to be a striking parallel between the imagination of history and the imagination of ethnicity: The entities that people discern within history, the periods of the past, in this region most conveniently structured by different states that ruled the area, are imagined as clearly bounded, almost uniform within and entirely different from one another. Therefore, if the post-Soviet period was characterized by corruption and disorder, the Soviet period is imagined exaggeratedly integer and orderly. The origin of something as big as the collapse of the Soviet state is sought in big politics and hardly ever in something as small as the corruption, embezzlement, and mismanagement in one's own environment. The decline of social norms, and with it the occurrence of ethnic conflict, is seen as an effect of geopolitical machination rather than one of its causes. In Bessarabia, most of my respondents thought the protesters on Maidan were naïve since they attempted to change political realities that were created somewhere far away from Kyiv. Or else they blamed the people who turned out on Kyiv's streets to be paid agents of these particular foreign forces. Exactly which outside force is to blame usually depends on a person's political tastes.

These new outside forces, be they suspected in Western Europe, or North America, appear to only demand and refuse to offer tangible benefits in return. Their goals remain unclear and sometimes appear deliberately obscured. The EU's arrogance towards Ukraine manifested itself in a lopsided deal whereby the EU had a long list of demands in exchange for a short list of vague promises. The most viable strategy with which people responded to the challenges of market economy are largely based on labor migration. This strategy has devastated village communities and can therefore hardly be a suitable alternative for those who keep the villages going.

Skepticism of Western demands has deep roots in the experience of decline. The economic supremacy of the West mocked the spirit of glory and victory cultivated in Soviet culture. Although many in Bessarabia admire the riches and orderliness they identify with Western Europe, they have a hard time seeing a cultural role-model in liberal individualistic societies. Things that have miniscule effects on the lives of people in Bessarabia, like gay pride marches in European cities, have been grossly inflated and have become representative of a dichotomy between a decadent, individualistic culture in the rich West vs. a natural culture, based on traditional values in post-Soviet societies. Ethnicity is often portrayed as a part of this bygone pristine culture, in which people naturally knew their place. Soviet society, although modern, industrialized and turbulent, was full of givens. There was no need to find one's ethnic identity in it, just as there was no need to reflect on one's gender, or to find a job. The state provided ready-made answers to all these questions. This order of seemingly clear social categories stands as a glaring contrast to contemporary uncertainties.

Part of the Ukrainian elite in 2013 chose to favor European integration. It would have allowed them to legalize their fortunes and make profitable investments. On the other hand, building closer ties with the West gave the elite little solid benefits to serve their electorate, besides the by now scorned promise of democracy and rule of law. For this reason, another part of the elite was frightened to lose their status. They stressed the cultural differences to the West and turned to Russia, ruled by a similarly kleptocratic elite, alas firmly centralized under the Kremlin's guidance and without a real perspective of ever profiting from the EU's expansion. Both parts of the Ukrainian elite, those oriented towards closer ties with the EU and those looking towards Russia, had an interest in linking this conflict to the region's past conflicts. They reinterpreted historic conflicts as conflicts between ethnic Russians and the non-Russian groups in the empire's periphery. Whenever conflict between ethnic groups becomes the focus of historiography, long past events offer themselves for reinterpretation through an ethnic lens. But for most people in Bessarabia there is little to profit from interethnic conflict.

Bessarabians did, as a consequence of the region's peripheral status, often not have the means to make their own rules. Instead, they needed to side with one or another outside force, with Russia or the Ottoman Empire, with the Soviet Union or Romania, and most recently with Russia or Ukraine. This tricky game of taking sides has had its local profiteers and therefore the periphery is no realm of innocence, but most of those who can hope to profit from sharpening ethnic dichotomies will do so far away from Bessarabia.

References

Primary Sources

Archive Files from Izmail State Archive (*by File Number*)

COLLECTION F4 *Vilkovskaya possadskaya uprava* [Vilkovo settler's council]

F4 D59 (1895) *Svedenie o kolichestvennom i natsional'nom sostave naseleniya* [Findings about the size and ethnic composition of the population]

COLLECTION F50 *Izmail'skaya uezdnaya finansovaya administratsiya* [Izmail uezd financial administration]

F50 D64 (1937–1939) *Spiski chinovnikov po natsional'nostyam (Izmail'skaya uezdnaya finansovaya administratsiya)* [Lists of state servants by ethnicity (Izmail uezd financial administration)]

COLLECTION F56 *Kantselariya izmail'skogo gradonachal'stva* [Chancellery of the Izmail civil administration]

F56 D37 (1835–1837) *Tsirkulariya ITsD o zapreshchenii brakosochitaniy raskol'nikov s pravovernimi* [Circular letter by the ITsD(?) about the prohibition of marriages between Razkolniki (i.e. Old-Believers) and Orthodox][1]

F56 D112 (1821–1830) *Delo o prinyatii v russkoe poddanstvo i poselenii v izmail'skom gradonachalstve bolgar, grekov, moldavan, bezhavshikh v Rossiyu ot Turetskogo iga v 1821–1830* [File about the acceptance of Bulgarians, Greeks, Moldovans who have fled the Turkish Yoke as Russian subjects and their settlement in the city-municipality of Izmail for the years of 1821–1830].

F56 D344 (1839–1841) *Raporty gradskikch politsiy o vypolnenii tsirkulariya Bessarabskogo voennogo gubernatora o zapreshchenii khristianam postupat' v prislugu k evreyam* [Rapports of municipal police about the implementation of the circular letter of the Military Govenor of Bessarabia about the prohbition for Christians to stand in the service of Jews]

1 The acronym in this file's title does not correspond to its content. The circular letter was sent by the Ministry of the Interior, the acronym for which is not ITsD but MVD (*Ministertsvo Vnutrenikh Del'*).

 | DOI:10.1163/9789004408029_010

COLLECTION F93 *Bolgradskiy sel'skiy prikaz* [Bolgrad rural councils]

F93 D332 (1851–1855) *Svidetel'stva, vydannye kolonistam na pravo vstupleniya v brak* [Confirmations of the right to get married, issued to Colonists]

COLLECTION F292 *Bolgradskaya gorodskaya uprava* [Bolgrad city council]

F292 D46 (1891) *Pasporta i bilety, vydannye zhitelyam goroda dlya vyezda v raznye goroda i sela Rossii* [Passports and permits issued to inhbitants of the city in order to travel to various cities and villages in Russia]

F292 D251 (1918) *Zhurnal registratsiy brakov za 1918 god* [List of the registered marriages for the year of 1918]

COLLECTION F312 *Izmail'skaya uezdnaya prefektura politsii* [Izmail uezd police prefecture]

F312 (1918–1940) *Opis' "Izmail'skaya uezdnaya prefektura politsii g. Izmail"* [Description of the file "Izmail uezd police prefecture, city of Izmail"]

F312 D49 (1930–1937) *Perepiska s bessarabskim okruzhnym inspektoratom politsii, komissriatami politsii gorodov Bolgrada, Kilii, Reni, Vilkovo* o *nablyudenii za deyatel'nost' russkoy i ukrainskoy natsional'nosti gorodov i uezda* [Correspondence of the Bessarabian District Police Inspectorate with police commissariats in the towns of Bolgrad, Kiliya, Reni, Vilkovo about observing the activities of the Russian and Ukrainian ethnicities in the towns of the uezd]

F312 D76 (1923–1940) *Documentele dreptilor Liceului din Bolgrad* [About the legal rights of the Bolgrad Lyceum]

F312 D138 (1937–1939) *Nablyudatel'noe delo za deyatel'nost' naseleniya russkoy i ukrainskoy natsional'nosti po Izmail'skomu uezdu* [Observation file on the activities of the population of Russian and Ukrainian ethnicity in Izmail uezd]

F312 D139 (1937–1940) *Nablyudatel'noe delo za deyatel'nost' bolgarskogo natsionalisticheskogo dvizhenie v Izmail'skom uezde 1937–40 gg.* [Observation file on the activities of the Bulgarian nationalist movement in Izmail uezd for the years of 1937–40]

COLLECTION F1023 *Ochag kul'tury sela Nerushay* [Culture center in the village of Nerushay]

F1023 D4 (1939) *Direktivnye ukazaniya Bukharestkogo obshchestva po rasprostraneniyu kul'tury o rabote ochaga kul'tury v sele Nerushay* [Instructions from the Bucharest based Society for the Dissemination of Culture for the activities of their branch in the village of Nerushay]

COLLECTION F1044 *Tsentr kul'tury v s. Galilesht' Izmail'skogo Uezda* [The Culture Center in the village of Galilesht' in Izmail uezd][2]

F1044 D1 (1927) *Otchet deyatel'nost'i tsentra i doklady sdelannye uchitelyami* [Reports about the activities of the center and lectures given by teachers]

COLLECTION F1139 *Tsentr kul'tury v sele Nerushay imail'skogo uezda* [The Culture Center in the village of Nerushay in Izmail uezd]

F1139 D1 (1927) *Postanovleniya ministerstva prosvyashcheniya o sozdanii i funktsionirovanii kul'turnikh tsentrov, tabel' tsentrov izmail'skogo uezda i ezhemesyachnye deyatel'nost'i tsentra za 1927g.* [Resolution of the Ministry of Education about the establishment and functioning of Culture Centers, lists of the centers in Izmail uezd, and monthly activities of the Center for the year of 1927]

COLLECTION FR30 *Bolgradskaya volostnaya pretura* [Pretura of Bolgrad district]

Fr30 D5 (1941) *Spravki o kolichestve, natsional'nom i professional'nom sostave naseleniya po selam volosti* [Documentation of the number, the ethnic and professional composition of the inhabitants of the district's villages]

Fr30 D46 (1942–1943) *Perepiska s primariyami sel uezda ob annulirovanii nezakonno vydannikh udostovereniy o ruminskoy natsional'nosti* [Correspondence with mayor's offices of villages in the Uezd about the annulation of illegally issued certifications of Romanian ethnicity]

Fr30 D193 (1943–1944) *Perepiska s Izmail'skoy uezdnoy prefekturoy primariyami i selvolosti ob ustanovlenii zhitelyam ruminskoy natsional'nosti* [Correspondence of the Izmail uezd Prefecture with mayor's offices and municipalities about certifying their inhabitant's Romanian ethnicity]

Fr30 D196 (1943) *Tsirkulariya bessarabskogo gubernatora i perepiska s izmail'skoy uezdnoy prefekturoy* [Circular letters of the Governor of Bessarabia and correspondence with the Izmail uezd prefecture]

Fr30 D206 (1943) *Perepiska s primariyami sel o kolichestve i natsional'nom sostave naseleniya* [Correspondence with mayors of villages about the number and the ethnic composition of their inhabitants]

2 The village was called *Desantnoe* after 1944.

COLLECTION FR35 *Primariya goroda Bolgrada izmail'skoy oblasti* [Mayor's office of the city of Bolgrad in Izmail oblast]

Fr35 D177 (1942) *Proshenie zhiteley o vydache im udostvoreniy o rumynskom poddanstve i natsional'nosti* [Petitions of inhabitants to be issued certificates of their Romanian citizenship and ethnicity]

Fr35 D178 (1942–1943) *Proshenya zhiteley o vydache im udostvoreniy o rumynskom poddanstve i natsional'nosti* [Petitions of inhabitants to be issued certificates of their Romanian citizenship and ethnicity]

Fr35 D179 (1942) *Prosheniya zhiteley o vydache im udostvoreniy o rumynskom poddanstve i natsional'nosti* [Petitions of inhabitants to be issued certificates of their Romanian citizenship and ethnicity]

Fr35 D179a (1942–1943) *Prosheniya zhiteley o vydache im udostvereniy o rumynskom poddanstve i natsional'nosti* [Petitions of inhabitants to be issued certificates of their Romanian citizenship and ethnicity]

COLLECTION FR37 *Primariya goroda Izmaila izmail'skoy oblasti* [Mayor's office of the city of Izmail in Izmail oblast]

Fr37 D26 (1940–1941) *Svedenie o kolichestve, polevom, natsional'nom sostave naseleniya goroda za 1940–41 gg.* [Findings about the number, gender and ethnic composition of the town's population for the years of 1940 and 1941]

COLLECTION FR262 *Ispolnitel'nyy komitet Kubeyskogo sel'skogo soveta* [Executive committee of the Kubey village council][3]

Fr262 D3 (1944) *Protokoly obshchikh sobraniy zhiteley sela za 1944 god* [Minutes of the general assemblies of the village's inhabitants for the year of 1944]

COLLECTION FR367 *Izpolnitel'nyy komitet Bolbokskogo sel'skogo soveta* [Executive committee of the Bolboka village council][4]

Fr367 D3 (1944–1945) *Protokoly obshchikh sobraniy krest'yan sela za 1944–1945 god* [Minutes of the general assemblies of the peasants from the village for the years of 1944–1945]

Fr367 D5 (1944) *Spisok voennoobyazannykh po sel'skomu sovetu za 1944 god* [list of men liable for military service in the municipality for the year of 1944]

Fr367 D6 (1945) *Protokoly zasedaniya ispolkoma sel'skogo soveta za 1945 god* [Minuets of the meetings of the executive committee of the village council for the year of 1945]

3 The village was called *Chervonoarmeyskoe* between 1945 and 2016.

4 The village was called *Kotlovina* after 1945.

Fr367 D95 (1959) *Protokoly obshchikh sobraniy rabochikh, sluzhashchikh i kolkhoznikov za 1959 god* [Minutes of the general assemblies of workers, employees and kolkhozniki for the year of 1959]

Fr367 D210 (1971) *Protokoly sobraniy o kandidatov v deputaty sel'soveta* [Minutes of the assemblies about candidates to join the village council]

COLLECTION FR415 *Izmail'skoe oblastnoe lektsionnoe byuro* [Izmail oblast bureau of lecturers]

Fr415 D10 (1947) *Temy lektsii dlya sel'skikh i kolkhoznykh klubov na 1947 god* [Topics of lectures for village and kolkhoz clubs for the year of 1947]

Fr415 D15 (1947) *Plany lektsiy po istorii i literature* [Lecture plans for history and literature]

Fr415 D22 (1948) *Metodicheskie razrabotki v pomoshch' lektoram* [Methodical designs as guidelines for lecturers]

COLLECTION FR445 *Izmail'skiy oblastnoy otdel narodnogo obrazovanye (oblono) gorod Izmail* [Izmail oblast Department of People's Education (OBLONO) the city of Izmail]

Fr445 D128 (1949) *Godovye otchety gorodskikh i rayonnykh otdelov narodnogo obrazovaniya o rabote shkol za 1948/1949 uchebnyy god* [Annual reports of urban and rural Departments of People's Education about the work of schools for the school year of 1948/1949]

Fr445 D156 (1949–1950) *Godovye otchety rayonnykh otdelov narodnogo obrazovaniya za 1949–1950 god* [Annual reports of rural Departments of People's Education for the years of 1949–1950]

Fr445 D184 (1950–1951) *Godovoy otchet Suvorovskogo rayonnogo otdela narodnogo obrazovaniya za 1950–1951 godov* [Annual report of the Suvorovo rayon Department of People's Education for the years of 1950–1951]

Fr445 D186 (1950–1951) *Godovye otchety rayonnykh i gorodskikh otdelov narodnogo obrazovaniya za 1950–1951 uchebnyy god* [Annual reports of urban and rural Departments of People's Education for the school year of 1950–1951]

Fr445 D209 (1951–1952) *Godovye otchety gorodskikh i rayonnych otdelov narodnogo obrazovaniya o rabote shkol za 1951 god* [Annual reports of the urban and rural Departments of People's Education about the work of schools for the year of 1951]

Archived Newspapers from Izmail Central Library (Alphabetically)

Kur'er Nedeli [Weekly Courier] Izmail weekly appearing every Saturday since 1998

Monitorul Oficial [Official Gazette] The Bulletin of the Romanian government, began to appear regularly in January 1877

New City Izmail weekly appearing every Thursday since 2010

Pridunayskaya Pravda [The Danube Region's Truth] Izmail based Soviet newspaper, which first appeared in 1940. In 1965 the newspaper was split into two publications, *Leninskiy Put'* [Lenin's Path], which covered news on Izmail's rural surroundings and *Sovetskiy Izmail* [Soviet Izmail], which reported news from the city. In 1991 *Leninskiy Put'* became *Pridunayskie Vesti* [Danube Region's News], and *Sovetskiy Izmail* first became simply *SI*, before being renamed *Sobesednik Izmaila* [Izmail's Interlocutor] in 2001.

Pridunayskie Vesti [Danube Region's News] Izmail newspaper appearing since 1991, one of the successor publications of *Pridunayskaya Pravda*

Sovetskiy Izmail [Soviet Izmail] Izmail newspaper that appeared under this name between 1965 and 1991, one of the successor publications of *Pridunayskaya Pravda*

Uezdniy Telegraf [The Uezd's Telegraph] Izmail weekly appearing every Wednesday since 1998, the pendant to Saturday's *Kur'er Nedeli*, which is produced by the same publishing firm

Secondary Literature

Encyclopedia Articles and Reference Books

"Berg, Lev Semenovich." 2005. *Bol'shaya Rossiyskaya Entsiklopediya Tom 3*. Moskva: Nauchnoe Izdatel'stvo "Bol'shaya Rossiyskaya Entsiklopediya."

"Derzhavin, Nikolay Sevast'yanovich." 2007. *Bol'shaya Rossiyskaya Entsiklopediya Tom 8*. Moskva: Nauchnoe Izdatel'stvo "Bol'shaya Rossiyskaya Entsiklopediya".

"Gogol' Nikolay Vasilevich." 1989. In *Russkie Pisateli 1800–1917*. Moskva: Izdatel'stvo „Sovetskaya Entsiklopediya" Tom 1.

"Istoriya Gorodov i Sel Ukrainskoy SSR–Odesskaya oblast'." 1978. Kiev: Institut akademii nauk USSR.

"Khronolgicheskiy Spravochnik Ob Okkupatsii Izmail'skoy oblasti (1941–1944 gg.)." 1950. Izmail: Izdatel'stvo "Pridunayskaya Pravda."

"Mogilyanskiy Nikolay Mikhailovich." 2012. *Bol'shaya Rossiyskaya Entsiklopediya Tom 20*. Moskva: Nauchnoe Izdatel'stvo "Bol'shaya Rossiyskaya Entsiklopediya."

"Pushkin, Aleksandr Sergeevich." 2007. In *Russkie Pisateli 1800–1917 Tom 5*. Moskva: Nauchnoe Izdatel'stvo "Bol'shaya Rossiyskaya Entsiklopediya."

"Putevoditel' Filial Odesskogo oblastnogo Archiva v g. Izmaile." 1966.

"Svin'in, Pavel Petrovich." 2007. In *Russkie Pisateli 1800–1917*. Moskva: Nauchnoe Izdatel'stvo "Bol'shaya Rossiyskaya Entsiklopediya."

Bibliography

Ahlberg, R., 1991. Das sowjetische Paßsystem—ein Instrument bürokratischer Herrschaft. Osteuropa 8, 802–817.

Amburger, E., 1966. Geschichte der Behördenorganisation Russlands von Peter dem Grossen bis 1917. Brill, Leiden.

Anastassova, E., 2006. "We are Bessarabians here": Identity, Tradition and Power in Southern Bessarabia. Anthropol. East Eur. Rev. 24, 59–65.

Anderson, B., 2006. Imagined Communities—Reflections on the Origin and Spread of Nationalism (Revised Edition). Verso, London.

Anikin, N.V., 2009. k voprosu o sovremennom samosoznanii gagauzov moldavii. Etnograficheskoe Obozr. 4, 17–25.

Appelbaum, A., 2017. Red Famine—Stalin's War on Ukraine. Allen Lane, London.

Arutyunyan, Y.V., 1974. Experience of a Socio-Ethnic Survey (Relating to the Tatar ASSR), in: Bromley, Y.V. (Ed.), Soviet Ethnology and Anthropology Today. Mouton, The Hague.

Baiburin, A., 2012. 'The wrong Nationality' Ascribed Identity in the 1930s Soviet Union, in: Baiburin, A., Kelly, C., Vakhtin, N. (Eds.), Russian Cultural Anthropology After the Collapse of Communism. Routledge, London.

Barbour, S., 2000. Nationalism, Language, Europe, in: Barbour, S., Carmichael, C. (Eds.), Language and Nationalism in Europe. Oxford University Press, Oxford.

Barth, F., 2000a. Enduring and emerging issues in the analysis of ethnicity, in: Vermeulen, H., Govers, C. (Eds.), The Anthropology of Ethnicity—Beyond Ethnic Groups and Boundaries. Het Spinhuis, Amsterdam.

Barth, F., 2000b. Boundaries and Connections, in: Cohen, A.P. (Ed.), Signifying Identities. Routledge, London.

Barth, F., 1969. Ethnic Groups and Boundaries—The Social Organization of Culture Difference. Waveland Press, Long Grove.

Bassin, M., 2016. The Gumilev Mystique—Biopolitics, Eurasianism, and the Construction of Community in Modern Russia. Cornell University Press, Ithaca and London.

Batyushkov, P.N., 1892. Bessarabiya—istoricheskoe opisanie. Ministerstvo Vnutrenikh Del, St. Petersburg.

Beissinger, M.R., 2002. Nationalist Mobilization and the Collapse of the Soviet Union. Cambridge University Press, Cambridge.

Berg, L.S., 1918. Bessarabiya Strana-Lyudi-Khozyaystvo. Ogni, Petrograd.

Bernsand, N., 2006. Othering Surzhyk in Implicit Metalinguistic Discourse, in: Törnquist—Plewa, B. (Ed.), History, Language and Society in the Borderlands of Europe. Sekel, Malmö.

Bernsand, N., 2001. Surzhyk and National Identity in Ukrainian Nationalist Ideology. Berl. Osteur. Info 17, 38–47.

Bernshteyn, S.B., 1949. Otchet o dialektologicheskoy poezdke v bolgarskie sela Moldavskoy SSR i Izmail'skoy oblasti USSR letom 1947 goda. Uchennye Zap. Instituta Slavyanovedeniya Tom I, 385–391.

Bilaniuk, L., 2005. Contested Tongues—Language Politics and Cultural Correction in Ukraine. Cornell University Press, Ithaca and London.

Bloch, M., 1989. The past and the present in the present, in: Bloch, M. (Ed.), Ritual, History and Power: Selected Papers in Anthropology. The Athlone Press, London.

Bloch, M., 1973. The Royal Touch—Sacred Monarchy and Scrofula in England and France. Routledge & Kegan Paul, New York.

Boeck, B.J., 2005. What's in a Name? Semantic Separation and the Rise of the Ukrainian National Name. Harv. Ukr. Stud. 27, 33–65.

Boneva, T., 2006. Continuity and Identity in the Local Community: A Long Term Perspective. Anthropol. East Eur. Rev. 24, 51–58.

Bosworth, C.E., Van Dozel, E., Lewis, B., Pellat, C. (Eds.), 1986. Mahalla. Encycl. Islam.

Brandes, D., 1986. Die Ansiedlung von Ausländern im Zarenreich unter Katarina II. Paul I. und Alexander I. Jahrb. Für Gesch. Osteur. 34, 161–178.

Brandes, D., Sundhaussen, H., Troebst, S. (Eds.), 2010. Lex. Vertreibungen Deport. Zwangsaussiedlung Ethn. Säuberung Im Eur. 20 Jhd.

Braudel, F., 2009. History and the Social Sciences—The Longue Durée. Rev. Fernand Braudel Cent. 32, 171–203.

Brodwin, P., 2002. Genetics, Identity, and the Anthropology of Essentialism. Anthropol. Q. 75, 323–330.

Bromley, Y.V., 1983. Ocherki teorii etnosa. Nauka, Moskva.

Bromley, Y.V., 1980. The object and the subject-matter of ethnography, in: Gellner, E. (Ed.), Soviet and Western Anthropology. Columbia University Press, New York.

Bromley, Y.V., Podol'niy, R.G., 1990. Chelovechestvo eto narody. Izdatel'stvo Mysl', Moskva.

Bromley, Y.V., Podol'niy, R.G., 1984. Sozdano chelovechestvom. Politizdat, Moskva.

Brubaker, R., 2004. Ethnicity without Groups. Harvard University Press, Cambridge MA.

Bulgar, S., 2017. Mobilizatsiya Gagauzov v "Trudovuyu Armiyu" v Gody Velikoy Otechestvennoy Voyny. Gramota 79, 35–44.

Bulgar, S., 2016. Uchastie Gagauzov v Velikoy Otechestvennoy Voyne 1941–1945 gg. Vestn. Bryanskogo Gosuniv. 2016, 28–36.

Burawoy, M., 2009. The Extended Case Method—Four Countries, Four Decades, Four Great Transformations, and One Theoretical Tradition. University of California Press, Berkley, Los Angeles.

Burbank, J., 2007. The Rights of Difference—Law and Citizenship in the Russian Empire, in: Stoler, A.L., McGranahan, C., Perdue, P.C. (Eds.), Imperial Formations. James Currey, Oxford.

Burke, P., 1990. The French Historical Revolution The Annales School, 1929–89. Stanford University Press, Stanford.

Cadiot, J., 2010. Laboratoriya Imperii: Rossiya/SSSR, 1860–1940. Novoe Literaturnoe Obozrenie, Moskva.

Cadiot, J., 2005. Searching for Nationality: Statistics and National Categories at the End of the Russian Empire (1897–1917). Russ. Rev. 64, 440–455.

Calinescu, M., 1993. Romania's 1930s Revisited. Salmagundi 97, 133–155.

Cash, J.R., 2011. Villages on Stage—Folklore and Nationalism in the Republic of Moldova. Lit, Münster.

Chandra, K., 2004. Why Ethnic Parties Succeed—Patronage and Ethnic Head Counts in India. Cambridge University Press, Cambridge.

Clay, C.B., 1995. Russian Ethnographers in the Service of Empire, 1856–1862. Slav. Rev. 54, 45–61.

Connor, W., 2011. Beyond Reason—The nature of the ethnonational bond, in: Baumann, G., Vertovec, S. (Eds.), Multiculturalism. Routledge, London.

Crowther, W., 1991. The Politics of Ethno-National Mobilization: Nationalism and Reform in Soviet Moldavia. Russ. Rev. 50, 183–202.

Cusco, A., 2017. A Contested Borderland—Competing Russian and Romanian Visions of Bessarabia in the Late Nineteenth and Early Twentieth Century. Central European University Press, Budapest.

Cvetkovski, R., 2014a. Empire Complex: Arrangements in the Russian Ethnographic Museum, 1910, in: Cvetkovski, R., Hofmeister, A. (Eds.), An Empire of Others—Creating Ethnographic Knowledge in Imperial Russia and the USSR. Central European University Press, Budapest.

Cvetkovski, R., 2014b. Introduction: On the Making of Ethnographic Knowledge in Russia, in: Cvetkovski, R., Hofmeister, A. (Eds.), An Empire of Others—Creating Ethnographic Knowledge in Imperial Russia and the USSR. Central European University Press, Budapest.

Demirdirek, H., 2008a. In the Minority in Moldova: (Dis)Empowerment through Territorial Conflict, in: Schmidtke, O., Yekelchyk, S. (Eds.), Europe's Last Frontier? Belarus, Moldova, and Ukraine between Russia and the European Union. Palgrave, New York.

Demirdirek, H., 2008b. Gagauz Autonomy and Ambiguous Citizenship, in: Heintz, M. (Ed.), Weak State, Uncertain Citizenship: Moldova. Peter Lang, Frankfurt a.M.

Derzhavin, N.S., 1914. Bolgarskiya Kolonyi v Rossii (Tavricheskaya, Khersonskaya, i Bessarabskaya Gubernii). Derzhavna Pechatnitsa, Sofia.

Dunn, E., Dunn, S.P. (Eds.), 1974. Introduction to Soviet Ethnography. Highgate Road Social Science Research Station, Berkley.

Eisenstadt, S.N., Roniger, L., 1984. Patrons, Clients and Friends—Interpersonal Relations and the Structure of Trust in Society. Cambridge University Press, Cambridge.

Elwert, G., 2002. Switching Identity Discourses: Primordial Emotions and the Social Construction of We-Groups, in: Schlee, G. (Ed.), Imagined Differences. Lit, Münster, pp. 33–54.

Elwert, G., 1997. Boundaries, Cohesion and Switching: On We-Groups in Ethnic National and Religious Forms, in: Wicker, H.R. (Ed.), Rethinking Nationalism and Ethnicity—The Struggle for Meaning and Order in Europe. Berg, Oxford, New York.

Eriksen, T.H., 1993. Ethnicity and Nationalism—Anthropological Perspectives. Pluto Press, London.

Fairbanks, C.H.J., 1999. Clientelism and the Roots of Post-Soviet Disorder, in: Suny, R.G. (Ed.), Transcaucasia, Nationalism and Social Change. University of Michigan Press, Ann Arbor.

Fairbanks, C.H.J., 1978. National Cadres as a Force in the Soviet System: The evidence of Beria's Career 1949–53, in: Azrael, J. (Ed.), Soviet Nationality Problems and Practices. Praeger, New York.

Fane, D., 1993. Moldova: Breaking loose from Moscow, in: Bremmer, I., Ray, T. (Eds.), Nations and Politics in the Soviet Successor States. Cambridge University Press, Cambridge.

Figes, O., 2002. Nataschas Tanz—Eine Kulturgeschichte Russlands. Berlin Verlag, Berlin.

Final Report of the International Commission on the Holocaust in Romania, 2004. International Commission on the Holocaust in Romania, Bucharest.

Fitzhugh, B., Bilaniuk, L., Lyon, K., 1996. Post-Soviet Anthropological Perspectives: An Introduction. Mich. Discuss. Anthropol. Post Sov. Eurasia 12, 1–5.

Flier, M., 1998. Surzhyk: The Rules of Engagement. Harv. Ukr. Stud. 22, 113–136.

Fowkes, B., 2002. Ethnicity and Ethnic Conflict in the Post-Communist World. Palgrave, New York.

Friedberg, M., 1991. How Things were done in Odessa—Cultural and Intellectual Pursuits in a Soviet City. Westview Press, Oxford.

Geertz, C., 1978. The Bazaar Economy: Information and Search in Peasant Marketing. Am. Econ. Rev. 68, 28–32.

Geertz, C., 1973. Thick Description: Toward an interpretive Theory of Culture, in: The Interpretation of Cultures. Basic Books, New York.

Gellner, E., 1983. Nations and Nationalism. Cornell University Press, Ithaca.

Gellner, E., 1980. A Russian Marxist Philosophy of History, in: Gellner, E. (Ed.), Soviet and Western Anthropology. Columbia University Press, New York.

Gelman, S.A., Wellman, H.M., 1991. Insides and essences: Early understanding of the non-obvious. Cognition 38, 213–244.

Gil-White, F.J., 2001. Are Ethnic Groups Biological "Species" to the Human Brain? Essentialism in Our Cognition of Some Social Categories. Curr. Anthropol. 42, 515–554.

Ginzburg, C., 1989. The Inquisitor as Anthropologist, in: Ginzburg, C. (Ed.), Clues, Myths and the Historical Method. The Johns Hopkins University Press, Baltimore.

Ginzburg, C., 1980. The Cheese and the Worms. The Johns Hopkins University Press, Baltimore.

Glass, H., 2014. Deutschland und die Verfolgung der Juden im rumänischen Machtbereich 1940–1944. Oldenbourg Verlag, München.

Gorenburg, D., 2006a. Rethinking Interethnic Marriage in the Soviet Union. Post Sov. Aff. 22, 145–165.

Gorenburg, D., 2006b. Soviet Nationalities Policy and Assimilation, in: Arel, D., Ruble, B.A. (Eds.), Rebounding Identities: The Politics of Identities in Russia and Ukraine. The Johns Hopkins University Press, Baltimore.

Gorenburg, D., 1999. Identity change in Bashkortostan: Tatars into Bashkirs and Back. Ethn. Racial Stud. 22, 554–580.

Gramatzki, H.-E., 2002. Die ukrainische Transformation. Rent seeking und andere Elemente institutioneller Reformstaus, in: Schorkowitz, D. (Ed.), Transition—Erosion—Reaktion: Zehn Jahre Transformation in Osteuropa. Peter Lang, Frankfurt a. M.

Grek, I.F., Russev, N.D., 2011. 1812 povorotniy god v istorii Budzhaka i "zadunayskikh pereselentsev." Stratum Plus, Chișinău.

Grosjean, F., 1982. Life with two languages. Harvard University Press, Cambridge MA.

Guboglo, M., 2012. Etnogenez kak predtecha sovremennykh identichnostey, in: Guboglo, M. (Ed.), Gagauzy v Mire i Mir Gagauzov. Izpolkom ATO Gagauziya, Komrat.

Guboglo, M.N., 2012. Etapi etnicheskoy mobilisatsii i etnopoliticheskogo vzrosleniya. Poluvekovoy opyt razvitiya Gagauzov, in: Guboglo, M.N. (Ed.), Gagauzy v Mire i Mir Gagauzov Tom 2. Izpolkom ATO Gagauziya, Komrat.

Guboglo, M.N., 2011. Sovremennaya yazykovaya situatsiya, in: Kvilinkova, E.N., Guboglo, M.N. (Eds.), Gagauzy. Nauka, Moskva.

Gumilev, L., 2002. Etnogenez i Biosfera Zemli. Izdatel'stvo Azbuka Klassika, Sankt-Peterburg.

Habeck, J.O., 2011. "Thank you for Being" Neighborhood, Ethno-Culture, and Social Recognition in the House of Culture, in: Donahoe, B., Habeck, J.O. (Eds.), Reconstructing the House of Culture-Community, Self, and the Makings of Culture in Russia and Beyond. Berghahn Books, New York, Oxford.

Haber, M., 2014. The Soviet Ethnographers as a Social Engineer—Socialist Realism and the Study of Rural Life, 1945–1958. Sov. Post-Sov. Rev. 41, 194–219.

Haimson, L.H., 1988. The Problem of Social Identities in Early Twentieth Century Russia. Slav. Rev. 47, 1–20.

Hann, C., 1997. The Nation-State, Religion, and Uncivil Society: Two Perspectives from the Periphery. Daedlus 126, 27–45.

Hartley, L.P., 1973. The Go-Between. Penguin Books, London.

Hatłas, J., 2011. The Gagauz People in Bessarabia. Slupskie Stud. Hist. 17, 191–199.

Hausleitner, M., 2004. Minderheitenpolitik in Grossrumänien zwischen 1918 und 1944, in: Schippel, L. (Ed.), Im Dialog: Rumänistik Im Deutschsprachigen Raum. Peter Lang, Frankfurt a.M.

Haynes, R.A., 2007. Reluctant Allies? Iuliu Maniu and Corneliu Zelea Codreanu against King Carol II of Romania. Slavon. East Eur. Rev. 85, 105–134.

Hilton, J.L., von Hippel, W., 1996. Stereotypes. Annu. Rev. Psychol. 237–271.

Hitchins, K., 1994. Rumania 1866–1947. Clarendon Press, Oxford.

Hobsbawm, E., 1990. Nationen und Nationalismus: Mythos und Realität seit 1780. Campus, Frankfurt a.M.

Hobsbawm, E., Ranger, T., 1983. The Invention of Tradition. Cambridge University Press, Cambridge.

Hosking, G., 2001. Russia and the Russians-A History. The Belknap Press of Harvard University Press, Cambridge MA.

Hosking, G., 2000. Patronage and the Russian State. Slavon. East Eur. Rev. 78, 301–320.

Hroch, M., 1998. Real and constructed: The nature of the nation, in: Hall, J.A. (Ed.), The State of the Nation—Ernest Gellner and the Theory of Nationalism. Cambridge University Press, Cambridge.

Hroch, M., 1968. Die Vorkämpfer der nationalen Bewegung bei den kleinen Völkern Europas. University Karlova, Praha.

Hrycak, A., 2006. Institutional Legacies and Language Revival in Ukraine, in: Arel, D., Ruble, B.A. (Eds.), Rebounding Identities: The Politics of Identity in Russia and Ukraine. The Johns Hopkins University Press, Baltimore.

Humphrey, C., 2002. Ist "postsozialistisch" noch eine Brauchbare Kategorie?, in: Hann, C. (Ed.), Postsozialismus—Transformationsprozesse in Europa Und Asien Aus Ethnologischer Perspektive. Campus, Frankfurt a.M.

Humphrey, C., 1998. Marx Went Away—But Karl Stayed Behind. The University of Michigan Press, Ann Arbor.

Ioanid, R., 2010. Romania, in: Bosworth, R.J.B. (Ed.), The Oxford Handbook of Fascism. Oxford University Press, Oxford.

Ioanid, R., 2000. The Holocaust in Romania—The Destruction of Jews and Gypsies Under the Antonescu Regime, 1940–1944. Ivan R. Dee in Association with the United States Holocaust Memorial Museum, Chicago.

Jernudd, B.H., 1989. The texture of language purism: an introduction, in: Jernudd, B.H., Shapiro, M.J. (Eds.), The Politics of Language Purism. Mouton der Gruyter, Berlin, New York.

Kaneff, D., 1998. When 'land' becomes 'territory'—Land privatisation and ethnicity in rural Bulgaria, in: Bridger, S., Pine, F. (Eds.), Surviving Post-Socialism—Local Strategies and Regional Responses in Eastern Europe and the Former Soviet Union. Routledge, London.

Kaneff, D., Heintz, M., 2006. Bessarabian Borderlands: One Region, Two States, Multiple Ethnicities. Anthropol. East Eur. Rev. 24, 6–16.

Kappeler, A., 2000. Kleine Geschichte der Ukraine. C.H. Beck, München.

Karklins, R., 1986. Ethnic Relations in the USSR, the Perspective from below. Unwin Hyman, Boston.

Kashu, I., 2014. U istokov sovetizatsii Bessarabii—Vyyavlenie „klassovogo vraga", konfiskatsiya imushchestva i trudovaya mobilizatsiya, 1940–1941 gg. Editura Cartier, Chișinău.

Kasianov, G., 2010. The Great Famine of 1932–1933 (Holodomor) and the Politics of History in Contemporary Ukraine, in: Troebst, S. (Ed.), Postdiktatorische Geschichtskulturen Im Süden Und Osten Europas—Bestandesaufnahme und Forschungsperspektiven. Wallstein, Göttingen.

Kettering, S., 1988. The Historical Development of Political Clientelism. J. Interdiscip. Hist. 18, 419–447.

King, C., 2000. The Moldovans—Romania, Russia, and the Politics of Culture. Hoover Institution Press, Stanford.

King, C., 1997. Minorities policy in the post-Soviet republics: the case of the Gagauzi. Ethn. Racial Stud. 20, 738–756.

Kisse, A.I., 2006. Vozrozhdenie bolgar Ukrainy. Optimum, Odessa.

Klaus, A.A., 1869. Nashi Kolonii—opyty i materialy po istorii i statistiki inostrannoy kolonizatsiy v Rossii. Tipografiya V.V. Nuswal'ta, St. Petersburg.

Knight, N., 1998. Science, Empire, and Nationality—Ethnography in the Russian Geographical Society, 1845–1855, in: Burbank, J., Ransel, D.L. (Eds.), Imperial Russia—New Histories for the Empire. Indiana University Press, Bloomington and Indianapolis.

Knudson Gee, G., 1995. Geography, Nationality, and Religion in Ukraine: A Research Note. J. Sci. Study Relig. 34, 383–390.

Kordan, B.S., 2008. The Mapping of Ukraine—European Cartography and Maps of Early Modern Ukraine, 1550–1799. The Ukrainian Museum, New York.

Kornai, J., 1980. Economics of Shortage. North-Holland-Publishing, Amsterdam.

Kornilovich, S., 1899. Statisticheskoe opisanie Bessarabii sobstvenno tak nazyvaemoy ili Budzhaka. Tipografiya I.M. Grinshteyna, Akkerman.

Kosienkowski, M., 2015. The Republic of Budjak: Next in line? New East. Eur.

Kotkin, S., 1991. Steeltown, USSR—Soviet Society in the Gorbachev Era. University of California Press, Berkley.

Kozlov, V., 1974. Problema etnicheskogo samosoznaniya i ee mesto v teorii etnosa. Sov. Etnografiya 1974, 79–92.

Kozlov, V., 1971. Etnos i Territoriya. Sov. Etnografiya 1971, 89–100.

Krushevan, P.A., 1903. Bessarabiya. Geograficheskiy, istoricheskiy, ekonomicheskiy, etnograficheskiy, i literaturniy spravochniy sbornik. Tipografiya A. V. Vasil'eva, Moskva.

Kryzhanovskaya, K.P., Russev, E.M. (Eds.), 1957. Ustroystvo Zadunayskikh Perselentsev v Bessarabii i Deyatel'nost' A. P. Yushnevskogo—Sbornik Dokumentov. Gossudarstvennoe Izdatel'stvo Moldavii, Chișinău.

Kuhn, T.S., 1996. The Structure of Scientific Revolutions. The University of Chicago Press, Chicago and London.

Kürti, L., Skalník, P., 2009. Introduction: Postsocialist Europe and the Anthropological Perspective from Home, in: Kürti, L., Skalník, P. (Eds.), Postsocialist Europe—Anthropological Perspectives from Home. Berghahn Books, New York.

Kushko, A., Taki, V., 2012. Bessarabiya v Sostave Rossiyskoy Imperii (1812–1917). Novoe Literaturnoe Obozrenie, Moskva.

Kushner, P.I., 1974. On some Processes Taking Place in the Contemporary Kolkhoz Family, in: Dunn, S.P., Dunn, E. (Eds.), Introduction into Soviet Ethnography Volume 1. Highgate Road Social Science Research Station, Berkley.

Kushner, P.I., 1951. Etnicheskie Territorii i Etnicheskie Granitsy. Izdatel'stvo Akademii Nauk SSSR, Moskva.

Kushnir, V.G., 1998. Narodsnavstvo Odeshchini. Hermes, Odessa.

Kuznetsov, A., 2008. Russian Anthropology: Old Traditions and new Tendencies, in: Boskovic, A. (Ed.), Other People's Anthropologies—Ethnographic Practice on the Margins. Berghahn Books, New York.

Lavender, A.D., 2006. Y-StrDNA. Encycl. Anthropol.

Lazarev, A.M., 1974. Moldavskaya sovetskaya gossudarstvennost' i bessarabskiy vopros. Kartya Moldovenyaske, Chișinău.

Lebedenko, O.M., Tychyna, A., 2002. Ukrayins'ke Podunav'ya—minule ta suchasne. Astroprint, Odessa.

Ledeneva, A., 1998. Russia's Economy of Favours—Blat, Networking and Informal Exchange. Cambridge University Press, Cambridge.

Livezeanu, I., 1995. Cultural Politics in Greater Romania: Regionalism, Nation Building & Ethnic Struggle 1918–1930. Cornell University Press, Ithaca.

Livezeanu, I., 1990. Between State and Nation: Romanian Lower-Middle Class Intellectuals in the Interwar Period, in: Koshar, R. (Ed.), Splintered Classes—Politics and the Lower Middle Classes in Interwar Europe. Holmes & Meier, New York.

Löwe, H.-D., 2000. Poles, Jews and Tatars: Religion, Ethnicity, and Social Structure in Tsarist Nationality Policies. Jew. Soc. Stud. 6, 52–96.

Magocsi, P.R., 2002. The Roots of Ukrainian Nationalism—Galicia as Ukraine's Piedmont. Toronto University Press, Toronto.

Magocsi, P.R., 1996. A History of Ukraine. University of Toronto Press, Toronto.

Makarchuk, S.A., 2008. Etnichna istoriya Ukrayiny navchal'niy posibnyk. Znannya, Kyiv.

Malinovski, B., 1932. Argonauts of the Western Pacific. George Routledge & Sons LTD, London.

Manz, B.F., 2003. Multiethnic empires and the formulation of Identities. Ethn. Racial Stud. 26, 70–101.

Marszk, D., 1999. Varietäten russischer Substandards. Handb. Sprachwiss. Russ. Ihrer Grenzdisziplinen. Harrassowitz, Wiesbaden.

Martin, T., 2000. Modernization or Neotraditionalism? Ascribed Nationality and Soviet Primordialism, in: Hoffmann, D.L., Kotsonis, Y. (Eds.), Russian Modernity—Politics, Knowledge, Practices. Macmillan Press, New York.

Mihaylova, A., 2006. National versus Regional Identity: The "Other" Romanians in Greater Romania. Balk. Stud. Etudes Balk. 2006, 9–23.

Moon, D., 2013. The Plough that Broke the Steppes, Agriculture and Environment on Russia's Grasslands, 1700–1914. Oxford University Press, Oxford.

Moshkov, V.A., 1907. Novaya teoriya proiskhozhdeniya cheloveka i ego vyrozhdeniya sostavlena po dannym zoologii, geologii, arkheologii, antropologii, etnografii, istorii i statistiki. Tipografiya gubernskogo pravleniya, Varshava.

Moshkov, V.A., 1902a. Gagauzy Benderskago uezda. Etnograficheskie ocherki i materialy gl. XI–XIII. Etnograficheskoe Obozr. 1902, 1–66.

Moshkov, V.A., 1902b. Gagauzy Benderskago uezda. Glavy XIV–XXIV. Etnograficheskoe Obozr. 1902, 1–91.

Moshkov, V.A., 1901a. Gagauzy Benderskago uezda. VI Semeynyya i obschestvennyya otnosheniya u gagauzov. VII Otnosheniya gagauzov k drugim narodnostyam. Etnograficheskoe Obozr. 1901, 1–49.

Moshkov, V.A., 1901b. Gagauzy Benderskago uezda. V. Svad'ba. Etnograficheskoe Obozr. 1901, 98–160.

Moshkov, V.A., 1900. Gagauzy Benderskago uezda. (Etnograficheskie ocherki i materialy) I. Territoriya, zanimaemaya gagauzamy, i ikh proizkhozhdenie. II: Obichai: rodiny i krestiny. III. Igry i razvlecheniya. IV. Tantsy, muzyka i penie. Etnograficheskoe Obozr. 1900, 1–89.

Mühlfried, F., Sokolovskiy, S., 2011. Introduction: Soviet Anthropology at the Empire's Edge, in: Mühlfried, F., Sokolovskiy, S. (Eds.), Exploring the Edge of Empire—Soviet Era Anthropology in the Caucasus and Central Asia. Lit, Münster.

Mulrine, S., 1999. Introduction, in: Mulrine, S. (Ed.), Gogol, Three Plays. Methuen Drama, York.

Naarden, B., 1996. "I am a genius, but no more than that." Lev Gumilëv (1912–1992), Ethnogenesis, the Russian Past and World History. Jahrb. Für Gesch. Osteur. 44, 54–82.

Palamarchuk, S., 2008. Zabytaya zemlya: istoricheskaya oblast' Bessarabiya. Astroprint, Odessa.

Pârâianu, R., 2007. Culturalist Nationalism and Anti-Semitism in Fin-de-Siècle Romania, in: Turda, M., Weindling, P.J. (Eds.), "Blood and Homeland"—Eugenics and Racial Nationalism in Central and Southeast Europe, 1900–1940. Central European University Press, Budapest.

Petrova-Averkieva, Y., 1980. Historicism in Soviet ethnographic science, in: Gellner, E. (Ed.), Soviet and Western Anthropology. Columbia University Press, New York.

Piattoni, S., 2001. Clientelism, Interests, and Democratic Representation, in: Piattoni, S. (Ed.), Clientelism, Interests, and Democratic Representation—The European Experience in Historical and Comparative Perspective. Cambridge University Press, Cambridge.

Plokhy, S., 2006. The Origin of Slavic Nations: Premodern Identities in Russia, Ukraine and Belarus. Cambridge University Press, Cambridge.

Popov, A., Kuznetsov, I., 2008. Ethnic Discrimination and the Discourse of "Indigenization": The Regional regime, "Indigenous Majority" and Ethnic Minorities in Krasnodar Krai in Russia. Natl. Pap. 36, 223–252.

Portnov, A., 2015. Post-Maidan Europe and the New Ukrainian Studies. Slav. Rev. 74, 723–731.

Raleigh, D.J., 2012. Soviet Baby Boomers—An Oral History of Russia's Cold War Generation. Oxford University Press, Oxford.

Razgon, A.M., 1982. Odesskoe obshchestvo istorii i drevnostey. Sov. Istor. Entsiklopediya.

Reid, A., 1997. Borderland—A Journey through the History of Ukraine. Westview Press, Boulder.

Renan, E., 2006. What is a nation, in: Bhabha, H.K. (Ed.), Nation and Narration. Routledge, London.

Renan, E., 1994. Qu'est-ce qu'une nation?, in: Hutchinson, J., Smith, A.D. (Eds.), Nationalism. Oxford University Press, Oxford, pp. 17–18.

Richardson, T., 2008. Kaleidoscopic Odessa—History and Place in contemporary Ukraine. University of Toronto Press, Toronto.

Richardson, T., 2004. Disciplining the Past in Post-Soviet Ukraine—Memory and History in Schools and Families, in: Pine, F., Kaneff, D., Haukanes, H. (Eds.), Memory, Politics and Religion. Lit, Münster.

Rjabtschuk, M., 2005. Die reale und die imaginierte Ukraine. Edition Suhrkamp, Frankfurt a.M.

Rossetti, F.C., 1934. Monografia Orașului Ismail. Tipografia I.H. Roitman, Izmail.

Roth, B., 1991. Sprachen, in: Bauer, H., Kappeler, A., Roth, B. (Eds.), Die Nationalitäten Des Russischen Reiches in Der Volkszählung von 1897, Quellenkritische Dokumentation Und Datenhandbuch, Band A. Franz Steiner Verlag, Stuttgart.

Rothschild, J., 1981. Ethnopolitics—A Conceptual Framework. Columbia University Press, New York.

Rouček, J.S., 1932. The Political Evolution of Roumania. Slavon. East Eur. Rev. 10, 602–615.

Ryasanovsky, N.V., 2000. A History of Russia. Oxford University Press, Oxford, New York.

Sakali, M.P., 2013. Kubey: Ocherkii i materialy istorii sela Kubey-Chervonoarmeyskoe v Bessarabii. FOP Petrov, Odessa.

Sapozhnikov, I.V., 2009. Zdanie Mecheti Proroka Mukhkhameda v Izmaile: Novye Fakty i Interpretatsii. Mater. Po Arkheologii Servernogo Prichernomorya 9, 243–268.

Sasse, G., Lackner, A., 2018. War and identity: the case of the Donbas in Ukraine. Post-Sov. Aff. 2018, 1–19.

Schmidt, C., 1991. Stände, in: Bauer, H., Kappeler, A., Roth, B. (Eds.), Die Nationalitäten Des Russischen Reiches in Der Volkszählung von 1897, Quellenkritische Dokumentation Und Datenhandbuch, Band A. Franz Steiner Verlag, Stuttgart.

Schmidt, C., 1990. Über die Bezeichnung der Stände (sostojanie—soslovie) in Russland seit dem 18. Jahrhundert. Jahrb. Für Gesch. Osteur. 38, 199–211.

Schmidt, U., 2008. Bessarabien—Deutsche Siedler am Schwarzen Meer. Deutsches Kulturforum östliches Europa, Potsdam.

Schneider-Deters, W., 2008. Die Ukraine, in: Schneider-Deters, W., Schulze, P.W., Timmermann, H. (Eds.), Die Europäische Union, Russland Und Eurasien—Die Rückkehr Der Geopolitik. Berliner Wissenschafts-Verlag, Berlin.

Schorkowitz, D., 2012. Cultural Contact and Cultural Transfer in Medieval Western Eurasia. Archeol. Ethnol. Anthropol. Eurasia 40, 84–94.

Schorkowitz, D., 2010. Geschichte, Identität und Gewalt im Kontext postsozialistischer Nationsbildung. Z. Für Ethnol. 135, 99–160.

Scott, J.C., 1998. Seeing like a State—How Certain Schemes to Improve the Human Condition have Failed. Yale University Press, New Haven and London.

Scott, J.C., 1969. Corruption, Machine Politics, and Political Change. Am. Polit. Sci. Rev. 63, 1142–1158.

Serbens'ka, O.A., Terlak, Z.M., 1999. Ukrainskiy yazyk dlya nachinayushchikh. Svit, L'viv.

Sergeyev, M.A., 1964. The Building of Socialism among the Peoples of Northern Siberia and the Soviet Far East, in: Levin, M.G., Potapov, L.P. (Eds.), The Peoples of Siberia. The University of Chicago Press, Chicago.

Shabashov, A.V., 2012. Gagauzy v Ukraine, in: Guboglo, M.N. (Ed.), Gagauzy v Mire i Mir Gagauzov Tom 2. Izpolkom ATO Gagauziya, Komrat.

Shlapentokh, V., 1996. Early Feudalism—The Best Parallel for Contemporary Russia. Eur.-Asia Stud. 48, 393–411.

Shnirelman, V., 2009. Stigmatized by History or by Historians? The Peoples of Russia in School History Textbooks. Hist. Mem. 21, 110–149.

Shnirel'man, V.A., 2006. Lev Gumilev: Ot "passionarnogo napryazheniya" do "Nesovmestimosti Kul'tur." Etnograficheskoe Obozr. 2006, 8–20.

Shornikov, P.M., 2012. Diskussii po voprosu o sozdanii avtonomii na yuge Moldavii i v pridunayskikh zemlyakh Ukrainy, in: Guboglo, M.N. (Ed.), Gagauzy v Mire i Mir Gagauzov Tom 2. Izpolkom ATO Gagauziya, Komrat.

Simon, G., 2008. Die Politische Krise der Ukraine. Ukr.-Anal. 2–7.

Skal'kovskiy, A.A., 1853. Opyt Statisticheskago Opisaniya Novorossiyskago Kraya Chast' II. Tipografiya Frantsova i Nitche, Odessa.

Skal'kovskiy, A.A., 1850. Opyt Statisticheskago Opisaniya Novorossiyskago Kraya Chast' I. Tipografiya Frantsova i Nitche, Odessa.

Skalnik, P., 1990. Soviet Etnografiia and the National(ities) Question. Cah. Monde Russe Sov. 31, 183–191.

Slezkine, Y., 1994. The USSR as a Communal Apartment, or how a Socialist State Promoted Ethnic Particularism. Slav. Rev. 53, 414–452.

Slocum, J.W., 1998. Who and When, Were the Inorodtsy? The Evolution of the Category of "Aliens" in Imperial Russia. Russ. Rev. 57, 173–190.

Sokolovskiy, S., 2012. Writing the History of Russian Anthropology, in: Baiburin, A., Kelly, C., Vakhtin, N. (Eds.), Russian Cultural Anthropology after the Collapse of Communism. Routledge, London.

Sokolovskiy, S., 2003. Rossiskaya etnografiya v kontse XX v. (bibliometricheskoe isseldovanie). Etnograficheskoe Obozr. 1, 3–54.

Solonari, V., 2010. Purifying the Nation—Population Exchange and Ethnic Cleansing in Nazi-allied Romania. The Johns Hopkins University Press, Baltimore.

Solonari, V., 2007. Patterns of Violence—The Local Population and the Mass Murder of Jews in Bessarabia and Northern Bukovina, July-August 1941. Krit. Explor. Russ. Eurasian Hist. 8, 749–787.

Solonari, V., 2003. Creating a "People": A Case Study in Post-Soviet History-Writing. Krit. Explor. Russ. Eurasian Hist. 4, 411–438.

Somers, M.H., 1994. The narrative constitution of identity: A relational and network approach. Theory Soc. 23, 605–649.

Spolsky, B., 2004. Language Policy. Cambridge University Press, Cambridge.

Stalin, J., 1994. The Nation, in: Hutchinson, J., Smith, A.D. (Eds.), Nationalism. Oxford University Press, Oxford, pp. 18–21.

Stefes, C.H., 2006. Understanding Post-Soviet Transitions—Corruption, Collusion and Clientelism. Palgrave, New York.

Steinwedel, C., 2007. Resettling people, unsettling the empire—Migration and the challenge of governance 1861–1917, in: Breyfogle, N.B., Schrader, A., Sunderland, W. (Eds.), Peopling the Russian Periphery—Borderland Colonization in Eurasian History. Routledge, London.

Steinwedel, C., 2001. Making Social Groups, One Person at a Time: The Identification of Individuals by Estate, Religious Confession, and Ethnicity in Late Imperial Russia, in: Caplan, J., Torpey, J. (Eds.), Documenting Individual Identity: The Development of Practices in the Modern World. Princeton University Press, Princeton.

Stokes, S.C., 2009. Political Clientelism, in: Goodin, R.E. (Ed.), The Oxford Handbook of Political Science. Oxford University Press, Oxford.

Subottina, I.A., 2011. Dinamika Chislenosti Gagauzov B XX–XXI vv., in: Guboglo, M., Kvilinkova, E.N. (Eds.), Gagauzy. Nauka, Moskva.

Subtelny, O., 2000. Ukraine—A History. University of Toronto Press, Toronto.

Sunderland, W., 2004. Taming the Wild Field—Colonization and Empire on the Russian Steppe. Cornell University Press, Ithaca and London.

Suny, R.G., 2001. Constructing Primordialism: Old Histories and new Nations. J. Mod. Hist. 73, 862–896.

Svin'in, P.P., 1816. Opisanie Bessarabskoy oblasti—Sostavleno vedomstva gossudarstvennoy kollegii innostrannykh del nadvornym sovetnikom Pavlom Svin'inym, 1816 goda, 1-go Yunya.

Szporluk, R., 1998. Nationalism after Communism: Refelctions on Russia, Ukraine, Belarus and Poland. Nations Natl. 4, 301–320.

Tebarth, H.-J., 1991. Geschichte der Volkszählung, in: Bauer, H., Kappeler, A., Roth, B. (Eds.), Die Nationalitäten Des Russischen Reiches in Der Volkszählung von 1897, Quellenkritische Dokumentation Und Datenhandbuch, Band A. Franz Steiner Verlag, Stuttgart.

Tel'pis, Y.M., 2000. Golod 1946–1947 godov v pridunayskom krae. Nauk. Visnik Izmailskogo Derzhavnogo Pedinstitutu 8, 12–16.

Tishkov, V.A., 2003. Rekviem po etnosu—issledovaniya po sotsial'no-kul'turnoy antropologii. Nauka, Moskva.

Tishkov, V.A., 1997. Ethnicity, Nationalism and Conflict in and after the Soviet Union—The Mind Aflame. Sage Publications, London.

Tishkov, V.A., 1992. The Crisis in Soviet Ethnography. Curr. Anthropol. 33, 371–394.

Tokarew, S.A., 1954. Die nationale Politik der Sowjetunion und die Aufgaben und Erfolge der sowjetischen Ethnographie, in: Völkerforschung—Vorträge Der Tagung Für Völkerkunde an Der Humboldt-Universität Berlin Vom 25.–27. April 1952. Akademie Verlag, Berlin.

Tonkin, E., 1992. Narrating our Pasts. Cambridge University Press, Cambridge.

Troebst, S., 2006. Postkommunistische Erinnerungskulturen im östlichen Europa. Bestandesaufnahme, Kategorisierung, Periodisierung, in: Troebst, S. (Ed.), Kulturstudien Ostmitteleuropas—Aufsätze Und Essays. Peter Lang, Frankfurt a.M.

Troebst, S., 2001. Die Autonomieregelung für Gagausien in der Republik Moldova—ein Vorbild zur Regelung ethnopolitischer Konflikte? Berl. Osteur. Info 76–78.

Troynitskiy, N.A., 1905. Pervaya vseobshchaya perepis' naseleniya Rossiyskoy Imperii, 1897 g. III Bessarabskaya Guberniya. Izdanie Tsentral'nogo Statisticheskago Komiteta Ministerstva Vnutrennikh Del, Sankt-Peterburg.

Tsyhanenko, L.F., 2013. Dzherela istoriyi Pivdennoyi Bessarabiyi (z davnikh chasiv do kintsya XIX st.). Izmaiyil'skiy derzhavniy humanitarniy universitet, Izmail.

Turda, M., 2011. Controlling the National Body—Ideas of Racial Purification in Romania, 1918–1944, in: Promitzer, C., Trubeta, S., Turda, M. (Eds.), Health, Hygiene and Eugenics in Southeastern Europe to 1945. Central European University Press, Budapest.

Turda, M., 2007. The Nation as Object: Race, Blood, and Biopolitics in Interwar Romania. Slav. Rev. 66, 413–441.

Urusov, S.D., 1904. Zapiski Gubernatora. Izdanie V.M. Sablina, Moskva.

van Meurs, W.P., 1994. The Bessarabian Question in Communist Historiography—Nationalist and Communist Politics and History-Writing, East European Monographs. Columbia University Press, New York.

Varese, F., 2001. The Russian Mafia—Private Protection in a New Market Economy. Oxford University Press, Oxford.

Verdery, K., 1996. What Was Socialism and What Comes Next? Princeton University Press, Princeton.

Verdery, K., 1993a. Nationalism and National Sentiment in Post-Socialist Romania. Slav. Rev. 52, 179–203.

Verdery, K., 1993b. Ethnic Relations, Economies of Shortage and the Transition in Eastern Europe, in: Hann, C. (Ed.), Socialism: Ideals, Ideologies, and Local Practice. Routledge, London.

Verdery, K., 1990. The Production and Defense of "the Romanian Nation," 1900 to World War II, in: Fox, R.G. (Ed.), Nationalist Ideologies and the Production of National Cultures. American Anthropological Association, Washington D.C.

Vermeulen, H.F., 1995. Origins and institutionalization of ethnography and ethnology in Europe and the USA, 1771–1845, in: Alvarez Roldán, A., Vermeulen, H.F. (Eds.), Fieldwork and Footnotes—Studies in the History of European Anthropology. Routledge, London.

Wanner, C., 1998. Burden of Dreams—History and Identity in Post-Soviet Ukraine. The Pennsylvania State University Press, University Park PA.

Webb, J., 1994. Krasnodar: A Case Study of the Rural Factor in Russian Politics. J. Contemp. Hist. 29, 229–260.

Weber, E., 1976. Peasants into Frenchmen—The Modernization of Rural France 1870–1914. Stanford University Press, Stanford.

Weber, M., 1996. The Origins of Ethnic Groups, in: Hutchinson, J., Smith, A.D. (Eds.), Ethnicity. Oxford University Press, Oxford.

Weber, M., 1990. Ethnische Gemeinschaftsbeziehungen, in: Winckelmann, J. (Ed.), Wirtschaft Und Gesellschaft—Grundriss Der Verstehenden Soziologie. J.C.B. Mohr (Paul Siebeck), Tübingen.

Wedekind, M., 2010. The Mathematization of the Human Being: Anthropology and Ethno-Politics in Romania during the late 1930s and early 1940s. N. Z. Slavon. J. 44, 27–67.

Wernhart, K.R., 1998. Ethnos—Identität—Globalisierung, in: Zips, W., Wernhart, K.R. (Eds.), Ethnohistorie—Rekonstruktion Und Kulturkritik, Eine Einführung. Promedia, Wien.

Willermet, C., 2006. Eve, Mitochondrial. Encycl. Anthropol.

Willerton, J.P., 1992. Patronage and Politics in the USSR. Cambridge University Press, Cambridge.

Wilson, A., 2002. The Ukrainians—unexpected Nation. Yale Nota Bene, New Haven.

Wimmer, A., 2008. The Making and Unmaking of Ethnic Boundaries: A Multilevel Process Theory. Am. J. Sociol. 113, 970–1022.

Yurchak, A., 2006. Everything Was Forever, Until It Was No More—The Last Soviet Generation. Princeton University Press, Princeton.

Index of Authors

Index of Subjects and Names

Printed in the United States
By Bookmasters